Southern Africa in Transition

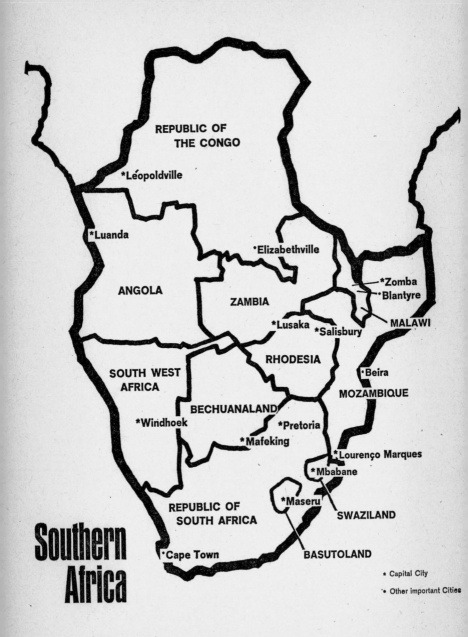

REPUBLIC OF
THE CONGO

*Léopoldville

*Luanda

ANGOLA

*Elizabethville

ZAMBIA

*Zomba
*Blantyre

*Lusaka *Salisbury

MALAWI

RHODESIA

SOUTH WEST
AFRICA

*Beira

MOZAMBIQUE

BECHUANALAND

*Windhoek

*Pretoria

*Mafeking

*Lourenço Marques

*Mbabane

REPUBLIC OF
SOUTH AFRICA

*Maseru

SWAZILAND

**Southern
Africa**

*Cape Town

BASUTOLAND

* Capital City

* Other important Cities

Southern Africa in Transition

EDITED BY

John A. Davis

AND

James K. Baker

PUBLISHED FOR

The American Society of African Culture

BY

FREDERICK A. PRAEGER, *Publishers*

New York · Washington · London

FREDERICK A. PRAEGER, PUBLISHERS
111 Fourth Avenue, New York, N.Y. 10003, U.S.A.
77–79 Charlotte Street, London W.1, England

Published in the United States of America in 1966
by Frederick A. Praeger, Inc., Publishers

Library of Congress Catalog Card Number: 65–13963

Printed in the United States of America

Contents

III. The High Commission Territories

IV. Zambia, Rhodesia, and Malawi

V. The Portuguese Territories

X. Nationalist Movements and Pan-Africanism

Preface

The papers in this volume were first presented at the Fourth International Conference of the American Society of African Culture (AMSAC), held at Howard University, Washington, D.C., in the spring of 1963. Recasting and editing papers given at a conference into a book is a prodigious task, especially when taken in stride with many other organizational responsibilities and duties. Late publication is nevertheless an unfair burden upon those of the writers who prepared their papers for publication in the first instance.

In spite of the passage of time, the decision was made to publish the papers because of their value in providing a basis for understanding what is presently happening in Southern Africa and because of the nature of the participants. Extensive revisions have been made in the case of most papers to bring them up to date. Editorial postscripts have been added at appropriate places in the text, providing a currency at publication date comparable to that of most magazines.

The situation in Southern Africa has undergone no basic change since the conference. Zambia has become independent (this was already assured at the time of the conference), but its independence is in doubt until the question of Rhodesia is resolved. The national revolts in Angola and Mozambique appear no stronger than they did in 1963. The High Commission Territories have been granted autonomous rule, as was expected at the time of the conference. The independence of Bechuanaland in September, 1966, could not have been foreseen in 1963, but this (like the case before the International Court of Justice on South West Africa) is merely an opening gambit in the struggle that will be determined finally by the conflict with and within the Republic of South Africa. The situation in South Africa has, to say the least, seen no improvement since 1963. The most recent development in Southern Africa has been Ian Smith's unilateral declaration of independence on November 10, 1965. (One of the principal speakers at the conference, the Reverend Ndabaningi

Sithole, leader of the Zimbabwe African National Union (ZANU), was placed in detention shortly after his return to Rhodesia.) This UDI has temporarily blighted all chances for an orderly resolution of the claims of the large African population against the political power of a small group of Europeans. Southern Africa is still in the balance.

The conferees at Howard included African national leaders, American and British scholars (some of whom were consultants in the developing governmental process in Southern Africa), African diplomatic representatives in this country, representatives of organizations interested in Africa, and political activists either concerned with planning for political action in Southern Africa or engaged in such activity. Papers presented dealt with the history, land, peoples, resources, and politics of the countries of Southern Africa, as well as with forms of nonviolent action, the nature of the nationalist movements, attitudes toward the use of force, the role of expatriate economic interests, the impact of Pan-Africanism, prospects for national and international action, U.S. policy toward Southern Africa, and the racial adjustment that must be faced after independence. Although the Congo is not usually included as part of Southern Africa, it is considered in this volume in so far as its significant forces and problems affect the area. (The nonferrous metals industries do not stop at the Congo border; nor does the threat of nationalist or national action, or the possibility for international action.)

Papers presented at the conference but not included in this volume were those of the Reverend G. Michael Scott, Honorary Director of the African Bureau, London; Daniel P. Biebuyck, Professor of Anthropology at the University of Delaware; Jeffrey Butler, Research Associate, African Studies Program, Boston University; and Griffith Nakubyana, at the time of the conference a student at Colgate University and U.S. representative of the United National Independence Party (UNIP) of Northern Rhodesia.

The sponsoring organization of the conference, the American Society of African Culture, has been in existence since February, 1957. It is composed of American Negroes who are scholars, writers, artists, teachers, and professionals, and is affiliated with the Society of African Culture, which has its headquarters in Paris. The organization has been concerned with the contribution of the Negro to world culture and with his economic, political, and social problems. Its publication, *African Forum: A Quarterly Journal of Contemporary Affairs*, is devoted to the political, social, economic, and cultural development of the Negro, especially in Africa and America.

Many persons helped in the preparation of the volume. Miss Brooke

Aronson organized the work as AMSAC's Director of Publications. Mrs. Dorothy Davis Lucas undertook the first technical editing of the manuscript, while Miss Ruth Zaslavsky did the typing and secretarial chores involved. Noel Kaplowitz is responsible for the painstaking updating of material that appears in the editors' postscripts. Finally, Arnold Dolin, of Praeger, was responsible for the final editing of the volume and through his work and confidence saved the book when others had given it up.

JOHN A. DAVIS
JAMES K. BAKER

December, 1965

Introduction

JOHN A. DAVIS

It is generally accepted by political scientists dealing with Africa that the United States has comparatively small economic and strategic interests in that continent. It is stated, for example, that only 5 per cent of American capital abroad is invested in Africa, little of it in black Africa. The proposition is beguiling, but essentially untrue.

First, as to economic interests, what matters is not the amount of money invested by the United States, but the importance of the resources in Africa and their availability to the West, through investment either by the United States or by its allies. Africa is rich in such natural resources as nonferrous metals, diamonds, and gold. Investments by the U.S. and its allies in Africa may not be porportionately large, but they are basic; the manufacturers of small automobiles, bicycles, ball-point pens, and plastic gadgets—certainly big business—could not exist without the nonferrous metals and minerals of Africa. And any doubt as to the depth of American interest in Africa should have been dispelled by the U.S. action in the Congo.

Professor Ferkiss in this volume, and Professor Hans Morgenthau elsewhere, suggest that America's interest in Africa is only a by-product of the East-West struggle. Both state that the United States is not engaged in a moral crusade in Africa to end imperialism and colonialism, to establish self-government and majority rule. They are right in the sense that American policy in Africa is inevitably linked to its total foreign policy. That foreign policy, for whatever reasons, is committed to competition and cooperation with Russia, to national self-determination and majority rule or consensus, and to the prevention of armed aggression by any nation, including Communist ones.

It is perhaps justifiable to say that American foreign policy attempts to keep the peace in terms of the lessons of the past. It is in this framework that American policy in Africa can best be understood. What are the lessons of the past? What foreign policy has resulted? How has this policy affected American policy in Africa? Where does American policy in Africa stand now?

World War I showed us that balance-of-power politics and denial of national aspirations in Europe, coupled with spheres of interest, colonialism, and imperialism abroad, were the road to war. The proffered alternatives were national self-determination, collective security, the economic underpinning of Western Europe by the United States and Britain, and the mandate system, under which "backward" peoples became the sacred trust of the civilized world.

These answers failed because the economic arrangements were faulty. International financial chaos led to the rise of fascism, whose threat was not met by collective security. Imperialist adventures, as in Manchuria and Ethiopia, and national aggression in Europe finally led to World War II.

After World War II, a broader commitment was made to collective security and to economic arrangements for underpinning it. The collective-security system has also provided for the evolution of colonies and trust territories to independence, under the supervision of the United Nations. This move has eased the competition between the world's two main contending forces over dependent areas. A source of major war has therefore been reduced. Most important, the contending powers have made it clear in advance where they *would* fight, and have thus avoided a direct confrontation resulting from a misinterpretation of their intent. Indeed, the situation as a whole has often led the two principal enemies to cooperate in the interests of the general peace. They have not always been able to keep their own allies in line, and minor confrontations have resulted—involving, at different times, France, Britain, Israel, and China.

In Africa, the main concern has been with the emergence to independence of former colonial or otherwise dominated areas. The process of leading Africa to independence has been a reasonably successful one (and, with the exceptions of Algeria and Egypt, not too painful) —at least until Central and Southern Africa were reached.

Two factors were basic to the liberating process: the transfer of power to indigenous national majorities and the support, indeed midwifery, of former colonial powers and the United Nations. The United States followed the lead and intentions of its allies, giving strong financial and technical support and a certain amount of pressure to get on with the job. It also moved with vigor to clean up its colonialism and imperialism at home (to use Wendell Willkie's phrase)—the American race problem. Since the United States had no effective presence in terms of people, skills, and investment in Africa, it had to pursue its policy through its allies and acquiesce in or guarantee their influence and position in the new nations of Africa after independence. The new African elites were trained in the metropole nations and were inevitably oriented toward them, even when ideologically in opposition to them.

In the case of the Congo, there was no colonial power either willing or capable of bringing the former colonial areas to nationhood. The Belgians had made no preparations for independence; there were only six university graduates among the indigenous people at the date of independence, and there was no suffrage in the Congo for anyone. They were faced with an area of large tribal groupings mainly geographically defined; and sectional and tribal differences had been exacerbated by the policies of the Force Publique. Panicked by what seemed to them the sudden rise of Congolese nationalism, the Belgians granted independence precipitously. The results are well known. Yet to date U.S. policy has been satisfied. The Congo is a unified nation, government has remained in the hands of moderates; Russian and Chinese attempts to take advantage of the situation and to precipitate a war of national liberation have been thwarted, and Belgian influence in the Democratic Republic of the Congo is unabated. In the crucial test this was achieved by the direct intervention of the United States in the Congolese civil war, at considerable loss of confidence in America among Pan-African leaders.

The government of the Congo is, at this writing, still under the military leadership of General Mobutu. The future is uncertain, but the calm and the goals achieved may be more apparent than real. In recent months, seven African states have undergone military coups; this has caused sighs of relief in some quarters, since it is assumed that military rule will mean an end to the radical threats and to Pan-African involvement. Although the situation varies from state to state, this may be too quick a judgment; African military leaders are not from the same social background as their Latin American counterparts, nor are they the ministrants of large family interests. In any event, as pointed out by James T. Harris in this volume, the major task in the Congo remains the building of efficient indigenous administrative and military classes that understand and are dedicated to the building of a modern state and a national political community through processes of group reconciliation.

In the rest of Southern Africa, American policy is faced with the intransigence of Portugal, which regards Angola and Mozambique as overseas provinces, integral parts of Portugal not eligible for independence; with Britain's rebellious colony of Rhodesia, under the leadership of Ian Smith and his Rhodesian Front government, which insists on independence without committing itself to eventual majority rule; and with the Republic of South Africa's commitment to a color-caste society and "self-governing" Bantu reserves within its own borders and in South West Africa. America and Britain are on a collision course with South Africa, Portugal, and Rhodesia; but before examining the risks involved to all of Africa and the world, and the choices available to the United States, it should be noted that the rest of Africa is not static and that a major technique of liberation has greatly jeopardized its stability.

In the process of orderly liberation in Africa—designed to prevent Africa from becoming a battleground where Russia and China could exploit national wars of liberation—the United States and its allies became proponents of, or tacitly approved, the principle of one man, one vote. There was no other way to break the power of colonial councils, with their official majorities, the representatives of special interests, of tribes and chiefs. Those local forces that had power, indigenous as well as European, would neither seek independence nor meet the national ambitions or rising expectations of the masses and the new elites. One man, one vote also provided a national consensus for liberation. Thus African nations came into existence with electoral arrangements that it had taken Britain eight centuries and the United States three and a half centuries to reach. It will be difficult, to say the least, for African nations to develop free institutions in societies with no middle class and with little class-role differentiation in terms appropriate for private and public functions in a modern state. Black African states, with some exceptions, are primarily poor peasant societies, with small elites, a growing modern labor force in industry, commerce, and transportation (with the consequent appearance of labor unions), and a developing small entrepreneurial class. They are rich in traditional culture that socialized their people in a harsh environment. The political movement has been from one dominant mass party to oligarchy to one-man rule, and now, too often, to one-man military rule. One is reminded of Aristotle's statement that it was the middle class that saved states.

African states face the additional difficulty of having to build national communities in areas artificially created by the colonial powers, where tribal rivalries are rife. Nor have they had wars of national liberation to serve as a basis for forming such a national community. Far more important, the structures of the states and of the political parties have provided no checks against the centralized organization of power, no provisions for bargaining or the establishment of reciprocal obligations between competing groups, and no protection of the minority against the will of the majority—or, in Calhoun's sense, no requirement of concurrent majorities. This is not to advocate impotency in government, but rather structures and processes that require the working out of a basic consensus. If, as

Talcott Parsons says, the building of a community requires the reconciliation of groups, then the creation of political structures requiring conciliation and compromise as a basis for organizing power is as desirable as basic political and ethical principles.

To make matters worse, African politics has too often been ideological, reflecting the European training or experience of African elites. As Gabriel Almond has pointed out, the success of British and American free institutions has resulted from the tendency to practice market politics: The voter group asks for programs, services, and policies in return for its votes. Indeed, it might be told to ask for certain things when it cannot comprehend its own best interest. The politician serves as an honest broker between groups, resolving the conflicting claims pragmatically in terms of the best that can be done in a given situation. The game is played with a more or less clear understanding of the primacy of the needs of the total political community, basic concepts of the rights of the individual and of minorities, and of the rule of law. It requires a society relatively free of rigid classes, groups, or sections whose in-group commitments prevent compromise with other groups in the interest of the total community— a condition long lacking in continental Europe. It also requires well-understood roles in the governing process for the executive, the parliament, the courts, the military, business, labor, the church, etc. It will take time to build such societies and such a political climate. In the meantime, much can be gained by the kind of political structure that breaks up power, requires group consensus to achieve political goals, protects the individual, and renders some recourse for the politically defeated and the minority.

The job of providing for the orderly emergence of African states outside Southern Africa is not yet finished, and African states, through their own disorder, may yet become battlefields of the Cold War. Be this as it may, Western Europe and the United States cannot stop pushing for majority rule, immediate or eventual. The same imperatives exist and indeed in greater force. If the transition does not take place in an orderly fashion under the tutelage of the West, then disorder, wars of national liberation, and even world war may take place through the instigation of the East. While the governmental process is shored up elsewhere in Africa, the liberating process must continue in Southern Africa. What are the stakes, and what are the choices open to American policy?

The stake is an orderly Africa, immunized from the world conflict. The process is liberation. Yet this will put in jeopardy one other stake —the considerable nonferrous metals and mineral resources in Southern Africa—especially in the Congo, Zambia, and the Republic of

South Africa—all now owned and exploited by the West. Professor Wolfe's paper in this volume reveals the interlocking nature of the Western companies involved in this exploitation, assumes that native majorities will control Southern Africa in the future, and suggests that the best way for the companies to maintain their position is to join the "wave of the future." It may not be that easy, nor will the enlightened liberal capitalism and self-interest approach of Taylor Ostrander ensure success.

The keys to the orderly development of Southern Africa and the reconciliation of group interests in new political communities are the white citizens of the Republic of South Africa and Rhodesia and the government of Portugal. The Republic of South Africa alone is rich enough and strong enough to draw all of Southern Africa into a race war of national liberation, with Chinese or Russian participation. The pressures on South Africa are considerable, as Britain moves to surround the Republic and to infiltrate its territory with states ruled by African majorities. This challenge to South Africa is heightened, as explained by Angie Brooks, by the case before the International Court of Justice, brought by Liberia and Ethiopia, charging South Africa with a violation of its obligations under the League of Nations mandate system with regard to South West Africa. The Republic is accused of unilaterally changing the legal status of the former League of Nations mandate, of applying apartheid in violation of its obligations under the mandate, and of failing to account for its actions to any international body. The United States has supported British actions against South Africa. The two nations now have in force an arms embargo against the Republic which has been joined by Sweden, Denmark, and Switzerland.

While the pressure increases from the outside, South Africa's internal policies become more abhorrent. Apartheid is legally made more rigid daily in every facet of public, social, and economic life. Black leaders are banned, executed, or jailed, and white liberals are harassed by confinement and prosecution.

In Portuguese Angola and Mozambique, the picture is one of tragedy and little hope, as the papers of George Houser, John Marcum and Allard Lowenstein, Douglas Wheeler, and Eduardo Mondlane reveal. The nationalist revolts in Angola have been effectively crushed by the Portuguese, and the movement now exhibits increased factionalism and disorganization. There is doubt that the Congo will continue to be a hospitable base of future operations against Angola. The rebel zone has been reduced to the mountains in northern Angola. In U.N. debates over Angola, the United States limited itself to saying that Portuguese refusal of self-determination threatened world peace and security. The U.S. opposed independence as a goal and opposed sanctions against Portugal. (The Portuguese have used American arms supplied under NATO arrangements, although they had agreed not to do so.)

According to reports from Tanzania, guerrilla activity started in Mozambique in September, 1964. (Dr. Eduardo Mondlane, one of the conference participants, left to return to Dar es Salaam to lead the activities of FRELIMO against the Portuguese in Mozambique.) FRELIMO now claims that as the result of its activities the Portuguese no longer control three of the northern provinces—Cabo Delgado, Zambezia, and Tete. On the whole, however, one must conclude that the Portuguese have the situation well in hand.

The same cannot be said of Portuguese Guinea, where guerrilla activity is on the increase and spreading northward. Disorder and economic disintegration appear to be increasing, and a considerable refugee problem has developed in Senegal.

Portugal has made some modifications in its policy toward natives in its "overseas provinces," which were and are the worst ruled in Africa. It is true that the Portuguese have less racial prejudice than any other Europeans. Miscegenation is not frowned upon, and there is an estimated population of mixed blood in Angola and Mozambique of 60,000 (much fewer in the latter than the former); neither country is in any sense a Brazil. The Portuguese have nonetheless viciously exploited African labor in the past by contract and forced labor. All Africans are now considered citizens, which has resulted in a slight increase in the number of Africans who can vote—a circumstance that in practice makes no difference, not only in terms of numbers, but also because there are no parties to vote for other than Portuguese parties (and, in Angola, only one of these). Some labor reform has been instituted, but contract labor exists under terms and conditions that would be interpreted as forced labor anywhere else in the world. Mondlane describes in this volume the labor system by which the Portuguese make some $10 million a year recruiting and shipping black labor to South Africa.

It is difficult to see how the United States can nudge the Portuguese into a position of self-determination for Africans. There is, first, the U.S. desire to hold on to the Azores. More important, the Portuguese are not interested in majority rule and free institutions at home —let alone, as Wheeler says, in mass education, social mobility, and economic development in their "overseas provinces." Quite apart from the issue of self-determination, there are no shared political and social values between the African nationalist leaders and the Portuguese rulers.

The Rhodesian conflict now threatens to telescope the whole process and bring either conflict or failure for British and American policy. On November 11, 1965, Prime Minister Ian Smith of Rhodesia proclaimed a unilateral declaration of independence from Britain. He thus forced action, either for or against his move and his principles, by Portugal, the Republic of South Africa, Britain, the United States, and several African states. Their activities were also reflected in the U.N. and the Organization of African Unity. Rhodesia, a self-governing Crown Colony since 1923, operating under a constitution granted in 1961, by its action violated the British tradition that independence in Africa is granted by Britain, followed by U.N. membership. Basically, it would appear from all the acts, negotiations, and counternegotiations that went on before Smith's action that he and his Rhodesian Front government were not willing to accept independence on a basis that would eventually guarantee rule by black Africans in Rhodesia, which now has 220,000 whites and 4 million blacks.

Smith's step challenged the whole British and American policy of gradual and orderly change to government by consent of the governed in Southern Africa, for it was taken at a time when neither could risk the direct action against which Smith could not prevail. Zambia, which produces 300,000 tons of copper a year (taken together with Katanga's production, this represents 25 per cent of the world's copper), smelts her copper with Rhodesian coal, and exports it over Rhodesian railroads to the port of Beira in Mozambique. As the war in Vietnam escalated, a copper shortage was developing because of labor troubles in Chile. In a sense, the interests of Communist China and Rhodesia coincided. The demand for copper became so strong that the United States in early 1966 released 200,000 tons from its reserves to keep the price down and placed controls on the export of copper from the United States. Should the war become a general one, the release of copper from its stockpile may come home to haunt the United States. Britain obtains two-thirds of her copper from Zambia.

The alternatives to some kind of cooperation with Rhodesia in order to get the copper out are extremely costly. The British own the Benguela Railroad, by which copper from Zambia may be shipped through Katanga and Angola to the port of Lobito. The cost is one-third more than shipping through Beira, and the line is operating near capacity; it could take only 120,000 tons of freight more in any year. There is also the possibility of using the rail, highway, and Lake Tanganyika route to the East African Railway and thence to Dar es Salaam or to Beira. This would be a most expensive and difficult route, as would be a truck route to Dar es Salaam. It has been estimated that newly developed Lockheed Hercules aircraft could fly the copper out at reasonable cost, but they are unlikely to be available in the near future.

Should alternative sources for export of copper become available, however, Ian Smith still has a trump card, for he could cut off the cheap metallurgical coal from Wankie which is used to smelt Zambian copper and for which there are no other sources in Africa. Indeed, for a short time he placed a $14 a ton royalty on coal from Wankie. Zambian ore production is also dependent on the electricity from the Kariba Dam power plants, which, unlike the dam, are located on the Rhodesian side of the border. The Zambian mines are wet mines, and they and Zambia depend to a great measure on electricity from the Kariba Dam. In reply to Zambian pleas, the British have sent an RAF fighter squadron and RAF troops to protect the dam and the power plant, but they are stationed on Zambian soil.

The UDI has put a strain on Britain's relations with Pan-African leadership in general and with her own former colonies in particular. On December 5, 1965, the OAU demanded that Britain crush Rhodesia by force within ten days, or African nations would break diplomatic relations with her. Former colonies referred to the swiftness with which Britain had used force against her black subjects engaging in insurrections. The OAU set up a five-man committee to work out strategy against Rhodesia, including the use of armed force. The committee is composed of representatives of Ghana, Zambia, Tanzania, Kenya, and the United Arab Republic. At this date, only Tanzania, Guinea, Senegal, Niger, Ghana, Mali, the UAR, and Mauritania have broken relations with Britain, and there is considerable evidence to indicate that such rupture is more apparent than real. The Pan-African movement has been humiliated by the unwillingness of its friends in the West and by its own weakness. The OAU meeting of prime ministers in Addis Ababa on February 28, 1966, which fell into a wrangle over seating Ghana, accomplished nothing.

The British have maintained that, although they would not use force against the illegal Rhodesian government, they would bring it down by economic sanctions. The British have insisted that Rhodesia is legally a colony, and thus sanctions under Chapter VII of the U.N. Charter do not apply, since that article refers to sanctions against nations that threaten international peace. Prime Minister Harold Wilson addressed the Security Council on December 17, 1965, the same day Britain imposed an oil embargo on Rhodesia. On December 21, the Security Council passed a resolution calling on member nations not to recognize the new government and to impose an economic boycott, including an embargo on oil and arms. The resolution called upon Great Britain to provide a new constitution for the colony to replace the one of 1961. The basic action was left to Britain and her allies.

Prime Minister Harold Wilson was able to gain support for his program against Rhodesia at the meeting of the Commonwealth nations in Lagos, which he addressed on January 11, 1966. African hostility was allayed by his promise not to restore government in Rhodesia under the constitution of 1961 when the rebellion was broken, an issue on which President Nyerere was especially firm. Wilson promised an interim government under the governor general, representative of all opinion and races in Rhodesia. Government would be restored after satisfactory amendments had been added to the 1961 constitution. In a speech before his National Assembly on December 14, 1965, President Nyerere had insisted that Britain should commit herself to *eventual* majority rule in Rhodesia. Britain has not yet made such a commitment to black rule in Rhodesia, as she has done in East Africa.

British action to date has included the following: the oil embargo mentioned above and an arms embargo previously effected; the prohibition of all trade with Rhodesia, with the exception of parts for the airways, the Kariba Dam and power plant, and the railroad; and the freezing of all Rhodesian assets in Britain except those of commercial banks. Britain has made it a crime to export tobacco from Rhodesia, which means that a buyer now cannot legally obtain title to tobacco; if he fails to gain possession before the re-establishment of the legal government, he may very well have a total loss. Britain normally buys one-third of the Rhodesian tobacco crop, and the tobacco auctioning is now underway.

The banning of oil from Rhodesia has also prevented the normal flow of gasoline, oil, and kerosene from the Umtali refinery in Rhodesia to Zambia. Rhodesia cut off oil to Zambia on December 18, 1965. Through an airlift organized from Dar es Salaam, Britain, with U.S. assistance, has kept the flow of oil products going into Zambia. Trucking from Dar es Salaam to Zambia is also being used.

The United States has backed British sanctions by banning the export of oil, oil products, arms, and ammunition to Rhodesia and the import of sugar into the U.S., even turning back sugar on the high seas. This seems to be as far as the United States has the legal authority to go. By working with American companies, the United States is stopping the sale of oil to Rhodesia produced outside the U.S. by American companies, and the purchase from Rhodesia by the U.S. of tobacco, lithium, and chrome. These measures, which are carried out with the cooperation of American companies, are at this writing still underway.

In spite of the array of economic sanctions, Rhodesia is faring well from all accounts. Her most difficult problem has been an act of nature, not man—a drought in Matabeleland which is wiping out the cattle and reducing the Matabeles to the point of starvation.

Rhodesia still has several moves that she has not made. I have already mentioned her ability to stop the shipment of coal from Wankie necessary to the smelting of copper ore in Zambia, and her control of the Kariba power plants. It is reported that Rhodesia has countered British RAF units by putting her own fighters in the Caprivi strip. In addition, some 500,000 workers from Malawi work in Rhodesia, and Ian Smith has banned the migration of all new labor from Malawi, Mozambique, and Zanzibar. Half of the white miners in Zambia are Rhodesian, and many of the rest are South African. Malawi, which buys essential goods from Rhodesia, has sterling currency that Britain has blocked for Rhodesia. It can be expected that Rhodesia will demand currencies other than her own from Malawi, 40 per cent of whose governmental budget is subsidized by Britain.

Rhodesia is selling her sugar below the world market price and raising the price at home approximately two cents a pound to compensate producers. Her tobacco will be sold to the Republic of South Africa, Portugal, and the Netherlands, which claims that it has no legislative authority for trade sanctions against Rhodesia.

With regard to money, Rhodesia recovered more than half of her £24,306,000 in Britain before UDI. She produces gold herself, and her holdings have increased from £500,000 before UDI to £3.5 million, which she is selling to countries other than Britain. In addition, it is reported that the Republic of South Africa has made rand credit available to Rhodesia, which can be exchanged for other currencies. The French role is not clear, but France abstained in the Security Council vote on Rhodesia, and a French business mission has visited the colony.

The rebellious colony has nothing to fear from African resistance at home. The riots in the townships around Salisbury and Bulawayo, and the strike in Bulawayo, were easily quelled by the police. With the help of scores of informers, the police have jailed nationalists and intimidators, and they protect all workers. The nationalist movement in Rhodesia is split into ZAPU and ZANU, and both Joshua Nkomo and Ndabaningi Sithole have been rusticated along with their workers. Rural Africans are too poor and uneducated to be involved, and the chiefs have repeatedly shown in indabas that they are on Smith's side.

There is also nothing for Smith to fear from black African nations. Rhodesia has 12,000 regulars and 46,000 army reserves, according to her reports, and she considers these adequate to repel any threat of invasion. Nkrumah has been ousted from Ghana and Ben Bella from Algeria. Guinea, Liberia, and the Ivory Coast have troops on each other's borders. The UAR is bogged down in Yemen. Morocco has its own internal unrest, and the Sudan is faced with a secessionist movement in its south. Nigeria is recovering from her own military coup, as are Dahomey, Congo (Léopoldville), and Upper Volta. The armies of Kenya, Uganda, and Tanzania are now being retrained after their own relatively recent mutinies.

Oil sanctions appear to be the most threatening to Rhodesia, and the refinery at Umtali has shut down several times. However, crude oil is now being shipped from Portuguese Angola to Beira, and the Republic of South Africa is trucking oil to Beitbridge in Rhodesia in amounts equal to half of the colony's requirements under rationing. Rhodesia is planning with the help of South Africa to run a railroad to Beitbridge that would link with the Rhodesian railway system at Rutenga or West Nicholson, thus bypassing the railroad from South Africa through Bechuanaland. South Africa has warned all foreign oil companies in her country that restrictions on their sales for Rhodesia will not be tolerated.

The crux of the matter, then, is continuing Portuguese and South African support of Rhodesia and the availability of the South African rand. South Africa will take the colony's tobacco and sugar. The Handels Institute of South Africa, a federation of industrialists, is cooperating with the Rhodesian Promotion Council to develop new industries in Rhodesia and to take her products.

The Republic of South Africa, in view of U.N. action against her, has a vested interest in proving that economic sanctions will not work against Rhodesia. In addition, Britain's economic sanctions may well cast Rhodesia permanently on the side of South Africa, a matter of some importance when one considers the dependence of Malawi and Zambia on Rhodesia and of Mozambique upon South Africa. Zambia normally purchases heavily from both Rhodesia and South Africa.

It has been pointed out that Britain will grant independence to Bechuanaland and Basutoland in 1966, and Swaziland in the near future. Also, sometime during 1966, the International Court of Justice may well decide that the Republic of South Africa has violated its commitments with regard to South West Africa. Before the end of the year, therefore, South Africa may face two black nations within its territorial boundaries, with another soon to appear. Within the next few years, its relations with South West Africa will undoubtedly be altered. At the least, its own racial arrangements will be put under considerable strain; at the most, it will face another black African state on its borders. South Africa will certainly try to counter these developments by increasing its economic influence over the newly independent areas, and in this sense, if Rhodesia is successful, South Africa will have gained one major step in such a program.

In this situation, the Security Council's committee of experts concluded that while economic sanctions, if universally applied and effectively enforced over a considerable period, would be effective against South Africa, the Republic would not be readily susceptible to such sanctions. The United States has not been willing to go beyond an arms embargo on South Africa, for it does not feel that it is legally justified under Chapter VII of the U.N. Charter; moreover, it feels that sanctions will not resolve South Africa's internal problems, but exacerbate them.

U.S. interests in South Africa are not so considerable that they cannot be risked through further action against the Republic. With the exception of gold, all the raw materials provided by South Africa can be obtained in good supply elsewhere. U.S. investment in South Africa is about 14 per cent of all foreign investment in the Republic, 28 per cent of its investment in Africa, and 1 per cent of its total foreign investment. New investment in South Africa will be curtailed by the U.S. program to improve its balance of payments. America maintains space-tracking facilities in South Africa, and the base at Simonstown is useful to U.S. naval ships en route to Vietnam. These are not considerable stakes in terms of the foreign policy that the United States must follow in Africa if it is to complete the organization of peace in Africa as an integral part of the peace of the world. If South Africa wins now, the holocaust in Africa will certainly eventually be much greater.

As Gwendolen Carter notes in this volume, it is the return from gold production that finances the booming South African industrial and commercial complex. The United States is slowly coming to the realization that there is not enough gold in the world to support the concept of convertibility of currency for a nation where gross national product at home and abroad is so great. American balance-of-payments problems are a reflection of the demand for the dollar and the goods and services it represents, not the reverse. The steps that the United States has already taken will increasingly work a hardship on nations committed to the dollar. The central reserve unit scheme is a step away from gold. It would be ironical indeed if the effectiveness of sanctions against South Africa came to rest finally upon the abandonment of gold convertibility by the major nations of the world.

Short of such an eventuality, the papers in this volume indicate that the period of transition for Southern Africa may be tragic years for the continent, and, indeed, threaten the peace of the world. For vigorous and complete economic sanctions must be applied against South Africa over a long period of time in order to be effective; otherwise, Africa will eventually resolve its race problem by force. And the Chinese could not wish for a more satisfactory approach to racial matters in terms of their aims.

I

The Republic of South Africa

African Nationalist Movements [*]

GWENDOLEN M. CARTER

In a continent within which African political control has spread in the past few years with breathtaking and unprecedented speed, South Africa provides the striking exception. Nowhere else in Africa is exclusive white control of political and economic life held with such determination and buttressed by such strength. As a result, the efforts of one of the oldest African nationalist movements on the continent have so far proved ineffective in South Africa, even though that country possesses a relatively high proportion of Africans (and other nonwhites) with professional and industrial skills. Furthermore, the constant and almost universal condemnation by countries outside, as well as inside, the continent has failed as yet to persuade South African whites to share their control.

Far from removing restrictions on nonwhites and those who support their aspirations, the South African Government has intensified such restrictions in recent years. As justification for this trend, it points to the growing militancy of nonwhite demands and actions and to what it calls "the South African solution to the racial problem," the planned development of Bantustans—i.e., semi-autonomous African areas within the present territory of South Africa. The first of these Bantustans has now been created in the Xhosa-speaking territory of the Transkei, and seven other areas are slated progressively to receive this status. Above all, however, South African whites justify their own distinctive policies by the "uniqueness" of the South African scene.

No one can deny, in fact, that South Africa has distinctive features not duplicated elsewhere on the continent. Since the great exodus from Algeria has reduced the number of Europeans in that country from 1 million to 100,000 (1964), South African Europeans comprise three-quarters of all those whites who regard Africa as their permanent

* This paper appeared, although in somewhat different form, in *The Massachusetts Review*, Autumn, 1963, pp. 147–64. It was revised and updated by the author in the spring of 1965.

home. Moreover, the proportion of whites to nonwhites—1 to 4—is far higher than it has ever been elsewhere on the continent: In Southern Rhodesia, it was 1 to 18 in 1961; in Kenya, 1 to 109 the same year; and in Tanganyika, 1 to 440 in 1962.

Moreover, whites have lived in South Africa far longer than anywhere else on the continent. The Dutch made a way station at the Cape as early as 1652, and the Huguenot French and Germans, who mingled with the Dutch to form the modern Afrikaner, came to Africa within sixty years of that original settlement. By the eighteenth century, the white settlers were spreading far outside the boundaries that the Dutch East India Company sought to impose and were exhibiting those qualities of independence and love of the land that helped to promote their emotional separation from Holland. English-speaking South Africans, who came from 1820 on, also have deep roots in the country, far deeper than those which white Rhodesians have been able to sink since 1890 or white Kenyans since the turn of the century.

The very length of time that whites have lived in South Africa led to a constitutional situation different from that of other multiracial territories in Africa. It is easy to say today that white South Africans should never have been given unrestricted control of their country, but in 1909–10 most people considered that the grant of Dominion status to South Africa was a great liberal measure in line with the constitutional advance within the British Empire that had brought Canada, Australia, and New Zealand to full internal self-government. It was not widely recognized before World War I that local white settlers' control might be coercive. Be that as it may, the fact is that South African whites have had complete control of their country since 1910.

What made this control different from that exercised *de facto*, if not fully *de jure*, by white residents in Southern Rhodesia and, at an earlier date, in Kenya was not only numbers, length of residence, and constitutional form, but also occupational make-up. Only in South Africa has there been a white group that has known the sting of being (or nearly being) of poor-white status. The United States has also seen the effects of tension over the economic competition of Negroes and poor whites, and the desperate efforts of the latter to retain a position of social superiority. In South Africa, the problem has been still more serious. In the early 1920's, the progressive impoverishment of the land on which most Afrikaners lived (hence the name Boers, or farmers) drove an increasing number into the cities to look for work. There they found that the English-speaking residents (against whom they still felt the resentments of defeat in the Anglo-Boer War, 1899–1902) were in control of all industry and commerce. Still more galling to them was the fact that the unskilled jobs, the only ones they were then equipped to take, were in the hands of Africans. As a consequence, South Africa faced the world's worst poor-white problem, with at least 60 per cent of the entire Afrikaner population either reduced to or threatened by poor-white status.

This situation has been solved, and today there are virtually no poor whites in South Africa. But it was solved by the creation of an area within the economy where jobs are reserved for whites and paid at inflated levels as a result either of legislation or of government-approved trade-union action. This area reserved for semiskilled or unskilled whites can be found throughout the economy: in the gold mines, with their legislative color bar; in the iron and steel industry, which was developed in the 1920's to provide jobs for Afrikaners as well as to promote South Africa's economic independence of Great Britain; in the administration; and, most dangerous of all, in the police. Clashes between the lower ranks of the white police and the Africans are routine. Sometimes these conflicts are over the incessant and often arbitrary enforcement of the pass laws, under which every male African, and increasingly also every female African, outside the reserves must have the requisite identity document on his or her person at all times. All too often, the handling by the police of these and other matters affecting Africans includes the use of violence as a means of reinforcing a sense of racial superiority.

Still more important and distinctive is the intense sense of Afrikaner nationalism that animates the Afrikaans-speaking majority among the white population. So strong is this sentiment that it may well be the most fervent nationalism existing on the African continent. It provides an internal cohesion that makes it difficult for Afrikaners to detach themselves from their community, and it exercises a constant pressure on the Afrikaner people to maintain a unified front against any internal or external forces.

Moreover, Afrikaner nationalism has its own political grouping, the ruling Nationalist Party, whose tightness of organization and control finds few parallels in other states with two-party systems. This party is directed by a network of paid professional organizers who supervise the activities of volunteer workers. These workers in turn concern themselves with every household in their own small area that has a professed or potential supporter. Thus there is an intimate and constant interaction between dedicated party workers and the Nationalist electorate, which reinforces unity both of purpose and of dogma.

One further unique feature of South Africa is its industrial development. No other country in Africa has had a genuine industrial revolution. South Africa's revolution arose out of the exploitation of the world's greatest supply of gold, whose recovery required large-scale operations and heavy mechanization to follow the ore-bearing rock deep underground. (Mining is now going on more than two miles below the surface on the Witwatersrand.) The returns of gold mining still underpin the development of the rest of the economy. But while mining (also of other metals and of diamonds) provides the basic wealth of South Africa, its iron and steel industry is as efficient and operates at as low a cost as any in the world. As an additional tier of production, the country has a wide range of secondary industries, most of which developed either during or since World War II. Thus not only for Africa, but even considered generally, South Africa has a fairly mature and well-balanced economy.

This fact has far-reaching consequences for relations between whites and nonwhites within South Africa. It makes essential a substantial use of nonwhites, particularly Africans, in the white-controlled economy. Because South Africa has a relatively small number of skilled white workers in proportion to the demands of its industrialization, Africans perform not only virtually all the nonskilled jobs in the so-called white areas, but also at least half the semiskilled jobs in industry and even some of the skilled ones (though they may not be so rated). As a result, whites and nonwhites are closely associated within the economic process, despite rigorous restrictions on their contacts when away from the machines. In fact, the whole South African economy is vitally dependent on the contribution made by Africans.

Despite these pressures toward economic integration, the legal restrictions on the acquisition of land by Africans outside the reserve areas and the virtual impossibility of Africans accumulating the resources needed to own even small manufacturing concerns give rise to a classically Marxist situation in which the means of production are in the hands of the white group controlling the government, and the landless proletariat provides the workers of industry.

The strain that would be induced anywhere by this situation is intensified in South Africa by the fact that the two groups are also differentiated by color, and that the landless proletariat is constantly subjected to the discriminatory provisions of the racial apartheid (apartness) policy.

But while the industrial situation in South Africa intensifies African bitterness and desire for change, it also gives the white population powerful means of curbing outward signs of African discontent. Only the white population, and in particular the government, can easily arm itself with punitive instruments of force. Perhaps still more important for maintaining control is the physical layout of the cities and the African townships. The whites live in more or less self-contained centers with their own transportation, public utilities, manufactures, and shops. In contrast, urban Africans nearly always live in townships that lie well outside the white cities but are almost wholly dependent on facilities controlled from within these cities. This dependence obtains not only for transportation but, still more important, for all kinds of power, for supplies, and for water. It was the cutting off of water from Langa Township, outside Cape Town, combined with the use of force by the police, that broke the African work boycott that had been launched in protest over the 1960 Sharpeville shootings and had temporarily threatened to cripple certain areas of the South African economy.

This, then, is the setting within which African nationalism must operate in South Africa. Unlike the situation everywhere else on the continent (except the Portuguese territories), Africans have no means of political representation outside the Transkei; they own none of the major means of production; they own virtually no land in freehold, even in the reserves. Moreover, African nationalists have always had to operate on the edge of illegality because of the rigorous restraints and laws that can be used to curb their activities. Thus African nationalism has little or no base of power in South Africa apart from representing by far the most numerous group within the country and from receiving such encouragement and potential aid as might come from Africans outside. African nationalist movements are hamstrung by law and practice and confronted at every turn by a militant white nationalism that is strongly organized, possesses the instruments of force, and, understandably, sees the rapid advance of African political control in the southern part of the continent as a potential threat to its own survival.

Despite these difficulties, African nationalism in South Africa established its own national organization in 1912—the African National Congress (ANC). Indeed, this organization had predecessors: the Native Education Association, which was formed in 1882 in the Cape and protested the pass laws two years later; the Native Electoral Association, founded in 1884 to organize the Cape African vote; and the Natal and Transvaal Native Congresses, organized after the turn of the century. On the eve of South African union, a national Native Convention considered the implications of the new structure of government for the situation of Africans and sent a delegation to the British Government to protest, though to no avail, the exclusion of non-whites from Parliament. The African National Congress (first named the South African Native National Congress), which was formed at Bloemfontein in the Orange Free State on January 8, 1912, built on this experience and named as its first President Dr. John L. Dube, the leader of the Natal Native Congress. In particular, the new ANC concentrated on opposing the pass laws and, after the 1913 Land Act, on the deprivation of Africans' land rights outside the reserves. More broadly, the objectives of the ANC were to achieve political and civil rights for Africans comparable to those possessed by whites, to aid the economic, social, educational, and industrial advance of Africans, and to establish a society in South Africa based on "racial unity and mutual helpfulness."

On certain demands like the abolition of the pass laws, there has never been division among Africans in South Africa. Over tactics, however, they have divided from time to time. In 1935, Africans were confronted with the Hertzog-Smuts United Party program of removing Africans with the franchise (i.e., those in the Cape who could meet literacy and economic qualifications) from the common roll, where they voted for the same candidates as did whites and qualified Coloureds, and placing them on a separate roll to elect three whites to the House of Assembly, the seat of power. The national African conference that met in response in Bloemfontein voiced a strong protest against this program, but could not prevent its enactment. The All-African Convention (AAC), established at the 1935 conference, was intended as a federal, coordinating organization uniting all African nationalist groups; but the ANC withdrew the next year and insisted on its own continued separate existence.

Despite this rebuff by the ANC, the AAC still tried to unite African, and subsequently nonwhite, organizations in a common front against discriminatory laws. Taking a new line in Bloemfontein on December 17, 1943, the AAC joined with a federation of Coloured organizations in the Cape that had been formed to oppose a newly established Coloured Affairs Department—and did so with such fervor that this effort to promote their separate development remained ineffective for some fifteen years. The program of what was called somewhat inaccurately the Non-European Unity Movement (NEUM) embodied not only a clear-cut repudiation of any notion of white trusteeship, but also a declaration of full equality between nonwhites and whites. Arguing, moreover, that nonwhites aided the government's policies of white supremacy whenever they cooperated with government-sponsored bodies affecting nonwhite interests and conditions, the NEUM called on all nonwhites to boycott such bodies whether they existed inside or outside the reserves.

Despite their militant attitude, the AAC and NEUM had relatively little influence except in a few areas of the Transkei and in the western Cape. The ANC continued to be the most significant representative of African opinion. But the ANC itself was far from unified over tactics. Those ANC leaders who had decided to serve in the Native Representative Council—which the government had set up as a sounding board for African opinion at the same time qualified Cape African voters were removed from the common roll—felt that they should not put forward demands during World War II. But growing restlessness at lack of action led to the establishment in 1944 of the Youth League, which worked within the ANC but demanded positive measures to publicize African opposition to discrimination.

In several respects, the year 1946 marked a turning point for both African and Asian organizations. A membership revolt within the South African Indian Congress (SAIC) changed what had been a predominantly middle-class and rather cautious organization urging civil rights for Asians into a militant group ready to work jointly with Africans. This new attitude led in 1949 to a formal alliance between the SAIC and ANC to work together to publicize and seek remedies for their common grievances.

The ANC also decided that the Native Representative Council was worthless as a channel of communication to the government and therefore boycotted it. But this was much less than the ANC's more active members demanded, the more so as others were gaining the limelight. This was particularly true of the strike of 60,000 African miners, who also provided a startling demonstration of the potentialities of organization when they marched in orderly fashion from the mines outside Johannesburg into the city. Blaming the strike on South African Communists, the government arrested 159 persons and subsequently prosecuted 52 of them, most of them Communists, for promoting an illegal strike, all strikes by Africans being illegal. Subsequently, steps were taken to prevent organizers from having access to the mines, but few people who had witnessed the demonstration would forget the latent power that it represented.

The militancy urged by the ANC Youth League was finally adopted in 1949 as the program of the Congress as a whole. Coupled with the threat to African organization implicit in the broad definitions included in the 1950 Suppression of Communism Act, this new attitude transformed the ANC from a forum of discussion to an activist group seeking to change conditions through mass demonstrations and pressure. The South African Indian Congress had already undertaken a two-year campaign of passive disobedience against the residential segregation embodied in the Asiatic Land Tenure and Indian Representation Act of 1946. Working closely with the SAIC, the ANC called a defiance campaign in 1952 to publicize its opposition to what were called "the unjust laws," notably the pass laws, but also other measures, including the Suppression of Communism Act.

The defiance campaign brought about both a high point in ANC success and a split. During the campaign, more than 8,000 volunteers deliberately courted jail sentences to demonstrate their grievances and on release helped to organize the 100,000 members in urban and rural areas to which the ANC had swelled. But after an extended court case, at the end of which African and Asian leaders were convicted of "statutory Communism" (i.e., Communism as defined in the 1950 Act), Dr. James Moroka, President of the ANC, who had previously been the candidate of the more militant younger members, repudiated the campaign and thereby drastically shook the movement. Moroka was replaced in December, 1952, by ex-Chief Albert Luthuli, who, though he did not court a jail sentence, had been forced to give up his chieftainship because of his endorsement of the defiance campaign. Despite a persistent series of banishments and restrictions to his own area, Luthuli has continued to provide at least titular leadership within the organization. But by the time of his election, the defiance campaign was already petering out for lack of money. It came to an end after the Criminal Laws Amendment Act of 1953 instituted severe penalties for advocating passive resistance to a law.

The next important landmark in the history of the ANC was the establishment in 1954 of the Congress alliance between the ANC, the SAIC, the small South African Coloured People's Congress, and the white Congress of Democrats (which stood for complete equality regardless of race or color and in this and other ways sought a radical reorganization of South African society). Meeting at Kliptown in the Transvaal on June 26, 1955, a large gathering, called the Congress of the People, widely representative of both urban and rural areas, adopted the Freedom Charter, which combined a declaration of traditional civil and political rights with a broadly socialist approach to the redistribution of land and national wealth.

To the government, the Freedom Charter appeared as such a threat to the existing social and political structure that it became the key document in the long-drawn-out treason trials that were launched with a mass arrest in December, 1956, of 156 persons, most of them African but including all races. Until March 29, 1961, when the trials finally ended with a verdict of "not guilty," persistent but unsuccessful efforts were made to prove that the Congress alliance was the spearhead of an organization of national liberation that was part of an international Communist-inspired movement to overthrow governments in all countries where certain sections of the population did not possess full political and economic rights. In bringing in their verdict, the judges declared that they found no evidence in the millions of words presented to them that the ANC was Communist-directed or that it was prepared to use violence to achieve its obvious objective of gaining rights for Africans within South Africa.

One of the few positive results of the treason trials from the point of view of Africans was that from time to time the trials facilitated a degree of communication between groups of the accused that would be impossible under normal conditions. It is sometimes said that the success of the Alexandra bus boycott of 1957—perhaps the most impressive demonstration yet made of African solidarity, and one that awakened far more white sympathy than had the passive-resistance campaign—was due to the direction afforded by those on trial, who, incidentally, were never kept in jail. But the immobilization of so many prominent ANC leaders seriously weakened that organization and indirectly prepared the way for the open split in the African nationalist movement in 1959.

None of the tactics adopted by the ANC after the defiance campaign had satisfied the younger group of activists within the organization. Although the ANC called a successful one-day stay-at-home strike on June 26, 1957, to commemorate the signing of the Freedom Charter, this activist group saw little sense to, or results from, such tactics. Moreover, it viewed the Congress alliance with suspicion, fearing that it had brought the African nationalist movement too much under the influence or control of Asians and whites. By 1955, this group had become known as the Africanists, and in their newspaper, *The Africanist*, edited by Robert Sobukwe, they preached what they called the original doctrine of the ANC, as formulated in 1912 and as revived and strengthened by the ANC Youth League in the 1940's. Obviously, they were affected also by the independence drive of African states following Ghana's achievement of sovereignty on March 6, 1957, and by the slogans of the Pan-African movement.

Sobukwe formally left the ANC in 1958; in April, 1959, he was elected President of the newly formed Pan-Africanist Congress (PAC), the name taken by the Africanists when they broke away from the ANC. Once again the African nationalist movement was split between two rival organizations, but this time, in contrast to the earlier split between the ANC and AAC, the differences were not only over tactics but also over allies. Under Luthuli's leadership, the ANC had remained loyal to the Congress alliance with its white, Asian, and Coloured components, in particular because this association demonstrated Luthuli's desire for a multiracial or, more particularly, a nonracial South Africa within which people would be free to associate without regard for race or color. To Sobukwe and the PAC, in contrast, the basis of any reconstituted society in South Africa had to be African since, they argued, it is the Africans who are indigenous to the country, form the majority of its population, and provide most of the labor.

The ANC and PAC also differed more than did the ANC and AAC in the constituencies to which they made their appeal. The earlier African nationalist movements concentrated on the urban literate, used English as their medium of communication, and thought in terms of change *within* the existing structure. Their approach was more comparable, therefore, to that of American Negroes in their attempts to improve their conditions within the United States than to that of African nationalists in West or East Africa with their drive for African majority control and independence. Many of the Pan-Africanists are highly educated (Sobukwe himself was lecturer in Zulu studies in the Department of Bantu Studies at the University of Witwatersrand from 1953 until 1960), but they have made a deliberate and quite successful attempt to communicate their own aspirations to African migratory workers in their own native languages and through examples and idioms that the workers understand in terms of their own experiences.

Such an appeal to rural Africans had been made successfully in the Eastern Provinces of the Cape during the defiance campaign, and the PAC built on this experience. The Pan-Africanists were particularly successful, however, in using this approach to migrant workers in the townships outside Cape Town where the ANC was relatively weak. By making understandable to them both the existing political system in South Africa and the PAC's objectives for a future in which Africans would play the major role, the Pan-Africanists developed a closer relation between intellectuals and illiterates, and between urban and rural, than had any earlier African nationalist group. How effective this relationship became was demonstrated on March 30, 1960, after the Sharpeville crisis, when 30,000 Africans made a peaceful and disciplined march from Langa and adjoining townships into Cape Town and as easily terminated the demonstration on promises to Philip Kgosane, a young PAC leader, that unfortunately were not kept, of opportunities to discuss with the government the PAC demands: the abolition of the pass laws and a £1-a-day minimum wage.

The differences between the ANC and the PAC both in approach and in choice of allies operate to keep the two apart; but common adversity and the desire of ANC leaders to retain a dominant role in the nationalist movement have brought them together from time to time. When the PAC launched its campaign against the pass laws on March 21, 1960, and almost immediately, and contrary to its plans, became involved with the police at Sharpeville, with a resulting loss of sixty-seven African lives, Luthuli immediately called for a national day of mourning on March 28. This appeal led to an almost complete work stoppage in the African townships outside Johannesburg, Durban, and the cities of the eastern Cape. Luthuli also publicly burned his pass, calling on all Africans to follow his example. The government immediately rushed a special law through Parliament that banned both the ANC and the PAC for a year (a ban that has been extended each subsequent year). Under an ensuing state of emergency, thousands of Africans, including Luthuli and Sobukwe, were detained, and also many persons of other races who were known to sympathize with African aspirations. Sobukwe was subsequently given a three-year jail sentence after a trial in which he refused to recognize the validity of the law under which he was tried, since Africans had no share in formulating it. Luthuli was again banished to his home in Natal. In so far as these two nationalist organizations can now operate within South Africa, it must perforce be underground.

Despite the banning of the ANC and PAC as organizations, certain of their former members and others concerned with rebuilding unity in African ranks made a series of efforts to reach a basis of agreement. These efforts were, in part, in response to the insistence on unity by African leaders of other countries. The most substantial of these efforts within South Africa took form at what was called the Consultative Conference of African Leaders, held on December 16–17, 1960, under the chairmanship of Jordan Ngubane of the Liberal Party, with all participants attending in their individual capacities. This conference agreed to establish a continuation committee to prepare for a more representative gathering of Africans, optimistically named the All-in African Conference. The purpose of this conference was to consolidate African unity along lines suggested at the December meeting, and to consider an action program that might include an appeal to the government to call a national convention of all South Africans to work out a new constitutional framework for the country.

Before the All-in Conference was held, however, divisions had already wrecked the hope that it would establish a new level of African unity. From the first, former PAC members made it clear that they were not interested in participating in a multiracial conference as such. Subsequently, these members withdrew from the continuation committee, charging that it was distorting the mandate outlined at the December meeting by making the multiracial character of the coming conference its dominant theme. Others, like Ngubane, felt that the principle of unity agreed on in December must be adhered to at all costs, and urged that preparations for the larger conference should be suspended while these differences of opinion were ironed out. When they became convinced, however, that the coming conference was being shaped to the particular purposes of certain former ANC members, that extreme left-wing elements were exerting a distorting influence from behind the scenes, and that there was no chance of postponing the conference, Ngubane and others, though not all the Liberal Party members, also withdrew from the committee. Despite these withdrawals, all those who had been on the original committee, were arrested or sought for arrest on March 20, 1961, five days before the conference was convened.

When the All-in Conference took place at Maritzburg, on March 25–26, 1961, the predominance of ANC songs and slogans suggested that it had been turned into a partisan gathering. The effect of the meeting tended, therefore, to be divisive rather than unifying. This fact was underlined when former PAC supporters openly distributed pamphlets condemning the stay-at-home demonstration that the Maritzburg conference had planned to coincide with the proclamation of the Republic, on May 31, 1961. A further factor in the failure of the demonstration seems to have been the disillusionment of many former ANC supporters over the failure of the All-in Conference to aid African unity. In addition, there were powerful external pressures to prevent the demonstration: the government put on a mass show of strength by mobilizing military and civilian forces; municipalities threatened the loss of passes; and some employers warned there would be loss of pay or dismissal for absence on those days. In the end, therefore, the All-in Conference and its plans for the anti-Republic demonstration seemed only to have alarmed the government and, if anything, to have widened the gulf between the supporters of the two former nationalist African organizations. Moreover, an effort to establish a representative United Front of the ANC, PAC, SAIC and an allied South West African National Union to operate outside South Africa for the purpose of influencing international public opinion against the government's apartheid policies was never fully implemented and the Front broke up in 1962.

In these projects and activities, ex-Chief Albert Luthuli, the ANC's best-known and most respected member, has played little direct role because government-imposed bans have restricted him to his own Natal district throughout almost all of his presidency of that organization. Yet Luthuli's clear-cut philosophy and his open stand in support of human values have made his influence a strong one within the ANC and among all Africans, and, to a lesser degree, among non-Africans. A devout Christian, with close links to organized Christianity in other countries, Luthuli is as much a spiritual as a political leader of his people. His forcefully expressed opposition to all forms of discrimination is based on his belief in the inherent worth and dignity of all men. His abiding objective is to help to build a society in which race will be irrelevant in considering either contributions or position. Thus he sees the working together of different racial groups in South Africa less as an organizational arrangement than as a beginning of that new society for which he strives.

Luthuli's earlier support of nonviolent passive resistance to discriminatory laws was rooted in his conviction that men must stand openly for what they believe but not in such a way as to cause physical damage to others. Thus, while he was continuously critical of laws that had an unequal or degrading effect, Luthuli until recently was no less firm in his opposition to violence as a means of changing existing conditions. As it became increasingly difficult and even impossible to find avenues through which to exert pressure on the government, Luthuli gradually became convinced, however, that major changes could not be achieved without violence. While he would greatly prefer nonviolent tactics, he has been pressured by circumstances into agreeing reluctantly that it seems unlikely there are other routes to change than sabotage, violence, and even racial war.

Robert Sobukwe, leader of the former PAC, also espoused nonviolence in the past, but as a tactical measure rather than as a matter of conviction. His approach has always been political rather than spiritual. Moreover, Sobukwe is a Pan-Africanist in a multiracial situation. He originally opposed a nonwhite alliance with Asians and Coloureds almost as much as any working together with whites, though both these PAC attitudes are now substantially modified. He denies the validity of laws that have not been passed by a predominantly African legislature, and he thinks in terms of a future society that has been shaped by an African majority. Far more than is true of Luthuli (despite Luthuli's continued responsibilities for a small Natal community), Sobukwe's objective is to establish an African mass movement that will bind together the peasants, migrant workers, and those living close to or below subsistence in the urban townships.

Both Luthuli and Sobukwe have mistrusted the government's program to establish Bantustans within South Africa as outlets for African energies and aspirations and, hopefully, as magnets to draw back from urban townships many of the Africans now more or less permanently domiciled within them. Luthuli has declared that the Bantu Authorities Act of 1951 and the Promotion of Bantu Self-Government Act of 1959 established a "fraudulent form of local government." His most obvious successor in the ANC, Nelson Mandela, the so-called "Black Pimpernel," who had a striking success in moving from one part of the country to another until captured by the authorities late in 1962, shared these sentiments. Paradoxically, Mandela, like the rival cousins—Chief Kaiser Matanzima, the Chief Minister of the Transkeian Legislative Assembly, and Paramount Chief Sabata, head of the Tembu tribe, who sincerely but ineptly opposed the Bantustan program—is a member of the Tembu royal household.

Though African nationalist leaders have generally stigmatized the Bantustan program as an attempt by the government to divide Africans to achieve better control over them, the government, in turn, can point to the fact that the United Transkeian General Council accepted the Bantu Authorities system in 1955. (The system came into operation a year later.) Moreover, at its 1961 session, the Transkeian Territorial Authority, the statutory body under this Act, requested the current form of self-government for the Transkei. Both moves—the original acceptance of the Bantu Authorities system and the subsequent demand for self-government—apparently resulted from the belief of many Transkeian African leaders that the current political opportunities in their territory, though limited and ultimately controlled by the central government, provide better outlets for self-expression than can be found by Africans elsewhere in the Republic.

In certain areas, violent, though largely hopeless, resistance to government-appointed chiefs and to the Bantu Authorities system has reflected the bitter opposition of rural Africans to what they regard as tightening government control. Moreover, the Zeerust uprising in 1957 and the resistance in Pondoland and Tembuland in 1960 and 1961 evidenced an interaction between urban nationalism and rural discontent. In Pondoland, the Congress alliance played a larger role than the PAC in supporting the unrest; in Tembuland, the PAC led. Thus, prior to being banned, both African nationalist groups had established to varying degrees the urban-rural alignments they recognize as essential for ultimate success. This earlier resistance in the African reserve areas to the new structure of authority raised questions as to the African reaction to "Bantustan" status for the Transkei. So far, however, political maneuvers between Chief Matanzima's Independence Party and Paramount Chief Victor Poto's Democratic Party have provided adequate outlets, though anti-government unrest is not far below the surface. It is not without significance either that African nationalist leaders, both inside and outside the country, now recognize that areas achieving Bantustan status might form the base for their future operations.

For a time, an increasing use of sabotage by African nationalists was a cardinal feature of their activities. After the failure of the May, 1961, demonstration, Mandela made a formal statement to the press that only violent methods remained. This turn to violence was formally approved by the ANC and the Congress alliance later in 1961. Late in 1962, the PAC also adopted this policy. In mid-December, 1962, the Spear of the Nation organization (*Umkonto We Sizwe*) sent a letter to South African newspapers declaring, on what it called the first anniversary of its campaign of violence, that "we have adopted this course because almost every avenue of legal and constitutional struggle has been closed by the State." It also stated that the "mass political movement is the cornerstone of the struggle against white supremacy" but that the government's policies had brought about a situation "in which the only real answer will be a direct test in the field of armed struggle."

While violence was originally restricted to inanimate objects, the explosion of a time bomb on January 18, 1963, in the building housing the provincial headquarters of the Nationalist Party and the offices of *Die Nataller* (the only Afrikaans newspaper in Natal and the spokesman for the provincial Nationalist Party) was interpreted as the beginning of terrorism without regard to human life. Violence against nonwhites has long been practiced by the police and other agents, and has been particularly noticeable in the Durban locations and in the Transkei. Indiscriminate though very limited killing of whites, as attributed to the terrorist Poqo group (said by the government to be the activist arm of the PAC), was new in the South African scene, however, and added a further dimension to the fear that was beginning to grow within the white population. This fear led to a tacit, if somewhat reluctant approval by most whites of the drastic measures taken by the government under the 90-day detention clause of the Criminal Laws Amendment Act, 1963, through which it apparently traced and ultimately broke by late 1964 both African resistance efforts and the small, largely white African Resistance Movement, which sought through sabotage to publicize its opposition to government policies.

Are there other alternatives to counterviolence in the South African situation? In two instances, white-directed political parties have African members and thereby provide bridges, however slight, across which discussions can be held between individuals of different racial groups on matters of national policy. The Liberal Party, which was formed in 1953, adopted a year later the long-term aims of universal suffrage and of removing racial restrictions on membership in Parliament, basing this policy on the argument that since South Africa depended on the labor of all its people, all should ultimately have equal political rights. Following a long series of discussions, all reference to an interim qualified franchise was finally officially deleted at the Liberal Party's Congress in May, 1960, at Cape Town, and replaced by a vague statement that the transition to universal franchise should be brought about "with the minimum possible dislocation." This change in the party platform led to the resignation of many moderate white members and to a transformation of the Liberal Party into an organization which, though still very small, has an African majority. At no time have the Liberals been able to win an election in a white constituency and such importance as they continue to have is largely the demonstration their white members provide of their belief in a nonracial society.

The second political party with some, though very small, African membership is the Progressive Party, which in 1958 followed the Liberal Party in breaking away from the United Party. The Progressives are more gradualist in their approach to African political rights than are the Liberals, but they accept the necessity for a qualified franchise common to all groups, for nonwhite representatives in Parliament, and for a bill of rights. The original eleven Progressive members in Parliament, who had been elected in 1958 on the United Party ticket, continued to hold their seats as Progressives from 1959 to 1961, but despite the fact that the party polled 69,042 votes, only one Progressive, Mrs. Helen Suzman, was returned in the 1961 general election.

Thus, while both the Liberals and the Progressives have some tacit or actual support—the former because of their program, the latter because they provide a liberal spokesman in Parliament—neither has had the electoral appeal necessary to have an impact on South African politics and policies. In contrast, the total results for the October, 1961, general election, together with a by-election held early in 1963, show that the Nationalist Party, with its predominant Afrikaner base, has continued the steady increase in voting strength demonstrated in the 1953 and 1958 elections, and in the republican referendum in 1960, and has gained the support of between 53 and 54 per cent of the white electorate.

What then does the current South African situation suggest for the future? Probably a Sparta, with control retained in the hands of the white population through an increasing use of force. Indeed, in the long run, violence from each side can be expected to stimulate greater and more irrational use of force by the other. But even so, it will be a Sparta that is dynamic because of its economic growth and because of the political dynamism of its two rival nationalisms: Afrikaner and African.

Afrikaner nationalism embodies a deep group sentiment intensified by fear for its own national survival; there are divisions of opinion within the Afrikaner group over both tactics and policies, but the pressures toward unity are almost overwhelming. What is new in the current situation is the growing solidarity of all South African whites under internal and external pressures and a common fear of what they might lose if they share political control with nonwhites. In contrast, both the nonwhite groups and the Africans themselves are still divided over tactics, allies, and the meaning and potentialities of the Bantustans, with no obvious signs of attaining formal unity in the foreseeable future. Yet African nationalism in South Africa has numbers on its side and the trend of events on the African continent.

The appalling dilemma faced by all groups in South Africa is that efforts to change, as well as to maintain, the existing structure threaten to end in violence. Excluded from all the normal channels of exerting influence, Africans and other nonwhites inevitably favor internal acts of sabotage and external sanctions to cripple the highly developed South African economy. This is so even though such damage would have its most serious impact, at least immediately, on the standard of living of urbanized Africans and other nonwhites. The government holds the major instruments of force and is probably restrained from using them chiefly because of their unfortunate effect on international public opinion. On either side, however, frustration or an unplanned crisis could precipitate a breaking point regardless of the consequences.

What of the possibilities of partition? Any division of South Africa's territory that did not provide equitable shares of land and of industrial, commercial, and mineral resources would impose unacceptable losses upon Africans, while such a partition would require a complete reorganization of the life of white South Africans. Thus few of the latter would be willing at present to explore such a possibility even though it might seem to offer one way out of the current impasse, particularly if the Bantustan program is genuinely implemented.

Barring so drastic a reorganization of society at the southern end of Africa, the situation holds the classic elements of tragedy. The two major groups within South African society stand in ever sharper opposition to each other, and yet are ever more interconnected and interdependent. Here in this most mature of all economies in Africa, there might have been a demonstration that the pressures on different races to work together were stronger than those which separate them: so far, the course of events has intensified division rather than woven together the ties of common interest.

White Politics

LESLIE I. RUBIN

At the last general election in the Republic of South Africa, in October, 1961, the Nationalist Party, led by Dr. Verwoerd, was returned to power with an increased majority and with the reaffirmed support of the electorate for the government policy of apartheid. The electorate that made this decision is white, and all the members of the House are white.[1] The Africans—numbering 11 million out of a population of 16 million [2]—were objects of the political process, not participants in it. Whether the African should have any say in the government of the Republic, the nature and the extent of the political rights that should be granted to him, and how and when they should be granted were among the issues raised in the election.[3] Around these issues, four distinguishable policies were presented to the electorate: those

[1] The South African Parliament consists of two chambers, the House of Assembly and the Senate. The Senate has a membership of 54, partly nominated by the government, partly chosen by an electoral college composed of members of the House of Assembly and members of the respective Provincial Councils. The House of Assembly—the effective organ of the legislature—comprises 160 white members; 156 are chosen by the direct vote of the white electorate in single-member constituencies, and 4 are elected by Coloured voters voting on a separate roll to represent constituencies in the Cape Province. At the date of the election in 1961, out of a Coloured population numbering 1,509,258, approximately 100,000 were eligible as voters, and of these approximately 25,000 had registered to vote.

[2] According to the last South African census, in 1960, the composition of the population was: African, 10,907,780; white, 3,088,492; Coloured, 1,509,258; Asian, 477,125. The total increase in the population since the 1951 census was 3,311,212, of which 2,347,706 were Africans.

The 1964 estimate is: African, 11,934,742 (68.3 per cent); white, 3,372,482 (19.3 per cent); Coloured, 1,642,556 (9.4 per cent); Asian, 524,220 (3 per cent). Total population, 17,474,000.

[3] Of the 156 seats, 70 were uncontested—50 represented by the Nationalist Party, 20 by the United Party. The registered electorate for the remaining 86 seats was 1,029,696. Of this number, 800,590 went to the polls.

of the Nationalist Party, the United Party, the Progressive Party, and the Liberal Party.[4] These policies combined to make up the pattern of white thinking on future relations between the white man and the African in the Republic.

The Nationalist Party and Apartheid

When the Nationalist Party came into power in 1948, the new doctrine of apartheid had not received precise definition. It had proved effective during the election as the focal point of a campaign that condemned the United Party of Field Marshal Smuts for pursuing a laissez-faire policy in relation to the influx of Africans into the cities. It had served as a slogan, under cover of which Nationalist politicians were able both to play on the white man's ever present fears of "black domination" and to assert that it was intended to deal justly with the African by giving him every opportunity to pursue his own development separately. Clearly the new policy was committed to increased separation of the races, but once in power, the Nationalist Party was compelled to face the question of how this increased separation was to be achieved.

Two conflicting views emerged among the supporters of the party. The first was advanced by the Dutch Reformed churches and a number of Afrikaner intellectuals: "By a policy of free and separate development, we must understand the territorial separation of European and Bantu, and the provision of areas which must serve as national and political homes for the different Bantu communities and as permanent residential areas for the Bantu population or the major portion of it." [5] The other view was put by Dr. Malan, the first Nationalist Prime Minister: "If one could obtain total or complete territorial apartheid, everybody would admit that it would be an ideal state of affairs. It would be an ideal state, but that is not the policy of our party. . . . When I was asked in the House on previous occasions whether that was what we are aiming at . . . I clearly stated . . . that total territorial separation was impracticable under present circumstances in South Africa, where our whole economic structure is to a large extent based on Native labour." [6] Earlier, Dr. Malan had

[4] A fifth party, National Union, was represented in the House by one member in 1963. Its policy did not differ significantly from that of the United Party. The party itself has since gone out of existence, its solitary parliamentary representative having joined the United Party.

[5] The apartheid policy of the S.A. Bureau of Racial Affairs as set forth in *Integration or Separate Development?* (Stellenbosch, 1952).

[6] Hansard, House of Assembly, April 12, 1950, cols. 4141–42.

said, "The principle of apartheid . . . is that we have two separate spheres . . . not separate territorial areas." [7]

The scruples of the intellectuals and the churches were brushed aside by the politicians. The policy of the Nationalist Party crystallized soon after it came into power as one of "keeping South Africa white" (baasskaap [mastery] was the popular cry), and a repressive policy was instituted. The party was content to leave the African what he in fact is—part of the multiracial society of South Africa—but was determined, within that society, to subject him to rigid controls and restrictions designed to maintain the supremacy of the white man. During the period 1948–59, numerous discriminatory laws were passed. There were laws providing for separate residential areas; [8] separate transport and separate accommodations in public institutions (e.g., waiting rooms in railway stations and counters in post offices); [9] and separate education, requiring Africans to be educated in their vernacular at certain levels.[10] Africans were denied the right to strike; [11] provision was made for the reservation of certain skilled occupations for whites; [12] rigid control of racial classification was introduced; [13] and in certain circumstances Africans were deprived of the protection normally afforded by the law.[14] There is a law that denies to an African who has since birth resided continuously in a town the right to have living with him in that town for more than seventy-two hours a married daughter or a son who has reached the age of eighteen.[15] There is another law that makes it a criminal offense for a white person and a nonwhite person to sit down publicly to a cup of tea together anywhere in South Africa, unless they have obtained a special permit to do so.[16] A third law empowers a policeman to enter and search, without warrant, "at any reasonable time of the day or night" premises where he has reason to suspect an African boy of eighteen years of age is committing the criminal offense of residing with his father without having the necessary per-

[7] Ibid., September 2, 1948, col. 1486.
[8] Group Areas Act No. 77 of 1957.
[9] Reservation of Separate Amenities Act No. 49 of 1953.
[10] Bantu Education Act No. 47 of 1950.
[11] Native Labour (Settlement of Disputes) Act No. 48 of 1953.
[12] Industrial Conciliation Act No. 28 of 1956. S. 77.
[13] Population Registration Act No. 30 of 1950.
[14] Natives (Prohibition of Interdicts) Act No. 64 of 1956.
[15] Natives (Urban Areas Consolidation) Act No. 25 of 1945, as amended. S. 10(1) (a) and (c).
[16] Proclamation No. 164, July 4, 1958, pursuant to S. 1(4) read with S. 1(i) (vi) of the Group Areas Act No. 77 of 1957.

mission to do so.[17] There are the pass laws, which impose rigorous control over the African's right to enter and leave the urban areas, subject him to constant police surveillance, and cause the arrest, and often the imprisonment, of hundreds of thousands of men every year.[18] An authoritative estimate in 1958 put the average number of arrests of Africans for pass-law and related offenses at 1,000 per day.[19]

These are some of the laws that constitute the implementation of the policy of apartheid during a period of fifteen years. Almost every aspect of the life of the African—social, economic, political—has been subjected to rigid legislative control, exercised, as a rule, by the administrative act of an official, without the right of recourse to a court of law. Alan Paton, commenting on these laws in 1959, wrote of "the illusion that apartheid propagandists are trying to foster abroad, that apartheid is a noble ideal." [20] In 1960, the International Commission of Jurists investigated the rule of law in South Africa and reported: "While the deep sociological problems confronting the Government of South Africa certainly cannot be minimized, it is manifestly apparent that the pursuit of the present policy constitutes a serious encroachment upon the freedom of all inhabitants, white and nonwhite alike." [21]

In 1950, the Nationalist Party decided to seek the opinion of experts on the question of whether the native reserves (the proposed Bantustans of today) could be used to carry out complete territorial apartheid. The Commission for the Socio-Economic Development of the Bantu Areas within the Union of South Africa, under the chairmanship of Professor F. R. Tomlinson, was required "to conduct an exhaustive enquiry into . . . a comprehensive scheme for the re-

[17] Government Notice No. 804, June 13, 1958, read with Act No. 25 of 1945, as amended. S. 10(1) (c).

[18] Natives (Abolition of Passes and Coordination of Documents) Act No. 67 of 1952. According to information furnished by the Minister of Justice in Parliament in 1957, 174,392 cases were sent for trial for offenses against curfew regulations, pass laws, and regulations relating to the production of documents; a further 52,631 cases (including a considerable number relating to control of movement) were sent for trial for offenses under the Natives (Urban Areas Consolidation) Act, as amended. (Hansard, House of Assembly, 1958, II, cols. 341–43.)

[19] Muriel Horrell, *A Survey of Race Relations in South Africa, 1957–8* (Johannesburg, 1959). During 1961, 375,417 Africans were convicted of influx-control and pass-law offenses. This figure was given to the House of Assembly in reply to questions by the Minister of Justice in February, 1963. (*The Star* [Johannesburg], February 9, 1963.)

During 1962, the number rose to 384,497. (Horrell, *A Survey of Race Relations in South Africa,* 1963 [Johannesburg, 1964].)

[20] In his Foreword to Leslie Rubin, *This Is Apartheid* (London, 1959).

[21] *South Africa and the Rule of Law* (Geneva, 1960).

habilitation of the Native Areas with a view to developing within them a social structure in keeping with the culture of the Native and based on effective socio-economic planning." The Tomlinson Report was presented in 1954, and a summary of the full report became available to the public in 1956.[22]

The report was a bitter disappointment to the proponents of territorial apartheid. While the Commission rejected the policy of integration of white and African and recommended separate development as the only alternative, it showed clearly that development of the Native Areas into a homeland for the African people was an undertaking bristling with problems, calling for urgent action, and involving great financial cost. It recommended the urgent expenditure by the government of £104 million within ten years to relieve the economic backwardness of the areas, urged white industrial development in the areas, and proposed that the African peasant be granted freehold title to land. Dr. Verwoerd, then Minister of Native Affairs, rejected these proposals. The government contended that a total of only £36 million was required and voted an initial amount of £3.5 million.

The most important conclusion of the Tomlinson Commission related to population growth in South Africa. It estimated that by the year 2000, the total population would be 31 million, comprising 21 million Africans, 1.5 million Asians, 4.5 million whites, and 4 million Coloureds. The Commission concluded that even if its proposals were put into effect, the reserves could, by that date, not accommodate more than 70 per cent of the African population—i.e., there would still be 6.5 million Africans in the white areas. Thus, under a policy designed to increase separation of the races, a progressively larger number of Africans would be living in the white areas.

The census returns of 1960 showed that in a period of 9 years the African population in the urban areas had increased by almost 1 million and that the nonwhite population as a whole was increasing almost twice as fast as the white population. In Johannesburg, the largest city (with a population of 1 million), the African population has increased almost 5 times as much as the white population since 1951. In Pretoria, formerly the only city where the whites outnumbered the Africans, the Africans had achieved a slight majority in 1960.[23]

While the Nationalists preached—and promised—apartheid, inte-

22 U. G. 61/1955 (Pretoria: Government Printer), p. xviii. The full report runs to 18 volumes; the 51 chapters cover 3,755 pages, and contain 598 tables and an atlas of 66 large-scale maps.

23 Keesing's Contemporary Archives (Bristol), May, 1961, p. 18090; December, 1962, p. 19132.

gration of the African within the multiracial society of South Africa proceeded apace. Henry Allen Fagan, a distinguished Afrikaner, a former Chief Justice of South Africa, and Minister of Native Affairs in the Nationalist Cabinet of General Hertzog before World War II, writing in 1959, referred to a twenty-year apartheid plan announced when the Nationalist Party came to power: "More than half of the twenty-year period has elapsed, with a Government in power that is pledged to carry out the policy of separation and is straining every nerve to do so. Yet no sign can be detected of even a commencement of the only process which can bring about the separation of White and Native . . . viz., the mass withdrawal of Bantu labour from the European industries." [24] By 1959, criticism of the government's policies, both within the country and beyond, was mounting. The worsening of relations between white and African led to growing concern among supporters of the government as well as among its opponents. A small but influential group within the traditional ranks of Afrikaner nationalism became more outspoken in their condemnation of the injustices inflicted upon the African and in their demands for fulfillment of the long-delayed promises of opportunities for separate development. At the United Nations, world opinion was hardening. The insistent protests of the new African states were an important factor; but it was the indisputably repressive character of the policy of apartheid that determined attitudes and policies in the outside world. It became increasingly difficult for nations only too anxious to understand the white man's problems to condone his policies. South Africans, many of whom were Nationalists, began to ask questions about positive apartheid. Negative apartheid—the whole apparatus of harsh laws separating white from nonwhite in the white areas—had been achieved, but where was Dr. Verwoerd's promised "South Africa in which the Bantu and the white man can live next to one another as good neighbours and not as people who are continually quarreling over supremacy"? [25]

In 1959, the government announced its intention of proceeding with the creation of self-governing Bantu states. The Promotion of Bantu Self-Government Bill was passed in that year, and came into force on June 30, 1960. It abolished existing parliamentary representation of the Africans,[26] established eight Bantu "national units," and

[24] *Our Responsibility* (Cape Town, 1959).

[25] Dr. Verwoerd, quoted in Hansard, House of Assembly, January 27, 1959, col. 154.

[26] Since 1936, the Africans of the Cape Province have been represented in the House of Assembly by three white members; the Africans of all four provinces by four white members in the Senate.

provided for the conferment of legislative powers upon Bantu territorial authorities. In a white paper explaining the background and
objects of the bill, the government declared its purpose to be "provision for the gradual development of self-governing Bantu national
units" and quoted the Prime Minister as having said that "if the various Bantu national units show the ability to attain the required stage
of self-sufficiency, they will eventually form a South African commonwealth together with white South Africa, which will serve as its core
and as guardian of the emerging Bantu states."

In fact, this law did not grant the Africans self-government. It deprived them of any say whatsoever in the government of the country,
and granted to them, instead, a system of local government subject
to the control of the white Parliament of South Africa. Furthermore,
in tying these subordinate legislative powers to the creation of tribal
units, the government was pursuing a policy of "divide and rule." Differences of language, tradition, and custom undoubtedly exist among
the African people, but they are of minor significance. To contem-
plate the permanent organization of the African people on the basis
of tribal units is to disregard the fact that more than half of them
live outside the tribal areas, and to ignore the fast rate of increase in
the number of Africans living in the white areas. All the reliable evidence (including expert Nationalist opinion—i.e., the Tomlinson
Commission) shows that the African is becoming increasingly part
and parcel of white South Africa. On this point, Professor de Kiewiet
has said: "That it is easy to demonstrate the powerful hold that the
old beliefs and habits of the tribe still have upon him cannot dis-
prove that he is a member of the total South African community . . .
irreversibly a part of the total life of South Africa. The true problem
of South Africa is to what degree and by what means the process of
adjustment and integration is to be continued. It would be easier to
drive the white man out of South Africa than the black man out of
the society the white man has created." [27]

The government went ahead with its proposals under the new law.
The first territorial authority to be constituted, that for the Transkei,
held its first session in 1959. It consisted of chiefs and other tribal
representatives, including a number nominated by a government official. It was empowered to exercise administrative powers subject to
the control of the government. All enactments made by the authority
require the approval of the government before they take effect. It
must be borne in mind, too, that all chiefs hold office at the pleasure

[27] "Fears and Pressures in the Union of South Africa," *Race Relations Journal*
(Johannesburg), XXII, No. 3 (1955).

of the government; they are appointed, and may be deposed, by the President.[28]

The reaction of the people of the Transkei to the "self-government" offer was swift and violent. Serious disturbances occurred in Pondoland from May, 1960, on, involving loss of life and destruction of property. The main cause of the disturbances was resentment that the chiefs' acceptance of the Bantu Authorities system and the government's appointment of chiefs had been effected without consulting the people.[29] Despite vigorous government measures, including the introduction of strong police reinforcements equipped with Saracen armored cars and helicopters, mass arrests, and, ultimately, the proclamation of a state of emergency in the affected areas, the disturbances continued. On January 5, 1961, it was officially announced that order had been restored, but the state of emergency continued. In September of that year, a government official stated that it would not, at the request of the Territorial Authority, be lifted "now or in the near future."[30]

In the meantime—in April, 1961—the annual meeting of the Transkeian Territorial Authority had taken place. It proved to be a historic gathering. The assembly of 120 chiefs and headmen, having spent some time presenting various grievances (among them a complaint that they were unpopular with the people because of opposition to the Bantu Authorities system, coupled with a demand that the government provide them with firearms for their protection), passed a unanimous resolution calling on the government to grant self-government to the Transkei.

The immediate reaction of the government was one of caution. The Minister of Bantu Administration and Development stressed the need for building up an adequate body of public servants and indicated that the territory might look forward to self-government within a few years. Discussions followed in Pretoria between representatives of the Authority, the Minister, and the Prime Minister, Dr. Verwoerd.

In January, 1962, Dr. Verwoerd informed Parliament that it was the intention of the government to grant self-government to the Transkei, and that it was hoped that the new system would be in

[28] H. R. Hahlo and Ellison Kahn, *The Union of South Africa* (London, 1960), p. 800; Muriel Horrell, "Bantu Authorities and Self-Government," *Race Relations Journal*, XXVI, No. 2. On July 18, 1958, the Minister of Justice stated that thirty-five chiefs and headmen had been deposed since January 1, 1955. (Hansard, House of Assembly, July 18, 1958, col. 514.)

[29] An Administrative Commission set up to inquire into the causes of the disturbances reported in October, 1960, that many complaints about the Bantu Authorities system were justified. (Keesing's Archives, October, 1961, 18367.)

[30] *Keesing's,* October, 1961, p. 18367; January, 1962, p. 18572.

operation during the first half of 1963. A new constitution would be granted providing for an African parliament with considerable powers that would be increased later, the details of the constitution to be worked out in consultation with the "Bantu leaders of the Transkei."

Following discussions between the government and a committee of twenty-seven chiefs and headmen appointed by the Transkeian Territorial Authority, the main provisions of the proposed constitution were announced in March, 1962. A Legislative Assembly consisting of sixty-four appointed chiefs and forty-five elected members would choose a prime minister who would appoint a cabinet or executive council. The Assembly would be empowered to legislate, *inter alia*, on internal affairs, agriculture, and social welfare. The South African Government would remain responsible for defense, external affairs, internal security, posts and telegraphs, public transport, immigration, currency, public loans, customs and excise, and "some aspects of justice." All laws passed by the Assembly would require the assent of the President of the Republic. In May, 1962, the Territorial Authority adopted the constitution, the President announcing that he expected the Assembly to be established by the middle of 1963.

In an official statement after he had first announced the proposed grant of "self-government," Dr. Verwoerd said: "The new South Africa which is being constructed by the measures announced today holds within it great promise for the building of friendship and cooperation between the races. It furthermore guarantees to each the retention of his own identity. All the nations of the world which seek to protect human dignity and the right to self-determination should give South Africa a fair chance to establish and develop its own commonwealth of nations." [31]

What are the facts? A measure of local government, entirely subject to the overriding control of the white government of South Africa, is to be *imposed* upon the people of the Transkei, who number 1.5 million. Such limited powers as are vested in the Assembly are effectively in the hands of the appointed chiefs, who hold 64 out of the total of 109 seats. The people of the Transkei have not been consulted by the government. There has been consultation with a number of chiefs and headmen, all of whom hold office by virtue of government appointment, are paid by the government, and may be deposed by the government at any time. In Pondoland, which represents a quarter of the area of the Transkei, a state of emergency, first imposed in November, 1960, remains in force. Its effect is, *inter alia*, to prohibit meetings of more than ten Africans without permission

[31] *Keesing's*, January, 1962, p. 18572.

and to empower the authorities to prevent any person from entering or leaving the Transkei.

This is the "positive" apartheid of 1963. On analysis, it is seen to be not a solution to South Africa's problems, but a retreat into the realm of fantasy: a plan to retribalize, forcibly, 11 million Africans who have become "irreversibly a part of the total life of South Africa."

The United Party—"White Leadership with Justice"

The policy of apartheid is opposed by the United Party, the official opposition, with 50 seats in the House of Assembly (against 105 held by the Nationalist Party). Formerly led by General Smuts, it receives support mainly from the English-speaking section, but a number of non-Nationalist Afrikaners are to be found in its ranks.

For some years after it was defeated in 1948, the United Party's policy in relation to the African remained vague and ambivalent. It shared with Nationalist Party policy the basic concept of white supremacy, but differed from it as to the methods to be employed in maintaining the dominance of the white minority. The methods were indicated in broad terms; they were not formulated precisely. Where the Nationalist Party program talked of "territorial and political segregation," the United Party promised to seek a "satisfactory solution" that would enable the African to develop along his own lines within a general framework that rested on the need to preserve "Western civilization."

The Nationalist Party was again returned to power in 1953. A strong body of opinion within the United Party attributed its defeat at this election to the inadequacy of the party's African policy. It was contended that the electorate had not been offered a sufficiently clear alternative to the policy of apartheid. As a result of this criticism, a new policy was formulated in 1954.

Under this policy, the United Party accepted economic integration of the white and the African as both a fact and an inevitable continuing process, but stood for social and residential segregation. White leadership must be maintained, but "Western civilization must be shared in practice with all nonwhites who have developed the capacity for taking joint responsibility for our future well-being in this subcontinent. . . . The Natives should gradually be given a more definite and secure place within the orbit of our Western way of life." [32] United Party spokesmen now talked of "white leadership with justice," but

[32] Quoted in Gwendolen Carter, *The Politics of Inequality* (New York and London, 1958).

the party—with an eye always on the Afrikaner vote in the rural areas —tended, more and more, to retreat from the practical implications of the new policy it had formulated. In 1957, the new leader of the party, Sir de Villiers Graaff, in the course of a statement on the party's industrial policy, talked of the need for protecting white workers against unequal competition from nonwhites.[33] As the general election approached, liberal trends within the party were kept in the background, and the claims of the party to be as determined as the government to ensure the dominant position of the white man became the theme of its leaders' speeches. But these concessions to the fears and prejudices of the white South African were made to no avail. The general election of 1958 produced a third defeat for the United Party.[34]

This repulse did not deter the party from vigorously opposing the government's Promotion of Bantu Self-Government Bill, concerning which Sir de Villiers Graaff said: "While this Parliament rules over the Bantu it is right that they should have representation in this House. . . . If there is a case for removing the Natives' representatives, then surely the time for their removal is when the new Black dominions of Dr. Verwoerd have gained their independence, and when the Bantu permanently settled outside the reserves are living in those Black dominions and earning their living there." [35] At the National Congress of the party, which took place later in the year, the party's policy in regard to African representation was formulated. It was decided that the former representation in the Cape Province should be restored, and representation added in the remaining three provinces; that there should be separate rolls for African voters, the franchise to be subject to a qualification based on "responsibility"; that the representatives of the Africans should, as before, be white; that the number of representatives should be limited to eight.

This was an advance on the party's previous policy, in that it conceded the African's right to representation throughout the country, instead of in the Cape Province alone. On the other hand, the representation was to remain white and separate, and the right to vote was to be limited to "responsible" (the term was not defined) Africans only.

For purposes of the last general election, held in October, 1961, the United Party entered into an alliance with National Union, a new party with little support from the electorate, vigorously critical of the

---

[33] Hansard, House of Assembly, March 23, 1957, col. 3606.

[34] The Nationalist Party showed a net gain of seven seats (ten gains and three losses), the United Party a net gain of one seat (ten gains and nine losses). (*Keesing's*, May, 1959, p. 16158.)

[35] Hansard, House of Assembly, May 18, 1959, col. 1652.

implementation of government policy, but urging separate development of white and nonwhite based on justice to both. In a pre-elec-
tion statement, issued jointly with National Union, the United Party,
for the first time, put forward federalism as a basis for future political
relations between white and African. But the proposal was stated in
the most general terms. It was announced that the party accepted a
"race federation in which all groups will be represented in the Central Parliament . . . on a basis which provides justice for all groups."
On three questions, however, policy was stated more specifically. The
party recognized as a fact the existence of a settled urban African
community, urged "more rational and sympathetic application" of
the pass laws, and proposed that provision be made for freehold
ownership of land by urban Africans.

Once more, the Nationalist Party was returned to power. In the
Parliament thus chosen to govern South Africa for another five years,
the United Party holds fewer than one-third of the seats, but this fact
does not reflect the support it received from the electorate. In the
contested constituencies, the total vote polled by the Nationalist Party
numbered 370,000; that by the United Party together with National
Union 336,000; and that by National Union 50,000.[36]

The United Party probably enjoys the support of almost half the
white electorate, but it is a support that offers no prospect of the
party's return to power in the foreseeable future. For the African, its
policy has come to be looked upon as fundamentally indistinguishable
from the government policy of apartheid, in that both rest firmly on
the concept of white supremacy.

The Progressive Party

In 1959, twelve members of the United Party resigned in protest
against the party's indecisive and equivocal racial policies, but retained their seats as representatives of the new Progressive Party established later in the year. The Progressive Party announced a policy providing for participation in government by "all suitably qualified citizens of a defined degree of civilization," and for a constitution entrenching fundamental human rights, providing safeguards against the
domination of one race by another, and making membership of the
party available to all citizens over the age of eighteen, regardless of
race or color.

In the general election of 1961, the party lost all but one of its seats
to the United Party, but succeeded in polling an aggregate of 69,000

[36] *Keesing's*, November–December, 1961, p. 18449.

votes.[37] Since then, the party has had no success in its attempt to win over supporters of the United Party. In March, 1962, the party contested fourteen seats in the elections to the Johannesburg City Council, and lost all to United Party opponents, including those in which the Progressive candidates were sitting members.

The party has African members, but their number is small since its policy of a qualified franchise is not calculated to attract African support. The qualifications [38] are sufficiently high, in the light of the educational opportunities of the majority of the African people, to ensure that the number of Africans entitled to vote would remain small.

The solitary representative of the Progressive Party in Parliament, Helen Suzman, is an effective critic of government policy and a courageous defender of African rights. But she represents a party that has clearly failed to gain any significant support from the electorate. Obviously, white South Africa is determined to reject even a moderate concession to the African demand for political rights.

The Liberal Party—Nonracial Democracy

The Liberal Party has no representatives in Parliament. Its four members—two in the Senate, two in the House of Assembly—all representing the Africans, lost their seats when African representation was abolished in 1960 by the terms of the Promotion of Bantu Self-Government Act. One of them, Margaret Ballinger, had held her seat continuously since the inception of separate African representation— a period of twenty-three years. She was generally recognized as the outstanding figure in the parliamentary fight against the forces of white supremacy.

The party was founded in 1953, shortly after the Nationalist Party had been returned to power for the second time. It grew out of a Liberal Association composed of a number of interracial discussion groups throughout the country.

The constitution of the party sets forth the following principles: (1) the essential dignity of every human being irrespective of race, color, or creed, and the maintenance of his fundamental rights; (2) the right of every human being to develop to the fullest extent of his ability consistent with the rights of others; (3) the maintenance of the rule of law; (4) the right of every citizen to participate in the government and other democratic processes of the country regardless of race, color, or creed.

[37] *Keesing's*, January, 1962, p. 18572.
[38] Either school standard eight, or school standard four together with certain material qualifications.

The party proposes extension of the franchise on the common roll to all adult persons, under a constitution incorporating an entrenched bill of rights based upon the Universal Declaration of Human Rights. It stands for a system of government based upon the wishes of all the people. "The future constitution of South Africa must be established by the consent of the people as a whole, and this consent can best be expressed by a National Convention, representative of every section of the people." [39]

The policies of the Liberal Party have been rejected by the white electorate,[40] but the party's activities, within Parliament and outside, have played a significant part in influencing white opinion and building up African support for a nonracial society. During the seven years that the party enjoyed parliamentary representation, its members provided the only concerted, unequivocal opposition to apartheid, and this opposition reflected the views of a group comprising all sections of the population. They constituted, furthermore, the recognized voice of the African people in the South African Parliament. Their consistent refusal to make any concessions to white prejudice tended to expose the indecisiveness of United Party policy and to strengthen liberal trends within the United Party.

Outside Parliament, the Liberal Party has gone ahead steadily with the construction of a growing nonracial oasis within the Nationalist desert of apartheid. The party's membership, predominantly white when it was founded ten years ago, is today predominantly African, and the party is closely identified with every aspect of the African's lawful resistance to apartheid. The Liberal Party recognizes that it has an extraparliamentary role, and accepts boycotts, strikes, and other nonviolent measures as methods of opposition to government policies which are legitimate in a country that denies the vote to the majority of the people. Whites and Africans share office in the party's national and regional committees, campaign together in elections, combine in protests and demonstrations, and cooperate in numerous other activities. During the emergency of 1961, a number of leading white and African members of the party, including the national chairman, were detained for a period of three months.

Alan Paton, national president of the party, has written: "The Liberal Party is a nonracial party. All its policies are nonracial. It believes

[39] *Non-Racial Democracy: The Policies of the Liberal Party* (Pietermaritzburg, 1960).

[40] In the general election of 1961, it contested two seats and lost both by a substantial vote. In one, the Liberal candidate forfeited his deposit. It has been defeated by substantial majorities in all the elections for white seats it has contested.

that nonracialism is the only sure foundation for a multiracial society of such complexity as ours, and that our problem can only be dealt with by people of all groups working together."

The Liberal Party is hampered by the growing network of apartheid restrictions, and the threat of proscription [41] hangs over its head. But it shows no signs of being intimidated. It takes its stand firmly on the belief that the only hope for a stable future in South Africa lies in the achievement of nonracial democracy.

As for African opinion, the African National Congress, too, has consistently asked for democratic government in which all the people —irrespective of race—will participate,[42] and has in many instances cooperated with the Liberal Party; on the other hand, the party has encountered hostility from the Communist group and from the Pan-Africanists.

Increasingly, the choice before white South Africa tends to crystal-lize into the choice between white domination (the policy of the present government when it is judged by its actions and its laws rather than by its promises and its plans) and nonracial democracy, with white leadership poised in a state of indecision between the two.

The promises and plans—total territorial apartheid—are under searching examination by a growing number of Afrikaner intellectuals and churchmen. How long will it take before they realize that apartheid is a pipe dream? And when they have, which will they choose— white domination or nonracial democracy? But these questions must be posed within the framework of the major question: How much time is left to white South Africa to make any choice at all?

Postscript [43]

The first Bantustan came into existence in November, 1963, when elections took place for 45 out of the total 109 seats in the Transkei Legislative Assembly. The overwhelming majority of these elective seats went to Chief Victor Poto, who opposed apartheid and stood for a policy of multiracialism, but his opponent, Chief Kaiser Matan-zima, an avowed supporter of apartheid, received the votes of most of the 64 government-controlled chiefs and thus became Chief Min-ister.[44] The fact that Matanzima and his government hold a minority

[41] The African National Congress and the Indian National Congress, with which the party cooperated, as well as the Pan-African Congress, have already been proscribed.

[42] Jordan K. Ngubane, "The Hardening Temper of the African," *Race Relations Journal*, Vol. XXIII, Nos. 2 and 3 (October, 1956).

[43] Based on information available as of April 1, 1965.

[44] Horrell, *Survey of Race Relations in South Africa*, 1963, p. 98.

of the elective seats in the Transkei Parliament is an eloquent commentary on South Africa's policy of separate development. It adds emphasis to the opinion of a distinguished South African judge who said, "Bantustans are places where votes can be safely exercised by nonwhites without influencing the real balance of power in the country. The ballot papers in a Bantustan box might as effectively be dropped into a well as into a ballot box, from the point of view of real legal power." [45]

None of the promised Bantustans for the remaining African population—approximately 10 million—has yet been established, and a recent policy statement by Dr. Verwoerd indicates a trend away from territorial separation. Addressing the South African Parliament in February, 1965, he reaffirmed the determination of his government "to maintain white leadership for all time . . . by force if necessary," declared that *territorial separation was not the essential part of the policy of apartheid,* and went on to emphasize the need for maintaining separation between white and African in the white areas. This new version of apartheid is, in a sense, no more than recognition of the growing and irreversible movement of Africans, in response to the demands of industrial development, from the reserves and the rural areas to the white man's cities. But it also means that white South Africa is moving back toward the *baasskaap* of 1948, with an alarming disregard of internal African discontent, hostility from independent Africa, and the mounting concern of the international community.

Within South Africa, however, government policy—suppression of internal resistance and defiance of external pressure—is receiving increased support from the white electorate. In Provincial Council elections held in March, 1965, the Nationalist Party won seats, for the first time in the history of Afrikaner nationalism, in the traditionally English-speaking strongholds of Durban and Pietermaritzburg. The image of Dr. Verwoerd and his party as the expression of an exclusive Afrikaner nationalism is being transformed. He and his party are now coming to symbolize the strong government required to defend the white man—Afrikaner and English-speaking South African alike—against the combined forces of militant black nationalism and the hostility of the outside world.

In this situation, support for the vague policies of the United Party can be expected to dwindle, and the government's prospect of a substantially increased majority at the next election to grow. The United Party's record reeks of equivocation. It seeks the participation of non-

[45] The Honorable O. D. Schreiner in his Presidential address to the South African Institute of Race Relations, January, 1964.

whites in the government of the country, but within the framework of "the maintenance of white leadership for the foreseeable future." In Parliament, it responds to government measures relating to the African by a voting pattern which fluctuates between qualified opposition and outright support. Some of its members outbid the Nationalists in playing on white fears of being "swamped" by a black majority. All of them join the Nationalists in rejecting the moderate multiracial policy put forward by Helen Suzman of the Progressive Party.

Extra-parliamentary opposition to apartheid faces growing obstruction. The Liberal Party has had leaders banned, members subjected to arbitrary detention, and its multiracial activities impeded by legislation and police interference. The National Union of South African Students (NUSAS) faces similar obstacles and, in addition, has come under severe government attack following the conviction of some of its leaders on charges of sabotage. Both organizations are constantly "smeared" by the Minister of Justice as Communist. Leaders of the Christian churches (excluding the Dutch Reformed Church, which, save for a few dissident voices, supports apartheid) speak out bravely, often fighting the prejudice of their own congregants as well as the policies of the government. They have been warned by the Minister of Foreign Affairs to cease interference in political matters, and the threat of the Native Laws Amendment Act—which empowers the government to prevent racially mixed services—hangs over their heads. The Women's Defence of the Constitution League (The Black Sash) continues its dignified protests and its aid to the victims of apartheid, but in the face of increasing police interference and administrative obstruction.

During 1963 and 1964, South Africa experienced violent resistance to apartheid, including many acts of sabotage. The government responded ruthlessly. Hundreds were detained in solitary confinement for periods of 90 days and more, informers were active, the homes of respectable citizens were searched, and many trials took place resulting in sentences of death and long terms of imprisonment. As a further guarantee of internal security, there has been large-scale expansion of South Africa's military forces.[46]

Notwithstanding widespread intimidation, a small number of whites (individually and through the organizations mentioned) continue to oppose apartheid and to identify themselves with African goals. Except for these, white South Africa appears to have been persuaded that a fortress composed of military power and the apparatus of a police state will furnish permanent protection against violent

[46] Colin and Margaret Legum, *South Africa: Crisis for the West* (London and New York, 1964), pp. 204–12.

internal resistance, the hostility of independent Africa, and mounting pressures from the international community.

But beneath the apparent state of security, buttressed by a buoyant economy, there lurks a sense of isolation and fear. The Minister of Justice has claimed that internal resistance to the regime has been crushed, but planned violence continues.[47] The United Nations has, so far, been unwilling to implement decisions calling for action against South Africa, but international pressures are bound to come to a head if the decision of the International Court of Justice on South West Africa, expected in 1966, goes against South Africa. And if, until now, independent Africa has failed to mount effective intervention, how much longer can 3 million whites postpone the inevitable day of reckoning with 280 million Africans, for whom the eradication of apartheid remains a central article of faith?

[47] On March 12, 1965, three Africans were arrested at the railway station at Germiston, in possession of a suitcase containing dynamite, chemicals, and bomb casings; on March 8, 1965, four Africans were sentenced to terms of imprisonment for being members of the banned Pan-African Congress. Evidence was brought forward that they planned to escape from prison, kill the white warders and their families, and go to Tanzania for guerrilla training, planning to return to South Africa with supplies of bombs.

Discussion

THOMAS KARIS.   [*Professor Karis raised provocative questions about Professor Carter's assertion of the African nationalists' position that only through the use of force could the African be a political person in South Africa.*] What is the purpose of violence as the acceptable means of political success, as apparently adopted by the leadership of both ANC and PAC? Is the purpose to remove the Nationalist Government from power and to replace it by a successful revolutionary group within South Africa? Or is the purpose to remove the Nationalist Government from power and bring into power a white group with whom African nationalists can work? Or is the purpose to produce a situation that will compel international intervention? [*Professor Karis believed that the chaos necessary to bring about foreign intervention would have to be of such magnitude as to be beyond the power of the South African Government to control.*] As long as the government can bring law and order back into being, it is very difficult to imagine intervention by foreign countries. [*More consideration, Professor Karis thought, should be given to whether, if violence was to become an African nationalist policy, it could be controlled by the nationalist leaders, since otherwise this obviously would mean a course of indiscriminate killing and resultant holocaust lacking in purpose and hardly meeting a definition of "policy."*]

BLOKE MODISANE.   South Africa is a country of very interesting definitions and, of course, fascinating clichés. One of the most exciting clichés is that Africans are inherently somewhat inferior and almost hopelessly ignorant, and that even education fails to make an impression on them.

I think I must be unintellectual because it seems I can't understand certain definitions as applied to us in South Africa. For instance, when Mr. Charles Swart was Minister of Justice, he said it is incorrect to say that Africans are killed by the police. The police do not shoot at Africans, he said, Africans die as a result of a clash with the police. I am not terribly sophisticated, so I don't understand the distinction.

Sometimes, I even find it difficult to try to understand eloquent expositions of apartheid. To me, apartheid is a reality of life. It is something that I live with, and it is something that I have to live with, like the fact that 45.6 per cent of African children between the ages of one and four die from malnutrition. But perhaps I understand that fact because there were six children in my family; two of them died of malnutrition, and the statistic begins to mean something.

The most frightening aspect of apartheid is that in South Africa there are no longer human beings; there are only masks, and the masks wear two colors: white and black. The creation of these masks has been deliberate and calculated; it is almost as if we pray to God to bless us with this condition. For 300 years, the whites of Africa have taken away from the black man the lines of definition differentiating one human being from another, and they have left a round mask that has no definition—a mask that is just a mask of color. And it is not even positive; it is negative in many respects. It is called non-European; it is called nonwhite; it is a negative extension of what is white. Sometimes, in a generous mood, people refer to this mask as John or Jim, but usually it is a negative extension.

Somehow human beings can't stomach the idea of exterminating other human beings. It is rather difficult. So first they must dehumanize, depersonalize people. The convenience of this sort of thing is that people can be destroyed as they are destroyed in South Africa because they have been invested with a subhuman image. But they have also said that Africans are like children, and this is true.

You see, all good children learn from their parents. After all, education is a system of reproducing knowledge, simulating the knowledge of other people. In this respect, Africans, too, have assimilated the idea of the white man, and he, too, sees only the white mask. And so today, because of various currents, these people, white and black, are in a position where they are going to destroy each other. One says, "We are going to kill this thing," and the other says the same thing. It is the same as when a man continues striking at a snake long after he has lost his power to injure him. But somehow the human being continues to beat and somehow in his mind he wants to continue to exterminate the physical existence of the snake. This is the way people are killing themselves in South Africa. This is the way they are leading themselves into an explosive situation.

Of course, we say we are unable to help the situation, that there is a commitment of history, that there is nothing we can do about it, that we are like figures in a great tragedy, actors in a fate that has been handed to us from above, players who can do nothing but play out the play. This is the sort of thing that takes place in South Africa. People feel a sense of hopelessness, and that is precisely the point. They have destroyed themselves as individuals, and there is nothing as individuals they can do about the situation.

Some people don't seem to realize that the African is now saying that South Africa must assume a democratic morality. The Africans are saying we do not want to negotiate with you for power. We say we are the majority in South Africa and our country must be ruled by the majority. Nobody is going to bargain us out of our country; nobody is going to exist as a separate racial entity in South Africa. We are all going to exist as South Africans, or we are all going to perish gloriously together. This is what is going to happen, for the fact is that the racial differences are not so fundamental.

Our contention is that since somebody is going to die in this fight, it is absolutely vital that those people who choose death must also choose the right to define why they want to die. I want to die so that my daughter 500 years from now or my son 500 years from now will never be faced with the problems I am faced with today. I don't believe in cutting up South Africa and giving the white man a certain section and somehow protecting his rights. I don't know race groups. I can protect the rights of individuals only because in the end this is what we are—we are individuals. You can be any color you like; you can be indigo blue; you are an individual and this is the right I am going to protect.

When Jefferson stood up and spoke rather eloquently about the rights of man, somebody should have whispered to him that some men were black. Apparently, he didn't know it, because there were a lot of slaves whom he forgot to release before he made this speech on liberty and the rights of man.

You start at the beginning; and if you make a mistake at the beginning, the situation of today is created. I am a despised human being in South Africa today. The day my daughter was born, I held her in my arms and said to myself, "I have committed a life into slavery; I have committed it into the hands and placed it at the foot of the master." And sometimes I feel that if we have to destroy each other in order to emphasize this fact, even to America, that we are doing this so that there will never be a Mississippi again, never be an Arkansas again, then South Africa's fight will have been to vindicate the color of black. Thereafter, when the color of black is seen, one will say that this is the color I can be, all I have to do is put a little color on my face! And we say this because we know the complete humiliation, the shame, the complete shame of being black in South Africa. This is what they have taught us. Fortunately, we don't have the right to make other people ashamed of their color. Now, they are not any longer going to make us ashamed of being black. The color of men is unimportant.

LEWIS NKOSI.   First, I will take up Professor Carter's suggestion that there may be benefits to be derived from Dr. Verwoerd's Bantustans and that we thus might consider cooperation. I think it should be made quite clear here that the African people in South Africa regard the Bantustans as shams and are not prepared even to consider them. And that is not because we do not see the need of exploiting the Bantustans against Dr. Verwoerd, but we are opposed to working within a framework that has been formulated for us without consultation. It is very important that the African people make any white man or minority group understand that in Africa the black people will not allow anybody to arrogate to himself the right to decide the future of the African people.

Next, I should like to comment on some minor points in the papers presented here this afternoon. I think Professor Carter said in her very good paper that when the Union of South Africa was first formed in 1910, some thought that this was a liberal and progressive act by Britain. I think I would differ somewhat with this suggestion. I think that Britain knew very well that she was handing the African people over to the tender mercies of a reactionary white minority. If this was not clear to Britain, the African nationalist leaders made it sufficiently clear through a delegation sent to His Majesty's Government at that time. I do not think that the British Government ever regarded African rights as of any importance. They did not do so in 1919, and, in a presently comparable situation, there is no reason to believe that the British Government will regard African rights as important today in determining the Southern Rhodesian question.

I would suggest that the reason Britain today is reluctant to hand over the black majority in Southern Rhodesia to white minority rule is simply that there is the reality of black organized power in Southern Rhodesia today, which could threaten to disrupt any state that gains dominion status on the basis of white supremacy. In South Africa, there was not a sufficiently organized black power in 1910, so we were handed over to the present white rulers in South Africa.

I am making this point because it is very important to understand that the African people in South Africa regard Britain as partially responsible for the rather ghastly and disastrous mess that has occurred in that Republic under Dr. Verwoerd's rule. The situation has been made more intolerable by the mischievous British Government's supplying of the South African regime with great quantities of arms for the ruthless suppression of black people. I think the black people will remember that Britain played a major role in our sufferings. One would think that after having achieved this major crime in 1910, Britain would try today to mitigate her guilt by doing just the opposite, supplying arms to the people who are prepared to die for freedom in South Africa today. But, of course, we do not expect Britain to do this. We do not expect anything, in fact, from the countries of the West.

It is sufficiently clear that Dr. Verwoerd exists today in South Africa because of the support given to him implicitly or explicitly by the Western countries, and I think that we would be deluding ourselves if we ever thought that Britain or even the United States of America is ever going to take any action whatsoever against the Verwoerd regime until such a time as we are prepared to take up arms ourselves.

The other comment I want to make briefly is on Professor Rubin's remarks about the Liberal Party in South Africa. I would be less than frank if I did not say that the actions of the Liberal Party in South Africa have been appreciated by the African people of South Africa. The party has played a part in the liberation struggle there. Where I do differ with Dr. Rubin is regarding his suggestion, which seems to me fantastic, that any party can do anything to achieve a change within the present legal framework in South Africa. And I say this although I am not peculiarly bloodthirsty. Unlike Mr. Modisane, I am not prepared to die. I would die very unwillingly, but I think that the situation has reached such proportions in South Africa that it is important for people outside to realize that there is no legal framework through which extraparliamentary struggle can take place and achieve anything.

I must also point out that the Liberal Party recently issued a statement through its national chairman, Mr. Peter Brown, in which it specifically condemned violence just after a recent race riot, and disassociated itself from any acts of sabotage taking place in South Africa today. In view of this, I find the statement fantastic that anybody, especially if he belongs to the white ruling class in South Africa, should presume to condone violence when it takes place. Professor Rubin neglected to mention the fact that

Mr. Patrick Duncan recently resigned from this political party because he regarded it as too difficult to be lawful in an unlawful state.

In South Africa, the people are going to end up with tragedy and are not going to be left with much choice. It would be much better if the tragedy could be averted by outside, nonviolent methods; but I cannot see the necessary change ever occurring through nonviolent means in view of what is happening in the world today.

MORLEY NKOSI.   [*Mr. Nkosi, commenting on the papers, found that Mr. Rubin's paper was biased in terms of the Liberal Party and that Miss Carter's paper was not up to date. He evidently also did not approve of Miss Carter's failure to note the part played by African labor in creating South African productivity.*]

It is virtually impossible that the Bantustan framework should be open to negotiation. However, we are willing to ask a few questions of those people who think that the Bantustan policy might work:

What happened to the financial allotment that was to be given to the Bantustans? Do you realize that it was suggested and in fact accepted by the federal government? The money that was allotted was said to be for the development of the Bantustan only. It is not so. That money is going to be utilized, and it has already been utilized, for the development of areas other than the Bantustan. I am willing to talk about it, but I am not willing to compromise the principle because it is not possible to balkanize South Africa. At any rate, the policy of the Bantustans is an absolute sham, as has been proved by the government's appointing the kind of chiefs who will see to it that this situation is perpetuated *ad infinitum*. The Bantustans in no way lend themselves to African rehabilitation; they are, in actuality, a dormitory for cheap labor. The South African Government is trying through the Bantustans to make sense out of a situation—a situation it created and out of which no sense can be made.

II

South West Africa

Historical Background
and Current Problems

F. JARIRETUNDU KOZONGUIZI

For more than fifteen years, South West Africa has been on the agenda of the United Nations. Throughout this period, discussion has been confined mainly to consideration of the appalling conditions under which the people there live; very little attention has been given to the pressing problem of determining the country's status—legal and otherwise—on the basis of its historical status. The U.N. approach to this problem has been paternalistic, with trusteeship offered as the only "practical" solution. There has been little regard for the historical fact that the people of South West Africa were once effective owners of their lands and proud administrators of their country.

Historical and Legal Status

The legal status of South West Africa up to the outbreak of World War I was clear in fact and in law. South West Africa was a territory in the ownership of its people, on which the aggressive German Imperial Government had forcibly imposed its administration, after almost exterminating the inhabitants and appropriating their land and cattle. Had the nations of the world used that simple criterion in determining the future of the country, the present international dispute over legal technicalities might never have arisen. But instead, the League of Nations took the view that the people of South West Africa were "not yet able to stand by themselves under the strenuous conditions of the modern world." A clash of external interests ensued, and the interests of the people in South West Africa were compromised: The country was declared a Mandate of the Union of South Africa. It was to report annually to the League of Nations' Permanent Mandates Commission.

The League of Nations, while recognizing the "well-being and development" of the people of South West Africa as important, never spoke of this well-being in such explicit terms as "independence" or "self-determination." Thus the idea of eventual self-government, although implicit in the Mandate arrangement, was never made clear. This vagueness is not surprising, considering that the forces of imperialism and colonialism were at that time determining the destiny of the world; the mandate system was created by the big powers to divide the spoils of war. Although the principle of treating those people "not able to stand by themselves" as a sacred trust of civilization was inserted in the Covenant, the economic interests of the great powers were not ignored, for the Covenant stipulated that "equal opportunities for trade and commerce of other Members of the League" should be secured. South Africa—even before her assumption of the mandate—saw South West Africa not as a "sacred trust of civilization" but as a field for territorial expansion and aggrandizement. In 1919, some of the discriminatory land legislation of South Africa was extended to South West Africa "to safeguard the interests of the white population."

Thus the confusion over the international status of South West Africa is not merely the result of the difficult nature of the problem, as has been suggested in the United Nations and in the International Court of Justice, but the logical outcome of the ambiguity of the 1920 Mandate, when diametrically opposed positions were taken, though not openly proclaimed. The League regarded South West Africa as a "sacred trust of civilization" and opposed its incorporation into South Africa. South Africa, on the other hand, regarded South West Africa as a spoil of war and proceeded practically and internally, while denying publicly and internationally, to treat South West Africa as its possession not merely administratively but also constitutionally.

The legal instruments for the determination of the legal status of South West Africa since the defeat of Germany are: (1) the Treaty of Versailles, especially Articles 118–119, which represent a complete renunciation by Germany of all her rights and titles to her overseas possessions, including South West Africa, in favor of the Principal Allied and Associated Powers—the United States, the British Empire, France, Italy, and Japan; (2) the decision of the Supreme Council of the Principal Allied and Associated Powers, including the concession that the mandate for South West Africa should be held by South Africa; (3) Article 22 of the Covenant of the League of Nations, which declared that the principle of the well-being and development of indigenous peoples was a sacred trust of civilization which should be applied to the colonies and territories formerly governed by Germany; (4) the Mandate for South West Africa, which defined the degree of authority, control, and administration to be exercised by the South African Government and the obligations of that government to South West Africa; (5) Article 96 of the Charter of the United Nations, on the basis of which opinions have been sought by the U.N. General Assembly from the International Court of Justice, and Articles 92–94, on the basis of which application for compulsory jurisdiction has been filed against South Africa in the International Court; and (6) Article 37 of the Statute of the International Court of Justice, under which the jurisdiction in the dispute concerning the South West Africa Mandate has been transferred or passed on from the Permanent Court of International Justice to the International Court of Justice.

It was in 1949 that the U.N. General Assembly first sought an advisory opinion from the International Court of Justice based on the following questions: (1) What is the international status of the territory of South West Africa? (2) Does the Union of South Africa continue to have international obligations under the Mandate for South West Africa, and, if so, what are those obligations? (3) Are the provisions of Chapter XII of the Charter applicable, and, if so, in what manner, to the territory of South West Africa? (4) Has the Union of South Africa the competence to modify the international status of the territory?

The position of the United Nations on these matters as stated to the Court was that: (1) the mandatary regime in South West Africa was considered temporary, to continue until such time as the mandated territory and its inhabitants were able to stand by themselves; (2) the status of the territory could be changed by concurrent action of the mandatary and Council of the League, provided that the change was consistent with the principles embodied in Article 22 of the Covenant; (3) the granting of independence to a mandated territory at a time when the whole territory and its inhabitants were able to stand by themselves was a change consistent with the principles of the mandate system; (4) the possibility of revocation in the event of a serious breach of obligation by the mandatary was not completely precluded, and the International Court or Council of the League or both could decide on such revocation; (5) annexation was not considered compatible with principles of the Mandate, but it was accepted that independence could not be achieved until the whole territory and its population, and not merely the white minority, were able to stand alone; (6) the consent of the Principal Allied and Associated Powers to termination of the Mandate was unnecessary.

South Africa argued that the international status of South West Africa had undergone a change with the dissolution of the League of Nations and that, since the signatories of the Versailles Treaty no longer had any right to modify the status of South West Africa or to sanction any fresh disposition of the territory without South Africa's consent, there was consequently no international legal document presently in force limiting the administrative powers of South Africa with respect to the territory of South West Africa or enjoining South Africa to continue its treatment of the territory as a separate international entity. Therefore, South Africa alone had the competence to modify the international status of the territory. In short, the South West Africa Mandate had lapsed with the dissolution of the League. Since the Mandate had lapsed, South Africa's international legal obligations had lapsed. The provisions of Chapter XII of the Charter did not apply to South West Africa because, in South Africa's view, the United Nations was not the legal successor to the League of Nations.[1]

The Court held that South Africa continued to have international obligations in the administration of South West Africa under the international Mandate assumed by her in 1920, which corresponded to the sacred trust of civilization referred to in the same article and contained in Articles 6 and 7 of the Mandate. The Court further concluded that the General Assembly of the United Nations was legally qualified to exercise the supervisory functions previously exercised by the League of Nations with regard to the administration of the territory and that South Africa was under an obligation to submit to the supervision and control of the General Assembly and to render annual reports to it. The Court also said the dispatch and examination of petitions formed a part of that supervision. On the issue of the determination and modification of the international status of South West Africa, the Court stated that this decision rested with South Africa, *acting with the consent of the United Nations*.[2]

Although the U.N. General Assembly endorsed the opinion of the International Court, South Africa rejected it except for the part declaring that South Africa was under no obligation to place South West Africa under trusteeship. The deadlock continues.

[1] *International Status of South West Africa*, ICJ Pleadings, Oral Arguments, Documents 1950, pp. 72–84, 273–317.

[2] *International Status of South West Africa*, Advisory Opinion: ICJ Reports 1950, p. 128.

In 1960, Ethiopia and Liberia instituted legal proceedings against South Africa, alleging: (1) that South Africa had violated and continued to violate Article 2 of the Mandate and Article 22 of the Covenant of the League of Nations by (a) failing to adopt measures necessary and appropriate for the effectuation of the provisions of those Articles and by taking affirmative action which denies their fulfillment, (b) practicing apartheid in South West Africa, (c) adopting and applying unjust laws to South West Africa, and (d) suppressing rights and liberties of the inhabitants of South West Africa; (2) that South Africa had violated and continued to violate Article 6 of the Mandate by its failure to render to the General Assembly annual reports of the administration of the territory; (3) that South Africa had violated and continued to violate Article 2 of the Mandate and Article 22 of the Covenant by the exercise of powers of administration and legislation over the territory inconsistent with the international status of the territory; and (4) that South Africa had violated and continued to violate the Mandate and Covenant by refusing to transmit to the General Assembly petitions from the inhabitants of South West Africa addressed to the General Assembly and by preventing them from appearing before United Nations bodies. The Court was asked specifically to uphold its advisory opinion of 1950, in addition to upholding the foregoing allegations.

In 1961, South Africa replied to the allegations by submitting to the Court preliminary objections stating that the applicants had no *locus standi* in the proceedings and that the Court consequently had no jurisdiction on the following grounds: (1) by reason of the dissolution of the League of Nations, the Mandate for South West Africa was no longer (later amended to "had never been") a "treaty or convention in force" within the meaning of Article 37 of the Statute of the Court; (2) neither Ethiopia nor Liberia was any longer "another member of the League of Nations," as Article 7 of the Mandate requires for *locus standi*; (3) no *dispute* in the sense contemplated by Article 7 of the Mandate was involved in the matters presented by applicants for adjudication; and (4) there was in any event no "dispute" which could not "be settled by negotiation" within the meaning of Article 7.[3]

In its judgment of December 21, 1962, the Court ruled as follows: (1) Article 7 of the Mandate was a treaty or convention still in force within the meaning of Article 37 of the Statute of the Court; (2) the dispute was one that was envisaged in Article 7 and could not be

---

[3] *South West Africa Cases (Ethiopia v. South Africa; Liberia v. South Africa), Preliminary Objections, Judgment of 21 December 1962: ICJ Reports 1962*, p. 319.

settled by negotiation; and (3) the Court was consequently competent to hear the dispute on its merits.

There is a yet unused instrument that I believe *must* be taken into account in the determination of the legal status of South West Africa. In my view, the jurisdiction of the Court in this dispute as well as its future rulings on matters related to South West Africa should have as a basis the terms of the Declaration on the Granting of Independence to Colonial Countries and Peoples, adopted by the U.N. General Assembly in 1961. Recognizing the "passionate yearning for freedom in all dependent peoples and the decisive role of such peoples in the attainment of their independence," it declares that "All peoples have the right to self-determination, and by virtue of that right to freely determine their political status and freely pursue their economic, social and cultural development."

Consideration of the legal or political status of a territory or country cannot disregard the question of sovereignty. Once this is decided upon and it is understood that sovereignty historically rests with the people of the territory as confirmed by the Declaration, questions on the status of the territory could be easily disposed of.

The question of sovereignty with regard to South West Africa was raised on several occasions during the days of the League of Nations, but the members of the Permanent Mandates Commission deliberately refrained from presenting a decisive position, limiting their consideration to such questions as nationality of the mandated populations, international conventions affecting the territory, and loans and investments of the mandatary *in behalf of* the mandated territory. What I am stating here has already been hinted at in a separate opinion by Judge M. Alvarez on part of the advisory opinion of 1950.

As stated earlier, even in the compromise of 1920 over South West Africa, the idea of eventual self-government can be logically assumed as implicit. The League of Nations ushered in a new order in world affairs through the mandate system. Former enemy colonies were no longer regarded as "spoils of war" but rather as "sacred trusts of civilization." Under the trusteeship system, terms such as "self-government" are used with respect to *all* territories—a trend that led, in 1961, to the Declaration on the Granting of Independence to Colonial Countries and Peoples, which re-established the historical position of these areas. World order from now on should not be governed by powerful feudal interests or oppressive mercantile monopolies or military supremacy, but should be determined by the sacred rights of peoples in their own areas. World order presupposes that interdependence of nations and peoples shall be governed by the principles of political freedom, opportunities for social equality, and majority rule—proclaimed cornerstones of Western democracy, but never practiced in the past in colonial areas.

The Declaration should clear up the confusion over the international status of South West Africa, because it vests in the people of South West Africa the sovereign right to determine political status, thus providing an effective legal foundation in international law. I submit that this is the only just and correct basis on which the consideration of this question should and must rest.

Tribal and Political Divisions

Let us turn now to a survey of the political groupings in South West Africa.[4] There are two main political organizations: the South West Africa National Union (SWANU), and the South West Africa People's Organization (SWAPO). SWANU is national in character, SWAPO is tribal.

Until 1959, African politics in South West Africa were mainly on a tribal basis, and even today tribal forces have a strong influence on political groupings. From the point of view of SWANU, which was formed to destroy the tribal basis in politics and to spearhead the liberation movement on a much more militant and progressive basis, the present intratribal conflicts in South West Africa are advantageous to the achievement of unity on a national basis.

What are the tribal and other significant groupings in South West Africa, particularly as they are related to the political situation, and what are the conflicts that divide them?

The Ovambo people are divided into seven subtribes. The chiefs and/or headmen of five of these subtribes—Ondongo, Ongandjera, Ukualuzi, Ukuanjama, Ukuambi—are supporters of the administration of South West Africa and the Government of South Africa. The headman of the Onkolongazi has not been articulate politically, and the headman of the Ombalantu is definitely against the government and for freedom.

The Okavango people are divided into six subtribes, the chiefs or headmen of which have all expressed satisfaction with the South African Government.

There is a so-called detribalized, or urban, group whose members may still have relations in Ovamboland and Okavango, but who were

[4] The following is excerpted from a statement written by Mr. Kozonguizi in August, 1962. The statement was included in a paper written for the conference by the Reverend Michael Scott, a petitioner before the United Nations for South West Africa since 1949. Mr. Scott was unable to attend the conference, and his paper is therefore not included in this volume.

born and/or have lived in urban areas in the Police Zone.[5] This group
is treated by the administration in exactly the same way as are the
tribal groups in the zone. SWANU has considerable strength in this
group, and some of the SWAPO leaders are also from it.

From the Northern Reserves of Ovamboland, Okavango, and
Kaokevel, the South West African Native Labour Association recruits contract workers. Those workers classed as "A" (able to do
heavy work) go into the mines of the building construction industry;
those classed as "B" (able to do work that requires ordinary strength)
are sent into domestic service in the hotels or in the homes of individual whites; those classed as "C" (able to do light work only)
become shepherds on farms or work as domestics. The C class often
includes children under sixteen who have been recorded as eighteen
or over.

There is also a strong political organization in the Caprivi Zipfel,
which is fighting for freedom, although the chiefs in the area have
not been articulate.

The Coloured community in South West Africa may be divided
into two main groups. The Rehobothers (or Basters), who are indigenous to South West Africa, live in the Rehoboth Gebiet, where,
unlike the Africans in the reserves, they can own land and enjoy
some amount of freedom of movement. The Cape Coloureds, who
are from South Africa, are spread throughout the territory and are
not allowed to own land in the Rehoboth Gebiet.

The Basterraad is a council of Rehobothers who act as advisers
to the Magistrate in charge of the Gebiet. The Magistrate is the
chairman of the Council just as, in the African locations, the Location Superintendent is the chairman of the Advisory Board. The
Basterraad does not support the government, although it once advocated some form of self-government for the Rehoboth Gebiet on
the basis of the 1923 Agreement.[6] Today the Burgher Association,
which voices the political aspirations of the bulk of the Rehobothers,
rejects that Agreement and stands for a federal constitution for South
West Africa. On several occasions the Burgher Association, upon the
urging of the younger generation of Rehobothers, has invited

[5] The Police Zone comprises the southern two-thirds of South West Africa's
territory. Within the zone, Africans are not allowed to work, travel or live without a government permit. Even the purchase of a railway ticket is forbidden
without a pass. The zone also contains a number of African reserves to which
residents are likewise confined unless they obtain a government or white-employer
permit.

[6] In 1923, the South African Government offered the *raad*, or traditional council of the Rehobothers, official status as an administrative organ of the government
in South West Africa.

SWANU officials to Rehoboth to explore a working relationship. There is a small, dissident group in the Burgher Association that is pro-government and anti-African.

When the Lutheran Church in South West Africa decided to work closely with the Dutch Reformed Church, which is linked to the government, some Rehoboth adherents of the Church decided to break away, thus leaving two Lutheran Church groups in the area.

Among the Coloured population, there are several other organizations that have political affiliations. The South West African Coloured Organization was founded in 1958 and is under the presidency of J. S. van de Roos, a teacher in Keetmanshoop. It supports the administration. The South West African Coloured Teachers Association was founded in 1958 and also has a harmonious relationship with the administration. Its president is a Rehoboth teacher, J. P. Titus. There are several parent-teacher associations, the most important of which is the one in Windhoek. The principal of the Government Coloured School there plays an important role in the organization. Most of its supporters, however, opposed the establishment of the South West African Coloured Council in 1962, and have also opposed the new township to be built for the Coloureds in Windhoek. Present at the opening of the Council—which is nothing but a "Coloured authority" with the same functions as Dr. Verwoerd's Bantu authorities—was J. van der Wath, South Africa's Deputy Minister for South West African Affairs.

The prime mover in the establishment of the Council was A. J. Kloppers, who came to South West Africa from South Africa to be a teacher in the Coloured School of Windhoek, where he became one of the founders of the South West African Coloured Teachers Association. His record is that of an opportunist. When he had a disagreement with his colleagues while he was Secretary-General of the Teachers Association, he sought the friendship of such African teachers as Berthold Himumuine, pretending to be an advocate of a merger with the African Teachers Association. When he disagreed with his principal at the Windhoek school, he joined the staff of the Roman Catholic African School there, and told the African teachers that he did so as a step against racialism and tribalism. Then, he lured the Roman Catholic Coloured children away from the Coloured School to his new school, at the same time that he was pressing Roman Catholic authorities to introduce apartheid in the school by creating a Coloured section, which subsequently became the Coloured Roman Catholic School. Mr. Kloppers is now principal of that school. When Kloppers went back to the Cape, he associated with the leaders of the Teachers League of South Africa to create the impression that he was progressive. (Many of the South West African Coloured students in the Cape were supporters of the non-European unity movement of which the Teachers League was a part.) It was then that he launched the South West African Coloured Organization on a pro-government platform that called for the establishment of the Coloured Council.

In short, the South West African Coloured Organization, the South West African Coloured Teachers Association, and the South West African Coloured Council all accept apartheid.

The Herero group, unlike the Ovambo or Okavango, is a homogeneous one, at least linguistically speaking. Division within it is on a residential basis. After the Germans had destroyed the tribal and, to some extent, the social organization of South West Africa, the South African Government placed the Hereros in various reserves. It is significant that the present split among the Hereros is to some extent based on this residential division. There are six main Herero reserves. None of the chiefs or headmen of these reserves supports the government, although otherwise there are divisions among them.

There is also an urban group among the Hereros. Within this group, there are the employees or former employees of the government or of the municipality of Windhoek who have moved to Katutura and support the South African Government actively, and there are the intellectuals—mainly teachers and government employees—who are active in professional and cultural organizations, such as the South West African Teachers Association and the South West African Progressive Association, as well as the Jeugbond (Youth League), a religious-cultural organization.

Several issues precipitated the split among the Hereros. Certain Hereros—among them the headmen in the Okotjituuo and Waterberg reserves, together with the Munjuko group of the Epukiro Reserve—were not satisfied with the election of Clement Kapuuo as successor to Hosea Kutako, chief of the Aminius Reserve and Paramount Chief of the Hereros. The split would be aggravated in the event of the death of Chief Kutako or a United Nations solution of the South West African question, and the way would thus be opened for a new political alignment, unless a *modus operandi* is reached by the warring factions in the meantime.

A second cause of division is the succession to the headmanship in the Epukiro Reserve. A long history of dispute over the succession of headman Gerson Hoveka has resulted in the Munjuku group's refusal to accept him as headman. At one point, the issue was put to a vote and the Hoveka group won. The South West African administration, however, would not approve Hoveka as headman. It accepted instead

Chief Munjuku II, of the Munjuku group. The situation today is that Chief Kutako works with the Hoveka group and regards the Ovambanderus (another of the Epukiro Reserve groups) as part of the Herero group under his (Kutako's) paramountcy, and the Munjuku group regards the Ovambanderus as an independent group with Munjuku as chief in his own right, having equal status with Kutako. The Munjuku group seems to ally itself with Headman Tjatjitua, of the Waterberg Reserve, and the other headmen who oppose Kutako.

Another issue, which to some extent may also be regarded as a basis for division among the Hereros, is the church question. In 1955, the bulk of the Hereros withdrew from the Rhenish Mission Church (German Lutheran Church) and established their own Herero church, called the Ongerki Jeruuano (Protestant Unity Church), under the Reverend Teinhard Ruzo. The new Herero church, however, does not have much support in the Otjohorongo Reserve or in part of the Epukiro Reserve, although in the latter both the Munjuku and Kutako groups support it staunchly.

When the South West Africa National Union was launched, in September, 1959, it had the support of Chief Kutako. Kutako's deputy, Clement Kapuuo, was a member, and several of Kutako's councilors—Isaskar Kambatuku, Aaron Kapere, and Frans Tjueza—made up the party's National Executive Committee. In April, 1960, however, these councilors withdrew from the SWANU Executive Committee, and SWANU and Kutako parted ways. The councilors had wanted the same kind of control of SWANU that they now have over SWAPO. Kutako was to issue all statements, and SWANU was to be a cosignatory. When SWANU refused to attach itself to one tribe, the councilors accused SWANU of: (1) opposing the appointment of Clement Kapuuo as deputy chief; (2) being extremists who stood for violence (Hereros were urged not to contribute to the defense fund for the fifteen people who were charged with public violence); (3) backing Chief Munjuku in his fight against Chief Kutako; (4) exposing Chief Kutako's secrets, i.e., in asking about Allard K. Lowenstein and the other American visitors to South West Africa; (5) wanting to steal the Chief's money, which was being sent from the United States; (6) opposing the United Nations and misleading the people in South West Africa. All Hereros, including myself, were asked to resign from SWANU. Only three Council members mentioned above and Kapuuo, chairman of the Council, did so.

SWANU had no part in the appointment of Kapuuo as deputy chief. This was strictly a tribal matter. Some Herero members of SWANU, at the invitation of the Herero Council, did take part in the deliberations, but as individuals, not as members of SWANU.

Furthermore, SWANU had no official link with the Munjuku group. SWANU has members from the Munjuku group just as it has from the Kutako and Hoveka groups. (An interesting sidelight: If SWANU had wanted to get into the struggle between Hoveka and Munjuku, it would have been obvious for my party to back Hoveka, since he is my cousin, the son of my mother's brother, and I visit him often.)

Regarding SWANU's either "stealing" from Kutako or "revealing his secrets," neither is true. As for the "secrets," we warned against the visiting Americans because, although they were given the names of SWANU leaders, they did not come to see the leaders. The accusation of stealing money is based on an incident connected with financial assistance that was offered by an American organization in a letter addressed to SWANU, OPO (Ovamboland People's Organization, which later became SWAPO), and Chief Kutako. SWANU wrote to the organization requesting that its share be sent directly to the party, and someone in the United States then sent a photostat copy of this letter to Kutako. A twisted version of the incident was used by Kutako's Council in its campaign against SWANU. (The director of the U.S. organization has subsequently agreed that it was perfectly valid for SWANU to make this request; he has also reported that the SWANU letter was never given to anyone outside of the organization, thus leaving the question open as to how the letter got to Kutako.)

SWANU's position on the United Nations is that the people be told about the shortcomings and difficulties of the organization so that they will know what can and cannot be accomplished by it.

This is the background of the present lack of cooperation between Chief Kutako (of the Hereros) and SWANU. It should be stressed, however, that SWANU does have Herero members, including the bulk of the urban Hereros and the Hereros in Okotkituuo and Waterberg reserves. The Munjuku group supports the political stand of SWANU. The 10,000 members who belong to SWANU, however, belong not as tribesmen but as African nationalists.

The Nama people, like the Hereros, are divided into several reserves. Like the Ovambos, they are also divided into several groups, or subtribes. None of the Nama chiefs or headmen supports the government. The Nama tribe is distinguished by its high sense of solidarity and capacity to maintain unity. Whatever intratribal quarrels there are among the Namas are known only to themselves. Not even the division between the majority that belongs to the African Methodist Episcopal Church and the minority still in the Rhenish Mission Church is allowed to interfere with political unity. Chief Samuel Witbooi, who resides in Krantzplatz Reserve, supports SWANU, and thousands of his followers are members. Chief Witbooi, however, does not allow his support of SWANU to stand in the way of his long-standing friendship with Chief Kutako. Although he has asked Kutako to cooperate with SWANU, he does not interfere with Kutako's independence to choose allies.

The government tried to abolish four of the reserves in which the Namas reside because of antigovernment activity there. In January, 1959, the government forcibly removed the Reverend Markus Kooper, a cousin of Chief Witbooi, from Hoachanas Reserve to Itsawisis Reserve because of a suspicion that he was the leader of the resistance. The government thought that the people would follow, but they refused to move and nothing more has been done about this.

A small group of Namas have formed the South West Africa United National Independence Organization (SWAUNIO), whose president, Gertze, is the former chairman of the SWANU branch in Keetmanshoop. Although the aims of the group are identical with those of SWANU, membership is limited to Namas. The group was formed by Gertze to allow the Namas to have a platform for the Namas in the same way that SWAPO was formed for the Ovambos. SWAUNIO's slogan is "The yellow people must be heard independently."

The Damara people can be divided into two groups, the tribal and the urban, both of which are led by Chief David Goraseb, who wholeheartedly supports SWANU. The tribal group resides in Soris-Soris and in Okambahe Reserve. Of the urban group, those who are active politically support SWANU, except for Fritz Gariseb, who left SWANU with the members of Chief Kutako's Council. Many of the Damara teachers and other civil servants, as is the case with the Hereros and Namas, are active in their professional and cultural organizations.

The Bechuanas, under headman Albert Mootseng, who lives in the Aminius Reserve, do not support the government. The headman's son, Gerhard Mootseng, is a loyal member of SWANU, and after the visit of the United Nations investigating committee, the headman himself announced that he would support SWANU.

SWAPO's members are mainly from the Ovambo tribe, more particularly those Ovambos who are working or have worked in the Police Zone. SWAPO does not give information on the number of paid-up members or even of those registered in its books. Figures from 55,000 to 100,000 have been cited, more often by those outside South West Africa, but such figures are the result of wishful thinking, based on the expectation that, because SWAPO is essentially an Ovambo organization and the Ovambos number about 200,000, SWAPO can claim half of that number. The strength of SWAPO's following can be determined only on the basis of those who do not support the tribal chiefs in Ovamboland, and even then all those who do not support the chiefs are not necessarily SWAPO supporters. In the Police Zone, SWAPO has the support of Chief Kutako's Council, but it would be more appropriate to say that SWAPO supports Chief Kutako, for it is SWAPO members who are in Kutako's Council rather than the other way around. SWAPO does have a few members from other tribal groups, but in the main these are people who have left SWANU or who hold a grudge against the SWANU leadership.

SWANU has 10,000 members listed in its register at headquarters in Windhoek. SWANU is backed by Chief David Goraseb, of the Damaras; the Damara Reserve residents and the urban Damaras (although one of Chief Goraseb's representatives in Windhoek, Fritz Gariseb, supports Chief Kutako and SWAPO); Namas in Hoachanas and Berseba reserves and the urban Namas; and those Coloureds in the urban areas who are opposed to the South West African Coloured Council. Although the bulk of the urban Ovambos support the party, SWANU has a very small following among the other Ovambos. SWANU's political stand also enjoys the support of the following Herero groups: Chief Munjuku II, headman Tjatjitua, and Teinhardt Maekopo. The Hereros in Tses Reserve also support SWANU, as does the "Union" group (originally from South Africa) in urban areas, mainly in Windhoek and in the Aminius Reserve under headman Mootseng.

SWAPO's policies are expressed mainly through Kutako's Council or through the press of the white Liberal Party in South Africa, which definitely supports SWAPO. (Most of the SWAPO members in Cape Town are registered members of the Liberal Party. Some of the Liberal leaders—e.g., Patrick Duncan and Ernest Wentzel—and the Liberal press, notably *Contact*, are very hostile to SWANU.) SWAPO gives the impression abroad of being neutral but pro-West.

SWANU is violently (but independently) against Western imperialism, although not necessarily pro-East in the Cold War. The purpose of SWANU is to unite and rally the people of South West Africa into one national front and to work with allied movements in Africa for the propagation and promotion of the concept of Pan-Africanism and unity among the peoples of Africa.

The U.N. Position—
And a Projection for the Future

ANGIE BROOKS

At the First Session of the U.N. General Assembly in 1946, the Assembly took the position that South West Africa should be placed under U.N. "trusteeship arrangements" with a view to self-determination and ultimate independence for the peoples of that territory. The Government of the Union of South Africa was invited to submit proposals to effect such arrangements. This position was not changed up to the Seventeenth Session of the General Assembly, in 1962–63. Certain important decisions of the United Nations in the last four years, however, are of great significance and are indicative of a new approach to the problem of South West Africa by the United Nations.

I should first discuss some underlying factors giving rise to these decisions. [*Miss Brooks' paper here delineates the background for and present legal position of the case on South West Africa pending before the International Court of Justice, wherein South Africa contests both the jurisdiction of the Court and the competence of the petitioning parties (Ethiopia and Liberia). This matter is discussed in detail in the preceding paper. As a significant addition to this historical-legal summary, Miss Brooks calls attention to Resolution 1361 of the Fourteenth General Assembly Session, which pointedly refers the member governments to the legal processes available to them as previously set forth by the Twelfth Session in Resolution 1142A, the pertinent portion of which reads:*]

Draws the attention of Member States to the conclusions of the Special Report of the Committee on South West Africa covering the legal action open to Member States to refer any dispute with the Union of South Africa concerning the interpretation or application of the Mandate of South West Africa to the International Court of Justice for adjudication in accordance with Article 7 of the Mandate read in conjunction with Article 37 of the Statute of the Court.—Eds.]

As would be expected, the African states, as former League of Nations members, considered it an obligation to foster the cause of their brothers although doing so incurred some financial deprivation for themselves. Thus the Liberian Government, as a former League member, took the initiative in filing a contentious proceedings in the International Court of Justice against South Africa; Ethiopia joined in the proceedings.

The important decision of the United Nations to establish effective U.N. presence in the territory of South West Africa was set forth in Resolution 1566 of the Fifteenth General Assembly Session. In consideration of its own obligations and the concern of the community of nations to promote the well-being and interest of the people of South West Africa, the Assembly invited the FAO, WHO, UNESCO, and the U.N. Children's Fund to undertake urgent programs in their respective fields to assist the indigenous inhabitants of South West Africa. The resolution further urged the cooperation of the Government of South Africa in this endeavor.

At the same session, the General Assembly adopted Resolution 1568 (XV) inviting the South West Africa Committee, in addition to its normal tasks, to go to South West Africa immediately to investigate the situation prevailing in the territory and to ascertain and make proposals to the General Assembly on: (1) conditions for restoring a climate of peace and security; and (2) the steps that would enable the indigenous inhabitants to achieve a wide measure of internal self-government designed to lead them to complete independence as soon as possible.

South Africa's reaction to these two resolutions was not only to refuse the technical agencies entry to South West Africa, but to deny visas to the Committee to go to South West Africa or to enter South Africa for talks with the government. Indeed, the South African Government threatened to arrest the members of the South West Africa Committee if they entered without visas, and simultaneously ruthlessly intensified its policy of apartheid.

In spite of this rigid attitude of South Africa, the United Nations continued its effort to effect a U.N. presence in South West Africa. At its Sixteenth Session, the Assembly adopted Resolution 1702 (XVI), in which it stated its deep regret that the Government of the Republic of South Africa had prevented the Committee on South West Africa from entering South West Africa. It solemnly proclaimed the inalienable right of the people of South West Africa to independence and national sovereignty and established a U.N. Special Committee for South West Africa. The Committee's mission was to accomplish or envisage the means to accomplish the following: (1) a visit to the territory of South West Africa before May 1, 1962; (2) the evacuation from the territory of all military forces of the Republic of South Africa; (3) the release of all political prisoners without distinction as to party or race; (4) the repeal of all laws or regulations confining the indigenous inhabitants to reserves and denying them all freedom of movement, expression, and association, and of all other laws and regulations that establish and maintain the intolerable system of apartheid; and (5) preparations for general elections to the Legislative Assembly, based on universal adult suffrage, to be held as soon as possible under the supervision and control of the United Nations.

The Assembly urged the South African Government to cooperate fully with this Special Committee. Notwithstanding the hostility of the Government to the Special Committee and, indeed, to most members of the United Nations, representatives of the U.N. were admitted for the first time into the international territory of South West Africa. However, severe limitations were imposed by the South African Government, which refused to admit the Special Committee as a whole into South West Africa and South Africa, but invited two of its members, the Chairman and Vice-Chairman (from the Philippines and Mexico, respectively), to come to South Africa and to visit South West Africa. At the same time, South Africa stated that nothing in its actions was to be construed as recognition of the competence of the United Nations to act with respect to South West Africa.

The Special Committee as a whole confirmed the information furnished by the prior South West Africa Committee and the petitioners before the Fourth Committee and concluded as follows:

It is obvious from the report of the Chairman and Vice-Chairman that, although they were in the Territory for more than nine days and visited only such limited places as were included in the itinerary arranged by the South African Government, the Chairman and the Vice-Chairman saw and heard enough of the conditions to be able to confirm the previous findings and conclusions of the General Assembly on the conditions prevailing in the Mandated Territory.

The Foreign Minister of South Africa, Eric Louw, taking issue with this conclusion, drew attention to a document (to which the Fourth Committee was not privy) that he claimed was a joint communiqué issued by the Chairman and Vice-Chairman of the Special

Committee and the Government of the Republic of South West Africa. He further claimed that the document (1) established that existing conditions in the territory of South West Africa held no threat to international peace and security; and (2) contained evidence that nullified the allegations of the governments of Liberia and Ethiopia before the International Court of Justice.

Representing the Government of Liberia on the Fourth Committee, I asked the Foreign Minister to reply to the following questions from Committee members:

1. Why did the Government of the Republic of South Africa not invite the Special Committee as a whole to go to South Africa and South West Africa, and, especially, why was the only African representative on the Special Committee not included among those who were invited?

2. What was really the underlying reason for extending the invitation if the Government of the Republic of South Africa did not consider the invitation to two of the representatives of the Special Committee to be a tacit recognition of the competence of the United Nations re South West Africa?

3. Is it to be construed that the real reason for the invitation was to make use of the presence of the U.N. representatives in the territory as a garb for the production of a document that the Republic of South Africa purports to be valid, a document that can be used in behalf of South Africa in the case before the World Court? The Chairman and Vice-Chairman of the Special Committee have denied being a party to the so-called joint communiqué. The Foreign Minister of South Africa insists that the joint communiqué contains evidence that nullifies the allegations of the governments of Liberia and Ethiopia against his government.

The Foreign Minister declined to reply to these questions; but it must be especially noted that even if it were true that the U.N. representatives were a party to such a document, such an act would have been *ultra vires*, since the terms of reference of General Assembly Resolution 1702 did not include authorization by the United Nations to issue such a communiqué; instead, the Committee was to report its findings to the United Nations.

It is no secret that the South African Government applies its policy of apartheid against the indigenous inhabitants of South West Africa just as it does against the people of Indian origin and the Africans in South Africa. All evidence tends to prove that the South African Government has violated the letter and spirit of the Mandate agreement and its undertaking under Article 22 of the League Covenant with respect to South West Africa.

Tirelessly and unswervingly, the United Nations continues its efforts to achieve the goal for the people of South West Africa as envisaged in the Mandate agreement and the Charter of the United Nations. At its Seventeenth Session, it adopted its sixty-sixth resolution on the question of South West Africa (1805, XVII), in which it condemned the continued refusal of the Government of the Republic of South Africa to cooperate with the United Nations in the implementation of its resolutions, especially Resolution 1702, concerning South West Africa.

In operative Paragraph 5 of Resolution 1805 (XVII), the Secretary-General is requested to appoint a U.N. Resident Representative for South West Africa to carry out the terms of Resolution 1566 in relation to the coordination of the economic and social assistance that the specialized agencies will provide. The Assembly urged the South African Government to refrain from using the territory of South West Africa as a base for the accumulation (for internal or external purposes) of arms or armed forces. In view of the anxieties expressed by a large number of member states, it also urged member states to refrain from any action likely to hinder the Assembly resolution on South West Africa, and directed the Special Committee on the Implementation of the Declaration of the Granting of Independence to Colonial Countries and Peoples to discharge *mutatis mutandis* the tasks assigned to the Special Committee for South West Africa.

However, the Government of the Republic of South Africa, through its Permanent Representative at the United Nations, has already informed the Secretary-General that it would not be able to agree to the appointment of a U.N. Resident Representative for Technical Assistance in South West Africa, and that it cannot consider whether any outside expert advice will be necessary. The question of South West Africa, like the question of the Portuguese overseas territories, presents serious problems for the United Nations, but the United Nations does not despair. It is its intention to have South West Africa placed under trusteeship for a brief period as a means of achieving self-determination and independence for the territory.

Certainly, the game carried on by the South African Government cannot last forever; for just as in the case of Algeria and the other territories ceded to the Principal Allied and Associated Powers under the Versailles Treaty, South West Africa will be free. The sovereign states of Africa share the concern of their brothers and cannot be expected to stand idly by while the indigenous inhabitants of South

West Africa continue to be treated ruthlessly because they desire to be free. There is a limit to human endurance; it should be no surprise if these people rise up to repel the force exercised by South Africa against them, break the shackles that bind, and take their rightful place among the community of nations.

May God help them to become free and independent.

Discussion

ALEX QUAISON-SACKEY.   I approach the problem of South West Africa from two aspects, peaceful and violent. The peaceful aspect can be divided into legal and political. In 1950, the World Court gave an opinion that South West Africa is an international territory, that it does not belong to South Africa, that the Mandate is still in existence, and that the United Nations has supervisory functions to perform in the territory. In our 1960 conference of African states in the United Nations, we were told that only two of our members, Liberia and Ethiopia, had been members of the League of Nations and therefore had status before the Court. Accordingly, all of us decided that the Court should be asked to determine whether the Mandate had been carried out by South Africa. I suppose it is very important to understand exactly what is meant by the Mandate of South West Africa. We had believed that when, in 1919, the great powers, as it were, sold away this territory, the Mandate was given to Her Majesty to be administered for her by South Africa (South Africa being in the Commonwealth); we believe, therefore, that there is a legal point as to whether South Africa got a Mandate by theft or whether Her Majesty in England had the Mandate and gave it to South Africa. However, the resolution was made, and so the great powers and leaders expressed the opinion that the welfare of the people should be cared for, the territory should not be used as a military base, and the idea of internationality should always be upheld.

Now, this has not been done. Therefore, the governments of Liberia and Ethiopia, in their own sovereign right and on behalf of the African states, have raised this issue with the Court. All of us are supporting Liberia and Ethiopia financially in this very expensive legal procedure.

Now, what about the political aspect? Political action can take place in the territory itself (as has been described by Miss Brooks) and in the United Nations. I think we have done a lot in the United Nations by bringing out the issue at this time, for the very fact that African states are opposed to South Africa threatens international peace. If we have not used violence, it is because we believe in the principles of the Charter (and possibly because we are not strong enough yet to attack). Action in the United Nations has been good, and I think that the resolution passed in 1961—that is, the setting up of the Committee to hold an investigation in the territory—was a landmark. The resolution anticipated that the Committee would look into the Legislative Assembly, the evacuation of South African military forces and bases, the forcible removal of Africans from village to village, and so forth. This, then, was a very important resolution, and was fully supported by the United States. The United Kingdom, which should have taken a strong stand, abstained. We had hoped that with South Africa's departure from the Commonwealth, the position of the United Kingdom would be stronger.

The reaction of the South African Government to the United Nations has not been very good. Foreign Minister Eric Louw said, and I am quoting: "One of the main contributing factors toward the feeling of lack of confidence in the U.N. by the Western nations is the growth of the African bloc. They are today in full control of the United Nations." He went on to say that this had come as a shock to the Western delegations, made aware of the power of the African bloc by the U.N.'s sanction and resolution against South Africa in the 1962 session. Newspapers that are no friends of South Africa—the *New York Times*, the *Washington Post*, the London *Times*, and others—all expressed their concern about this resolution, contending that the U.N. had no power to pass such a resolution and that the resolution contributed to a feeling among Western states that the United Nations had lost prestige.

In March, 1963, Louw said: "We live in difficult times, and the outlook is perhaps a bit darker than people think. I do not wish to sound unduly pessimistic, but we are in the fullest sense involved in a cold war. We do not know what is going to happen, but we do know that we as South Africans are determined to hold what we have and oppose all attempts at black domination." This is the reaction of the South African to the African nations in the United Nations and to the United Nations itself.

But, apart from the U.N., action in the territory itself is vital. It is true that in the formative period of an independence movement it is necessary for the leaders to run away and organize, arouse world opinion, and get attention focused on the problem. But it is essential that organization in the territory itself should produce agitation, riots, and attrition—all geared to molding opinion. We have the South West Africa People's Organization, the South West Africa National Union, and other, smaller splinter groups, and there is no valid reason why they should not come together in the territory with one strong leader to deal with the South African Government. They have all the legal and moral right on their side. It is accepted by all people that South West Africa cannot be a territory of South Africa, and so it should be very clear that it is impossible for South Africa to revoke the Mandate unilaterally. It is true that some of us have in fact considered the question of whether it would be possible for the United Nations to consider revoking the Mandate, but our legal experts tell us to wait, for the issue is before the International Court. They add that a year or two of waiting is not a bad thing, but a year or two in the life of a nation, of a people struggling for independence, can be very long indeed.

Now I must emphasize the responsibility of the great powers. How is it that South Africa is allowed to import arms from the United States, from the United Kingdom, and from France? I do not see why pressure should not be brought to bear by a powerful country like the United States against South Africa on the question of South West Africa. It seems that the leaders of the U.S. delegation to the United Nations are coming more and more to accept this view, and their actions for the past two years have been good. I think they have seen the problem. Certainly, if the United States and the United Kingdom would say to South Africa that South West

Africa is not hers, it would be an important step toward solving the problem.

ACHKAR MAROF.   For us, South West Africa is symbolic of many wrongs. First of all, the country represents the two foremost evils in Africa: racism and colonialism. Second, and to me this is the most important, South West Africa represents the failure of the United Nations, the failure of the international community to discharge its obligation.

Now, this may sound like a very strong expression, but the facts, as they have been pointed out by Mr. Kozonguizi and Miss Brooks, are most discouraging. In other words, year after year we discuss this problem of South West Africa; we bring about resolutions, good resolutions, and nothing is done. The only new element that has appeared is the report before the International Court of Justice. Why is the U.N. incapable of implementing its own decision in the territory? No matter what you call it—a mandated territory or any other name—it is obvious that South West Africa is an international territory. The U.N. has taken a stand to resolve the problem created there by the South African Government, but so far it has been incapable of doing anything. This calls for a closer look at the United Nations.

What is the United Nations but its members? What can the U.N. do if the members are not willing to do it? And when I say the members, I mean those members who are really in a position to do something, the big powers, the great powers. But the situation is that the big powers without exception, and I emphasize without exception, are not ready to implement the resolution.

So, meanwhile, the Africans face the International Court of Justice. We know what will probably happen: The Court will render a judgment stating that South Africa is violating the Mandate in South West Africa and therefore should hand it over to the United Nations. It is very likely, according to what we have witnessed this last year, that the Government of South Africa will not abide by such a judgment.

Then what will happen? Liberia and Ethiopia, on behalf of the African states, may go before the Security Council, in accordance with Article 94 of the Charter. And what will happen in the Security Council? The same big powers there will very likely take the same position; in other words, they will do nothing, because no one of the great powers, I'm afraid, is prepared to fight for the freedom of South West Africa. That is the hard reality of the situation in the United Nations. A number of speeches will be made, a number of resolutions offered; and a number of petitions will come before the United Nations. But so long as the big powers who, after all, have been robbed of something that belongs to us, the United Nations, refuse to take the territory from South Africa, these other actions in the U.N. are without meaning.

Now, as to the U.N. resolutions, who can apply sanctions effectively against South Africa? Obviously, those countries who have substantial relations with South Africa. So we come back to the same big powers and we come back to the same position of theirs, that they are not willing to do anything. Ambassador Quaison-Sackey referred to the way Resolution 1761 calling for sanctions was voted on. Let me say that precisely all those countries capable of implementing that resolution voted against it.

The problem is to fight and destroy a fascist regime in South Africa. The only realistic solution is the cooperation of the nationalists in South West Africa and in South Africa. Whenever that is achieved, no matter how, then both the South African and the South West African problems will be resolved.

In the meantime, the struggle now being waged all over Africa, mostly in the southwestern and central parts, is also likely to help South West Africa. The geographical position of South West Africa is such that it is almost unthinkable that a half-million people in such a large and sparsely settled area can wage alone any kind of efficient war of liberation. The struggle for liberation for the rest of this part of Africa will influence very greatly South West Africa. The independence of Angola, when it comes, will be a very positive element in the solution of South West Africa; so also will the coming independence of Northern Rhodesia.

This is the position today. Everybody knows that the U.N. has been successful only when the big powers have agreed on the action to be carried out. Unless the big powers and most of the Western powers agree to exert pressure on South Africa, to boycott effectively, the solution of the South West Africa problem will still take some years to come.

JACOB KUHANGUA.   First, may I congratulate you for your wisdom in initiating such a gathering as this one. I am sure all African people join me in delaring that your demonstration of good will and spiritual encouragement will always be remembered in the furtherance of the bonds of unity and solidarity between the people of Africa and the Americans of African descent.

After the formation of the United Nations, in 1946, the South African Government refused to place South West Africa under the United Nations Trusteeship. In the same year, a delegation led by the late Jan Smuts, who was then Prime Minister, came to the United Nations vainly seeking legal integration of South West Africa into South Africa. The South African Government thereafter ignored every resolution passed in the United Nations regarding the serious situation prevailing in South West Africa. The South African minority government is deceiving itself by refusing to recognize the dramatic changes that have occurred in Africa and all over the world in recent years. Although the Government of South Africa, as has been indicated, is fighting a losing battle, its policy of apartheid causes unbearable suffering among the African population of my country. I call to the attention of the entire civilized world the inhuman laws and unbearable conditions imposed upon the people of South West Africa.

Let me define apartheid to those who are not familiar with it. The regime of Prime Minister Hendrik Verwoerd is no different from the regime of Adolf Hitler, and the practice of apartheid is no different from the Nazi persecutions. There are many concentration camps erected in my country. South Africa, in violation of the Mandate, has ruthlessly applied this apartheid policy in South West Africa with increasing intensity, and continues to do so with utter contempt for public opinion and with complete disregard for the United Nations. The South African Government has set up a regime of military and police terror in our country. The police are well armed with modern weapons against the defenseless women and children of my country. In short, the government is cruelly persecuting and physically eliminating the people of my country who are fighting for freedom and independence. The African population have been deprived of political and civil rights, and they are the victims of arbitrary action on the part of the white colonizers. By means of force and arms, the colonizers are suppressing any attempt at improving the prevailing situation. And that is precisely what we say constitutes a threat to international peace.

But you have the assurance from me that independence is about to be won in South West Africa.

BRIAN BASSINGTHWAIGHT.   A great deal has been said about South West Africa and the legal and historical position of this country; but one point that perhaps needs more emphasis is the question of education in South West Africa.

Under the present setup, all African students are educated under a system known as Bantu education; [1] because of this very fact, almost all schools (and there are not many) are empty, and most students who want to get higher education seek it outside the territory. It so happens that most of our students who go to the outside go to places like Dar es Salaam, where they stay for perhaps more than a year awaiting scholarships, which they do not receive in most cases. By the time some scholarships are available to them, they have almost given up hope of obtaining a higher education.

In South West Africa, there are no universities or other institutions of higher education, and the situation is really a very tragic one. In a country of roughly 700,000 people, we find that we do not have more than 10 university graduates. Sometimes we are successful in getting scholarships, but in most cases students wait for years without getting aid from any source. If we are to govern ourselves one day, something has to be done about education in our country.

Finally, I am glad this conference has emphasized once again the importance of unity among South West Africa's political parties, in order to better assist in the liberation of our country, since for so many years we

[1] EDITORS' NOTE: The cornerstone of Bantu education is the use of language, that most subtle and profound socializer, to limit and restrict the African's frame of reference. According to its architect, Dr. Hendrik Verwoerd, the aim of Bantu education is to condition the African to inequality and separate development. Accordingly, all instruction is in the African vernacular, while elementary reading, writing, and arithmetic are emphasized so that the child may follow simple instructions.

have been looking to the outside, to the United Nations, to other African states.

THE REVEREND MARKUS KOOPER.   All I will say here in connection with what has been said is that this conference would do very well if it could determine a course of action that would motivate the big powers, and particularly the country in which this conference is held, to institute those economic sanctions against South Africa as resolved by the United Nations last year [1962].

Editors' Postscript*

Everyone concerned with Southern Africa has been waiting for more than four years for the International Court of Justice to render a decision on South Africa's administration of South West Africa. At this writing, that decision is about to be made. If the Court decides against South Africa and recommends U.N. administration, as expected, the issue will probably be brought before the Security Council. Since the U.N. Charter obligates the Council to uphold decisions of the International Court, a legal rationalization for inaction will have been removed. The United Nations will then be faced with a decision that could determine whether the future of Southern Africa will be decided by violence or by peaceful means.

In the meantime, the United Nations has continued to condemn South Africa. Despite the confusion and intrigue that resulted from the visit of the Special Committee on South West Africa, the same committee formally rejected the joint communiqué that was allegedly issued by its Chairman and Vice-Chairman and the South African Government. Following the debate on South West Africa, the General Assembly adopted a resolution urging members to "refrain from the supply in any manner or form of any petroleum products to South Africa." Voting against the resolution were the United States, the United Kingdom, South Africa, Portugal, Spain, and France. American and British reluctance openly to oppose South Africa in the United Nations continued through 1964, when both powers abstained from voting on a resolution that called upon South Africa to desist from setting up Bantu homelands in South West Africa.

During 1965, the Special Committee on Colonialism began to emphasize the economic aspects of South African domination and reported to the General Assembly that Africans working for foreign companies in South West Africa are forced to exist under conditions of virtual slave labor. They are, for example, denied by law the right to strike or to refuse to obey employers' orders regardless of conditions.[1]

On January 12, 1965, the Committee called upon the General Assembly to condemn South Africa for granting concessions to companies that were draining South West Africa of its mineral wealth. Outcries against the systematic exploitation of the country by monop-

---

* This and all subsequent Editors' Postscripts were written during the summer of 1965.

[1] *Africa Digest*, XII, No. 4 (February, 1965), 109–10.

olists and politicians have even been heard from within the white community itself. In the summer of 1963, for example, the leader of the Opposition in the South West Africa legislature, Mr. Niehaus, asked for a commission to investigate the irregularity surrounding the granting of a concession to a group who, according to Niehaus, were already "up to their ears in the diamond industry." [2] He then produced a list of persons involved that read like a roster of the most prominent Nationalists in South Africa.

Among the African population, conflict continued between SWANU and SWAPO, as well as among leading personalities within the various political parties. Ethnic conflict also occurred as the Coloured and Baster communities came to an open split in March, 1964. The Coloured Organization, which is pro–South Africa, declared it did not want Basters living in its townships, teaching in its schools, or belonging to its organizations. At the same time, there were signs of increasing unity among the anti-government groups. In October, 1963, a National Liberation Front was formed to represent all parties and groups in the country. A month later the South West Africa Freedom Fighters' Open United Front was established, with headquarters in Dar es Salaam.

Meanwhile, the South African Government has had to plan a course of action should the ICJ decision go against her. Some prominent South Africans have reportedly expressed the view that the government would simply take over the territory by military means in defiance of the United Nations.[3] On the other hand, there has also been talk of yielding the territory to the United Nations, or—a more likely course—offering to make it an independent Bantustan under South African guardianship.

The South African Government, in response to international pressures, did send the Odendaal Commission to South West Africa to advise on the development of the territory. The Commission's report stated—in the classic tradition of divide and rule—that cultural and linguistic differences made central government impossible. It recommended, instead, the setting up of several African Bantustans and a five-year development plan. Each Bantustan would have a legislative council consisting of chiefs, headmen, and a few elected members. The councils would control "all legislative and administrative functions except for defense, foreign affairs, internal security and border control, posts, water affairs, power generation and transport," [4] which would remain in the hands of Pretoria.

[2] *Ibid.*, XI, No. 1 (August, 1963), 25.
[3] *Ibid.*, X, No. 5 (April, 1963), 168–69.
[4] *Ibid.*, XI, No. 5 (April, 1964), 150.

At this point, the United States and Great Britain reportedly warned South Africa that any attempt to establish Bantustans while the issue of South West Africa was still before the International Court of Justice would be followed by an injunction against South Africa in the Court and by United Nations intervention.[5] Dr. Verwoerd promptly announced to Parliament that a formal decision on the creation of Bantustans in South West Africa had been postponed. Nevertheless, the government decided to go ahead with economic projects and also purchased 158 white farms in areas designated as future Bantustans.

Shortly before this action, 154 Hereros and Damaras had fled to Bechuanaland. Although the refugees told British authorities they were students seeking education, it is widely believed that the mass exodus was politically organized and that the men were destined for Dar es Salaam, where they were to await assignment to guerrilla training camps.[6]

[5] *Ibid.*, XI, No. 6 (June, 1964), 186.
[6] *Ibid.*

III

The High Commission Territories

The People:
Their History and Government

D. V. COWEN

Introduction

The three High Commission Territories of Basutoland, Bechuanaland, and Swaziland have been subject to British control in one form
or another since the latter half of the nineteenth century. Although
they are geographically either surrounded by, or wedged into, the territory of the Republic of South Africa and are economically closely
tied to it, and although, with Britain's concurrence, provision was
made in the South African constitution more than fifty years ago for
their possible incorporation as an integral part of South Africa, they
continue to be governed independently of the Republic by a High
Commissioner who is answerable to the British Government through
the Colonial Office.

Although the territories are often spoken about collectively, each
has its distinctive character and problems. Of the interests and problems they do have in common, the most striking is a growing sense of
frustration and urgency—a need for each to resolve its own harassing
problem and to achieve a firm sense of direction with maximum deliberate speed. Unless their present malaise is tackled vigorously, imag-
inatively, and, above all, quickly, they may come to be known in history as Britain's lost opportunity in Africa.

Basutoland

The African population of Basutoland is approximately 800,000, of
which some 650,000 reside in the territory; the remaining 150,000
(approximately half the adult male population) find employment as
migrant laborers in South Africa—in the mines and on the farms, in
industry and in domestic service. There are some 2,000 white persons

in Basutoland, of whom half are South African citizens. Among the whites there are a bit fewer than 250 missionaries, about 230 traders, about 200 officials, more than 100 school and university teachers, and some 60 artisans.

With an annual revenue struggling toward U.S. $5 million, Basutoland does not quite pay its way, but relies on the British Government for the funds to develop its economy and social services.

The land of Basutoland is owned communally by the Basotho people and is held in trust for the nation by the Paramount Chief. Rights of user are allocated by the chiefs to their subjects, but the area of arable land available to each family is only about six acres. And each year the pressure of a growing population increases ominously. Industrial development has been negligible, and such mineral wealth as exists—including small deposits of diamonds—is still undeveloped.

The dominant feature of Basutoland's economy is the migrant-labor system. As long as this system prevails, there will exist a built-in obstacle to agricultural improvement and economic development, for the system obliges approximately half of the adult male population to spend years working in the Republic of South Africa, and badly disrupts decent family and social life in Basutoland.

Basutoland's main potential economic asset is water. The territory is a natural reservoir and an obvious source of hydroelectric power for an enormous area of Southern Africa. It is also the source of South Africa's major river, the Orange River. The development of hydro-electric power could galvanize the economy and be Basutoland's salvation. But this would require a capital investment of some U.S. $30 million, and would almost certainly need the cooperation of the Republic of South Africa.

The Basotho have fortunately been spared the divisiveness of tribalism. Linguistically homogeneous, they have a strong sense of national identity—the Paramount Chieftainship having served powerfully to symbolize the unity of the nation from the days of the great Moshoeshoe, who formed the Basotho nation from resident tribes in the early part of the last century and sought the protection of the British Crown for Basutoland. At the same time, tensions are developing between the hereditary chiefs, who are still influential, and the ever growing body of politically conscious commoners. Indeed, the search for a formula that will peacefully accommodate both chiefs and commoners in a mutually acceptable polity is one of the most harassing features of Basutoland's constitutional development.

Until very recently, the pattern of administration in all three territories was much the same. Full power to govern by proclamation was vested exclusively in Her Majesty's High Commissioner, the various councils and committees of the inhabitants of the territories being advisory only. The High Commissioner's headquarters were, and still are, located in Pretoria and Cape Town. In each territory, however, he appoints, and delegates certain powers to, a Resident Commissioner who works under his direction.

The Basotho were the first to ask for an effective say in their own government. As early as 1872, some of the leading chiefs requested representation in the Cape Parliament and were refused. In 1903, an advisory Basutoland Council was established. Only after many attempts and long years of waiting have the Basotho achieved any legislative representation.

In September, 1955, the Basutoland Council passed Motion 90, requesting that the Council be given power to make laws in all internal matters. In May, 1956, the Secretary of State for Commonwealth Relations said that he was willing to consider proposals along these lines, subject, however, to certain conditions. Among these conditions was one that would have prevented any proposed Basutoland legislature from making laws affecting the 2,000 whites residing in the territory. Needless to say, this condition was rejected by the Basotho.

The Basutoland Council then proceeded to appoint a committee with power to draw up—in consultation with an independent adviser —comprehensive proposals for a new constitution. In due course, specific proposals were published in a lengthy report. They were unanimously accepted by the Basutoland Council and, in substantial measure, implemented by Her Majesty's Government, which, on the basis of the proposals, introduced the present Basutoland constitution in 1960.

A few obvious and immediate gains were made through this constitution. Whereas under the old dispensation, the powers of the Basutoland Council were advisory only and did not extend to the whole field of government, under the new constitution the competence of the Legislative Council covers the whole field, being legislative in a wide range of matters, though it remains advisory in an important area reserved to the High Commissioner. Again, any suggestion of a color line in empowering the legislature was firmly rejected. "Fancy" franchises and reserved seats were also rejected, and the principle of democratic common-roll elections for both the Basotho and the 2,000 whites lawfully resident in the territory was adopted. The elections to the legislature are, however, at present indirect; directly elected local government bodies serve as the electoral colleges.

In the unicameral legislature, the democratic principle was given further extension so as to increase the elected element from 36 per cent to 50 per cent—the remaining 50 per cent of the members obtaining their seats by virtue of their chiefly birth or through nomination by the Paramount Chief. It would not have been possible to get approval in the Constitutional Committee or in the Basutoland Council (both of which consisted mainly of chiefs) for a great degree of popular representation; without that approval, negotiations with the Secretary of State would have been hamstrung.

Although executive decisions were no longer possible without consulting the people's representatives, the new Basutoland constitution was not particularly progressive. Under it, a political party could win an overwhelming victory at the polls without being able to control either the legislature or the executive—and this is what has happened. The constitutional proposals fully recognized that this sort of divorce between power and responsibility was unhealthy. But there was, for the time being, no alternative. For some eighty years, virtually no steps had been taken to establish the foundations of fully responsible government; this could not be achieved at one stroke.

What was needed was a framework that would inevitably set the course for more democratic and responsible government, build up pressures for development, not incite too much opposition among the more conservative and influential Basotho, and afford, above all, a period of training in modern democratic government.

Today, after three years under the 1960 Constitution, the Basotho are demanding radical steps forward: full democracy, full responsibility, the establishment of the Paramount Chief's position on a sound basis, and either immediate independence or the fixing of an early date for independence. A Commission for Constitutional Revision, to which I am pleased to be the adviser, is now working on the subject.

Party political development in Basutoland is vigorous. Founded in 1952, Ntsu Mokhehle's Basutoland Congress Party is probably the strongest. Chief Leabua Jonathan's Basutoland National Party, which places more emphasis on integrating the traditional way of life into a modern structure, also has considerable support. Toward the end of 1960, dissension within the leadership of the Basutoland Congress Party came to a head, and B. M. Khaketla, then Deputy President of the Congress Party, resigned and formed the Basutoland Freedom Party. This party has recently amalgamated with Chief S. S. Matete's Marema Tlou, which was formed in 1957 with the creation of unity between chiefs and commoners as one of its avowed objects. A small Communist Party exists—sniping (as yet ineffectively) at everyone, and especially at the powerful Congress Party. Finally, within the last few months, a Labour Party has been formed, mainly among the migrant laborers working in the Republic. In its recently published manifesto, it seeks, among other objectives, cooperation with the Republic on the basis of good-neighborliness.

There are some in Basutoland who see in all this proliferation of party activity the danger of weakening the struggle for freedom and independence and of encouraging a policy of divide and rule. This is the view of Josiel Lefela, veteran freedom fighter among Basutoland's politicians, who has called for a National Liberation Front. The danger, no doubt, exists; but the Basotho are patriots and not fools, and offsetting the proliferation of parties (which, after all, is not unnatural in a free country in the formative years of democracy), there has recently been formed the Pan-African Solidarity Congress (PASCO)—an alliance between the Basutoland Congress Party and like-minded parties in Swaziland and Bechuanaland.

Bechuanaland

Physically, Bechuanaland provides a complete contrast to Basutoland. Bounded by the Republic of South Africa, Southern Rhodesia, and South West Africa, Bechuanaland is somewhat larger than Texas. It is not a shortage of land but a shortage of water that is the main factor in the life of the 350,000 Africans, 3,000 Europeans, 700 persons of mixed blood, and 300 Asians who live there. Cattle-raising and dairying are the slender props of the economy. Although deposits of coal have recently been discovered, Bechuanaland is a poor and as yet undeveloped country with an annual revenue of less than U.S.$ 3 million.

Approximately 113,500 square miles of the country have been reserved for occupancy by the African peoples. (Land is allocated by the chief for the use of his subjects much the same way as in Basutoland.) More than 100,000 square miles, much of the area desert, are undeveloped Crown lands. In addition, there is an area of some 5,000 square miles comprising land owned by the Tati Company and blocks granted in perpetuity to the British South Africa Company, where Europeans can buy farms with freehold title.

The history of Bechuanaland's association with Great Britain has some points of similarity with that of Basutoland. It was another great African chief, Khama III of the Bamangwato, who helped to bring Bechuanaland directly under the British Crown.

Actuated by the same fears as Moshoeshoe of Basutoland for the integrity of his country and the safety of his people, Khama, from the time he acceded to the chieftainship in 1872, made representations to the High Commissioner that his country and people should be taken under the direct protection of the British Crown. In this, he received the potent backing of Cecil Rhodes, who shrewdly saw in Bechuanaland the essential passageway to what is now Rhodesia; for the Germans, meanwhile, had occupied South West Africa, and Bechuanaland was therefore the corridor between German South West Africa and the Boer Republic of the Transvaal. In 1885, the whole of Bechuanaland was declared to be under the protection of Her Majesty Queen Victoria. The southern part of the area later became part of the Cape Colony and is now an integral part of the Cape Province of the South African Republic; the northern part has remained a British Protectorate administered by the High Commissioner.

In 1895, ten years after the declaration of protection, the British Government proposed to hand over the administration of Bechuanaland to Rhodes's British South Africa Company. Chief Khama, supported by two other principal tribal chiefs, promptly went to England to protest. Their protest was effective: The price for continued protection by the Crown was land on which the Crown could build a railway, which today runs from Mafeking to Bulawayo.

Despite a long struggle for improvement by great representatives such as the late Tshekedi Khama, constitutional development of the territory has been much slower even than in Basutoland.

In 1920, two advisory councils, representing respectively the European and African inhabitants of the Protectorate, were created; they were to be consulted on certain items of government policy. The European Advisory Council, which met twice a year under the presidency of the Resident Commissioner, was made up of eight members elected to represent the European inhabitants in the eight electoral areas into which the Protectorate was divided. The African Advisory Council was composed of the chiefs of the eight principal tribes as permanent ex officio members, and thirty-two other members selected by tribal or district councils for the thirteen divisions in the Protectorate. The Resident Commissioner served as president, and there were to be not more than seven other government officials as members.

The method of selection or appointment to the African Advisory Council varied from area to area, but until very recently the democratic elective principle was little in evidence. The Resident Commissioner was authorized to consult the African Advisory Council on a range of matters affecting Africans only, such as those concerning chiefs, African courts, customary law, and tribal organization.

In 1950, a Joint Advisory Council was established, consisting of eight members of the African Advisory Council elected by that Council, the eight members of the European Advisory Council, and seven government officials. In April, 1958, the Joint Advisory Council passed a resolution "that in the opinion of this Council the time has come when a Legislative Council should be formed and empowered to assist in the Government of the Territory." Thereupon, in April, 1959, it was announced that the Secretary of State for Commonwealth Relations was prepared to consider proposals for the establishment of such a Council.

A Constitutional Committee, consisting of four European and four African unofficial members of the Joint Advisory Council and four government officials, was appointed to assist the Resident Commissioner in the formulation of proposals. The Committee's report, duly endorsed by the Joint Advisory Council, was published in November, 1959. After it was published, certain modifications recommended by the Resident Commissioner and the High Commissioner were agreed upon, and, in July, 1960, the Secretary of State announced his approval of the proposed constitution.

The new constitution came into force in May, 1961. It provides for a Legislative Council of thirty-five members, of whom fourteen are either government officials or government appointees. The twenty-one elected members consist of ten Europeans elected directly by Europeans in ten constituencies, ten Africans elected indirectly by the old African Advisory Council (which continues in existence and now acts, in addition, as an electoral college), and one Asian elected by Asians throughout the territory by postal vote.

This constitution spurred the Bechuana immediately into the organization of political parties whose aim is to have the constitution superseded by a more democratic and less race-conscious structure. The most conspicuous defects of the constitution are: (1) the principle of parity between African and European representatives (the so-called "50-50 principle") despite the overwhelming majority of Africans in the territory; (2) the absence of common-roll elections, and the presence of communal representation—always a canker in the body politic; and (3) the disparity of treatment between Africans and Europeans in regard to the method of election—direct elections being favored for Europeans, indirect elections for Africans. Last year, in the United Nations, Britain's representative conceded that in so far as Bechuanaland's constitution was based on the principle of racial parity, it was "essentially of a transitional nature," and there can be no doubt that popular opinion in the territory is becoming increasingly opposed to it.

Party political organization in Bechuanaland is now making rapid progress. The Bechuanaland People's Party, founded in December,

1960, and led by K. T. Motsete and P. Matante, is the Bechuanaland counterpart of the Basutoland Congress Party. A defectionist section of the Bechuanaland People's Party, with apparently leftist sympathies, led by M. K. Mpho, also calls itself the Bechuanaland People's Party.

Unlike Basutoland, Bechuanaland faces a possible danger of tribal division; there are some eight principal tribes in the territory, perhaps the best known being the Bamangwato (the tribe of Tshekedi Khama and Seretse Khama) and the Bangwaketse under Chief Bathoen II. In 1959, the Bechuanaland Federal Party was formed with the aim, *inter alia*, of working toward the unity of the tribes. And recently, Seretse Khama, secretary of the Bamangwato tribe, was reported to have formed a new party, the Bechuanaland Democratic Party. Chief Bathoen of the Bangwaketse is also active in politics. It is earnestly to be hoped that these developments will not exacerbate tribal differences, as has happened in other African territories.

Swaziland

Smallest of the three territories in both size and population, Swaziland is economically the most prosperous and politically the most challenging.

Since Swaziland is favored by a good climate, abundant water, fertile soil, and considerable mineral wealth, her economic viability is assured. Afforestation and irrigation schemes have made possible a valuable and growing export of sugar, wood pulp, and fruit. More than a million tons a year of high-grade iron ore from the Bomvu Ridge fields are under contract to two Japanese steel firms; and a $30 million railroad is now under construction from Bomvu Ridge to the Mozambique border, where it will join a railhead to Lourenço Marques.

While the African population is the smallest of the three territories, the European population is the largest and, by far, the most influential. About 250,000 Swazi (Africans) live and work in the territory, and an additional 8,000 to 10,000 find employment as migrant laborers in South Africa, principally in the gold and coal mines of the Transvaal. There are approximately 10,000 Europeans in the territory; in addition, there are some 2,500 people of mixed blood (called Eurafricans or Coloured people).

Most of the Swazi still live in a rural environment under a semi-feudal regime of traditional law and custom and within a subsistence economy; but a steadily increasing number are becoming modernized and urbanized as the industrialization of Swaziland gets under way.

For example, trade unionism among the Swazi is a recent and potentially very significant development. And there are, today, at least two modernly conceived political parties in the territory under Swazi leadership (the Swaziland Progressive Party and the Swaziland Democratic Party).

The Europeans in the territory include civil servants, missionaries, teachers, merchants, and farmers, and, increasingly, they are providing the initiative for, and assuming control of, the territory's expanding commerce and its industrial and mining activities. It has been estimated that about 75 per cent of the Europeans in Swaziland are South African citizens. A large number of them reside and own property both in the Republic of South Africa and in Swaziland; under the existing laws, many of them exercise citizenship and franchise rights in both countries. On the other hand, Swazi living in South Africa are not accorded political rights in that country.

The Eurafrican community is a middle-class group consisting mainly of farmers, artisans, and traders. This community has for many years been accorded a separate status under the laws of Swaziland, being treated as neither Swazi nor European. In addition, there are a number of persons of mixed blood who choose to live as Swazi under Swazi law and custom.

The story of how Swaziland came under European jurisdiction reflects little credit on human nature. In the 1880's, the then Paramount Chief of the Swazi, Mbandzini, granted to acquisitive Europeans (both Boers and Britons) innumerable overlapping concessions for farming and mining. Disputes over ownership arose that threatened to erupt into violence. Government intervention became necessary. In 1890, a form of condominium by the United Kingdom and Transvaal (South African) governments was provisionally established, to be replaced four years later by a convention that gave the Transvaal Republic powers of protection, legislation, jurisdiction, and administration over Swaziland. As a result of the Boer War, these powers passed in 1903 to the Governor of the Transvaal, and, three years later, they were transferred to the High Commissioner, with whom they remain to this day.

Although the Swazi have begun to win back land and mineral rights that were carelessly granted to Europeans, these rights lie close to the heart of some of the present wrangling in regard to proposed constitutional advance.

About 51.5 per cent of the total land area of Swaziland is set apart for occupation by the Swazi. The major portion of this land (approximately 38 per cent of the territory) consists of so-called Swazi areas. which are scattered in blocks throughout the territory. The balance of the land allocated for the Swazi is from two sources, in approximately equal shares: (1) land purchased over the years by the Swazi people and held in trust by the Paramount Chief on behalf of the people, and (2) Native Land Settlement Areas, vested in the Swaziland Government. Approximately 45 per cent of the land area of the territory is held by private persons in freehold under Roman-Dutch law or under mining concessions. The major part of this privately owned land (about 43 per cent of the whole of Swaziland) is held by Europeans. The remaining area of the territory consists of government-owned freehold land, unallotted Crown land, and townships. African and European land holdings are inextricably mingled.

The territory's political and constitutional advance presents the most backward and discouraging picture of all three territories.

For some forty years the administration of Swaziland has been based on a division between "purely European affairs" and "Native (or Swazi) affairs." Thus, in 1921, an elected European Advisory Council, representative of the European community, was established "to advise the administration on purely European affairs." At present, this Council consists of ten members (one representing each of the electoral divisions of the territory), together with the Resident Commissioner, the Deputy Resident Commissioner, and six other official members appointed by the Resident Commissioner, who presides over the Council. The leader of the elected European group is C. F. Todd, a prominent South African lawyer and director of companies, who has interests, and is a registered voter, in both countries.

On the other hand, the focus of the traditional Swazi tribal structure is the Ngwenyama, or Paramount Chief, Sobhuza II. He acts in consultation with two traditional councils. The smaller of these, the Liqoqo, consists of the Ngwenyama's kinsmen and a few chosen advisers. The larger council, which normally acts only when matters have been referred to it by the Liqoqo, is known as the Libandla (or Swazi National Council). In theory, and in its largest extension, it is a council consisting of all the adult males in the nation. In practice, however, it is made up of all the chiefs and persons, of whatever rank, who have been co-opted to it. The Libandla is recognized, under Swazi custom, as the final body from which approval for any contemplated act of legislation by the Ngwenyama should be obtained.

The first serious steps toward constitutional reform were taken in April, 1960, by Sobhuza II, who invited a small group to hear his views on the subject:

We regard the European Advisory Council as having a lower status than our Council. We cannot meet the Advisory Council in its present stage as an Advisory Council; and in order that we should join it, let its status be raised to that of a Legislative Council. Only then can we come together.

As for election of representatives to this Legislative Council, the Paramount Chief said:

I think a solution to that would be that the Advisory Council, the European public, should elect their own men under their system of election, and we would get our men, chosen in the way we are wont to do, and then those men will meet and legislate for the country.

The constitutional planning which has taken place in Swaziland is very largely within the framework of the Chief's ideas. Following upon his pronouncement, in November, 1960, the Secretary of State authorized the appointment of a committee to make proposals for a Swaziland constitution. A committee was thereupon appointed consisting of representatives of the European Advisory Council, the Ngwenyama in Libandla, and the British Administration, under the chairmanship of the Resident Commissioner of Swaziland, B. A. Marwick.

On the Constitutional Committee—though not on its working committee—there were initially three members of the Swaziland Progressive Party (an African nationalist party which was at the time the territory's only political party), although they were given their places on the committee as members of the Libandla and not as members of a recognized political party. They were J. J. Nquku, then the President of the party; Dr. A. P. Zwane, the General Secretary; and Mr. Mabuza, a member of the Executive Committee. The Eurafrican community was not accorded any representation, notwithstanding the fact that it constituted a substantial minority and was treated under the laws of Swaziland as a separate group possessing a separate status.

Soon after the Constitutional Committee began its work, a conflict developed between the Swazi traditionalists and some of the white settlers on the one hand, and the Swaziland Progressive Party on the other hand. The members of the party on the committee were informed that it was expected that discussions for reform would proceed "within the framework of the Paramount Chief's proposals." They were reminded particularly that their views concerning adult suffrage were quite unacceptable to the Paramount Chief.

In May, 1961, the members of the Progressive Party on the Constitutional Committee, having failed in a request to have a constitutional adviser appointed for the committee as a whole, decided that their position on the committee was untenable and approached me to assist them. I agreed: (1) to advise the party on the whole subject of constitutional reform in Swaziland and to assist in drafting proposals, having due regard for the interests of the traditional tribal structure, the white settlers, and all other relevant interests; and (2) to consider and advise upon what steps could be taken to achieve the party's goals at an early date with the minimum friction among the various interests in the territories.

Meanwhile, dissatisfaction with the Eurafricans' position and with the procedures of the Constitutional Committee was being expressed by the Eurafrican Welfare Association on behalf of the Eurafrican community of Swaziland. And during August, 1961, they too asked me to represent their interests, having outlined their grievances to me and made constructive proposals for improvement. They emphasized that they were a substantial minority group in danger of being forgotten. They pointed out that, although they pay taxes in the same way as Swaziland's whites, they have no political representation whatever. They are by law excluded from the vote for the European Advisory Council and, unless they wish to live a tribal life, are not regarded as part of the country's political structure.

They complained about the lack of adequate financial support for schooling for their children; they resented the fact that there were differential rates of pay for white, Eurafrican, and African artisans; and they regretted the fact that they had not been given representation on the Constitutional Committee, although in the laws of Swaziland they are regarded as a separate group. They reported that when giving evidence to the Constitutional Committee, they had asked for some special provision to be made for them because they feared that, under King Sobhuza's scheme, they would be swamped on a common roll confined to whites and Eurafricans, inasmuch as the whites greatly outnumbered them. They had, however, been summarily informed that they had made no case for additional nominated representation because the Committee felt that if they got on the common roll, they would have enough representation on the Legislative Council.

The spokesmen of the Swaziland Eurafrican community explained to me that they considered themselves to be a group only by rejection, exclusion, and legal definition. They did not wish to perpetuate group distinctions on a racial basis and hoped to work for the eradication of all laws which treated them as a separate group with a separate status. For this reason, they favored the introduction of a genuine common voters' roll on a broad suffrage that would include Swazi as well as whites and Eurafricans. At the same time, they said that, until non-racialism developed in Swaziland in practice as well as in theory, they would like some provision for the "nomination of interests not otherwise represented." They made it quite clear that they did not wish to merge their identity either with the Swazi or with the whites. On the contrary, they were for submerging their identity as a separate group with a distinct legal status in a Swaziland nationhood that would embrace all Swazilanders irrespective of race or color. I have dealt with the position of the Eurafricans at some length because it is clear their interests have been neglected and because there is a danger that, in the clash of more powerful and obvious forces, they may again be forgotten.

On September 20, 1961, the proposals I had prepared on behalf of the Swaziland Progressive Party and the Eurafrican community were sent to the Constitutional Committee. In essence, the proposals were for a Legislative Council consisting of a clear majority of unofficial elected members, who were to be elected on a single common roll with universal adult suffrage. In addition, there was to be provision for ensuring representation by the technique of reserved seats for the Swazi traditionalists and for the white and Eurafrican minorities.

These recommendations were categorically rejected. And in March, 1962, the Constitutional Committee issued its own proposals. After setting out its ultimate objectives in an exemplary way, namely to "make Swaziland a state whose people would have equality of citizenship, irrespective of race, color, or creed," it proceeded to outline proposals that are rather difficult to relate to these objectives.

The Committee recommended that there should be a Legislative Council consisting, in addition to the Speaker, of four official members without a vote; twelve Swazi unofficial members elected by the Swazi National Council, serving as an electoral college; and an equal number of unofficial European members, elected separately on a "common roll consisting of Europeans and Eurafricans."

It has seemed to the Swaziland Progressive Party, to the Eurafrican community, and to a substantial number of Europeans, officials, and others in the territory that the Constitutional Committee's proposals are unacceptable, for several reasons:

1) They result in unhealthy racial-communal representation, whereby the Swazi are placed in one group and the whites and Eurafricans in another, a system calculated to perpetuate racial thinking in Swaziland and to sour race relations.

2) The 50-50 principle of racial parity between whites and Swazi is quite unfair to the Swazi, for it gives the whites at one jump an enormous accession of political power, coupled with their already overwhelming economic power. Numbering barely 10,000, they would come up from a position in which their present Advisory Council has

very little power—and then only in matters "affecting Europeans"—to a position in which they would exercise very substantial power over all persons in the territory.

3) The 50-50 principle is also quite unfair to the Eurafrican community, who would in all probability be "swamped" by the whites—and whites have not been slow to raise the swamping argument when there is talk of voting on a common roll with Africans.

4) The proposals make no provision whatsoever for democratic elections on a genuine common roll, including Africans as well as whites and Eurafricans. And unless this principle is implemented, in reasonably substantial measure, *from the very outset*, it would seem vain to speak of building a nonracial democracy in Swaziland.

More than a year has passed since the committee's proposals were published; they have been heavily and responsibly criticized in leading journals of opinion, and an inconclusive conference on the whole subject was recently convened by the Secretary of State in London. The various interests there represented took up prepared positions, and the Secretary of State and his advisers were left with the difficult task of doing what they could. In due course, it was agreed that everyone should go home and rethink the position.

The British Government's attitude at the date of writing has not been published. But it would be surprising if the 50-50 principle of racial parity were found acceptable, and, above all, it would be deeply disappointing to those who believe in nonracial democracy if the British Government did not insist upon an *immediate* and *substantial* start being made in Swaziland with democratic common-roll elections for Swazi, whites, and Eurafricans without regard to race, color, or creed.

Opportunities and Challenges

For some eighty years, Britain has been responsible for the government and well-being of these territories. The reasons for her involvement were mixed. Included among them was a good deal of what Sir John Seeley once called "a fit of absence of mind." There was a substantial measure, too, of genuine philanthropy and compassion, which yielded to the overtures of the Basotho and Bechuana peoples, who turned to Britain for protection against their white neighbors. And there was something, too, of that peculiar compound of economic and political imperialism tinged with sentimentality that led Cecil John Rhodes to proclaim, during the scramble for Africa, that "philanthropy was all very well, but philanthropy plus 5 per cent was better," and that enabled him to persuade Britain that Bechuanaland should be taken under protection as the "Suez Canal to the north."

But whatever the reasons might have been for Britain's original assumption of stewardship, the facts of stewardship and answerability for it are hard contemporary realities. There is certainly no compelling economic benefit to be derived by Britain from continued association with these territories. On the contrary, they are a financial burden; and manifestly they are a growing source of embarrassment. In 1962, for example, Great Britain's stewardship of the High Commission Territories was adversely criticized by the U.N. General Assembly. I have little doubt that world attention will increasingly be focused upon these territories and their problems. Time and again one hears senior British civil servants in the territories say, "We have no other interest here but to seek an honorable discharge." What, then, is the debt that must be honorably discharged?

Throughout the greater part of Britain's administration of the High Commission Territories, the policy toward them was determined by the expectation that some day they would be incorporated in the South African structure. The British Government was content to adopt the attitude of Mr. Micawber, hoping that some day something would turn up, and believing that it was unwise to allow the direction of political and economic development in the territories to get too much out of step with that prevailing in South Africa.

Naturally, I am not for one moment suggesting that it was ever the British Government's intention to go back on its oft-repeated pledge that incorporation would not be allowed without first consulting the peoples of the territories as well as the British Parliament. What I am suggesting is that for decades ultimate incorporation was in fact anticipated and that this expectation had a decisive influence on the shaping of policy.

In 1948, however, Dr. Malan's apartheid policy won the South African general election and put his party in power. This gave the British Government a jolt, but by no means a decisive one, for the opposition, the United Party, it was felt, might—in the tradition of British politics—return to power. The United Party favored ultimate incorporation of the territories; again, the British Government went on hoping for something to turn up, while the territories and their inhabitants languished.

When it became obvious in the late 1950's that South Africa was determined to pursue the way of apartheid, or separate development, and when it became equally obvious that the United Party's potential opposition was becoming increasingly hopeless, Great Britain openly committed herself to bring the High Commission Territories into the orbit of her general colonial policy and committed herself to guide them toward nonracial democracy and the maximum degree of self-government possible in their circumstances.

When Prime Minister Macmillan came to Cape Town in 1960, he said to Dr. Verwoerd in his famous "winds of change" speech:

> What is now on trial is our way of life. Our judgment of right and wrong and of justice is rooted in the same soil as yours—in Christianity and in the rule of law as the basis of a free society. It has been our aim to create a society which respects the rights of individuals—a society in which men are given an opportunity to grow to their full stature, and that must in our view include the opportunity of an increasing share in political power and responsibility; a society finally in which individual merit, and individual merit alone, is the criterion for a man's advancement, whether political or economic.

And he concluded this theme by endorsing a declaration made by the British representative at the U.N. General Assembly in 1959:

> We reject the idea of any inherent superiority of one race over another. Our policy is therefore nonracial; it offers a future in which Africans, Europeans, Asians, the peoples of the Pacific, and others with whom we are concerned will all play their full part as citizens in the countries where they live, and in which feelings of race will be submerged in a loyalty to new nations.

Here, then, is the debt of honor acknowledged by Britain. A gauntlet, so to speak, was thrown down; and it was promptly taken up by Dr. Verwoerd, who, in his own turn, proclaims the virtues of his policy of racial differentiation and the development of "Bantu" states. Two ways of life and two philosophies of government are now in open competition in Southern Africa. Plainly there can be no compromise in the territories themselves on the basic issues; yet open conflict would involve great suffering and would have grave international implications, which both South Africa and Britain obviously wish to avoid.

If Britain fails in the High Commission Territories—if, for example, she cannot set the course deliberately and decisively toward nonracial democracy among the 10,000 whites and 250,000 Africans in Swaziland—such a failure would give powerful support to Dr. Verwoerd. For he would undoubtedly use it, as he uses the failure of so-called "partnership" in the Central African Federation, as an argument in support of his case that one cannot achieve harmony between whites and nonwhites by pious hopes—however eloquently expressed —or by trying to bring the creatures together by tying fancy constitutional knots in their tails. Nor would anyone find much comfort in pointing up the flaws in Dr. Verwoerd's own policies.

There is still a chance that the ideals to which Britain is now firmly committed in the High Commission Territories can be achieved; but this will call for great qualities, not only from the British Government but from the people of the territories themselves—black and white, chiefs and commoners. There is absolutely no room for complacency and self-deception. Only great damage can be done to these territories by those who would condemn Dr. Verwoerd, while expecting a nonracial democracy to spring into being without sweat and tears.

Meanwhile, time is running heavily against Great Britain and all concerned in the High Commission Territories. Real constitutional advance has already been far too long delayed, and each additional month of delay leads to growing frustration, misunderstanding, and bitterness.

It is for these reasons that I would ask you to fix your eyes, and maybe your prayers, on what is now happening in Swaziland. From the point of view of race relations and political significance in the over-all picture of Southern Africa, Swaziland is very much the key territory, for, in substantial measure, it presents South Africa's problems in microcosm. The hour for firm and principled action has now come. It would be a disaster if any new constitution that might be devised proved to be just another illustration of superficial and, ultimately, dishonored "partnership."

Editors' Postscript

In September, 1963, Prime Minister Verwoerd of South Africa offered to take over the High Commission Territories from Great Britain and to administer them as black Bantustans. Addressing himself to economic interests, he declared that the Republic was more willing and able to help her neighbors than was far-off, noncommittal England. In Great Britain, liberal opinion reacted by immediately calling for a crash program of assistance totaling some £27 million for three years. In Basutoland and Bechuanaland, majority opinion soundly repudiated Verwoerd's proposal. Only in Swaziland was there even a hint that union with South Africa might be acceptable.

Realizing that independent African states within her very borders were a distinct possibility, South Africa began a determined effort to control movement to and from the three territories. Barbed-wire fences and 24-hour patrols are now standard at all boundaries. Meanwhile, the territories continue to move toward self-rule.

In 1964, a new constitution for Basutoland was agreed upon, providing for a sixty-member National Assembly elected on a one-man, one-vote, nonracial basis. In addition, there is a thirty-three-member Senate, consisting of twenty-two chiefs and eleven nominees of the Paramount Chief, with powers of amendment and delay. The new constitution provides that "the request for independence will be confirmed one year after elections and take effect as soon as possible thereafter." [1]

These elections were held on April 29, 1965, and Basutoland became self-governing. The moderate Basutoland National Party, under the leadership of Chief Leabua Jonathan, won thirty-one seats (41.63 per cent). Chief Leabua favors friendly relations with South Africa and has declared that a Basutoland under his leadership would avoid policies detrimental to neighborly relations with the Republic. Nevertheless, she would continue to give political asylum to South African refugees if they did not interfere in Basutoland politics or use the country as a base for sabotage. The more radical Basutoland Congress Party, led by Ntsu Mokhehle, won twenty-five seats (39.66 per cent). Its program calls for land reform, industrialization, and reduction of traditional power. The middle-of-the-road Maramatlou Freedom Party won only four seats (16.49 per cent). However, on May 18, 1965, this party voted with the ruling BNP and helped to defeat a no-confidence motion proposed by Mr. Mokhehle.

On June 7, 1965, a BCP delegate appeared before the U.N. Special Committee on Colonialism in Dar es Salaam and asked that it declare the elections null and void because of South African interference. Meanwhile, full independence is expected sometime in 1966.

Bechuanaland, more than any other High Commission Territory, has enjoyed smooth progress toward independence and is now self-ruling. Responsibility for external affairs and internal security remains with the Queen's Commissioner. In the summer of 1964, a new constitution, designed to lead to independence, was agreed upon by representatives of all communities. It provides for a lower house to consist of thirty-two members elected on a universal-suffrage, nonracial basis; four members elected by the parliament itself; and two appointed officials. In addition, there is an advisory House of Chiefs.

In the first elections, the "cautiously nationalistic" Bechuanaland Democratic Party, led by Seretse Khama, won twenty-eight seats. Though favoring a policy of multiracialism within the country, the

[1] Africa Report, X, No. 6 (June, 1964), 20.

BDP supports friendly relations with South Africa. This policy could be significant in a territory which is viewed by South African refugees as an escape route to the north. Upon his victory, Mr. Khama received personal congratulations from Dr. Verwoerd, although he had been banned from the Republic until a few months before because of his marriage to an English woman.

The more radical and Pan-Africanist Bechuanaland People's Party, led by Philip Matante, won only three seats. The BPP opposes the nomination of chiefs to representative bodies and wants Bechuanaland to become a center of resistance for South African freedom fighters. The party has already helped many members of the South African Pan-Africanist Congress to make their way north.[2]

Swaziland, dominated by an alliance of Europeans and African traditionalists, lags behind the other two territories in political development. This alliance has, so far, successfully fought all attempts by the British Colonial Office and Swazi modernists to work out a system of parliamentary democracy. In October, 1963, there was a political explosion when it became known that Paramount Chief Sobhuza II had been receiving advice on how to thwart British plans for a multiracial society from a South African lawyer close to Dr. Verwoerd and reputedly a member of the secret Broederbund.

Early in 1964, nevertheless, Britain virtually imposed a constitution that represented a compromise between the 50-50 principle proposed by the European Advisory Council and the traditional Swazi National Council (that is, 50 per cent of the seats to Europeans and 50 per cent to African chiefs) and the nonracial, universal suffrage demanded by the modern nationalist parties. It provides for a legislature of four Europeans elected by Europeans only, four Europeans elected on a national roll, eight nominees of the Swazi National Council, and eight members, black or white, elected on a national roll. The Europeans on the national roll must first secure the nomination of twenty-five whites, virtually assuring the candidates' antipathy to nonracial politics. In addition, the constitution gives resident white South Africans (70 per cent of the European population) the vote, while black South Africans remain disenfranchised.

In the first elections, the European reactionaries and African traditionalists won a complete victory. Seventeen Africans and seven Europeans, all endorsed by the Imbokoduo Party of Paramount Chief Sobhuza II or the European United Swaziland Association of Carl Todd, won all twenty-four seats in the legislature. The four "white" seats on the national roll went to two Europeans and two African tra-

[2] *Africa Digest*, XII, No. 5 (April, 1965), 130.

ditionalists, while the eight seats appointed by the Swazi National Council went to seven Africans and one white farmer. All candidates put up by the four modern nationalist parties were defeated. The Ngwane National Liberatory Congress, led by Dr. Ambrose Zwane, emerged as the only party that could possibly form a serious opposition, receiving about 10 per cent of the votes. So far, Britain has firmly resisted demands for independence from Chief Sobhuza and the white farmers, remaining true to her promise of creating a political system based on a nonracial society.

Discussion

PAUL KHOTSO MOONYANE.   I should like to add to Professor Cowen's comments on Basutoland some details on the nationalist movement in that Protectorate, which is my home.

Changes in the High Commission Territories are the result of political movements, all of which have been established fairly recently. In the early 1940's, there existed some political movements in the British Protectorate of Basutoland, but as soon as the Basutoland Congress Party (BCP) was founded, all the older movements were absorbed into it.

The BCP started among a group of teachers in Maseru township under the leadership of Ntsu Mokhehle, who, after he obtained his M.Sc. in parasitology at Fort Hare University, became a teacher at the Government Primary School. He was an influential member of the Basutoland National Teachers' Association and was highly regarded by most of the teachers in the Basutoland African National Teachers' Association, a movement meant to protect the general welfare of the Protectorate's African teachers. Soon, however, Mr. Mokhehle and B. M. Khaketla, the then secretary and editor of the BCP magazine *Mohlabani* (*Warrior*), were charged with political deviation and expelled from their positions as teachers.

The Basutoland Congress Party strongly criticized the British local authority's discriminatory policies and its negligence in solving the economic problems of the Basutoland territory. It demanded the immediate Basutoization of the civil service, which was mainly composed of the British and recruits from South Africa. It had quite a number of followers, the most important being the Basuto working in the Union of South Africa.

The BCP had no real opposition, with the exception of a few warnings from certain missionaries who suspected that the movement had Communist elements in it, but from the beginning it was evident that some day it would clash with the chieftainship.

It would have been wise for the BCP to win the favor of the chiefs, the rulers of the nation, for through them it could bring the whole nation to its side and thereby more readily obtain British assent to reforms in the territory. This the party did not or could not accomplish, and it soon found itself faced with strong opposition from the chiefs, Basuto traditionalists, missionaries, and some of its own members who were now convinced that the party was no longer effectively representative of the Basuto. Basuto traditionalists opposed the BCP because it was against their mores and customs; the chiefs opposed it because they believed it would diminish their power; and the missionaries opposed it because they regarded it as antireligious.

The alienation of the chiefs was due, in part, to the fact that the English had succeeded in so separating them from the nation that, instead of playing the part of leaders, they became obstacles to the progress of the nation. In 1957–58, however, the chiefs began to realize their duties in a changing society. New parties were formed through which some of them took a direct or an indirect part in the political struggle of the nation. Instead of opposing, they took the course of independence, which one might have expected to originate with them.

First came the National Party of Chief Leabua Jonathan; then later, the United Front, Marema Tlou, of the Honorable Chief S. S. Matete. These parties either developed out of the old opposition to the BCP, or were formed with the idea of counterbalancing the radical ideas of the BCP with movements more favorable to Basuto traditions and customs. For example, the Basutoland Congress Party wants the Paramount Chief to be a constitutional monarch, a symbolic head of the nation, and nothing else. This idea is opposed by the chiefs themselves and by a good number of Basuto conservatives, especially now that the present Paramount Chief of the Basuto is concerned with the general welfare of the country. The BCP's unfriendly attitude and apparent desire to abolish the chieftainship also alienated the elderly Basutos; its hostility toward religious activities was another reason that people left the party, including the BCP's secretary, B. M. Khaketla.

The Basutoland National Party is similar to the Congress Party in policy and purpose, but, like all the newly formed movements, it is local and Basutoic in outlook, while the Basutoland Congress Party is broad in outlook and Pan-African, keeping in contact with the other African leaders of the continent. The BCP also maintains links with movements in Bechuanaland and Swaziland. (Indeed, in 1962, the leaders of nationalist movements in the three Protectorates met to form a united front.) These events, particularly the formation of a Communist Party, under the leadership of John Motloheloa, are being watched with suspicion and fear by the neighboring South African Republic. In a society that has been, for years, warned against Communism by the Catholic Church, the new movement has little appeal. Its literature, however, sells heavily. And there is not a reader who has not read papers and books sold by the clownish Mr. Motloheloa. The name Basutoland Communist Party makes surrounding South Africa shiver and creates fear among Western observers.

In summary, the people of Basutoland have to decide whether to go along with the conservative, tribal systems under the chiefs, their traditional, natural leaders, or to embrace a more intense nationalism in facing the Protectorate's problems. There is the problem of the Protectorates' falling under South African rule. Although the British have given the territories increasing responsibility in their internal affairs—Basutoland and Bechuanaland have their own legislative bodies—Britain's friendly relations with the Republic of South Africa trouble Protectorate Africans. Concomitant with this problem is that of economic development. If the British plans for industrialization of the Protectorates were undertaken seriously, Africans living in the territories would not have to work in the mines of South Africa and the Republic's work force would be seriously depleted. The resolution of these problems may well determine the course that much of Southern Africa will take.

IV

Zambia, Rhodesia, and Malawi

White Rule and the Federation of British Central Africa, 1889–1953[1]

ROBERT I. ROTBERG

Our opposition to federation is based on the simple fact that the Europeans of Central Africa . . . are aiming at a complete domination and exploitation of the black people of Central Africa. . . . Ladies and gentlemen, we are being betrayed by the British government, and it is high time that we tell the white people in this country that their support of this plan is not only dangerous to us but to their well-being and happiness in this country. This is our country.

—HARRY MWAANGA NKUMBULA
June 26, 1952

Central to the history of the Rhodesias (now Zambia and Rhodesia) and Nyasaland (now Malawi) in the three decades from the end of Chartered Company rule to the beginning of federation in 1953 was the estrangement of black and white. In Southern Rhodesia, the climate of race relations worsened during a period of outright settler hegemony. In the two northern protectorates the British Government steadily modified its concept of trust in order to take account of settler interests. At the same time Northern Rhodesia experienced a period of rapid industrialization, thereby further entrenching white paramountcy and causing Imperial policies to reflect an increasing ambivalence between European and African predominance. Eventually, this complicated combination of economic and social pressures brought about an imposed federation of three areas that had been developed along distinctly different lines.

In settler eyes, Southern Rhodesia was a white man's country. The typical settler was a landowner, dependent upon poor soils, rains that

[1] This paper was originally prepared early in 1963, before the author had completed the research on which his most recent publications were based. The present version has been revised and updated as of March, 1965.

sometimes failed, and an African labor force. By the advent of self-government, 23 per cent of those Europeans gainfully employed were farmers; a third of the members of the first post-Company Legislative Council were also men of the land. Twelve per cent of the working whites were engaged in mining. Gold remained an important source of foreign exchange, and chrome, asbestos, and coal were exploited increasingly. Unlike those of South Africa, however, the Southern Rhodesian mines were never sufficiently large or profitable to transform the Crown Colony's economy into one dependent exclusively upon minerals. Racial policies therefore were designed to cater to the economic interests of white Rhodesians generally, with emphasis upon those who tilled the soil.

Nearly all whites in Rhodesia supported one or another form of segregation after 1923. Fear of Africans was general in a land where whites were greatly outnumbered and were dependent upon a continued ability to master African discontent. Such fear "was not simply [derived from] the threat of economic competition, or even of political infiltration; it was a combination of these factors together with the shadow of miscegenation and the presence of a vast mass of people across a culture gulf which seemed unbridgeable." [2] The extreme solution to this problem was advanced by benevolent paternalists (who wished sincerely to preserve African society in isolation) and supremacists alike, but the middle road of pragmatic segregation was the only course ever acceptable to the mass of white Rhodesians. Dependent upon African labor as they were, most whites early realized that Africans, however denigrated, must be tolerated. Not all Africans could be shunted to the reserves. Not all could be "temporary" residents of an urban area when a steady work force was wanted. However, since Africans were inherently different from Europeans, they must remain apart whenever their labor was not required. Whites thought it was wrong to allow Africans to own plots in the towns or to permit any mixing that would lead to equality. Hence the concatenation of laws and actions that gave rise to so many African grievances and contributed so thoroughly to color-consciousness south of the Zambezi.

Land was basic to the African-European estrangement. A 1920 Order-in-Council finally demarcated the native reserves, but it did not disturb African rights to acquire and to hold lands in the same way as Europeans. Although few Africans had in fact obtained land outside the reserves, this realization impelled the government and a

[2] Richard Gray, *The Two Nations* (London, 1960), p. 19.

delegation of settlers and officials to urge rigid restrictions on land ownership. As a result, a commission under Sir William Morris Carter was appointed in 1925 to examine the problem in detail.[3] He and his colleagues, after receiving testimony from a variety of petitioners, concluded that segregation was the wish of the majority. The commission considered that closer association between the races was eventually inevitable. In the interim envisaged, the sources of friction should, it thought, be removed. The commission therefore recommended that part of the 43.5 million acres of Crown land as yet unalienated be designated Native Purchase area, the remainder to be retained for European use. After abandoning strict principles of equity, the commission decided that the amount of land that would be designated Native Purchase should be determined according to an arbitrary assessment of African "needs." [4] On that basis, it assigned almost 7 million acres to Africans and more than 17 million to Europeans. Nearly 18 million acres—dry, remote, and fly-infested—were retained by the Crown.[5]

The Land Apportionment Act of 1930, which embodied the Carter Commission recommendations, became effective in 1931, after which Africans were enjoined to leave white-owned lands or holdings in European rural and urban districts.[6] But, instead of diminishing, the number of Africans on "white" land rose considerably, creating still further problems. Because Africans were forbidden to own land in the "European area," they could not own houses in the towns, where they were permitted to reside only on the premises of their employers or in the urban "locations." It was cheaper to provide accommodation for single men than for families; thus, locations, "like the domestic servants' quarters in the suburban gardens, became a kind of barracks rather than homes," with all the attendant social evils.[7] Africans thereafter shuttled between urban areas and reserves, where most families remained. In the crowded, badly watered, overstocked reserves, pressure on the land grew until it approximated alarming proportions. Of the 96 million acres of land in Southern Rhodesia, 48 million were in the hands of 50,000 whites by 1931; 1 million Africans had rights to

[3] See *Report of the Land Commission 1925* (Salisbury, CSR 3–1926). Sir William Morris Carter also chaired land commissions in Uganda and Kenya.

[4] Cf. Lucy Mair, *Native Policies in Africa* (London, 1936), pp. 65–67.

[5] Colin Leys, *European Politics in Southern Rhodesia* (New York and London, 1959), p. 28.

[6] See Barry Neil Floyd, *Changing Patterns of African Land Use in Southern Rhodesia* (Lusaka, 1961), pp. 67–91; A. C. Jennings, "Land Apportionment in Southern Rhodesia," *Journal of the African Society*, XXXIV (1935), 298–308.

[7] Leys, *op. cit.*, p. 29.

28 million acres; and the remaining land was urban, forest, or unfit for cultivation.[8]

The Land Apportionment Act was designed to solve the problem of racial conflict in Southern Rhodesia. Segregation was believed to be the ideal answer to a broad spectrum of racial dilemmas. But just as practical apartheid constitutes sophistry, so Southern Rhodesia begged the symbiosis that has always characterized "settler" Africa. Europeans, south of the Zambezi as well as north of it, were dependent upon the efforts of Africans. The races could not be separated, for the minerals, which provided as much as half of the national income, and the white-owned farms, which provided much of the other half, could not be organized without African labor.[9] Similarly, the railway, the government, the professions, and all the many other forms of European endeavor were possible only because of the broad base of Africans who received a bare minimum wage.[10]

The threat of African economic competition was met by legislation that specifically denied to Africans the status of "employee" and thereby denied to them most forms of skilled employment.[11] The agreements provided that Africans could be employed in what normally were skilled positions only if they were paid a wage equal to that earned by whites. The Industrial Conciliation Act of 1934 contained an implicit and effective color bar, and Africans were rarely found in responsible positions in the urban centers. It created an artificial scarcity of skilled labor, with high rates of pay for whites. Job reservation also impelled a reliance upon immigration from South Africa and Europe and, in turn, channeled as much as possible of the resulting economic growth in the direction of whites.

The preservation of white superiority was central to settler and business thinking. The government of Southern Rhodesia faithfully reflected these concerns after 1923 by sharpened tools designed to effectuate segregation and by economic, political, and social policies intended to entrench white prerogatives more securely. The architect of a white Rhodesia was Dr. Godfrey Martin Huggins (later Lord Malvern), a British surgeon who emigrated to Salisbury in 1911 and served as the Prime Minister of Southern Rhodesia from 1933 to 1953. Huggins espoused the "two-pyramid" scheme of parallel racial

[8] Ibid., p. 14.

[9] See C. H. Thompson and H. W. Woodruff, Economic Development in Rhodesia and Nyasaland (London, 1954), pp. 11–17.

[10] For a modern discussion, see David Bettison, "Factors in the Determination of Wage Rates in Central Africa," The Rhodes-Livingstone Journal, XXVIII (1960), 23–38.

[11] William Barber, The Economy of British Central Africa (London, 1961), pp. 30–31, 41–42.

development in Rhodesia and appealed to the electorate on a segregationist platform.[12]

To implement his racial policies, the Prime Minister moved forward on two broad fronts: He sought to separate the pyramids effectively while providing a significant but insufficient amelioration of African living conditions in the reserves. In the second sphere, he acted to some extent in order to avoid censure by the British Government which, under the 1923 constitution, retained oversight of all legislation that subjected Africans to conditions or restrictions that did not apply to Europeans.[13] This oversight had been expressed earlier, but not actually used, after criticism was directed at the passage of the Juveniles' Employment Act (1926) and the Native Affairs Act (1927), but Huggins managed to consolidate his position at home and abroad sufficiently to make British oversight nugatory. In 1937, he contrived to transfer supervisory authority from the High Commissioner in Pretoria to the Secretary of State for Dominion Affairs, and thus eliminated an additional impediment to direct Rhodesian influence in those British deliberations which affected the Crown Colony.[14] After 1938, he even attended Empire (later Commonwealth) conferences as a demi-constituent member.

Under Huggins, Southern Rhodesia moved inexorably toward a fuller control of Africans. The Natives Registration Act of 1936 was modeled upon earlier local legislation and upon the "pass" laws of the Union of South Africa, which in turn were designed, after 1923, to prevent the influx of "undesirable" Africans into the towns, to obtain better service from African labor, and to implement segregation generally. Under the 1936 Act, all male Africans were required to carry a registration certificate (which embodied a tax receipt) on which could be endorsed the contract of service.[15] In addition, Africans were required at all times to carry either a pass that permitted the bearer to seek employment in an urban area, a document demonstrating that he was already working in the town, a certificate attesting to his gainful employment by lawful means, a letter from his employer vouching for his movements, or a visiting pass. The ordinance permitted policemen to challenge Africans at will, enabled the government to exert an almost total control of African life, denied Africans essential freedom of movement, and, to some extent, also denied freedom of employment.

[12] The name was derived from N. H. Wilson, *A White Standard of Living for Southern Rhodesia: The Two-Pyramids Policy* (Salisbury, 1933).

[13] These restrictions were removed only in 1961.

[14] See Gray, *op. cit.*, p. 153.

[15] *Ibid.*, p. 154.

As in Kenya, these actions not surprisingly increased African discontent. To make the expression of such displeasure more easily punishable, the Sedition Act of 1936 declared it illegal "to engender feelings of hostility between Europeans and others." [16] At the same time, chiefs, who considered themselves the powerless "dogs" and "women" of government, were given some jural and conciliar roles, and new funds were devoted to African agricultural development, African medical orderlies were trained, and new clinics were established in the reserves (there were only thirteen in 1936). Primary education, begun by the government in 1927, was encouraged for the first time, and a few "model" African locations were constructed near Bulawayo and Salisbury.

In the last decade before federation, pressures within Southern Rhodesia had introduced paternalism into the fabric of discrimination. Economic development and urbanization had made complete separation impossible as a real alternative for Rhodesians. Thus the growing interdependence of black and white brought about modifications in the "two-pyramid" scheme and, after African strikes in 1945 and 1948 had threatened white complacency, white attitudes underwent some further modernization consequent upon European awakenings and an influx of new immigrants.

Huggins realized that African dissatisfaction was dangerous. By the end of World War II, he became anxious to improve urban living conditions for Africans; he even sought to stabilize the indigenous population by making it easier for married couples to live in the towns. In many ways his thinking was more advanced than that of his white electorate, but a commission that investigated the main postwar strike advocated bigger doses of benevolent paternalism.[17] As a result, the Native Labour Board was created in 1947 to deal with wage disputes involving Africans, and Salisbury and Bulawayo established Native Administration Departments to supervise the locations and to administer them along modern lines. New housing was promised to alleviate the frightful overcrowding, squalor, and unhealthiness of the African ghettos. But implementation of the Native Urban Areas Act also brought hardship, for wives and children were evicted from quarters designed for single men or from housing situated in nonscheduled areas.

In a theoretically complementary way, the government sought to reform rural land holdings by the passage, in 1951, of the Native Land

[16] *Ibid.*, p. 155.
[17] *Report of the Commission to Investigate the Grievances Which Gave Rise to the Strike Amongst the African Employees of the Rhodesian Railways* (Salisbury, 1946).

Husbandry Act. This measure was designed to divide the reserves into individual holdings and to prepare the way for the introduction of Western forms of land tenure. In a break from the earlier segregationist pattern, it was also designed to drive Africans permanently to the cities, where they would labor for the white man, by depriving those Africans who did not actually farm reserve lands of any rights to ownership in the reserves at all.[18]

On the eve of federation, whites continued to dominate Southern Rhodesia. The franchise, which had always remained open to a few relatively wealthy Africans, was effectively denied to any who might have qualified as a result of postwar prosperity. After Huggins had pledged to "close the common roll to Africans for the foreseeable future," the 1951 Electoral Act raised both the means and educational qualifications for the vote, thereby preserving what Huggins called "civilized government, which is the only important thing." [19] Discrimination was also intensified during a period of renewed white immigration. Post offices, railways, hotels, and urban shops all maintained the barriers of segregation. Africans were unable to use "white" facilities of any kind; they were regularly treated with that unthinking callousness and lack of courtesy that has done so much to exacerbate racial animosities in Southern Africa.

Northern Rhodesia and, to a lesser extent, Nyasaland, drifted gradually into the white orbit during the three decades before 1953. Theoretically, the Colonial Office exercised a trust on behalf of the African people of both protectorates until such time as they would be "fit" to govern themselves. But, as Europeans settled on the lands north of the Zambezi River, they came to figure in colonial considerations. Their influence, particularly in Northern Rhodesia, grew in accordance with changing economic and political circumstances and as a result of their own ability to convert the colonial administrative apparatus to their own ends.

When the Colonial Office assumed direct control of Northern Rhodesia in 1924, it began to administer the new Protectorate on lines familiar elsewhere in British tropical Africa. A government, with its secretariat and its executive and legislative councils, was established in the usual pattern. An education department, concerned initially with rural African schooling, was established, the first inspectors employed, and, by direct supervision and financial encouragement, the govern-

[18] See *Report of the Mangwende Reserve Commission of Inquiry* (Salisbury, 1961), pp. 34, 164–79.
[19] Quoted in Gray, *op. cit.*, p. 309.

ment attempted to improve facilities throughout the territory.[20] But until after World War II nearly all schooling, in Northern Rhodesia as in Nyasaland, was directed by Christian missionaries. The government also extended "indirect rule" to Northern Rhodesia after 1929; "native authorities" and "native courts" were established, as they were in Nyasaland, but the actual administration of the rural areas remained in the hands of European district commissioners who were themselves responsible for roads, taxes, law and order, justice, and all the other concomitants of British overrule. Even in Barotseland, where Lewanika had been succeeded as Paramount Chief by Yeta III, the Resident Commissioner, charged originally with the tendering of advice, came to govern the special protectorate within a protectorate in a manner effectively direct. The Lozi, unlike the Ganda, submitted easily. They kept the trappings of traditional monarchy and lost much of its substance. Elsewhere, chiefs were beholden to the government for their positions and their emoluments, although the government usually refrained from interfering too frequently in their selection or installation.

The government of Northern Rhodesia exercised its "trust" only passively. Despite official pronouncements during the 1920's and 1930's that were meant to ensure "paramountcy of native interests," the government expended the greater part of its energies and capital on behalf of the small white population.[21] In 1930, Lord Passfield (Sidney Webb), the Labour Secretary of State for the Colonies, stipulated that African development should be a "first charge" on the Protectorate, but as late as 1938 an official report disclosed the "very striking disparity" between the amount of money spent on projects that would further white enterprise (on the "line of rail") and that spent on or for Africans.[22] White farmers were assisted by research and maize marketing. In the African areas, there was little official attention paid to agricultural improvement, and almost nothing was done to prevent disease from decimating herds of African-owned

[20] See files C 1/8, C 2/3, C 2/4, B 1/1/A 1569, Lusaka Archives, for material on education in Northern Rhodesia. See also G. C. Latham, "Native Education in Northern Rhodesia," *Proceedings of the General Missionary Conference of Northern Rhodesia* (Lovedale, 1928), pp. 63–74.

[21] "I have always understood that we were here primarily to exploit the tropical belt in the interests of the Empire while at the same time taking care to protect the legitimate interests of the autochthonous peoples." H. C. Donald C. Mackenzie Kennedy, in the Legislative Council, December 20, 1932, quoted in *Northern Rhodesia Debates*, XII (1932).

[22] Alan Pim and S. Milligan, *Report of the Commission Appointed to Enquire into the Financial and Economic Position of Northern Rhodesia*, Col. No. 145 (1938), p. 95.

cattle. Africans were discouraged from competing with European tobacco and maize farmers by a series of administrative and economic actions that discriminated against "native" crops. The worst forms of South African and Southern Rhodesian job reservation were at first avoided, but Africans were never afforded equal opportunity to learn a skilled trade. Yet African tax payments during the interwar period were about equal to European private and corporation payments.

In the two protectorates, the colonial governments shared power with the local whites. An end to Chartered Company rule in Northern Rhodesia transformed the Advisory Council into a Legislative Council, where settler views were expressed effectively to the detriment of African interests. Originally composed of 9 British officials or nominees and 5 elected Europeans (the electoral roll never enfranchised more than 4,000 whites and a very few Asians), the Council included 7 of these "unofficials" after 1929. In 1938, parity of representation was granted, and government and officials each occupied 8 seats.[23] Three years later, another member joined each side, and in 1945 the official majority was discarded as four new unofficials were added to the Council. Subsequently, the unofficials obtained increased prerogatives and sought, once again, that home rule on the Southern Rhodesian pattern which had eluded them since 1917. But the government responded after World War II to indigenous fears and overseas opinion by retaining the ultimate reins of power in its own hands.[24]

It had been Sir Harry Johnston's idea to develop neighboring Nyasaland "by educating the Black Man and introducing the Yellow Man, and establishing ourselves in the more healthy districts so that we may direct these operations *in situ*."[25] After his departure, however, the government came to share its oversight of African rights with the small number of white planters and businessmen resident there. The Legislative Council, which was constituted in 1907, was composed of four officials and four nominated European unofficials, one of whom usually was a missionary charged with the protection of African interests. Thereafter, the leisurely calm of local affairs was punctuated only infrequently by disagreement between the two Council factions. Cooperation within the Council merely mirrored har-

[23] One unofficial, Lt. Col. Stewart Gore-Browne, was nominated by the Governor to represent "native interests."

[24] Governor Sir Hubert Young, in the Legislative Council, December 1, 1934, quoted in J. W. Davidson, *The Northern Rhodesian Legislative Council* (London, 1948), p. 41.

[25] Quoted in Roland Oliver, *Sir Harry Johnston and the Scramble for Africa* (London, 1957), p. 254.

monious relations without; fewer than 1,800 whites lived in Nyasaland before World War II, and, unlike their compatriots elsewhere in Central and East Africa, they were never sufficiently numerous to effect a total derogation of the principles of colonial trust. The planters were assisted in their quest for land and labor, and, although complete protection of indigenous interests was impossible wherever such rights clashed with white demands, African initiative and responsibility were generally recognized and accorded their due. Yet it was not so much the quality or degree as it was the mere existence of inequality that was resented.

African grievances were real in Nyasaland and, in time, they were expressed in nationalist forms. But the government took little notice of African opinion until 1948, when the number of official and unofficial representatives on the Legislative Council was increased to nine. For the first time, two Africans and an Asian were included. The Africans were appointed by the Governor from a list of names submitted by the African Protectorate Council (a central "native authority"), and the Asian was selected from a slate forwarded by the Indian Chamber of Commerce. A third African and another official were added in 1953, and in 1956 five Africans were elected as representatives of the Nyasaland African Congress.

Africans of both protectorates were most profoundly affected by the exploitation of copper in Northern Rhodesia. Chester Beatty, an American engineer, first proved that a much richer zone of sulphide ore lay below the layer of oxidized Rhodesian copper.[26] In 1929–30, the Copperbelt experienced its first boom; white and black labor was attracted from all over Southern Africa, towns were built, and mine shafts were constructed. During the 1931–36 depression, the boom abated, but the Rhodesian companies weathered the crisis more easily than most and emerged as low-cost producers dependent upon abundant supplies of African labor and ores that were technically easy to treat. World War II, the Cold War, and the Korean War boom (which lasted until 1956) brought great wealth to Northern Rhodesia. At the same time, the Protectorate was transformed from a rural land of essentially subsistence producers into one where large numbers of Africans became permanent urban dwellers. Likewise, the mines proved a magnet for migratory labor, and the impoverished villages of both Nyasaland and Northern Rhodesia consequently were denuded of men seeking the cash with which to pay their taxes and support themselves in the new money economy.[27]

[26] See Kenneth Bradley, *Copper Venture* (London, 1952), pp. 78–81.
[27] See Godfrey Wilson, *An Essay on the Economics of Detribalisation in Northern Rhodesia* (Livingstone, 1941), I, pp. 37–56.

During the years immediately before and after World War II, Africans flocked to the new towns of Rhodesia, and the administration found itself faced with a scale of urban employment that went beyond anything in any Crown Colony in Africa. There the confrontation with white rule was more immediate and direct. Africans were paid badly, but they managed somehow to live and to bring up families.[28] Government and the mining companies provided housing that Africans said was inadequate and sanitation that was primitive. Conditions of employment, particularly underground in the mines, were rarely ideal.[29] But the Copperbelt strikes and riots of 1935 and 1940 signified a discontent generated as much by the pinpricks of discrimination as by sharp economic grievances.[30] When whites, too, came to the new industrial centers, they erected a color bar that prevented African advancement and compelled Africans to experience their inferiority in oppressive new ways. Although the tenor of discrimination became more strident in the years after World War II, the rise of African nationalism paralleled it and eventually made a mockery of well-intentioned paternalism and that "partnership" which later constituted an excuse for continued settler dominance.

Between the time a charter was granted to the British South Africa Company in 1889 and the creation of the Federation of Rhodesia and Nyasaland in 1953, schemes for incorporating one or more of the Central African territories within a broader union had excited settlers and officials alike. In 1927, the British Government announced that "some form of closer union between the territories of Central and Eastern Africa appears desirable.[31] A commission, under the chairmanship of Sir Edward Hilton Young, was therefore appointed to investigate and to report, bearing in mind the "Imperial duty" of safeguarding the welfare and interests of the indigenous population. In 1929, the commission dismissed the idea of such a large grouping, and was divided on the wisdom of establishing a smaller federal unit to include the two Rhodesias and Nyasaland.

The commission rejected any proposals that placed "any further tracts with a large native population under the Government of South-

[28] Gray, *op. cit.*, p. 117.

[29] See the Minutes of the Livingstone Welfare Association, May 5 and July 7, 1934.

[30] See *Reports of the Commission Appointed to Inquire into the Disturbances in the Copperbelt, 1935 and 1940* (Lusaka, 1935 and 1940).

[31] *Future Policy in Regard to Eastern Africa*, Cmd. 2904 (1927). For a fuller discussion of this period, see Robert I. Rotberg, "The Federation Movement in British East and Central Africa, 1889–1953," *Journal of Commonwealth Political Studies*, II (1964), 141–60.

ern Rhodesia until that Government has demonstrated its ability to cope with the extensive native problems that already confront it." [32] The majority felt that there were "many reasons for eventually linking Nyasaland and a part at least of Northern Rhodesia with the Northern Territories," and urged the British government to avoid "the forging of any fetters which might bind [trans-Zambezia] permanently to the south." [33] It wanted Britain to maintain the independent status of the two protectorates in order to safeguard African rights. As far as Central Africa was concerned, the Hilton Young report faithfully reflected the various factors for which British policy should account. Yet the commission was unable to offer a striking solution, and its report did not immediately effect new constitutional or territorial arrangements.

But the deliberations of the Hilton Young commission had threatened European hegemony in Northern Rhodesia and had consequently acted as adrenalin to the heart of amalgamation. In 1930, whites were again stirred to action by Lord Passfield. His *Memorandum on Native Policy in East Africa* [34] simply reaffirmed the doctrine of trusteeship and paramountcy of African interests as it had been enunciated in different circumstances by the Duke of Devonshire in 1923. The *Memorandum* made it clear that African interests would prevail should their interests and those of immigrant races conflict. This was established policy for Kenya, but now Lord Passfield had explicitly extended the Duke of Devonshire's statement to Northern Rhodesia. Furthermore, Lord Passfield indicated that immediate steps "to ensure strict conformity" were to be taken.[35] He promised equality of opportunity in the purchase of Crown lands and the provision of easy credit. Taxation was to be limited to an amount that would not upset customary life, and, moreover, African development was henceforth, he decreed, to be the keystone of colonial policy.

Europeans reacted swiftly. Unofficial members of the Northern Rhodesian Legislative Council demanded an immediate conference in London:

To subordinate the interests of civilized Britons to the development of alien races whose capability of substantial further advancement has not

[32] *Report of the Commission on Closer Union of the Dependencies in Eastern and Southern Africa*, Cmd. 3234 (1929), pp. 90–92.

[33] *Ibid.*, p. 261. Governor Maxwell of Northern Rhodesia also regarded amalgamation as "not being in the interests of the people of this territory, European or native." (Maxwell to Passfield, December 2, 1929.)

[34] Cmd. 3573 (1930), pp. 3–5.

[35] *Ibid.*, p. 6

been demonstrated appears to be contrary to natural law. . . . [Thus] faced with the declared determination of the Imperial Government to prefer the interests of barbarous races to those of their own, [we] may seek and find sympathy and aid . . . from neighboring colonies enjoying freer institutions and more equitable opportunities.[36]

They were refused the conference—their views being deemed "wholly irreconcilable with the considered policy of His Majesty's Government." [37] Furthermore, the Secretary of State in 1931 telegraphed Governor Sir James Crawford Maxwell that:

His Majesty's Government . . . are not prepared to agree to the amalgamation of Northern and Southern Rhodesia. . . . They consider that a substantially greater advance should be made in the development of Northern Rhodesia before any final opinion can be formed as to its future. . . . The European population is small and scattered . . . while problems of native development are in a stage which makes it inevitable that His Majesty's Government should hesitate to let them pass even partially out of their responsibility.[38]

Lord Passfield thus encouraged a fatal liaison between two Rhodesias in differential states of development. His attitude toward settler demands increased an insecurity fundamental to Europeans in Northern Rhodesia, and, long after Lord Passfield had retired from the scene, white Northern Rhodesians continued to clamor for self-government or amalgamation in order to ensure "the subject" more control over "his destiny and that of posterity." [39] Only thus did whites think that Africans could be "properly" controlled.

The depression ended local hopes for immediate white self-government in trans-Zambezia and even turned Leopold Moore, the perennially strident unofficial leader, toward amalgamation. In 1933, Moore explained:

It is going to take a long time—some months, possibly a couple of years —to bring about any change [but] if we definitely and clearly state time after time . . . that we do not wish to be governed by the Colonial Office, that we do wish to be absorbed in amalgamation with Southern Rhodesia, the Imperial Government will be forced to give way.[40]

[36] *Correspondence with Regard to Native Policy in Northern Rhodesia*, Cmd. 3731 (1930).

[37] *Ibid.*, p. 10.

[38] July 1, 1931, Sec/Ea/9, Lusaka archives.

[39] Leopold Moore, in the Legislative Council, April 6, 1933, quoted in Davidson, *op. cit.*, p. 95.

[40] On April 6, 1933, in the Legislative Council, quoted in *ibid.*, p. 96.

The Legislative Council unofficials then voted in favor of the amal-gamation of the Rhodesias. Two years later, after the Copperbelt riots, the unofficials again expressed themselves strongly in favor of ending Colonial Office control. Moore feared that Hitler would obtain Tanganyika and that Northern Rhodesia might therefore cease to be British. He told Huggins that the settlers of Northern Rhodesia wanted "to come in with you, not as partners and certainly not as rivals, but as an integral part of your country. We want what you have." [41] Meanwhile, in Southern Rhodesia, there was a large group that also sought amalgamation. It wanted to ensure a duty-free mar-ket for southern goods, a continued supply of African labor from the north, and, most important, a similarity of racial policy.

In 1936, all seven unofficial members of the Northern Rhodesian Legislative Council and thirty representatives of the three Southern Rhodesian parties met at Victoria Falls and unanimously resolved that amalgamation under the constitution of Southern Rhodesia "is in the best interest of all the inhabitants of both colonies." [42] With amalgamation, the delegates agreed, should come dominion status. They foresaw a joint Legislative Council composed of partly nominated and partly elected members, of whom three would repre-sent African interests. Separate laws would be maintained until altered by the new government of "Rhodesia." In time there would be a single high court, sitting in the joint capital of Salisbury. The Legislative Assembly of Southern Rhodesia supported the decision of the conference. But its agreement had been obtained only by provid-ing for a new sovereignty with greater powers than those which already were conferred upon the colony.

In the north, two of the seven unofficials realized the extent of African opposition to amalgamation and agreed that it could be detrimental to indigenous interests and therefore a derogation of Imperial trust. Lt. Col. Arthur Stephenson and Gore-Browne termed their colleagues' demands preposterous. Governor Sir Hubert Young of Northern Rhodesia and the Secretary of State agreed. The latter simply reiterated the policy laid down in 1931.[43]

Huggins refused to bide his time, however, for he feared "creeping blackness" from the north. Southern Rhodesia's Prime Minister char-

[41] Correspondence in Sec/Ea/9, Lusaka archives.

[42] Sec/Ea/9. But see Colin Leys and R. Cranford Pratt, *A New Deal in Cen-tral Africa* (London and New York, 1960), p. 9.

[43] *Report of the Rhodesia and Nyasaland Royal Commission*, Cmd. 5949 (1939), pp. 113–14. See also Governor Young to the Secretary of State, June 20, 1936; Ormsby-Gore to Young, August 20, 1936; Macdonald to Huggins, July 31, 1936.

acteristically applied pressure on the British Government and spoke of overtures toward a union with South Africa. New discussions took place at the Coronation celebrations, bringing about a meeting in 1937 attended by the Secretaries for Dominions and Colonies, the Governors of both Rhodesias and Nyasaland, the Prime Minister of Southern Rhodesia, and Gore-Browne. As a result, a Royal Commission, chaired by Viscount Bledisloe, former Governor-General of New Zealand, was appointed to inquire "whether any . . . closer cooperation or association between Southern Rhodesia, Northern Rhodesia and Nyasaland is desirable and feasible, with due regard to the interests of all the inhabitants, irrespective of race . . . and to the special responsibility of Our Government . . . for the interests of the Native inhabitants." [44]

The Bledisloe Commission spent three months in Central Africa. The whites of both Rhodesias naturally pleaded for that racial security which only amalgamation could ensure. Africans in the northern territories, however, were unanimous in opposing any ties to Southern Rhodesia.[45] Africans had worked there, and compared treatment of Africans in the colony unfavorably with that in the protectorates. A Cewa chief told the Commission that there was no respect in Southern Rhodesia "like there is here in our country." [46]

After hearing lengthy evidence on these lines, the Commission, in a labored, ambiguous way, brought forth its inconclusive compromise. The territories will probably "become more closely interdependent in all their activities, and . . . identity of interests will lead them sooner or later to political unity." But, if nothing else, it was clear to the Commission that Africans in the Protectorates were strikingly opposed to withdrawal of the Crown's oversight, and that these fears were well founded since the racial policies in Southern Rhodesia remained restrictive.[47] It therefore refused to urge any rapid develop-

[44] Cmd. 5949, p. 4.

[45] Leopold Moore, in a Legislative Council debate on the Commission's report (June 6, 1939), dismissed African opinion: "All this talk about Native evidence. . . . Their opinion is not worth anything at all. . . . They put it off on the grounds that the Natives would not like it. Well, the Natives have got no grounds for liking it or disliking it; we are running the show, and we shall be running it for at least a generation, and possibly two or three." (*Legislative Council Debates,* 33 [1939], p. 251.)

[46] Evidence to the Bledisloe Commission, quoted in Gray, *op. cit.,* p. 192.

[47] "It is the fear that the balance is not fairly held between the two races in Southern Rhodesia that alone prevents a recommendation being made for immediate amalgamation; the avowed policy of segregation, under the name of 'Parallel Development,' and the institution of colour bar stand in the way." (Cmd. 5949, p. 252.)

ment of that identity of interest which existed between the territories and deferred the implementation of real unity indefinitely.[48] Instead it proposed that Nyasaland and Northern Rhodesia be amalgamated and that an interterritorial council be established to coordinate governmental services without executive authority.

The Commission's report angered Central African Europeans. Huggins stormed to London to present his case directly. Sir Cosmo Parkinson, reporting on Joint Colonial-Dominion Office discussions with the Southern Rhodesian Prime Minister, indicated that the policy supported by Northern Rhodesia's Governor Sir John Maybin and the Northern Rhodesian Executive Council had been followed: "The only point which has clearly emerged is . . . that native policy is the crux of the whole question." [49] Moore resigned from his Northern Rhodesian Legislative Council seat and was returned unopposed in the subsequent by-election. Unofficials complained inside and outside of the chamber. Various local Northern Rhodesian European political associations and the so-called European Protection League condemned the Bledisloe Report:

> The time when the native can express an opinion with an intelligent appreciation of the issues involved is too distant to allow the question of his agreement or disagreement to affect the question of amalgamation. The Southern Rhodesia [native policy] is both wiser and juster. The native's interests are protected and he is being educated to become a good agriculturalist.[50]

But World War II intervened, and the British Government thereafter concerned itself with more immediately important matters until 1944. In the interim, agitation for amalgamation continued in Northern Rhodesia, unofficials speaking regularly in its favor. But, in 1943, when Roy Welensky (later Prime Minister of the Federation of Rhodesia and Nyasaland) moved that "Northern and Southern Rhodesia be amalgamated under a constitution similar to that now enjoyed by Southern Rhodesia," [51] his motion was opposed by some

[48] *Ibid.*, pp. 217–18. Gore-Browne also wrote: "No number of years spent in discussion or investigation will ever make the white settler in either Southern Rhodesia or the Union abandon his privileged position—nor can I picture the Imperial Government coming round to the settler point of view. All that part of the report seems to me just the expression of pious hopes, and not worth the paper it is written on." (Gore-Browne to Dame Ethel Locke-King, March 25, 1939, Gore-Browne Papers, unpublished.)

[49] Parkinson to Maybin, August 8, 1939, Sec/Ea/14, Lusaka archives.

[50] Luanshya resolution, August 23, 1939, Sec/Ea/14.

[51] On November 25, 1943, in *Legislative Council Debates*, 46 (1944) p. 76.

legislators who felt that federation would be more desirable than amalgamation; by Gore-Browne, at the time a nominated member for "native interests"; and by numerous Africans in both Nyasaland and Northern Rhodesia. Thereafter, Northern Rhodesia's white leadership began to move away from its support of outright amalgamation toward other forms of unity. In 1944, this tendency was encouraged by the Secretary of State for the Colonies' announcement that his government had concluded that amalgamation, "under existing circumstances," could not be regarded "as practicable." [52] At the same time, a Central African Council was formed to coordinate research, medical and educational policies, economic development (including a customs union), and to further the sharing of transport and communications systems.[53] Huggins called it "nothing more than a sop" but agreed to its formation as a step, however small, toward amalgamation.[54]

The growth of African nationalism and Dr. Daniel F. Malan's unexpected victory in the South African elections of 1948 added new considerations. This time, however, booming copper production in the north made that territory economically the stronger of the two Rhodesias. The south pressed fervidly for unity and, in 1948, at a meeting in Lusaka, settler representatives from both territories agreed to seek "federation," since "amalgamation" was abhorrent to the British Labour Party, then in power at home, because of African fears. Welensky, after a visit to London, told his Broken Hill constituents that if whites were to make an approach to London he believed that they would not be ignored.[55] Africans immediately grew apprehensive, the congresses and territorial councils of both Nyasaland and Northern Rhodesia protested to their respective governors and to the Secretary of State, while in London interested individuals like Dr. H. Kamuzu Banda attempted to make African views known to members of Parliament. The Northern Rhodesian African Congress memorialized against the dangers of "federation." [56] The second Victoria Falls Conference, in 1949, nevertheless brought together white leaders in the Rhodesias and Nyasaland to decide upon a new scheme for closer association. A resolution in favor of federation was passed unanimously.

[52] "Existing circumstances" referred to the divergent "native policies." Quoted in Alexander John Hanna, *The Story of the Rhodesias and Nyasaland* (London, 1960), p. 248.

[53] See *The British Territories in East and Central Africa 1945–50,* Cmd. 7987 (1950), pp. 29–31.

[54] Quoted in Hanna, *op. cit.,* p. 249.

[55] *The Bulawayo Chronicle,* August 19, 1948.

[56] Congress memorandum, July 15, 1948.

In the months that followed, northern Africans at home and abroad condemned any federation that would forge permanent links to Southern Rhodesia. Paul Sikazwe told the Northern Provincial Council:

> Every African in Northern Rhodesia does not want to be federated with Southern Rhodesia. If a man is given good food and he vomits it, can he again eat what he has already vomited? Most of us know that our friends in Southern Rhodesia are slaves.[57]

The Labour Colonial Secretary also spoke against the federal concept. But in early 1950, a new Labor Council Secretary, at the behest of his permanent staff, called for a fresh examination of the federal issue. The 1951 London conference was attended by the chief officials of the four governments concerned; they concluded that differences in racial policy need no longer divide the Central African territories or stand in the way of closer association.[58] The officials thought a federation would save the Rhodesias from apartheid, and that it could provide a rational foundation for swift economic development. African opposition, however, intensified.

At the third Victoria Falls Conference, in September, 1951, white settlers and government officials from all three territories met with African leaders and the secretaries of state for the colonies and the Commonwealth in an attempt to transform the London conference recommendations into a workable federal scheme. Huggins sought modifications in the closer association report, but he was opposed by the British ministers and by Africans, who spoke strongly against any form of federation. The conference ended in a deadlock. But the Labour Party lost the October, 1951, general election, a Conservative government resumed the colonial reins, and a new Secretary of State, Oliver Lyttelton (later Lord Chandos), announced that a federation was urgently needed and that another conference would be summoned, despite African dissatisfaction, to draw up final plans for a Central African union. He trusted that Africans would accept federation once the benefits it would bring were clear.[59]

Talks between Huggins, the respective governors, and the secretaries of state took place in January, 1952. The hurried Lancaster House Conference of April, 1952, boycotted by Africans from the protectorates, issued a report embodying the changes desired by Hug-

[57] *Proceedings* of the Northern Provincial Council, April, 1950.
[58] *Central African Territories: Report of a Conference on Closer Association,* Cmd. 8233 (1951).
[59] See *Closer Association in Central Africa,* Cmd. 8411 (1951).

gins and Welensky, and took the form of a draft federal scheme.[60]

Africans continued their vociferous opposition in the protectorates, despite constant administrative attempts to persuade them otherwise, and in Britain the African national congresses of both territories, the representative councilors, and the provincial councilors all expressed heartfelt dissatisfaction with a plan that would subordinate their own interests to those of the white settlers. They were "protected" Africans in treaty relationship with the Crown. How, they asked, could treaties be altered without the consent of the parties involved? Africans of all classes feared the extension of Southern Rhodesia's policies of racial segregation to the northern protectorates. They feared pass laws, new social indignities, and the loss of their land to white settlers. Dr. Banda spoke for many of the more articulate opponents of the Federation when he said that the concept was rejected because it would deprive us "of our right to eventual self-government."

> It is not I, the agitator in London, who is opposing federation. It is my people at home. You cannot bring to Central Africa partnership by force. . . . We, the Africans of Nyasaland and Northern Rhodesia, are people. Some of the clauses of the Atlantic Charter which Mr. Roosevelt and your Mr. Churchill signed guaranteed territorial integrity and the right of any people to choose the form of government under which they would live. We, the Africans of Nyasaland and Northern Rhodesia, are people under the provisions of the charter and this clause.[61]

Liberals in Britain also voiced protest, and there was an important current of antifederal sentiment in Parliament.[62] But strategic, geographic, economic, and humanitarian sentiments, often sincere although misguided, were allowed to carry the day.

The final intergovernmental meeting took place in London in January, 1953. Africans from Northern Rhodesia and Nyasaland again boycotted the deliberations, and the resultant federal constitution embodied further emasculations of reservations meant to protect Africans.[63] In March, Parliament approved federation. In April, the elec-

[60] *Southern Rhodesia, Northern Rhodesia, and Nyasaland: Draft Federal Scheme Prepared by a Conference Held in London in April and May 1952,* Cmd. 8573 (1952).

[61] Report of a public meeting at Church House, Westminster, on January 23, 1953.

[62] A summary of parliamentary opinion is contained in W. F. Gutteridge, "The Debate on the Central African Federation in Retrospect," *Parliamentary Affairs* (1957), pp. 210–19.

[63] See *Report by the Conference on Federation Held in London in January 1953,* Cmd. 8753 (1953).

tors of Southern Rhodesia (46,355 whites, Asians, and Eurafricans and 380 Africans—of 2.4 million Africans, 150,000 whites, and 10,000 other) ratified the scheme. It came into legal being on August 1, 1953.

Cynics said that the Federation was created in order to further white settler political ambitions. But there were others, both in 1951–53 and in subsequent years, who agreed with a wistful governor of Northern Rhodesia: "There was then recognized the great opportunity, perhaps the last opportunity, to create an influential State in Africa where colour and race were to become of no account." [64]

Color and race continued to be of importance. Post offices were finally desegregated, but a disregard for the avowed principles of partnership finally compelled believers to regard their support for the federal government in a new light.[65] Lands were not taken away from the Africans of Nyasaland and Northern Rhodesia, as they had feared, but discrimination was injected into the medical service, advancement opportunities generally were denied to Africans in federal employ, and looming large in African minds was the total failure of the Federation to live up to its original promises. Africans saw that partnership was not implemented. They discovered that the façade of multiracialism obscured a multitude of discriminatory sins. When they realized that not even the most qualified among them could ever hope to play a substantial part in the government of Rhodesia and Nyasaland, they reverted to their earlier struggle for territorial self-government, an achievement that they believed to have been unduly delayed by the arrival of federation. The agitation of the middle 1950's was abortive. But in 1959 the rising tide of African nationalism swept new leaders to the shores of the independent political kingdom. Arrests followed riots, but prison proved an excellent political school, and, after their release, agitators eventually became cabinet ministers and officials of the Crown. Simultaneously, the waters of nationalism eroded the Federation's foundations and made its continued existence that much more precarious. Its official collapse occurred at the end of 1963.

[64] Arthur Benson (former Governor of Northern Rhodesia), in a letter to the editor of The Times (London), February 20, 1961.
[65] See Rotberg, The Rise of Nationalism in Central Africa: The Making of Malawi and Zambia, 1873–1964 (Cambridge, Mass., 1965), ch. 10.

Southern Rhodesian Nationalism
in the East Central African Conflict

THOMAS M. FRANCK

In six African countries, spanning two-thirds the length of Cecil Rhodes's broad red ribbon from Cape to Cairo, contemporary nationalist movements have attained catharsis by the violence of popular reaction against the imposition of functional union by outsiders. Uganda, Kenya, Tanganyika, Nyasaland, and Northern and Southern Rhodesia have all experienced that catharsis. In the process, they have developed their national identities. They have also developed a sense of regional identity, in large part by struggling together to earn the right to be separate.

The Federation of the Rhodesias and Nyasaland had its cathartic effect on black nationalism, even in Southern Rhodesia, but it was a muted catharsis, far less rewarding than those of the Central and Eastern territories. For, unlike Northern Rhodesia, Nyasaland, Uganda, and Tanganyika, Southern Rhodesia had never been set by Britain on the road to African paramountcy. By 1953, the beginning of the Federation, white supremacy had for thirty years been deeply entrenched in Southern Rhodesia. This development was presided over largely by one man, Sir Godfrey Huggins (Lord Malvern), the Prime Minister. He, and Sir Roy Welensky on behalf of Northern Rhodesia, began immediately after World War II to revive the idea of federation. They made sure that the old Central Africa Council, a limited interterritorial association, did not function successfully and that true interterritorial cooperation could be bought by Britain only at the higher price of full political unification. The inclusion of a third party to this union, Nyasaland, was rather an afterthought—one that Huggins accepted very reluctantly and only at a further price: the implied promise that Britain would never exercise its undoubted constitutional power to end or alter the Federation except at the request of a federal parliament controlled by white settlers of Northern and Southern Rhodesia.

To the fewer than 50,000 whites of Northern Rhodesia, federation meant an opportunity to come under the umbrella of a white-settler–controlled federal legislature, in lieu of a government at Westminster whose dilettantish tendency to appease Africans was even then suspect. To the Southern Rhodesians, it meant release from a staggering debt and a bleak economic future by cutting themselves into the wealth of the Northern Rhodesian copper belt. To Britain, it meant a release from the burden of meeting the annual Nyasaland deficit and an economically "sensible" solution to the remote and enigmatic legacy of Cecil Rhodes. To the British liberal, it meant the promise of a new deal in Central Africa: "partnership"—albeit one ostensibly described by the new Federation's Prime Minister as the "partnership between a horse and rider." Federation disappointed all these expectations. If it did not disappoint African expectations, it was only because there were none. Yet it is perhaps a little surprising, and a measure of federation's failure, that it failed to give Africans even the promised economic benefits that were to be the compensation for postponement of their political aspirations.

In the first three years after federation, Rhodesian companies distributed £130 million in interests, dividends, and other earnings and put another £80 million back into their own plants and pockets. The percentage rise in annual incomes of the African and the white wage earner was almost parallel—but a 14 per cent rise in the African worker's average annual income of £106 is not impressive when set against a 12 per cent rise in the white worker's average annual income of £1,127.

The African may not have been able to predict these economic trends in 1953, but he had a healthy sense of logical deduction. The European was promoting federation. Why? To maintain and extend his political supremacy. Why did displaced English country squires, tobacco farmers, and industrialists—notorious as a tribe for their political reticence and apathy—now *want* political power? To entrench their economic paramountcy, of course. If, as a by-product, Africans' wages, like other commodity prices, proved able to sustain an increase, so much the better. But, above all, federation was a device to preserve at least the *relative* economic *status quo* between the races.

The Southern Rhodesian African, however, had less to lose by federation than did his Northern Rhodesian or Nyasa cousins, if only because he entered the union with less power and less prospect of gaining any. To him, as to the American Negro, progress by "seizing the controls" was scarcely imaginable. White paramountcy had existed in Southern Rhodesia since the final defeat of King Lobengula in the decimating Matabele War and the suppression of the Mashona uprisings. By 1897, Southern Rhodesia, unlike Northern Rhodesia and Nyasaland, had been won by the white man on the field of battle. When Southern Rhodesia entered the Federation, its 178,000 white residents could boast of 55 years of uninterrupted peace and of a docile native population whose members cheerfully knelt before the visiting *bwana* from the Native Affairs Department, who stoically submitted to carrying half a dozen passes and were glad of the opportunity to take work under compulsory labor contracts at rates of 30 cents a day. To oppose federation was to be "rude" to the commissioners—and that was a crime punishable by caning. At a time when apartheid was becoming virulent just south of the Limpopo, the Southern Rhodesian African was told to be glad he was not living in South Africa; and indeed he was. The African of Northern Rhodesia and Nyasaland could look north and see progressive and liberal Tanganyika. The African of Southern Rhodesia could look south and see Dr. Malan and M. Strijdom.

Not surprisingly, therefore, it was the Nyasa African National Congress, organized in 1944 and operating in Southern Rhodesia through the ranks of the 117,000 Nyasa migrant laborers in the colony, that gave an early impetus to Southern Rhodesian nationalist action and organization. Action preceded organization, as it often does in Africa. In November, 1956, there were violent riots in Harari township led by Nyasas and largely economic in origin. The riots shook the complacency of nearby Salisbury, whose all-white residents had smugly believed that "it couldn't happen here" because they had found the key to the care and handling of the native. More important, it shook the Southern Rhodesian Africans, who had almost come to believe that "it couldn't happen here." No amount of organization could have had the effect of the white police superintendent's having to ask George Nyandoro, of the Southern Rhodesia African National Youth League, to intervene to restore order.

As the Youth League's tactics were inspired by the Nyasa Congress, so its policy was inspired by the Gold Coast Convention People's Party and its Youth League. African socialism is more apparent in the early writings of the Youth League leaders, particularly in their demands for "socialization of industry," than in the platforms of the Northern Rhodesian and Nyasa nationalist movements—reflecting the larger urban industrial proletarian component in the Southern Rhodesian black population.

In 1957, guided by the more experienced Nyasas and a few well-disposed Europeans, such as Anglican agricultural missionary Guy Clutton-Brock, the Youth League was transformed into the Southern Rhodesian African National Congress. The Youth League's more radical leaders, James R. Chikerema and George Nyandoro, were passed over for the presidency in favor of the more "moderate" Joshua Nkomo, who was believed to have a wider base of appeal. From the beginning, the Congress suffered four major handicaps: its moderation, outside intervention, inside rivalry, and government harassment.

The three successive leaders of Southern Rhodesian nationalism were all men sympathetically inclined toward cooperation with the European community and commerce, but this did them little good. The Congress was banned in 1959, its leaders arrested. With this began a cat-and-mouse game between the white regime and the nationalist movement—consisting of jailing and releasing, banning and rescinding the ban—the end of which is not yet in sight. The nationalist political movement, this time called the National Democratic Party, was laboriously rebuilt under the successive leadership of Mr. Mawema and Leopold Takawira. Takawira's credentials of moderation included an executive appointment with the multiracial but white-led Capricorn African Society (which at one time had favored federation). When Takawira was succeeded, it was by Joshua Nkomo, who had been in Ghana when the Congress was banned and had gone into exile in London. His stay abroad had not altered his image as a leader of "moderate" aims and goodwill toward the European, willing to work toward African emancipation "a step at a time," and anxious to convert Europeans to his ideology of cooperation. Nkomo spent endless hours addressing polite but unresponsive European audiences and moving among the small salons of European liberals in Salisbury and Bulawayo. African voices were heard to mutter that Nkomo had not only contrived to avoid arrest but was making no effort to have the more radical detainees released.

Even with Chikerema and Nyandoro out of the way, however, an antimoderation faction was organizing both within and outside the ranks of the party. African reaction against their own moderate leadership was a natural response both to a deterioration of the African position in the Federation and to white repudiation of moderation in their own ranks. Prime Minister Welensky, in an all-or-nothing gamble to win independence for the Federation under white supremacy, had succeeded in introducing new and unfavorable constitutional "reforms" and franchise laws. In Southern Rhodesia, the white liberalism of Garfield Todd was repudiated by the white voters for trying to give the Africans a few thousand votes and a few more shillings a week. The African activists, impressed with the Mau Mau performance in Kenya, encouraged the making and throwing of petrol bombs and sanctioned violence and intimidation. Nkomo was characterized as a J. Alfred Prufrock, enchanted by European salons and wondering, "Should I, after tea and cakes and ices, have the strength to force the moment to its crisis?"

Thus unforced, the crisis occurred nevertheless in the form of increased spontaneous violence, rioting, bombing, shootings. Inexorably, there followed the suppression, on December 9, 1961, of the National Democratic Party. When, within two months, it had once more re-emerged with 20,000 members as the Zimbabwe African People's Union (ZAPU), Joshua Nkomo was again chosen as leader over the opposition of the radicals. But by this time the difference had narrowed.

Joshua Nkomo, as leader of ZAPU, consciously tried to create a new image of radicalism. While he could not, by temperament, shout with Dr. Banda at the Salisbury airport crowds, "Yes, I am an extremist!" Nkomo nevertheless moved to ally himself with the new temper of a movement chafing at the tradition of futile moderation and biennial suppression. The change in Nkomo first became apparent even before the NDP was forced to reappear as ZAPU. On February 16, 1961, a revolt within the NDP led by key lieutenants Takawira, Mawema, Mushonga, and Enoch Dumbutshena caused Nkomo to renounce his apparent agreement to at least that portion of the proposed new Southern Rhodesian constitution which allotted to Africans ("B" roll voters) fifteen of sixty-five seats in the new parliament and up to 25 per cent of the votes to elect the others.

This was an important change of policy. Nkomo's earlier apparent acquiescence in these proposals, which had been painstakingly negotiated under British auspices, had brought down on his head not only the wrath of his own radicals, but also the enmity of African nationalist leaders in Northern Rhodesia, Nyasaland, Cairo, and Ghana. The spokesman for Kenneth Kaunda's UNIP in Northern Rhodesia, Mr. Namulino Mundia, said, "Mr. Nkomo has let down our brothers and sisters." Lieutenants had to be dispatched to Accra in a not altogether successful effort to stop Ghana from writing off Mr. Nkomo and switching financial support to a rival. Dr. Banda's opposition to Nkomo was particularly apparent, and included allegations of laziness and dishonesty. Banda was believed by Nkomo's lieutenants to be backing a rival, Patrick Matimba, who did for a time threaten to create an effective rival movement (ZNP).

Thus harassed on the left, Nkomo moved to restore unity by assuming a more radical posture. He did so at first by renouncing his alleged constitutional agreement with Prime Minister Whitehead. The banning of the NDP, coinciding with a rise in spontaneous violence, was Whitehead's *quid pro quo*.

After Nkomo reorganized his third political manifestation of the nationalist current, the Zimbabwe African People's Union, neither he nor his party had much inclination toward a policy of moderation and cooperation. As history would have it, the stiffening African attitude coincided with what appeared to be a slightly more flexible and cooperative initiative by the white leadership. There were some gestures toward African trade-unionism, plans to reform the discriminatory land policy, and the Southern Rhodesian legislature even repealed the law making it an offense for "any native" to have sexual intercourse with a "white woman or girl." The concessions were too little and, as it transpired, too late.

Not surprisingly, the first victims of the Africans' new, hard line were not the European reactionaries, but the white liberals and their African counterparts. The ZAPU executive who was arrested for his part in one of Dr. Terrence Ranger's freedom marches to desegregate a toilet had to face his leader's recriminations for wasting time. The whole effort by multiracial groups to desegregate swimming pools, hotels, bars, restaurants, and cinemas, although it was beginning to show some results, now seemed to ZAPU a diversion and dissipation of effort. "First we must have political control. When we have that, we will desegregate things," said the new Nkomo, paraphrasing Dr. Nkrumah's injunction to seek first the political kingdom. Yet even Nkomo knew that in Southern Rhodesia the political kingdom was not at hand. While awaiting it, would there be any harm in picking up a handful of seats for Africans in the legislature, the cinemas, the bars?

The withdrawal from "multiracial" projects was accompanied by an intensification of pressure against Africans who did not wholly subscribe to the new line, ranging from Jasper Savanhu, member of the Federal Assembly and Sir Roy Welensky's "favorite African," to Reuben Jamela, who, as leader of the Southern Rhodesian Trade Union Congress, refused to ally his unions to the political purposes of ZAPU. Jamela, with the backing of the International Confederation of Free Trade Unions, tried to establish a tradition of unaligned "responsible" trade unionism which, understandably, was to ZAPU indistinguishable in the labor field from political "moderation." ZAPU retaliated by expelling Mr. Jamela in July, 1962, and backing a breakaway, the Southern Rhodesia African Trade Union Congress, headed by Thomas Mswaka, which, by November, 1962, appeared to have the affiliation of twenty-two unions, including the important Transport Workers and Railway Workers Union. (There were, however, more breakaways from the ATUC which further confused the scene. Significantly, each group accused the other of "moderation.")

The new policy had its severest test when applied to the actions of

Nkomo himself. In the next move of the cat-and-mouse game, the Whitehead government, disappointed that its "liberal" advances had gone unrequited, banned ZAPU in the fall of 1962, while Nkomo was on a visit to Northern Rhodesia. Considering the protracted preparations that had gone into the dragnet operations accompanying the banning of ZAPU, the seeming coincidence of Nkomo's absence must have been a deliberate strategy to confront him with an embarrassing choice between the "reasonable" and "unpopular" on the one hand, and the "popular" but "unreasonable" on the other. The Whitehead regime no doubt expected Nkomo to jump again to the side of reason and moderation. And so, instinctively, he did, seeking exile in Tanganyika where he could continue to be useful to his cause, rather than face a futile but politically expedient martyrdom in a Rhodesian prison. Again it required a second thought, in part induced by external pressure, for him to adhere to the new policy and to return to Southern Rhodesia to face restriction and rustication in various "little Siberias" established by Southern Rhodesian ministries.

Nevertheless, by the end of 1962, the image of militancy still seemed to elude Mr. Nkomo. White leaders could exploit this for their own ends—thereby exposing the disingenuousness of their search for a moderate African leader. The new Prime Minister, Winston Field, has declared that ZAPU would remain under ban and that most of its leaders would not be permitted to participate in the formation of a successor, but that this stricture would not apply to Nkomo.

Most advantageous of all to the white leaders was the growing dissension in the African camp. Originally, it was merely a dispute over personality and ideology, and turned mostly on the Southern Rhodesian Africans' assessment of Joshua Nkomo's leadership qualities. By the end of 1962, however, this purely "domestic" dispute had become a part of larger African disputes, particularly between the governments of Ghana and Tanganyika. With the blessing of most East and Central African leaders, the Reverend N. Sithole returned from exile in Dar es Salaam to overthrow the leadership of Nkomo. While the latter proclaimed the establishment of People's Caretaker Councils, Sithole organized a rival political party, the Zimbabwe African National Union (ZANU). Although ZANU charged Nkomo with the familiar allegation of moderation, ZANU attracted a large number of prominent university and professional Africans, thus leaving itself open to the counterallegation of being a party of intellectuals. Street-fighting between the rival groups continued, while the Field government had matters pretty much its own way. Worst of all, the division between Nkomo and Sithole began to take on ugly tribal aspects. Both Sithole and Nkomo were detained and in the three years that followed the reorientation toward radicalism and away from moderation, the African position steadily weakened. Where there had been hope of inspiration and catharsis, there was now only drift and despair. In one sense, Southern Rhodesian nationalists chose the very worst possible time to try to catch up with the militancy of the movements to the north. It was too late in 1962. The breakup of the Federation was willy-nilly, creating a white laager in Southern Rhodesia. The white settler had said, "All right, we'll let the black fellow have the two northern territories, but in return we intend to be masters down here." However misguided the assumption, it was basic to the victory of the conservatives at the polls in Southern Rhodesia at the end of 1962.

In another sense, it was too early. Northern Rhodesia and Nyasaland, free and reincarnate as Zambia and Malawi, will almost certainly not be able to bring effective pressure to bear on Southern Rhodesia until after they have had some quiet years to concentrate on the tremendous problems following the breakup of the Federation and their own emergence to independence. Might those few more years of grace for white entrenchment in Southern Rhodesia have been put to better use through "moderation" and "cooperation"? Has intransigent demand for an immediate transfer from white control to black—"one man, one vote, *now*"—boxed the Africans into a position that leaves them no room for maneuver?

In the abstract, the answer would seem to be "yes." But politics is not to be confused with logical abstraction. There are two reasons for the maneuvers of the Africans. By refusing all forms of cooperation, by focusing world attention and world pressure on the United Kingdom, black Southern Rhodesians compelled Britain to deny independence to the white government in Salisbury—something for which there is powerful pressure within the Conservative Party. Britain was forced for once to take a hard line against the aspirations of the Southern Rhodesian regime. Moreover, the Africans hope still to compel Britain to exercise a jurisdiction in Southern Rhodesia which the British say they are constitutionally bound not to do. Once the Federation was buried, Southern Rhodesia was released from that framework over which Britain still exercised some substantive constitutional control. With Northern Rhodesia and Nyasaland independent, it also becomes more and more difficult for Britain to intervene directly in Rhodesian affairs, particularly after the Mombasa and Aden bases are surrendered. British military power in Central Africa will soon have vanished.

Southern Rhodesian Africans have therefore been working against time, trying to compel British intervention in their colony before it is too late. Only by dramatic opposition to the present regime can they draw world attention to their cause. Paradoxically, their efforts have yielded more internal crisis than danger to the *status quo*.

In 1961, at the Salisbury constitutional conference, Sir Edgar Whitehead and Joshua Nkomo confronted each other, just for an instant, in mutual accommodation. Then they seemed to shrug and pass quickly in opposite directions. Neither was a free agent moving entirely by force of will; and this suggests the second reason why moderation has been rejected. Had Nkomo accepted the relatively generous offer proffered at the time by Whitehead, he would have been rejected as utterly by his own people as Whitehead was by his when he later tried to take a longer second step toward the halfway point.

The Africans are not the only ones plagued by bad timing. Had Whitehead's offer been made five years earlier, it might have been acceptable to the Africans as a start. But at that time it would have been totally unacceptable to the Europeans. In any event, the offer was made too late, and in the wrong way. It was based on a false assumption of an African nationalist leadership that no longer existed: the amenable African moderate—the Paul Mushonga of 1959, the Leopold Takawira of 1960, the Joshua Nkomo as he was until February, 1961 (and possibly still is in his heart of hearts). This was the elusive moderate who became the target of a desperate nationwide search, the "Build a Nation" campaign, the "Claim Your Vote" campaign, the vanished African, who had been so much in evidence for four decades, the indispensable African whose vote Sir Edgar, seeing himself even in the 1958 elections deserted by a majority of white voters, now desperately needed to stay in office. This was the African into whose shoes no leader, least of all Joshua Nkomo, could any longer afford to step.

The African masses rejected moderation during that crucial confrontation in 1961 because, under pressure of events outside Southern Rhodesia, events which may prove to be crucially unanalogous, they had learned a lesson. They had discovered the strategic plausibility of ultimate victory through temporary dramatic defeat. Used against the British, it was sometimes an effective tool in Gandhi's hands and, translated from pacifism to activism, was an even more effective one in the hands of Kenneth Kaunda and Dr. Banda. A noble defeat can have an undeniably stimulating effect on a people, arousing their pride, sense of identity, and will to win. The Mau Mau rebellion horrified many Africans and decimated the Kikuyu, but it was also the Dunkirk of East African nationalism. The old search for temporization and scraps of compromise had given way to the demand for drama, even a dramatic temporary defeat. This demand came to

Southern Rhodesian politics not primarily from the Southern Rhodesian leaders—for many of those who sensed it were already in jail—but from the grass roots. Nkomo could do nothing *but* turn down Whitehead's compromise, could do nothing *but* return voluntarily to accept detention. Kaunda, Banda, Kenyatta, Mboya, even Nyerere stood as symbols of successful courting of blows from colonial authority—blows that aroused, catalyzed, and enhanced their popular support almost as much as victory and far more than temporization. The question now is whether the Southern Rhodesian will retreat before African militancy or whether he will battle to the end.

The militancy to which Southern Rhodesian African leaders are now committed has a further purpose beyond directing the imagination and will of the African people. It is also intended to take some of the profit out of white supremacy. The thin line of railway along which the white-settler population is scattered is easy to harass and hard to defend. But more than that, each explosion, strike, boycott, and riot affects the public image of a community that cannot hope to live without importing capital and population. Both are now at dead center and on the verge of shrinking. Discouraging settlers, then, is no small success for African activism. In 1961, for the first time since federation, more whites (6,241 more) left the country than entered it. Capital is also evacuating Southern Rhodesia, harried by Kaunda's declared threat to impose a tariff wall at the Zambezi "and let the Southern Rhodesians eat the blankets they manufacture," and by the news that the copper companies are to move their headquarters back to Lusaka, leaving in Salisbury, with its empty Charter House and Livingstone House, the most impressive white elephant since the Mogul emperors built their splendid capital, Fatehpur Sikri, at an imposing site that turned out to have no water.

The European population, like that of Kenya before it, has suffered from its own exclusiveness. By seeing no Africans but their own servants, the Europeans have wrongly assessed the population ratios, not to mention popular temperaments. They have tended to believe that all the time in the world lay at their disposal. Now, too late, they see the need for action—but of the wrong kind. Their first reaction, like that of the Kenya settlers in the 1950's, has been to double their efforts to prevail, to withdraw the tentatively offered and now firmly rejected hand of "partnership."

The new militant African policy was most dramatically demonstrated by the sense of satisfaction felt by many African leaders when the Whitehead government was defeated. "This is very good news indeed. It could not be better." So said Kenneth Kaunda, according to the London *Times* of December 17, 1962. His response was widely shared, and not only because most African leaders have greater respect for the fairness of Winston Field than of Sir Edgar Whitehead. The defeat of Whitehead, in an electoral battle, was a demonstration of the power of the African nationalist movement. The Africans may not have elected Field, but they did defeat Whitehead. Since there was no effective choice before them, Whitehead and Field being captives of the same predominantly white electorate, this was the only palpable victory the Africans could have won.

Moreover, it did have two important side effects: It brought to power a government in Southern Rhodesia prepared to wind up the Federation, and it eliminated the liberals and moderates of both races. The leader of the moderate multiracial Central Africa Party, Ralph Palmer, garnered just eight votes in the African constituency of Highfields.

These tactics had been used in the north, too. To win, Julius Nyerere had to wipe out the moderate United Tanganyika Party. In Northern Rhodesia, it was Sir John Moffatt's moderate Liberal Party, for whose benefit the electoral system had been deliberately slanted. Had a handful, from 10 to 20 per cent, of whites and blacks chosen the "moderate" course, the independence of Northern Rhodesia under a nationalist government might have been delayed for years—perhaps disastrously. As it turned out, the Northern Rhodesian Liberals in the lower-roll constituencies polled an average of twenty-eight votes. Although there is genuine mutual admiration between the Liberal Moffatt and the nationalist Kaunda, the total defeat of the former, on November 6, 1962, accomplished a primary objective of the latter. Again, it can only be speculated whether these objectives, so suitable to Banda and Kaunda, are as appropriate to Nkomo. The defeat of Whitehead by Field released certain frontier go-for-broke spirits among the whites of Rhodesia which in turn led to the purge of Field when *he* appeared to be insufficiently extreme in suppressing African aspirations. The speculation can be resolved only by reference to the temper of the masses. The reasoning may be faulty, but it is very real: What was good for every nationalist movement from Sudan to the Zambezi must be good for Zimbabwe.

So far, we have assumed the existence of a mass nationalist movement in Southern Rhodesia, which exists to be led, but which also leads its leaders—a movement which, born, banned, reborn, and rebanned, flows along like a river, now above ground, now beneath. What are its characteristics?

After the banning of ZAPU the third time around in the cat-and-mouse game, it was decided to ignore the ban and not to re-form as a political movement, at least for the present. The new Caretaker "movement," while not a political party, is organized on a cell pattern that does not very substantially differ from ordinary political organization. There are, of course, rival groups, chiefly ZANU, anxious to fill whatever vacuum may exist or seem to exist. It seems highly improbable at the present that any of these stand any chance of displacing an underground ZAPU.

In the Zimbabwe African National Union (ZANU), led by the Reverend Sithole, ZAPU does, however, have a formidable rival. ZANU opposes the policies of ZAPU, including the decision not to reorganize as a political movement. It believes "underground" cells to be too complex a political framework for rural Africa. But most of all it opposes the continuing leadership of Joshua Nkomo.

And always lurking in the background is some more extreme alternative, a "General Chedu" and a Zimbabwe Liberation Army. In African consensual society, it is customary that alternatives which gather support are adopted into the movement to which they were an alternative.

That ZAPU is still the mainstream is beyond question, and was, indeed, demonstrated most dramatically in an election in which ZAPU did not participate. ZAPU was banned on September 20, 1962. In one week, 1,285 persons were arrested under Southern Rhodesia's Law and Order Maintenance Act and the Unlawful Organization Act (the former of which had caused the Chief Justice of the Federation, Sir Robert Tredgold, to resign with the charge that it "outrages almost every basic human right"). Altogether, 191 ZAPU leaders were rusticated to a 3-mile area of the native reserves, thereby, paradoxically, giving ZAPU the first legal opportunity to appear in these areas, which the government had hitherto kept closed to them. ZAPU files, vehicles, moneys were all impounded. All this makes the solidarity of the African people with ZAPU, demonstrated after such adversity, all the more dramatic.

After his February, 1961, *volte face*, Nkomo decided to ask the Africans to boycott the Southern Rhodesian constitutional plebiscite and the territorial elections. In this plea he was joined by a few European sympathizers, notably Garfield Todd and Guy Clutton-Brock. In the face of a heavily financed "Claim Your Vote" campaign to get 50,000 of the estimated 60,000 eligible Africans on the "B" roll, fewer than 11,000 registered, and of these fewer than 3,000 voted. There was no trace of intimidation on voting day. This result is particularly eloquent when one considers the votes in the 90 percentile produced by the exuberant Northern Rhodesian and Nyasaland elections. If the nationalist movement can claim the adherence of the abstaining 80 per cent of the *registered* African "B" roll voters and 95 per cent of the *eligible* "B" rollers—those "moderate" Africans chosen by Sir

Edgar Whitehead to lead the reconciliation of white and black—how near-unanimous must be the movement's support among the poorer masses deemed unqualified to exercise a "responsible, civilized" vote?

In at least five white "A" roll seats, a larger turnout of the enrolled "B" roll voters, with their maximum 25 per cent weight, could have swung these seats behind Sir Edgar Whitehead's United Federal Party. In only one seat did this actually occur, so that, in competition with Whitehead for the allegiance of the most "responsible" Africans in Southern Rhodesia (by Whitehead's UFP's own definition), ZAPU swept the boards. In no case was a "B" roll seat won by a candidate receiving more than 202 votes, thus making all 15 elections a sham. Fourteen of the 15 African seats were carried by Whitehead's United Federal Party, giving the victorious Africans and one Coloured member, unrepresentative though they are of their own people, a majority in Sir Edgar's caucus of 29—a sure kiss of death and an amusing nemesis for the party of Welensky and Huggins.

Impressive as this showing of African solidarity is, particularly as it repeats similar performances in connection with the government's and ZAPU's own 1962 plebiscites on the new constitution, there are still those who insist that support is obtained chiefly by intimidation. This would seem not to be so. No doubt there is great pressure brought to bear on the handful of Africans who have curried personal favor by working with the Southern Rhodesian or Federal governments. Such pressure compelled the first African Federal minister, Jasper Savanhu, to reconsider his role and eventually to tender his resignation. What is relevant is not whether coercion is used, but whether it *creates* the public will or is merely a *manifestation* of it. Who would have thought to condemn the freedom fighters of the Norwegian or French underground for their actions against "traitors" and "quislings"?

The Southern Rhodesian nationalists' impressive showing "at the polls" nevertheless leaves the future clouded. Speaking in Highfields Township on January 14, 1962, the late Dr. T. S. Parerenyatwa, Deputy President of ZAPU, told Africans that if they enrolled as voters, "it was the one thing which could prevent ZAPU acquiring independence and majority rule by the end of this year." Such promises create a danger of popular disenchantment. It is by no means clear that the Southern Rhodesian rank and file know that in choosing activism, as did the five northern territories, they have taken on in the Rhodesian settler a much more formidable opponent than was the British raj, and that victory will not necessarily follow as rapidly or easily as in the north.

The breakup of the Federation is now history, but, like the victory of the Rhodesian front in the Southern Rhodesian elections, this constitutes a victory for Southern Rhodesian black nationalism only in a moral sense, rather like self-immolation. More repressive laws are already before Parliament or in preparation to implement "community development"—the Southern Rhodesian version of apartheid. The coming fight to have this policy adopted may spell the end of the constitutional protection for the African, the Constitutional Council, and the independent judiciary, as it did in South Africa. Obligatory death sentences have been enacted for certain offenses against public order. The Land Apportionment Act, which allocates to the Europeans 51,410,000 of the best acres as against 41,950,000 for the Africans, is not, after all, to be repealed.

In fact, not politics but economics may prove to be the Africans' chief ally. After federation ended, Southern Rhodesia had to revert to an economy that had only just been saved from bankruptcy. Before federation, Southern Rhodesia's imports exceeded her exports by over 40 per cent. Secondary industry has expanded rapidly since then, but if the Northern Rhodesian markets for the products of this industry are cut off, the imbalance may now be even greater rather than less. In one of his rare political insights, Sir Roy Welensky has said publicly that he did not believe it possible, if federation failed, to maintain any kind of economic association between Southern Rhodesia and the other two territories because nationalist governments in Northern Rhodesia and Nyasaland would not buy Southern Rhodesian goods. If a rail line were to give Malawi and Zambia alternative access to the seacoast through Tanganyika, these nations would at once take a firmer line to support their suppressed brother Africans next door.

This is what the Southern Rhodesian nationalists are counting on. By defeating the UFP and federation in the Southern Rhodesian elections, they have earned an IOU from Dr. Banda and Kenneth Kaunda. One of Winston Field's first postelection gambits was to visit Dr. Banda to see that the IOU was not honored, using the 117,000 Nyasa wage-earners in Southern Rhodesia as barter. In the fairly near future, one would expect the economic relationship between Southern Rhodesia and her two former partners in federation to end. If it does, the Southern Rhodesian economy must choose between surrender or union with the Republic of South Africa.

If the latter option is chosen, the cause of black nationalism in South Africa will have been immeasurably strengthened both by the recruitment of a huge and militant black preponderance and by the elimination of the buffer zone separating them from the black nationalist states to the north. Dr. Verwoerd, in his white laager, is well aware of this and is said to have told Sir Roy Welensky that, in the event of a black uprising in Southern Rhodesia, he would do all in his power to bring the Rhodesian whites to safety in South Africa, but that he would not dissipate his armies in a futile second Matabele war.

The African believes that moderation is a policy that can be pursued only from a position of strength. This should not surprise us, for it is an aphorism he might well have learned from Washington. Its particular rationale in Southern Rhodesia is that only a policy of black extremism can compensate for the military and psychological handicap under which this nationalist movement operates.

Those who find this strategy unworkable—and so, indeed, it would appear to be—are fixed with the onus of contriving some other strategy that has not already been tried and found wanting. Those who believe that black nationalism's salvation in Zimbabwe must come not through a new strategy but from a new leader had better produce their man only after there is reasonable certainty that his appearance will do more than further fragment the nationalist movement. Lest, however, this be taken as a counsel of despair, it should be remembered that the logical incongruity of the African nationalist position in Southern Rhodesia is far exceeded by that of the position the white settlers are trying so desperately to maintain. The few logically constant factors one can perceive in the situation—time, economics, regional trends—are entirely on the side of the Africans.

It is most important, however, to remember that in Africa, as in any revolutionary situation, it is often not the predictable that occurs and not the logical that succeeds. Predictable factors will liberate Southern Rhodesia, but in a decade or more. The unpredictable—as in Zanzibar—may accomplish it tomorrow.

Editors' Postscript

The government of Prime Minister Ian Smith has pursued independence relentlessly. For over a year there have been countless harangues with the British Government, and threats have flowed freely from both sides. Emigration is up to about 1,000 whites per month, and the economy is stagnant.

Complete suppression of African nationalism is another hallmark of the present government. Immediately upon assuming office, Mr. Smith banned ZAPU and ZANU and arrested Joshua Nkomo and the Reverend Ndabaningi Sithole; for over a year, they have been restricted to remote parts of the country. Suppression continued as the Daily News, a newspaper designed for African readership, was banned for allegedly printing reports that were likely to cause alarm and to undermine the authority of traditional tribal chiefs. The International Press Institute termed this banning the most outrageous suppression of the press in 1964. P. van der Byl, Parliamentary Secretary for Information, summed up the year's activities as follows: "Already, Government has banned the African nationalist parties and restricted the political trouble-makers. The newspaper which supported them has also been banned. The political trouble-makers will never again be allowed to start new parties. They are finished." [1]

In the field of foreign policy, Prime Minister Smith began a determined effort to achieve independence, convinced that Britain was a threat to the Rhodesian idea of a white-led society. At the same time, the opposition Rhodesia National Party, headed by Sir Edgar Whitehead, mounted a vigorous campaign against a unilateral declaration of independence (UDI). Fearful of the economic and diplomatic isolation that might follow a UDI, the party advocated forgetting about the few extra powers that would be added by independence, in favor of maintaining a viable and prosperous economy.

At a constitutional conference held in London in September, 1964, Britain made it clear that the decision to grant independence lies entirely with the British Government and Parliament, and that they have a solemn duty to be satisfied that independence would be acceptable to the country as a whole. A UDI, Mr. Smith was told, would be considered an open act of defiance tantamount to treason. Serious consequences would surely follow, including the complete economic and diplomatic isolation of Rhodesia.

Mr. Smith, in turn, recognized Britain's right to be satisfied about the wishes of the people, and confidently declared that the majority of both blacks and whites were with him. He then announced plans to test public opinion, including a referendum of the electorate (80,000 voters out of a population of some 4 million) and a traditional indaba of 196 chiefs and 426 headmen. Although the British Government informed him beforehand that the indaba was not an acceptable method of testing African opinion, Mr. Smith went ahead anyway. The results of the referendum were 58,191 in favor of independence and 6,096 against, with practically all the 16,000 or so non-white voters boycotting the election. As expected, the chiefs and headmen—who are salaried employees of the Smith regime—after meeting secretly for a few days, declared unanimous support for independence. Neither Britain nor the United States accepted invitations to send observers. Lord Malvern, former Prime Minister of Southern Rhodesia, declared, "As for the indaba, that was a swindle. . . . Many of the

[1] *Africa Digest*, XII, No. 5 (April, 1965), 120–21.

Shona chiefs are rather dodderers. Their real powers and influence were destroyed at the time of the rebellion—1896." [2]

On February 22, 1965, the Rt. Hon. A. Bottomley, Secretary of State for Commonwealth Relations, and Lord Gardiner, the Lord Chancellor, visited Southern Rhodesia and were greeted at the Salisbury airport by 6,000 Africans carrying banners reading: "Release Nkomo"; "Majority rule, now"; and "One man, one vote." After being permitted a three-hour meeting with Nkomo, Mr. Bottomley requested a second visit and was promptly threatened with a crisis.[3]

On May 7, 1965, national elections were held with Smith's Rhodesian Front gaining a complete sweep of all fifty "A" roll seats. The opposition Rhodesia National Party won ten of the "B" roll seats, the other five going to independents. Again, the elections were boycotted by most nonwhite voters. Nevertheless, Mr. Smith found it appropriate to declare: "It seems to me that it is the real Rhodesian nation which has emerged." [4]

The overwhelming Rhodesian Front victory increases the likelihood of a unilateral declaration of independence, and tension is expected to mount during the coming months. African leaders have declared that such a move would be followed by guerrilla warfare.

[2] *Ibid.*, XII, No. 3 (December, 1964), 70.
[3] *Ibid.*, XII, No. 5 (April, 1965), 120.
[4] *Ibid.*, XII, No. 6 (June, 1965), 148.

The Economic Future of Central Africa

SAMUEL Z. WESTERFIELD, JR.[1]

Central Africa[2] has often been described as a dualistic economy. The Africans have traditionally been in subsistence agriculture; the Europeans have dominated the money, or market, economy. The primary contact of the Africans with the money economy has been through the cash sales of agricultural surpluses and the sale of their labor power to European agriculture and industry. It has often been stated that economic development takes place when there is an increase in per capita real income. We determine per capita real income by dividing the total real income by the total population. However, given the structure of a dualistic economy, it is quite possible for an income increase in the money economy to show a per capita income increase for the total population, even though per capita income in subsistence agriculture may have changed little or not at all.

It is necessary to be certain that the concept of economic development includes the indigenous economy of the Africans within its framework. In this frame of reference, we would conclude that economic development has taken place when two conditions have been satisfied: When the money economy increases in real terms, and when the per capita real income of the indigenous population grows over a period of time.

A widely held view is that economic development in Central Africa at the present stage of African culture is inconceivable without the government, management, skills, capital, and social values of Westerners. In this view, the indigenous population is thought to be incapable at present of applying the high-level technology of the West to the economic development of the region. Moreover, implicit in this position is the view that the Africans are really incapable of and will

---

[1] The views expressed in this article are the personal views of the author and not necessarily those of the U.S. Government.

[2] Throughout this paper, Central Africa is defined to include Malawi, Zambia, and Rhodesia.

not achieve the level of skill and competence associated with the Europeans. This view of the conditions for economic progress emphasizes the importance of the provision of basic amenities for Europeans in order to attract them to the area.

Increased export earnings are required for the rapid development of Central Africa, which does not yet have a full complex of industry. At present, the most important exports of the region are electrolytic copper, blister copper, tobacco, raw asbestos, chrome ore, tea, maize, zinc bar and ingots, cobalt metal, ferro chrome, and lead bar and ingots. However, copper has a widely fluctuating price, which of course means widely varying export revenues from this source; tobacco exports are also subject to similar variations in quantity and price.

The export earnings of Central Africa constitute a very large percentage of the gross national product. For example, in 1954, exports and imports of goods and services amounted respectively to £167.6 million and £151.9 million, while the domestic product was £304.7 million. Exports and imports of goods and services were therefore 55 and 49.9 per cent, respectively, of the GNP in 1954. In earlier and later years, they were also a high percentage of the GNP. Hence we see the great impact that international transactions have on income, employment, and output.

Central Africa must have a high rate of domestic savings and investment to ensure a high rate of economic growth. The funds for capital investment come from two major sources: export earnings and capital inflows from abroad. However, it is important to note that almost 75 per cent of export earnings is spent for imports. As a result, only 25 per cent is available for other foreign-exchange expenditure for the Central African economy. This situation raises difficult problems of acquiring sufficient revenues to service external debt.

The foregoing analysis follows closely the position of Stephen Enke[3] in his emphasis upon the skills and capital of the Europeans as requisite to economic development. Enke sums up his position by concluding that the Rhodesian experience contains valuable lessons for other underdeveloped areas with populations that have few skills. First, such a region must invest heavily in providing amenities for Westerners. Second, to a substantial extent, the basis for this investment will be the export earnings of the economy (which are subject to wide fluctuations and also high import propensities). Third, such an economy must attract a continuous flow of capital and immigrants.

[3] Enke, "Western Development of a Sparsely Populated Country: The Rhodesias," *The American Economic Review*, June, 1960.

Fourth, the indigenous population must be admitted into the market economy and share in the gains of economic growth.

Another view of economic development in Central Africa has been presented by a small group of professional economists in the industrial, financial, and academic spheres in Salisbury. The position of this group of economists was stated in a pamphlet entitled *Planning the Development of the Wealth of Three Nations*, published in November, 1960. The economists recommended the establishment of a "high development authority" that would be responsible for the organization of a development plan for Central Africa. The Phoenix group, as these Salisbury economists called themselves, noted that in 1959 per capita personal income for Europeans amounted to £580; for Asians and Coloureds, £235; and for Africans, £24. Even this low African figure included £11 of "subsistence income," which is probably overstated; at the time of the study, it appeared that African cash income did not exceed £15.

In projecting their target of a gross national product exceeding £1 billion by 1970, the Phoenix group set per capita income at £570 for the Europeans, £345 for the Asians and Coloureds, and £50 for the Africans. Thus we see that even in the projection of this "liberal plan," African per capita income would still be less than one-tenth of the European per capita income in 1970.

However, the plan does suggest that the European community should be prepared to accept a reduction in per capita income over the next decade. The Phoenix group also observed that the "illusion of racial harmony has been shattered, perhaps beyond repair—indeed, it is one of the most regrettable features of government policy that it has been framed with almost willful disregard of its effects on foreign investment reaction, or alternatively, that it has been based on a misguided belief that strong-armed tactics would draw a favorable response from overseas investments, notwithstanding the exactly contrary experience in South Africa." [4] The Phoenix economists also expressed concern about the flight of capital from Central Africa and noted that there is little prospect of achieving an environment more congenial to foreign investment without fundamental changes in the political arena. In the Phoenix view, the investment environment has continued to deteriorate in Central Africa. A lower level of investment would mean an additional burden upon exports. We have already noted the wide variation in the level of exports for raw-material–producing countries, and it would be very risky to attempt a forecast of the future export proceeds over the next decade.

[4] *Planning the Development of the Wealth of Three Nations* (Salisbury, 1960), pp. 7–10.

There is nothing in the Phoenix proposal that comes to grips with the fundamental questions involved in the achievement of full citizenship for the Central African community. A great deal of ground is covered in a rather general fashion, but it is not at all clear that the establishment of a high development authority along the lines suggested would do much to resolve the political and economic problems of the Central African community.

Still another view of economic development in Central Africa, while not identical with Enke's, fits very easily into his analysis. W. Arthur Lewis [5] has argued the case for economic development with "unlimited supplies of labor." The primary thrust of Lewis' analysis suggests that the Africans' economic position will improve when the European sector has to pay higher wages to attract the African from the agriculture sector. This is supposed to take place when the African's real wage in agriculture is higher than the real wage currently offered in industry. Under these circumstances, the industrial sector would have to pay higher real wages to attract the African. As long as real wages in industry are higher than the African real wage in agriculture, the industrial sector would have access to unlimited supplies of African labor without increasing the wage payment. This suggests that when the real wages rise for the African, he becomes a more integral part of the industrial economy and his greater income provides the basis for expanding consumption expenditures that will give impetus to the development of local industry. With a sufficiently expanding African income, the assumption is that the market will gradually become large enough to support more diversified and broadly based industry, including a capital-goods sector, which is common to all industrial nations.

It would seem that neither Enke's, the Phoenix economists', nor Lewis' view of economic growth in Central Africa represents the position of impatient African leadership in this region. Enke's view is that the primary impetus to economic growth in Central Africa has come from European management and capital. The African argument is that the indigenous population has a large degree of talent which is underemployed in the Central African economy, and that where the skills are not already present, they can be acquired rapidly with proper education and training. All the evidence suggests that the European labor force in Central Africa is not uniquely endowed with ability.

In an open labor market with trained African workers, it is clear that the Africans would dominate all the job categories from top

[5] Lewis, "Economic Development with Unlimited Supplies of Labor," *Manchester School of Economic and Social Studies*, XXII (May, 1954), 139–91.

management down through the unskilled groups. In a somewhat comparable situation, Negro labor, as well as Southern white labor, in the United States has been largely underemployed. The research of many labor economists, including Richard Lester at Princeton, concludes that Southern white labor and Negro labor are as productive as any other segment of the labor force once they have been exposed to training and the opportunity to employ their skills.

I remember a conversation in Salisbury with an able member of a management group during my visit to that city in the winter of 1960. I was then Dean of the School of Business Administration at Atlanta University and engaged in a search to enroll likely African candidates in our M.B.A. program. The executive with whom I talked was most enthusiastic about the proposed program, but "could not see where an African with an M.B.A. degree would be employed in Salisbury." This experience suggested how far apart the European and African leadership really were. In a different political context, Rhodesia would need not one but hundreds of competent Africans trained in the field of business administration, which would, of course, include a great deal of work in management, economics, finance, statistics, and accounting.

Normally, in the economic development process, surplus labor moves from agriculture to the urban community and into the industrial economy. However, there are immediate ceilings placed upon the African worker as he leaves "subsistence" agriculture for the market economy. The "color bar," including restrictions imposed by the absence of the opportunity to secure adequate training and education, prevents the upward mobility of the African worker and consigns him for his entire life to a condition of underemployment. If equal opportunity were open to the African worker, he would be in a position to contribute to an expanded national income and thus provide strong impetus to the formation of new and diversified business firms.

The utilization of new African training in an open economy would lead to the achievement of a much higher income and provide the demand necessary to support the establishment and expansion of light industry. Beyond this, a firm foundation would be laid for the gradual development of capital-goods production in selected areas where an early comparative advantage might be indicated.

We now turn briefly to a survey of Central Africa's resources.[6] The Kariba Gorge Project on the Zambezi River represents the most significant achievement of recent years in terms of its potential impact

[6] See William A. Hance, *African Economic Development* (New York, 1958), pp. 135, 178.

upon economic development. The completion of the Kariba Dam and hydroelectric facilities should eliminate any physical reason for the Central African region to be short of power for many years. This statement is not meant to suggest that power will be available for every conceivable consumption and industrial need. However, full utilization of these facilities will enable Zambia and Rhodesia to lay a firm foundation for the distribution of power for high-priority industrial and consumption requirements.

Malawi, Zambia, and Rhodesia all have substantial reserves of high-quality coal. Thus there is no problem of a prospective fuel shortage in physical terms. There are, however, difficulties in providing transportation for the delivery of the coal, but it would appear that this problem is one of manageable proportions. Kariba can make a substantial contribution to industrial growth. As noted earlier, Central Africa has a wide range of minerals, including copper, cobalt, petalite, chrome, and asbestos, to mention only a few of the most important ones whose production is of world-wide significance.

In Malawi, secondary industry is largely limited to the primary processing of agricultural produce. Zambia industry is mainly involved in the concentration, smelting, and refining of minerals. However, secondary industry is developing rapidly in Rhodesia; it now includes a rather wide variety of products. Mechanical and metal-fabricating industries are now being established, including ones for the production of wire, nails, plows, tubes, window frames, automobile radiators, and metal containers. The vehicle industry is also represented with a significant start in local production of automobiles and the assembly of bicycles. Some of the other leading secondary industries are building and construction, food and beverage, textile and clothing, and chemicals.

We must ask the fundamental question: Can we achieve full utilization of African labor at all levels of the Central African economy within the framework of a multiracial democratic society? The tragedy of this position is that there does not seem to be sufficient time for the European community to do all the many things it should have done much earlier. If Rhodesia should finally decide to attempt a closer relationship with the Republic of South Africa, the lines of the coming struggle would be sharply drawn. Should the present situation deteriorate very rapidly, prognostication with reference to the short-run economic future of the region would be impossible. We could continue to view with confidence the long-run future, but could speak far less confidently about economic development over the next few months and years.

We should realize how difficult it is to extrapolate future economic growth on the basis of past performance. Consider how far off the target a number of economists were when they forecast a high level of economic activity for the early 1930's in the American economy on the basis of its performance in the 1920's. The same difficulty of accurate forecasting would hold if one were to project the economic growth of Central Africa on the basis of the relatively high level of economic activity in recent years. Political and social upheaval in this region would effectively bring economic growth temporarily to a halt. Therefore, we must conclude that until the political problems of the region have been resolved, there is little that we can say with confidence about its immediate economic future.

Discussion

M. W. Kanyama Chiume.   If I appear to disagree with some of the remarks made by the three distinguished speakers who have preceded me, it is only because of our differences in experience. They are learned men working in classrooms. I am a politician actually living in Central Africa.

Their sources of information can be questioned, for those who now have a monopoly on the means of publishing books on Africa (apart from a few liberals whose attitude is not questionable) are mainly those who have prejudices and who would like Africa to remain where it was at the beginning of the twentieth century.

I think it was in 1958 that Lord Home, then Secretary of State for Colonial Affairs, came to Nyasaland and told us that the Federation was here to stay. We told him that if the Federation was to stay in Nyasaland we wanted him to go and convey to Her Majesty that it was going to stay over our dead bodies. The poor man did not understand. To him, Britain was such a mighty power that 3 million beggarly Nyasas had to obey. To him, the Europeans had acquired the right, as a result of their economic achievement, to do the thinking for the 3 million people of Nyasaland, and therefore he was shocked to hear a few Nyasalanders, some of them shorter than himself, telling him that the Federation was at an end.

Now, Lord Home did not realize that a long time ago in our country we had agreed that while you can fool some of the people all of the time, and you can fool all of the people some of the time, you cannot fool all of the Nyasalanders all of the time.

Why were we opposed to the Federation? Many people have the impression that the Federation was an institution imposed upon ignorant masses of Central Africans in order to improve their economic position. This is not the truth. The Federation was imposed upon 8 million people of Southern Rhodesia, Northern Rhodesia, and Nyasaland in order to prevent Nyasaland and Northern Rhodesia from becoming black states in the African continent. As the then Secretary for Colonial Affairs said, he wanted to create a political entity that would act as a buffer between Ghana's black nationalism to the north and white supremacy in South Africa. I want to assure you that the existence of Ghana is a blessing to Africa, and the existence of white supremacy in South Africa is not a thing we want to be perpetuated. Not a single inch of Africa is an extension of Europe, and we are determined, come what may, that no part of Africa shall remain dominated, be it South Africa, Mozambique, or Angola.

The white men of Southern Rhodesia had made up their minds to extend their influence beyond the borders of Southern Rhodesia. They had their eyes on Nyasaland as a part of their empire—a continuing source of cheap labor and a dumping ground for their cheaply manufactured goods. They also had their eyes on Northern Rhodesian copper to meet their national debt, which in 1953 amounted to about £134 million. Now we were not going to be part of these ambitions in spite of the fact that the Federation was being sold in attractive sugar-coated pills labeled an "experiment in moderation" and "an experiment in partnership which America and Britain cannot afford to see fail." As noted earlier, the partnership they envisaged was that of "rider and horse," the horse being the African who welcomed the European in Africa and the rider being the European made prosperous by Africa's natural resources.

What I say here is not in any way to suggest that we in Africa are waging a struggle against Europeans as such. We are not antiwhite in spite of all that has been said about us (although about that we could not care less); we are not dedicated to exterminating white men for the sake of extermination. A political animal, whether an African or a white man, is a human being. The existence of people of various races is to us an expression of the beauty of nature. Nevertheless, we are convinced that the existence of a few Europeans in any part of Africa is no justification at all for the African's being treated as a second-class citizen in his own country.

Therefore, we refuse to accept dictates from the United Kingdom, and we are determined, come what may, to fight for liberation. I want to make one correction here of what one speaker said. We are not dedicated to a policy of nonviolence in Nyasaland. We said that if Europe and Britain would behave, we would behave and follow a nonviolent pattern. If they do not, then we reserve the right to follow the course of conflict.

For nine years we have been involved in a very difficult battle. In 1954, we lost some lives in the heavily settled Miange and Cholo districts. In 1959, as many of you are aware, we lost some 50 to 60 lives. Dr. Banda, now the Prime Minister, and about 1,500 of us went to jail. Nevertheless, we were convinced that ours was a fight for truth and the Federation was nothing but an implementation of a big lie. On the 19th of December, 1962, Mr. Butler, a very able minister in the British Government, recognized the fact that while you can take a horse to the river you cannot force him to drink. The horse that was intended to be ridden in 1954 was allowed to get out of the Federation, and that horse is Nyasaland. The same British Secretary then recognized that one could not allow Nyasaland to get out of the Federation without allowing Northern Rhodesia to get out, too.

The problem, therefore, is really Southern Rhodesia. The whites there are convinced that they can hold on longer than many of us believe. Now I do not share the optimism of those who believe that Southern Rhodesia and South Africa will long endure as presently governed. For, as our Prime Minister said when Nyasaland became self-governing, "The independence of Nyasaland is absolutely meaningless unless and until the whole of Southern Africa is freed."

I hope I'm wrong in the impression I got from Mr. Westerfield that he regards the future of Central Africa, as far as economic development is concerned, as rather uncertain or gloomy. I would like to assure him that we do not share that view. As long as Southern Rhodesia is dominated by a few, I agree that the economic development of that country is doomed. But we in Nyasaland, and our friends in Northern Rhodesia, are now showing that when power is transferred to a majority of the people in a country, political stability is established.

When we took over the government in Nyasaland, for instance, there were only about 40 university graduates in the country out of a population of 3 million. This was no fault of our own. We were slightly unlucky in Central Africa because our climate was so good that we had a white-settler community, and also because the British Government imported skilled labor from Britain. For that reason, they did not consider it necessary to train our people as they train people in Ghana and other parts of West Africa, which were fortunate in having more mosquitoes than we. Of course, when we discovered that mosquitoes were a political asset in our national liberation, the Europeans had already discovered mosquito guns and DDT.

Anyway, since we took over, we have been able to send, out of our own humble means, 140 students to overseas countries to prepare themselves and to return and man the civil service of our country. Seventy-two years of colonialism produced 40 graduates; 1.5 years of self-government produced 140—an indication that progress cannot begin unless and until a majority has the control of the political key to their national resources.

As for illiteracy in Nyasaland, absolutely nothing was done except for some experimentation in the early 1950's. When we took over, we decided to launch a mass literacy campaign. In October, 1962, we selected three pioneer districts, and, in one district alone, from October to January, 1962, we trained, at no cost to them, 1,350 old men and women who were awarded certificates by the Prime Minister.

In the field of construction, the people in the villages are doing a tremendous amount of work in helping the Central Government to construct roads. The cooperative societies, which have in the past been frowned upon, now take a very vital part in the economic development of our country. In other words, the political power we have is now being used to mobilize our people into helping the Central Government. They are no longer mere spectators and laborers, but active participants in the government. This could not be without a change from government of the few to government of the many.

When I talk about mobilizing the forces of our country in order to help the Central Government to reconstruct Nyasaland economically, I know some of you might be wondering whether in doing so we may not be creating a dictatorship. I have been in this country now for about four weeks and almost invariably the question asked is whether Africa can stand democracy.

We in Africa feel that there is no one type of democracy. The French democracy of President de Gaulle is completely different from the British democracy, and the American democracy, in which Southern Democrats can unite with Northern Republicans to control legislation, is completely different from the Swiss democracy. It is wrong, then, for others to try to impose their own achievements or faults in form of government upon Africans, and to create the impression that if Africa does not follow their type of democracy, Africa is composed of dictatorships. There was democracy in Africa long before the word "democracy" was used. The people under their chiefs met and decided and discussed, sometimes perhaps more hotly than you discuss in your own legislatures in this country, the questions of building a house, cultivating gardens, constructing roads, and so forth.

In those discussions, people were allowed to say all they wanted, but, once a decision was made, it was expected that every citizen was going to follow the majority decision. That is the type of democracy that we feel should be followed in Africa. In the past, we could not afford to have too many people quarreling about leadership or how to achieve this or how to achieve that, because the more you quarrel the more opportunity you give your enemies. It was necessary, therefore, to organize strong political parties and to recognize strong leaders in order to meet the common enemy —just as, during the dark days of the 1940's, the British people thought it was necessary to rally around one common leader, Churchill, and to sink their differences in order to meet the common enemy.

When a strong political party emerges, even after self-government, it is not because its leaders are opposed to democracy, but only because it was necessary during the time of the struggle to have strong political leaders and strong political parties. In Nyasaland, there were a number of strong parties fighting against us. But we won the election and we feel no obligation to create an opposition party for the sake of its creation. If one arises, well, let it arise. As we see it, it is necessary to have a strong organization to fight the unholy trinity of ignorance, poverty, and disease, the insidious legacies left behind by the colonial powers.

I shall be failing in my duty if I do not point out again, in conclusion, that Southern Rhodesia is now the problem. If the great powers use their influence on the settlers in South Africa and Southern Rhodesia, as well as on the British Government, the white Southern Rhodesians and South Africans will not long be able to hold the reins. It is my hope and prayer, therefore, that the great powers, who have in the past been running with the hares and riding with the hounds, will now find it necessary for the sake of man to change their tactics.

ARTHUR N. L. WINA.   My comments will be confined mainly to Northern Rhodesia and the central area. It was not surprising to us in Central Africa that the decision to end the Federation was made. It was surprising only that others took so long to recognize the obvious—that it had to end. The Federation of Central Africa was an instrument in the hands of white nationalists to impose control over the masses in Central Africa. The Federation was a tool in the hands of the white settlers of Southern Rhodesia not only to dominate the whole of Central Africa, but also to exploit the mineral resources of Northern Rhodesia and the labor resources of Nyasaland. Not only was all this being done without the consent of the people of Northern Rhodesia and Nyasaland, but it was being implemented ruthlessly, regardless of the human rights of the people to their native soil, without even a pretense of democracy.

We have gone through a very difficult period in Central Africa, especially since 1953. Our political leaders have been arrested, deported, and imprisoned; even now there are people in prison in Nyasaland, Northern Rhodesia, and Southern Rhodesia only because they stood up and said that they did not believe in the Federation and were going to die seeking its destruction. When, therefore, the decision was made to end the Federation, you heard fresh reports of rejoicing in the streets of Lusaka; for those of us in leadership positions, however, it was a very sober moment, a moment to reflect on all the suffering that had been involved in the process of destroying the system.

The pronouncement of the end of the Federation by Mr. Butler means that we can look forward in the very near future to complete independence and to a democratic African government. The end of the Federation also means that we of Northern Rhodesia can muster our resources of copper, labor, and agricultural land in the interest of the people. It also means that on the borders of the Zambezi, adjacent to white-dominated Southern Africa, there will be an independent African state. This will have a psychological effect upon Southern Africa and can otherwise make a substantial contribution to the liberation of Mozambique, Angola, South West Africa, and, indeed, Southern Rhodesia.

Our commitment to Pan-Africanism is well known through our leader, Kenneth Kaunda, who is also chairman of PAFMECSA. As we see it, Pan-Africanism should develop in three progressive stages: (1) the liberation of Africa, (2) the achievement of some lesser forms of all-African unities, and (3) economic development and the raising of the peoples' standard of living. The breakup of the Federation is a contribution to the liberation of Africa and to Pan-Africanism.

The Europeans' illusion that they forever will be the happy riders astride the masses is ended. If the Federation was created to protect Europeans, the only "protection" now left to them in Northern Rhodesia is to learn to live in a country governed by Africans. The European must obey African laws; he must adjust himself to the reality that he cannot have the luxury of two homes, one in Africa and one in Europe. His home will be in Africa or elsewhere, and if it is elsewhere, it is to that place that he must go and make his home.

Those who have maintained that the breakup of the Federation would be followed by general deterioration will be proved wrong by what is actually happening in Northern Rhodesia now.

Mr. Chiume has indicated what the African government in Nyasaland has accomplished. The world was surprised to learn that the African government in Northern Rhodesia had seventy-three new company registrations, representing an investment of more than £3 million. This far exceeds the figure for any comparable period during the life of the Federation.

Indeed, for the same period in 1962, we had only twenty new companies and, against this, fifty bankruptcies. The key to economic development is not an imposed political system, but rather a democratic society in which the government is chosen by and responsive to the people. Businesses trust such a government because stability can be counted on. With stability, there is no longer a question of whether there is going to be a revolution the next day; any "revolution" will be carried out in the electoral process. There is no longer a question of who is going to prison next, or of arbitrary hangings, which is what is going on in Southern Rhodesia. People are being hanged in Southern Rhodesia now for the mere expression of disapproval of the government; they are being hanged merely for appearing in the United Nations and exposing some of the inequities in Southern Rhodesia.

Such a situation provides no basis for stability. We are proving in Nyasaland and Northern Rhodesia that, given the right to govern ourselves, we, and other Africans, can promote a higher rate of economic development than can the white-dominated systems of Southern Rhodesia, South Africa, and the Portuguese territories of Angola and Mozambique. There is a popular African saying: "We would rather misgovern ourselves than be governed without our consent. Seek ye first political liberty and everything else shall be added unto you."

Nyasaland has been granted the right to secede from the Federation, and Northern Rhodesia, which has established an African state under the very complicated constitution of 1962, has now also been granted the right to secede and anticipates independence at about the end of 1964. Southern Rhodesia, under the fascist government of Winston Field, is now resorting to any measures to maintain white domination. We fought against the Federation not because we do not like unity and cooperation with other African states, but because the Federation was created to guarantee the government of a minority over the majority. Liberation of Nyasaland and of Southern and Northern Rhodesia could never take place so long as the Federation existed. When we have achieved independence, our objective will be some other form of unity—this time, of course, of truly African countries.

With our independence, freedom will spread in Southern Africa. And it is here that Africans will count nations as being for or against them: Are you interested only in economic advantage, or are you interested in the human being and his rights? Big nations will be put to the test of whether they are on the side of supporting the right or of compromising the right in order to maintain or achieve short-term interests.

I take this opportunity to assure my colleagues who are here from Mozambique, Angola, South Africa, South West Africa, and, indeed, Southern Rhodesia, that as far as we of Zambia are concerned, their struggle is not theirs alone; it is also ours. They can count on us.

NDABANINGI SITHOLE.   In fairness to Mr. Nkomo and other ZAPU leaders, I think it only right and proper that I make certain comments in their defense, not because I resent criticism but because I must put criticism to right; in other words, I reserve the right to criticize criticism.

It is important to note that of all the British colonial countries, Southern

Rhodesia was the only British colony that was allowed to have a police force of its own and an army of its own. This has complicated our situation in Southern Rhodesia. This, of course, is not an apology for lack of independence on our part in Southern Rhodesia, but it does demonstrate some of the complicating factors.

Secondly, there is the fact that we in Southern Rhodesia have not had the benefit of the Colonial Office, as other British colonies have had in the past. For instance, any time an African leader was thrust into jail, if he fell under the jurisdiction of the Colonial Office, the Colonial officer just came along and opened the door of the jail. But we operate under a different and more complicated situation in Southern Rhodesia.

The next thing I would like to point out is that in 1923 Southern Rhodesia was granted a representative government, so that the white settlers there had the opportunity of electing their own members of Parliament. This situation did not obtain anywhere in other colonies of Southern Africa or West Africa.

Further, in Southern Rhodesia today it is unrealistic to talk in terms of an acceptable white leader. It does not matter how liberal the white leader may be, the African people are determined that they shall rule themselves. This is why we do not subscribe to the doctrine of multiracialism, but, rather, to the doctrine of nonracialism.

Important also is the fact that there are more foreign investments in Southern Rhodesia than in other neighboring territories. The European is spread all over Southern Rhodesia. He controls the land and practically every sector of the economy. This has made the task of Joshua Nkomo more difficult than that of any of the other leaders in our neighboring territories. Nevertheless, the African people deeply feel that it is their duty to liberate themselves, and we believe that with the support of the independent African countries, with the support of the freedom-loving people of the world, independence is bound to come to Southern Rhodesia as it has elsewhere.

There is a growing impression among the people of the world that if an African leader goes to jail, independence automatically follows, but, of course, that is not true. We have only to look at history. In South Africa for the last fifty years the African political leaders have been going to jail, but independence has not come. On the other hand, no political leader in Tanganyika, as far as we know, went to jail, but independence did come.

The problem in Southern Rhodesia is one of African majority rule against white-settler minority rule. In 1919, the first African political organization to fight for the political rights of the African was formed. In 1923 came the referendum, which was conducted only among the 13,000 white settlers. The referendum resulted in a new constitution being given to Southern Rhodesia by the British Government.

Under this constitution, the British Government reserved for itself the right to veto or disallow any laws that would affect the African people adversely. As the whites grew in strength, they entrenched themselves, and in 1930 they divided Southern Rhodesia into African and European lands, although European land can really be found only in Europe. The African people were deeply dissatisfied with the political setup, and in 1956 the Youth League was started. In 1957, the Youth League merged with a branch of the African National Congress. In 1959, the government became scared, so scared that they used the police force and army to round up all leaders, not only in Southern Rhodesia, but in Northern Rhodesia and Nyasaland as well, and put them in jail. In 1960, the National Democratic Party was formed, and then in 1961 it was banned because it was getting popular and strong. In December of 1961, the Zimbabwe African People's Union was formed. Again, as it grew in strength and became popular with the people, the government was terrified, and in 1962 that party was banned. But now the people in Southern Rhodesia have decided that they are not going to form another party; they are going to operate underground. They are no longer prepared to fight within normal channels or by constitutional means, not because they want to create as much disorder as possible, but because the laws in the country make it almost impossible for them to function as a normal political party.

Our present problem is the new constitution, according to which there are 65 members of Parliament, 50 of them white and 15 African. In other words, the legislature is 77 per cent white and only 23 per cent African. More than 90,000 whites are voters, as compared with 10,000 Africans.

Now the Africans feel very strongly that the country is fundamentally an African country and that this constitution cannot be accepted since it does not represent the majority of the people. Mr. Winston Field, the Prime Minister of Southern Rhodesia, who was elected by less than 1 per cent of the population, now demands independence for Southern Rhodesia. The African people ask themselves: What does this actually mean, independence for Southern Rhodesia before the establishment of a fully representative government? The African people can interpret this as meaning only that the demand for independence for Southern Rhodesia under the present constitution is intended to disinherit the African people. In other words, the whites would like to create another South Africa. Britain created South Africa in 1910 when she granted independence to that country before the majority of the people had the vote, and now Britain is presented with a similar proposition. But if independence is granted to the white settlers in Southern Rhodesia or if the white settlers declare themselves independent, then Africans have no alternative but to declare themselves independent also. This, of course, is a very serious matter. It means going into a full-scale war because if we accept the position of an independent Southern Rhodesia and a white-settler minority government, then we have given up the noble and glorious task of getting independence for ourselves.

Now the battle in Southern Rhodesia is not necessarily one that belongs exclusively to the African people of Southern Rhodesia. It affects people of Africa, it affects people of the world, people in America, people in Europe, people in Asia, people everywhere, and this is why it is very important that as many countries as possible should try to bring the necessary pressure to bear on the British Government and on the situation in Southern Rhodesia.

We in Southern Rhodesia do not believe in racialism. We believe people are people. We are fighting for our birthright. Some people say that the white people introduced democracy to Africa. But this is not true. The real introduction of democracy will be the task and duty of the African people. You cannot introduce imperialism at one and the same time with democracy. You introduce either imperialism or democracy, and what we are fighting for in Southern Rhodesia is democracy.

Abraham Lincoln defined democracy as a government of the people, by the people, and for the people. But the type of democracy that was introduced in Southern Rhodesia was government of the Africans by the whites for the whites. Now, we would like to make it government of the Africans, by the Africans, for the Africans. And we believe that with the support of the people here and elsewhere and with the determination of our people back home, we shall be able to establish Zimbabwe, a true democracy under which people of all races may live happily.

EDDISON ZVOBGO. There are two points that I would add. One concerns the history of Southern Rhodesia and the other is of a general nature that will bring the picture up to date.

Southern Rhodesia's history should also be viewed as part of South African history. Southern Rhodesia was on the frontiers of the Boer trek from the south, and the kind of political climate and government that we have in Southern Rhodesia since the coming of the Europeans is largely attributable to that fact. Hence, our situation is very different from that of our two neighboring countries to the north because the majority of the original settlers in our country came from South Africa. We then are the white man's frontier on the south, and, in that sense the white man is really fighting his last battle against black nationalism from the north.

Ever since the victory of our Northern Rhodesian colleagues in getting assurance that Northern Rhodesia could secede from the Federation, a profound change has come over Southern Rhodesia; the impact it has had on the white settlers is tremendous. They have since closed the gaps in their ranks. There is no such thing in my mind now at all as a liberal, moderate European, if there ever was such a thing. And already there is the talk about a Southern Rhodesian front, a precipitation of another general election in order to eliminate once and for all such moderates as Sir Edgar Whitehead and any other Europeans who want to compromise with African nationalism.

On the other hand, the Africans in Southern Rhodesia have, since Northern Rhodesia achieved its victory, closed their ranks, too. If historians such as Professor Franck could speak with certainty of African nationalism in Southern Rhodesia as being moderate as of last year, at the present moment it could not be described as moderate at all: Now dislike and hate are complete on both sides. The African nationalist no longer distrusts the white; he hates him, and so the Europeans realize just what can happen.

V

The Portuguese Territories

Nationalist Organizations in Angola:
Status of the Revolt *

GEORGE M. HOUSER

African organizations in Angola go back at least to 1923. The earliest known organization is the Liga Africana. This organization was, of course, government-approved; it remains today the only legal, secular, African organization permitted in Angola. Its aims were described at the Third Pan-African Conference held in Lisbon in 1923: "The Liga Africana has a commission for all the other native organizations and knows how to express to the government in no ambiguous terms, but in a dignified manner, all that should be said to avoid injustice or to bring about the repeal of harsh laws. That is why the Liga Africana of Lisbon is the director of the Portuguese African movement, but only in the good sense of the word, without making any appeal to violence and without leaving constitutional limits." [1]

In 1929, the Liga Nacional Africana (LNA) was founded in Luanda. The essential objective of the LNA was to secure better economic and social conditions through legal pressures. A similar group called the African Guild, later called Associação Regional dos Naturais de Angola, was established with a similar objective. For the next decade or so these organizations gave some outlet to the protests of Africans. But in the 1940's there were demands within the LNA to transform the organization into a mass movement. A clash of interests caused an internal crisis within the ranks of the leaders of the LNA. The Portuguese took advantage of this internal crisis by placing secret agents in the association and in the end were able to dominate the organization through people chosen by the Governor-General.

Another attempt at a legal organization of Angolans was the Associação Africana do Sul de Angola established by railway workers

* This paper was revised and updated by the author as of April, 1965.

[1] Thomas Okuma, *Angola in Ferment* (Boston, 1961), pp. 62–63; and *Angola: A Symposium, Views of a Revolt* (London, 1962), p. 106.

in Nova Lisboa. This organization was not long in existence before
the authorities interfered with it and killed it.[2] The first attempt at
a revolutionary political party was the Partido de Luta Unida dos
Africanos da Angola (PLUA).[3] This movement was a direct precursor
of one of the major nationalist political organizations in Angola today
—the Movimento Popular de Libertação de Angola (MPLA).

A legal organization in Angola is one that has registered with and
been certified by the Governor-General's office. The government
must know its officers, purposes, and where it hopes to function. If
it is political, it will not be certified, for only one party, the União
Nacional, is allowed to operate. This alone makes a farce of elections,
even though all "civilized" Angolans are granted the vote. Any political opposition is illegal, and must therefore operate secretly. Commenting on this, the U.N. Subcommittee on the Situation in Angola
said in 1961: "By prohibiting political activities and trade-union organizations, the Portuguese authorities were able to keep Angola out
of the world press, and to claim that the silence was proof of peace
and harmony in Angola." [4] This famous "silence" over Angola, however, had been broken a number of times before the 1961 events. In
1952, more than 500 Angolans addressed a petition to the U.N. protesting the injustices to indigenous peoples by the authorities and
asking the United Nations to help bring Portuguese rule in Angola
to an end.[5]

In 1957, the Policia Internacional para a Defesa do Estado (PIDE)
arrested four Africans for acts against the "security of the State." In
March, 1959, the PIDE arrested twenty-eight Africans. Among them
were two mechanics, twelve civil-service employees, eight nurses, a
clerk, a teacher, a student, a printer, a Catholic priest, and a writer.
Twelve others were named but not arrested as they were not in
Portuguese territory at the time.

In July, 1960, when Dr. Agostinho Neto was arrested, the people
of his village of Catete, near Luanda, marched in protest to the
headquarters of the administrator. A military police unit was dispatched to Catete and, in the clash between the police and the villagers, thirty-eight persons were killed.[6]

Events beginning in January, 1961, transformed the objective situ-

[2] *Angola: A Symposium, Views of a Revolt*, p. 107.
[3] *Ibid.*, p. 108.
[4] United Nations, *Report of the Subcommittee on the Situation in Angola*,
S/4993 (November 22, 1961), p. 122.
[5] *Ibid.*, p. 122.
[6] Okuma, *op. cit.*, p. 1.

ation in Angola. The "kingdom of silence" was at an end. The capture of the Portuguese luxury liner the *Santa Maria* by Captain Henrique Galvão attracted the attention of the world as reporters made their way to Luanda to await the arrival of Galvão. Never had there been so many international correspondents in Angola at the same time. The attack by Angolan nationalists on the Luanda prison with the objective of freeing the political prisoners shattered the conspiracy of silence in Angola. The indiscriminate reprisals by the Portuguese citizens against Africans in Luanda shocked most of the sixty visiting journalists and, through them, the rest of the world.

A Security Council meeting was called for March 15, 1961, at United Nations headquarters in New York. This day was marked not only by the beginning of an important debate in the international organization, but also by the beginning of the armed revolt. Thus, on one day, Angola suffered two shocks—one from abroad, the other internal. Subsequent events must be seen in the light of the beginning of the war of liberation.

We shall consider here only six organizations. Three of these groups, although in favor of eventual independence for Angola, are opposed to the present revolt and seem to have, on one level or another, some kind of cooperative arrangement with the Portuguese authorities. They are: the Movement for the Defense of Angolan Interests (MDIA), Ntobako, and Ngwizako-Ngwizani a Kongo (Ngwizako). The other three groups are not only committed to the struggle for independence, but accept the necessity of violence and warfare in order to accomplish this end. Two of them, the União das Populacões de Angola (UPA) and the Democratic Party of Angola (PDA), are now joined in the Angolan National Liberation Front (FNLA).

Movement for the Defense of Angolan Interests

The MDIA was founded early in 1961. Most of its leadership had previously been affiliated with the UPA. They broke away from the UPA not only because they had differences with some of the leadership, but because they disagreed with UPA policy in resisting the Portuguese through armed revolt.

The young men who founded the MDIA come mostly from the Bazombo, a large tribe of merchants and farmers of northern Angola. After breaking with the UPA, they reportedly held discussions with the leadership of the Zombo Peoples Alliance (ALIAZO, which later became the PDA), but apparently were not satisfied with positions that might have been offered to them in ALIAZO, and so decided to form their own group.[7] In 1963, however, the MDIA reportedly split into two wings: one, led by Augustin Kaziduki, joined the PDA; the other retained its independent position under Jean-Pierre Bala. As with many other political organizations, it is difficult to get reliable figures on the exact membership or size of the MDIA following. In his testimony of August, 1962, in Léopoldville before the U.N. Special Committee on Territories Under Portuguese Administration, Jean-Pierre Bala, Secretary-General of the MDIA, claimed 32,500 card-carrying members. But in his testimony before the Fourth (Trusteeship) Committee of the U.N. in late November, 1962, Mr. Bala said that the last membership card issued in the Congo bore the number 75,631. In addition, he claimed that his movement had the support of thousands of Angolans living in the territory, as well as of some 200,000 members of an Angolan religious sect.[8]

According to the two testimonies of Mr. Bala before the United Nations, the MDIA, faced with a choice between war or negotiation with Portugal, decided to make contact with the Portuguese Government. The party is committed to a nonviolent course of action.

There seems little doubt that the MDIA is maintaining some kind of relationship with the Portuguese and probably is receiving financial assistance from them, not only in the form of scholarships, but also to cover travel expenses of the delegations visiting Lisbon and Luanda.[9]

Ntobako

In 1961, the Portuguese Minister for Overseas Provinces is reported to have said that Ngwizako, MDIA, and Ntobako were the "only valid representatives of the Angolan people."[10] It would seem apparent from the record that even of these three organizations, the Portuguese would have greatest faith in the "reliability" of Ntobako.

[7] *Angola: A Symposium, Views of a Revolt*, p. 122.

[8] It should be noted that objective sources for actual membership in the various Angolan organizations are impossible to find. Official membership figures, in any event, are not as important as the mass following the organizations have. The effectiveness of the organizations cannot be judged by membership figures, but by actual programs being carried on.

[9] United Nations, *Report of the Special Committee on Territories Under Portuguese Administration*, August 15, 1962, p. 96: "During its visit to Léopoldville, the Committee heard the representative of the MDIA and from his statement in replies to questions is convinced that the MDIA is being used by the Portuguese Government solely for the purpose of being able to claim that it had the cooperation of some Angolan group."

[10] *Courrier d'Afrique* (Léopoldville), October 20, 1961.

According to the chairman of the organization, Mr. Angelhino Alberto, speaking before the Fourth Committee of the United Nations on December 4, 1962, Ntobako was founded in Léopoldville on December 8, 1960. In this same presentation, Mr. Alberto claimed that Ntobako had the phenomenal membership of 900,000. Its following comes from the Bakongo area of northern Angola.

Ntobako is opposed to a precipitate independence that would make Angola dependent on assistance either from Portugal or from other nations. The party wants independence, according to Alberto, alongside Portugal, within a multiracial society similar to that of Brazil. No target date for independence is given. There is only the expressed belief that in cooperating with the Portuguese authorities, progress will be made toward independence. In his statement before the United Nations, the closest Mr. Alberto came to criticizing Portugal was to say that he had seen, on his various trips to Angola, "that there was room for improvement in certain respects, for example, with regard to wages, medical care, education, and political freedom." He had found that the claims of the Portuguese Government were considerably nearer the truth than the allegations of Portugal's enemies.

When Alberto visited the United States in early 1962, the trip was arranged by the Portuguese-American Committee on Foreign Affairs, an organization registered as a foreign agent with the Department of Justice. Photographs released to the press at the time of this visit showed Alberto speaking to Angolan villagers and surrounded by Portuguese officers.[11] Later that year, it was reported that when Alberto left Léopoldville for Luanda, the Portuguese Ambassador to the Congo was at the airport to see him off.[12] In June, 1963, Ntobako was reported to have joined the MPLA's hurriedly formed Democratic Front for the Liberation of Angola. It is not known how far this alliance extended, though it is suspected that it was of a temporary nature, designed to catch the eye of a visiting OAU commission.

Ngwizako-Ngwizani a Kongo

Ngwizako was formed as a political party in February, 1960, in Léopoldville. Like Ntobako, it also finds its supporters among the Bakongo people of northern Angola. It is "spiritually" based in the area of São Salvador in Angola, and has had as its basic aim the reconstitution of the ancient Kingdom of the Kongo, which historically

[11] *Christian Science Monitor*, February 10, 1962, p. 10.
[12] *Courrier d'Afrique*, October 24, 1962.

was centered in São Salvador and included in its domain the Bakongo people in the former Belgian and French Congo as well as in Angola.

"Ngwizako is advocating," reads a petition to the U.N. Committee on Decolonization, "that a large portion of the Conventional Basin of the Congo which was annexed by Portugal to Angola in violation of Article 39 of the General Act of Berlin should regain freedom and sovereignty above all as a Monarchy. This Monarchy of Musikongo has nothing in common with monarchies in Europe or elsewhere. To us, it will always be the property of twelve free and sovereign clans of the Kongo." [13] The King referred to is "H.M. Pedro VIII, enthroned at San Salvador du Kongo on 9 September 1962, with the full agreement and cooperation of the Portuguese Government." [14]

Thus Ngwizako favors independence for Angola as a whole only because there is no other way to restore the old Kongo. The party is not involved in the current struggle. It speaks of using only "lawful means" to achieve its purpose. The chances of the party's achieving its ambitions are not great; yet one would do well to keep it in mind when independence for Angola approaches, for it would act as a disruptive element in the new country. As with the case of Ntobako, Ngwizako was reported to have joined a front organized by MPLA in June, 1963.

Democratic Party of Angola

The name Democratic Party of Angola was not adopted until late 1961. Originally this group, based in the area of the town of Maquela do Zombo near the Congo border of northern Angola, was a mutual-aid association of the Zombo people and was called Assomizo. It was established as a political organization under the name ALIAZO (the Zombo Peoples Alliance) in 1960, with headquarters in Léopoldville. The Zombos number about 750,000.

Before the revolt, ALIAZO was committed to passive resistance to Portuguese rule. When violence came, the outlook changed radically. As André Massaki, President of ALIAZO, explained: "In our region, where there had been no violence whatsoever, the Portuguese came and took all the educated people, especially the chiefs. Later they came back to some of our villages with trucks, and dumped out the clothing of the men who had been taken. Our people assumed they were killed—we have never heard from them again, and it was

[13] United Nations, *Special Committee on the Situation with Regard to the Implementation of the Declaration on the Granting of Independence to Colonial Countries and Peoples*, A/AC.109/Pet. 58 (March 8, 1963).
[14] *Ibid.*

then that some ALIAZO supporters began taking rifles and machetes and resisting the Portuguese military power." [15]

When Emmanuel Kunzika, Vice-President of ALIAZO, came to petition at the United Nations in November, 1961, the group already spoke for Angola as a whole, rather than merely for the Zombo people. He "threw an SOS to the United Nations . . . to disarm Portugal" and requested two U.N. commissions to penetrate Angola, one to ascertain facts and the other to establish the mechanisms for holding a general election.[16]

By late that year, ALIAZO had decided to drop its name, with its tribal connotations, and to adopt the name Democratic Party of Angola. In April, 1962, PDA joined in a united front with the UPA. The organization continues to maintain separate offices, except for those of its officers serving in the Angolan National Liberation Front (FNLA). In October, 1964, the youth wing of the PDA was reported to have rebelled against the alliance with Roberto, but the adults were able to beat back the rebellion for, as of April, 1965, Emmanuel Kunzika remained a member of the Front.

Movimento Popular de Libertação de Angola

The MPLA was founded at a clandestine conference of small, secret organizations held in Luanda in December, 1956. The objective was to form one large united popular liberation movement. The first manifesto of the MPLA, dating from this conference, briefly analyzed capitalist and imperialist domination of the African people, the essential aspects of Portuguese colonial domination in the political, economic, social, and cultural spheres, and denounced the attempted genocide of the Angolan people and the forced labor system. It also called on the Angolan people to join the struggle for the liquidation of Portuguese colonialism and warned that the struggle would not be successful "unless there is a united front of all Angolan anti-imperialist forces, without taking into account the social situation of individuals, their religious beliefs, or their philosophical tendencies, unless the broadest-based popular liberation movement of Angola is formed." From its very beginnings, the MPLA, then, has advocated the formation of a united front of all possible opponents of the Portuguese regime. In 1958, a group called the Movement for the National Independence of Angola (MINA) was formed; it later joined the MPLA.

[15] *The Guardian* (Manchester), September 20, 1961, p. 2.
[16] *Pétition pour l'Angola, presentée à la 16e Assemblée Générale des Nations-Unies à New York* (Léopoldville; undated document of ALIAZO).

The MPLA existed secretly inside Angola until early 1959. But on Easter Sunday, March 29, 1959, the PIDE began a concerted roundup of all those suspected of activities against the Portuguese regime. Nationalist leaders, many of whom were in the MPLA, were arrested and imprisoned. It was shortly after this that the MPLA decided to establish headquarters outside Angola. An office was opened in Conakrý with the approval of the Sékou Touré government. Guinea was far from Angola, however, and on October 30, 1961, the MPLA moved its headquarters to Léopoldville. MPLA membership was reported to be 34,800 in November, 1961. In his statement before the Special Committee on Territories Under Portuguese Administration on August 9, 1962, Mario de Andrade, then president of the MPLA, said there were 50,000 card-carrying active members and several thousand other active members who, for obvious reasons connected with the nature of clandestine political work, did not have cards.

One of the early MPLA pronouncements was the declaration to the Government of Portugal on June 13, 1960, signed by Viriato Cruz, then secretary-general of the party, and Mario de Andrade, then the president. In this declaration, the MPLA demanded: (1) the immediate recognition of the right of the Angolan people to self-determination; (2) complete and unconditional amnesty for and immediate liberation of all political prisoners; (3) permission to form political parties and guarantees of civil liberties; (4) the immediate withdrawal of Portuguese forces and liquidation of military bases on Angolan soil; and (5) convocation by the end of 1960 of a round table with representatives from all Angolan political parties and representatives of the Portuguese Government with a view to finding a peaceful solution to the colonial problem in Angola. The declaration affirmed the desire of the MPLA to liquidate colonial domination through negotiation. More than two years later, at its First National Conference, held in Léopoldville on December 1–3, 1962, the MPLA reaffirmed its willingness to negotiate with the Portuguese, provided certain minimum conditions were met.

The 1960 appeal to Salazar was answered by the assignment of fresh contingents of Portuguese troops to Angola. In November of that year, twenty-eight nationalists from Cabinda were shot in Luanda prison. The rumblings of revolt had started. Then came the *Santa Maria* incident, early in January, 1961, and, on February 4, the storming of the Luanda prison, the broadcasting station, and the army barracks. The next day, it is estimated, some 3,000 Africans were killed in reprisal, although the battle continued for two more days.[17]

[17] *Angola: A Symposium, Views of a Revolt,* p. 111.

The MPLA is generally thought to have organized this rebellion. And it is logical to accept this claim, for the MPLA had always been strongest in Luanda. In fact, this identification of the MPLA with the urban-dwelling, so-called assimilated Angolans was one of the problems that the 1962 Conference had to face. The MPLA, finding itself with men, some arms, and leadership, but with no apparent fighting front (MPLA strongholds such as Luanda, Cuenza Norte, and Melange are too deep in Angola for access from the Congo), was forced to re-examine its basic structure and position.

The December, 1962, Conference recognized fresh tendencies in the party: The most important was the "primacy of the interior over the exterior," growing out of the realization that there was too little contact between the party and the peasant masses. This position in turn entailed some major revisions in the MPLA program. The first was to emphasize African neutralism and minimize the ties to the East. The second was to cleanse the image of the party as one primarily of the "intellectual *assimilado*" (which, in effect, meant the so-called mulatto) by shaking up its personnel. Dr. Agostinho Neto, an African and a physician and poet with a history of arrests and imprisonments for nationalist activities, became president, and Mario de Andrade secretary for foreign affairs. Viriato Cruz resigned.[18] To strengthen organization, the MPLA emphasized a democratic centralism in all party matters.

Mario de Andrade, the other important MPLA figure, is also a poet. Somewhat younger than Neto (he was born in 1928, Neto in 1922), he is also more outspoken. De Andrade studied philosophy at Lisbon University and social science at the Sorbonne. He was active in a group of intellectuals centered around the magazine *Présence Africaine*, and was one of the organizers of the Conference of Negro Writers in Rome in 1958.

Soon after the return of Dr. Neto to the movement, Andrade actually withdrew from active participation in MPLA affairs. It was not until August, 1964, after Viriato Cruz had left the MPLA altogether, that Andrade returned.

It should be noted here that, superficially, Angolan nationalist movements are characterized by frequent splits as well as tendencies to form paper alliances. The MPLA has not been immune to such tendencies. Shortly before an OAU commission was to visit Léopoldville in order to decide which of the two main groups—UPA or MPLA—was to receive aid, the MPLA announced the formation of a Democratic Front for the Liberation of Angola. Ngwizako and

[18] See Ronald Segal, *Political Africa* (London and New York, 1961), for profiles of Neto and Cruz.

Ntobako were reportedly in the Front. Only one other public mention of this front has been made since then. The OAU, however, appeared not to have been impressed by this new grouping, for it was the UPA's own front which received official blessings. Shortly thereafter, the Congo Government closed down the MPLA office in Léopoldville. The organization's headquarters were thus transferred across the river to Brazzaville. In the latter part of 1964, the MPLA commenced military operations against the Portuguese in Cabinda.

The OAU commission visit had another effect on the fortunes of the MPLA: Viriato Cruz, usually considered to be on good terms with the Chinese Communists, left the movement and applied for admission into the UPA Front. Having waited some six months, Cruz was finally admitted in April, 1964.

Just as the MPLA has attempted to establish a united front of Angolan groups, so it has played a crucial role in establishing coordinating bodies of nationalist groups from various Portuguese colonies. In January, 1960, at the Second All-African People's Conference held in Tunis, De Andrade and Cruz initiated the organization FRAIN (Frente Revolucionaria Africana para a Independencia des Colônies Portugueses). Groups representing two other Portuguese territories (Guinea and Goa) joined the MPLA in this international front. The organization lasted for little over a year. About a month after the beginning of the revolt in Angola, a conference was held in Casablanca (April 18-20, 1961), and the CONCP (the Conference of the Nationalist Organizations of Portuguese Colonies) was born. Mario de Andrade was elected chairman. Fourteen delegates were present from ten organizations representing all the Portuguese colonies with the exception of Macao and Timor. A permanent secretariat was established in Rabat, where it carried on its work with the blessings of King Hassan II of Morocco. Marcelino dos Santos of Mozambique, the secretary-general of the CONCP, said the purpose of the organization was to proclaim "unity of action of the nationalist organizations in the all-out struggle for the immediate abolition of Portuguese colonialism and for freedom from all forms of oppression." [19] The organizations making up the CONCP are agreed upon the necessity of taking direct action.

Since Algeria gained independence, most nationalist groups, expecting violence to play a role in their struggle for independence, have made urgent overtures to the North African republic. Mario de

[19] This statement was made in testimony before the U.N. Special Committee on Territories Under Portuguese Administration on August 9, 1962.

Andrade was in Algeria to welcome Ben Bella back after his release from a French prison. The Algerian Premier has been most friendly toward the MPLA representatives. On February 3, 1963, he attended the ceremonies marking the opening of the MPLA office in Algeria. The MPLA has had offers of military equipment from Algeria. Furthermore, Ben Bella has offered to make volunteers available to the MPLA forces, and this offer has been specifically accepted by Dr. Neto.

A significant new development took place in early March, 1963. A new coalition called the Patriotic Front of National Liberation with headquarters in Algiers was announced. Under the nominal leadership of General Umberto Delgado, it is a coalition front of anti-Salazar Portuguese political exiles representing monarchist, republican, Roman Catholic, socialist, and Communist factions.[20] The discussions leading to the formation of this new group took place secretly in Paris in December, 1963. The official formation of this new front made quite clear what was understood to have been an MPLA policy for many years—namely, sympathetic ties with the Portuguese anti-Salazar elements. At its annual conference in December, the MPLA specifically encouraged the Portuguese democratic opposition in its efforts to overthrow Salazar. The basis for this front was established when General Delgado officially recognized the right of self-determination for the Portuguese territories. In September, 1962, Dr. Neto wrote to General Delgado to say that this recognition "makes it possible at this moment for us to consider the Portuguese opposition members as allies in the war against the fascist government of Salazar." [21] In 1964, however, the Front was reported to have split into pro- and anti-Delgado factions.

União das Populacões de Angola

The UPA was formed in 1954 as an organization of the Bakongo people. Its original name was the Union of the People of Northern Angola (UPONA). Its tribal base and its essential purpose were the same as those of Ngwizako at that time. UPONA and Ngwizako probably split over the question of who should be chosen King of the Kongo.[22] The early leaders of UPONA were Eduardo Pinock and Manuel Barros Necaca, Holden Roberto's uncle. A communication to the United Nations dated June, 1957, stressed that "this peti-

[20] *Christian Science Monitor*, March 4, 1963.
[21] *Ibid.*
[22] *Courrier d'Afrique*, October 18, 1961.

tion is not introduced by the country called Angola, but rather by the Kongo, which is an ex-independent territory with no treaty with Portugal."

In various communications and letters received by the American Committee on Africa from UPONA leaders, the position of the organization at this period of its development was made quite clear: The Ancient Kingdom of the Kongo was not conquered by the Portuguese. But, in 1884, by a bit of trickery, the King of the Kongo signed a note to the King of Portugal, under the impression that he was signing an expression of gratitude for gifts that the Portuguese King had sent him; if he had not been illiterate, he would have known that what he was signing was a missive in which he declared his fealty, loyalty, and submission to the King of Portugal. The Kongo territory, therefore, has a different status from the rest of Angola, which was conquered by the Portuguese, and it should be given its independence.

The development that was to make UPONA into a truly nationalist organization began early in 1958. In a letter to the American Committee on Africa dated February 9, 1958, a leader of UPONA said:

> It is of course very difficult to think of a restoration of the Ancient Kingdom of the Kongo, since Africa is not independent yet. For the time being, the thing which matters the most to us is the changing of the conditions now prevailing in Angola. The question of the restoration of the Ancient Kingdom of the Kongo will be considered later when better circumstances will allow it. We have been working for quite a long time with some leaders living in Luanda, because our objectives are in principle the same, and our delegation will represent the whole of Angola.

Shortly after this, the leadership of UPONA decided that one of their number should leave Léopoldville, where UPONA was organized but where it was impossible to take any action publicly, and go to an independent area of Africa in order to make contact with nationalist movements throughout the continent. Holden Roberto was chosen for this task, and by a very difficult overland trip, without any documents, he traveled up the west coast of Africa, finally arriving in Accra in October, 1958. In the next few months, Roberto became acquainted with key nationalist figures in Ghana, such as George Padmore and Kwame Nkrumah, and attended the First All-African People's Conference in December of that year. Largely because of Roberto's influence, UPONA became the Union of the People of Angola. A tribal group had been transformed, in intention at least, into a modern nationalist movement. Today, the UPA claims to have

40,000 registered members, in addition to more than half a million sympathizers.[23]

The statutes of the UPA outline the objectives of the organization. The motto of the party is: "For the national, territorial, and social liberation of Angola." The party is defined as "a political organization formed for all Africans, natives of Angola, without discrimination as to sex, religion, age, ethnic origin, or domicile." The main objectives of the organization are to obtain the territorial liberation of Angola, to promote understanding and unity among all Angolans, and to fight in conjunction with all Angolan nationalist organizations in a popular union for the liquidation in Angola of the Portuguese colonial regime.

The UPA is undeniably the backbone of the revolt against the Portuguese at the present time. It is not quite clear whether the events of March 15, 1961, were entirely planned by the UPA; no doubt the revolt spread spontaneously once the UPA-initiated strike of contract laborers on a Portuguese coffee plantation had started. A number of eyewitnesses from abroad (Gavin Young of the London *Observer*, Robert Young and Charles Dorkins of NBC, Professor John Marcum, and the writer) have traveled into rebel-held territory in northern Angola. They have all testified to the presence of several thousand UPA guerrillas operating in a territory not under Portuguese control. The UPA has its own trade-union affiliate, the LGTA, a women's organization, a youth organization (JUPA), and a medical organization to aid refugees (SARA).

The UPA has done a minimum in blueprinting the society of the future that it would establish. A suggested program was published in 1960 as part of the declaration of the steering committee of the organization. The document is a call to the peasants, the unemployed and the forced laborers, the women, the tribal chiefs, the youth, and the Portuguese to join in establishing a democratic regime. It contains an implied threat to the chiefs and the Portuguese colonists that they especially must join in the movement for independence, or risk having no place in the future free Angola. Both in this statement and in subsequent addresses by Holden Roberto, emphasis has been placed upon land reform. Roberto has commented: "Ownership of land is inherent in the Angolan way of life. Our people are sons of the soil for whom their land is a cherished possession. It is the deprivation of land among other things which has led to the sorry and poverty-stricken conditions of most Angolans." [24] Roberto added that if the Portuguese settlers resist to the end the independence of An-

[23] Press conference held by Holden Roberto in New York on March 15, 1961.
[24] From a speech delivered by Roberto in Washington, D.C., on December 12, 1961.

gola, then their land will be taken away from them and redistributed. If, however, independence comes through negotiation, the settlers will be accepted as citizens with the same rights as any Angolan. There is no indication as to how the land and agricultural reform will be implemented, other than that this will be the basis for a complete reformation of the economy of the country.

The UPA is the senior partner in a coalition with the PDA; together they form the Angolan National Liberation Front (FNLA) and the Provisional Government of the Republic of Angola (GRAE) in exile. The establishment of the GRAE was officially announced on March 27, 1962. The Prime Minister, Holden Roberto, was born in São Salvador in 1923. He received his primary education in Angolan missionary schools, and his secondary education in Léopoldville.[25] The Vice-Premier is Emmanuel Kunzika of the PDA. Although each party still maintains its own separate identity, all public statements are issued in the name of the FNLA or the Provisional Government. The Army of National Liberation (ALNA), of which Roberto is commander in chief, is the military arm of the FNLA and the Provisional Government. The General League of Angolan Workers (LGTA) is closely identified with the FNLA, The LGTA claims a membership of more than 8,000, 4,000 of whom are inside Angola in liberated portions of the country and in the ranks of the National Liberation Army.

Neither the UPA nor the FNLA has joined a coalition of nationalist organizations from other Portuguese territories. However, Roberto attended the first two All-African People's Conferences. In January, 1960, at the conference in Tunis, he was elected to the Executive Committee. Since he first left Léopoldville in 1958, and especially since the independence of the Congo made it possible for the UPA to operate openly and publicly, Roberto has traveled widely throughout Africa, Western Europe, and the United States. He also attended the Belgrade Conference of Nonaligned States in September, 1961. Although some Portuguese propaganda has described Roberto as "Communist-trained," he has never traveled to the Communist countries, except Yugoslavia. And while he has traveled several times to the United States, primarily for appearances at the United Nations, it would be as incorrect to call him a "stooge of the West" as to call him a Communist. He has said: "Our party is attempting to accomplish its aim without dependence on the ideologies of any outside groups. We are a nationalist party and we have a nationalist policy."

[25] See Segal, *op. cit.*, for profile of Roberto.

He has been especially critical of the United States because of its ties with Portugal and has called explicitly upon the United States and other countries "to abstain from giving any material assistance, including arms, to the Portuguese, who use these very arms to destroy the lives and liberty of Angolans." [26]

Although a large number of African states have given positive aid and assistance to the UPA and the FNLA, principal international support has come from Tunisia, the FLN in Algeria, and the Government of the Republic of the Congo. Algeria has helped most materially. Not only has a significant amount of military equipment been supplied, but Angolan guerrillas have been trained by FLN military personnel. On January 17, 1963, Premier Ben Bella said that the Algerian Government had put sixteen Algerian officers at the disposal of the FNLA to train Angolans.

Since the UPA and the FNLA are based on Congolese soil (the FNLA has offices in Tunis, Algiers, and New York), it is absolutely essential for good relations to be maintained with the Republic of the Congo. Relations with Kasavubu became strained following the independence of the Congo because the UPA no longer accepted the concept of a Bakongo state. Occasionally even now, there is a problem between the police of Léopoldville province and the Angolans who go back and forth from the capital city of Léopoldville to the Angolan border. But with the coming to power of Adoula in August, 1961, a solid relationship was established between the UPA and the Congolese Government. Adoula was most cooperative in permitting the UPA to operate widely in the Congo and even to establish several military bases.

Adoula's resignation and Tshombe's accession to power have not yet materially affected the fortunes of Roberto's organization. The Kinkuzu military base near Thysville remains in operation, and guerrilla raids continue to be made into Angola.

It should be noted that a meeting of foreign ministers of the Organization of African Unity in Dakar in August, 1963, recognized Roberto's group as the one to receive official OAU aid. The initials UPA have been used less frequently in public since that time. Roberto is now usually identified as Premier in the GRAE.

In spite of these signs of external support, the GRAE has suffered at least one severe internal shock. Roberto's decision to take Viriato Cruz into his Front precipitated a break between himself and his Foreign Minister, Jonas Savimbi, a young southerner. Savimbi an-

[26] From a speech delivered by Roberto in Washington, D.C., on December 12, 1961.

nounced his resignation from the Front at the Cairo OAU conference in July, 1964. He was soon followed by refugee clinic director Dr. José Liahuca.

The UPA is subject to three recurrent criticisms. The first—an especially popular one with the Portuguese—is that the movement is Communist or Communist-inspired. Two items are usually produced to sustain this argument: a forged document in Roberto's name to the effect that he intends to rule Southern Africa while Sékou Touré and Kwame Nkrumah share West Africa, and the contention that all anticolonialist movements are *ipso facto* Communist.

The second charge is that the UPA is a closed tribal and racial organization. It is true that the UPA has its principal strength in the north, but it has attracted among its militants and followers as well as its leaders, a goodly number from all parts of Angola. The commander of its armed forces inside Angola, João Baptista, killed in February, 1962, was from the south. Its present commander, José Kalundungo, is likewise from the south; its vice-president, Rosario Neto, is from the Kumbundu area. Among those in training at the military center in the Congo are even a number of pygmies.

Yet the defection of Savimbi and some other southerners will make it more difficult in the future for Roberto to disclaim the accusations of being based principally in the north. Parenthetically, it should be remembered that the GRAE recruits most of its fighters among the Bakongo refugees. Although some refugees from the south have trickled into Katanga, obvious strategic considerations have prevented the opening of a guerrilla offensive in that region.

To the charge of racism, Roberto has said: "We do not say to the Portuguese colonialist, 'You are a foreigner: go away!' We do not say to him, 'We are going to take over the running of the country and make you pay for your crime and those of your ancestors.' We do not want to supplant a hatred for the black with a new hatred for the white. We say to him, 'We are Angolans; banish from our lands all racism, all forms of oppression, of injustice, all attempts to keep our people in ignorance, and let us work together for the flowering of mankind and the enrichment of humanity.' " [27]

The third frequent criticism is that the UPA is terroristic. It is true that atrocities have been committed in the fighting—but they have been committed on both sides. The Portuguese, with their superiority in weapons and armed men, have far outstripped the Angolans in mass killings and cruelty. The UPA earned its reputation for atrocities largely on the morning of March 15, 1961, when ma-

[27] Press conference held by Roberto in New York on March 15, 1961.

chetes, spears, and crude homemade weapons (the only implements available) were used against the Portuguese. Once modern weapons started coming in, fighting was carried out in its more conventional form—with bullets and grenades. The charge of terrorism is now largely a semantic one. The Portuguese refuse to recognize the rebellion as such; they maintain the fiction that it remains an act of individual terrorists and gangsters.

Problems of Unity

Both the UPA and the MPLA have committed themselves to the ideal of a unified front, though the MPLA has been the more emphatic of the two.

"Our basic principle," said Mario de Andrade, "is the unity of the nationalist forces within the country, and of all the forces fighting Portuguese colonialism." [28] The MPLA sees unity being established through a front composed not only of the various political parties, but of the trade unions, youth organizations, women's organizations, and military organizations. According to the MPLA plan, the executive committee of the front would be elected by the national conference, composed of delegates, three from each cooperating organization, accredited by the supreme organ of each of the political parties and organizations participating.[29]

The UPA's reaction to these overtures has not been enthusiastic. "The men of the MPLA are talkers," said Roberto recently. "It's not by 'philosophizing' that one can triumph over barbaric colonialism. . . . That's why the FNLA talks less but acts more." [30] The UPA takes the view that a national front—the FNLA—has already been created and that the MPLA can join it at any moment it wishes to do so. The MPLA maintains that the front should be all-inclusive. "The Angolan youth, and the Angolan people as a whole," reads a slogan in the UPA *Juventude Revolucionaria*, "demands the unity of all true patriots around the FNLA. Concrete unity, not abstract." [31] In the end, then, the UPA *will* accept a front only on the condition of pure and simple integration into the FNLA.

The first unity attempt was made in November, 1960, before the

[28] From a petition presented to the U.N. Special Committee on Territories Under Portuguese Administration (Léopoldville, August 9, 1962).

[29] Statement to the press by Dr. Eduardo dos Santos, member of the MPLA Executive Committee, in Léopoldville on April 5, 1962.

[30] Aimé Diakanua, "*Rencontre avec Holden Roberto*," in the Léopoldville daily, *Actualités Africaines*. (Reprinted in *Angola: Information Bulletin* [Léopoldville], March 10, 1963.)

[31] *Juventude Revolucionaria* (Léopoldville), March 15, 1963.

revolt, and it almost succeeded. Representatives of the UPA (Roberto was out of the country at the time), ALIAZO, MPLA, and the Movement for the Liberation of the Cabinda Enclave (MLEC) met in Léopoldville. An agreement was reached for the creation of a front, and a drafting committee was organized, composed of MPLA, UPA, and ALIAZO membership. UPA left the front in December, shortly after Roberto's return, and the front was dissolved by February, 1961. Another attempt was made in April, 1961, when delegations of the MPLA, UPA, ALIAZO, and MLEC met again. A conference was planned for Monrovia in May to proceed with further plans. But these discussions in Liberia came to naught.

In August, 1962, at the time of Dr. Neto's return to Léopoldville from his years of confinement, another attempt was made to enter into discussions with the FNLA. Dr. Neto made the following unity proposal:

1. The fusion of our movements in order to form a unique movement. This fusion would be done rapidly although passing through conventional stages.
2. Close collaboration of our movements in their politico-military action, through the means of a common structure.
3. Following the advice of His Excellency, Osagyefo K. Nkrumah, the direction of the armed forces of our movements by a united command, supervised by a national council.[32]

Talks between representatives of the two groups were held in early August; those between Agostinho Neto and Holden Roberto, scheduled for August 12, were never held, however.

The UPA has criticized the MPLA for claims of carrying on an armed struggle against the Portuguese when there has been no evidence to this effect. At a joint press conference held early in the summer of 1961, Roberto and Commander João Baptista, chief of operations of the National Liberation Army, said: "We deplore the fact that certain groups are giving themselves the credit for the direction of the armed struggle and are thus sowing the seeds of confusion in public opinion when the National Liberation Army . . . is the only nationalist force which is carrying out military operations against Portuguese colonialism." In a speech before the Central African Students Association Conference on December 30, 1962, Roberto stated:

[32] Statement to the press by Dr. Neto in Léopoldville on August 10, 1962.

Certain African brothers allow themselves to be dangerously seduced by the rank verbiage of a kind of anticolonialist in lounging robes, the kind who makes his appearance in a capital often far from his native land, and puts forth beautiful anticolonialist theories, inspired by ideas which are completely un-African, the kind who calls himself progressive, and proclaims himself the great revolutionary, but never takes off his lounging slippers.

Adding to the distrust between the two major groups and their leaders have been the public attacks by the MPLA upon Holden Roberto. He has been accused of ordering the massacre of a small MPLA military unit captured by UPA militants in northern Angola, of being responsible for the death of Commander João Baptista, of having embezzled large sums of money, and of having preached tribalism, racism, and fraticidal warfare. The bitterness between the groups has become all the more severe.

In addition to discussions of the Angolan leaders themselves, there have been attempts at pressure and at mediation from other sources. Mr. Cleophas Kamitatu, then Congolese Minister of the Interior, called meetings of the principal Angolan organizations to discuss a common front in May, 1962. Discussions lasted for two days, but nothing new was decided.[33] President Kwame Nkrumah then convened a conference of all "freedom fighters" in Accra in June. One of its principal purposes was to achieve unity among contending groups in various Southern African countries, including Angola. Again, nothing concrete was achieved. African heads of state, such as Ahmed Ben Bella, have attempted to apply pressure by making their aid conditional upon unity being achieved. This, too, has not met with success, and continued aid seems to have been granted to both major groups by the Algerian Government.

Unification is theoretically desirable. The MPLA could provide a cadre of university-trained leaders, contacts abroad willing to help with the campaign, and more military strength. The FNLA would provide the broader mass base of peasant-cultivators, its own contacts abroad, and the territory that it now virtually controls in northern Angola. But such a union will be most difficult to form. First, the UPA feels that it is speaking from strength, and thus has less to gain from unity. It controls the border area in northern Angola and has the backing of the Congolese Government. It also has other significant backing, especially from the Monrovia powers, and is receiving overtures from the Casablanca powers as well. The UPA was the

[33] *Courrier d'Afrique*, May 18, 1962.

only Angolan nationalist organization accepted into membership of the Pan-African Freedom Movement of Eastern, Central, and Southern Africa (PAFMECSA) at the time of its conference in December, 1962, in Léopoldville. At the moment, it can claim to be the only group carrying on constant military operations against the Portuguese. Moreover, there is great hesitation among the UPA leaders, with their peasant-based organization, to align themselves with a group having a greater depth of intellectuals and well-educated members. There is a wall of suspicion between the less well-educated and the educated, the black and the mulatto, the unassimilated and the *assimilados*—a concomitant of the Portuguese colonial system.

Finally, ideological differences are slight; both claim to be neutralist and to look forward to social and economic reform and land distribution. The UPA tends toward a neutralism with a Western exposure, and the MPLA toward a neutralism with an Eastern exposure. But differences in ideology do not appear to be an essential factor in keeping the two parties apart.

Revolt in Progress

Only little more than six months after the events of March 15, 1961, the Portuguese Government claimed that the revolt was at an end. The Permanent Representative of Portugal to the United Nations wrote on August 4, 1962, to the U.N. Subcommittee on the Situation in Angola: "The situation in the territory of Angola must be considered peaceful and normal. No military operations are being undertaken; all that is taking place are limited police actions in the small area that had been affected by terrorism." [34]

The U.N. Subcommittee accepted neither the assertion that the situation was "peaceful and normal" nor the statement that current operations by the Portuguese were in the nature of "limited police actions." Its report said that "war by any definition of the term continues to be waged in Angola." [35]

The revolt has already achieved a certain limited success in that rebels are incontestably in control of a significant area in the north, although it is impossible to point to the exact boundaries of this area, for they shift constantly. But the writer knows from his own experience that there is no difficulty in crossing the border from the Congo into Angola and walking for many days through the forests. The people living in this area, now called Free Angola, are becoming ad-

[34] United Nations, *Report of the Subcommittee on the Situation in Angola,* A/5286 (November 15, 1962), p. 41.
[35] *Ibid.,* p. 43.

justed to wartime conditions. Although they face the constant threat of air bombings, their way of life is geared to eking out an existence from the land and prosecuting the war of liberation.[36] The FNLA does not claim to hold territory outside the north at this point. Holden Roberto, in his testimony before the U.N. Fourth (Trusteeship) Committee on November 30, 1962, said quite plainly that the southern part of Angola was almost entirely in the hands of the settlers.

Although there is a limited amount of information about the conflict in Angola, there is considerable evidence not only of the limited success of the revolt, but of its prosecution. Communiqués from both the Portuguese and the FNLA attest that military engagements are taking place. A Portuguese communiqué of June 8, 1962, reported that the army was limiting itself to patrolling and to liquidating "small nuclei of resistance still existing." [37] On September 13, 1962, the Portuguese military command at Luanda reported on the project called Operation North Wind in the Nova Caipemba area. The Portuguese claimed that heavy losses had been inflicted on the "enemy" concentrations and that much war material, as well as documents containing plans for future attacks, had been seized. The communiqué also said that "the army in Angola is permanently in action although this action is nearly always not very remarkable or spectacular." [38]

Commander José Kalundungo reported in early January that at least sixteen engagements had taken place in northern Angola between December 29, 1962, and January 7, 1963.[39] Most of the fighting took place near the villages of Buela, Noqul, Quimpeze, Kinzau, Bembe, and Nambuangungo. The report also said that the nationalist forces had attacked a Portuguese military convoy in the suburbs of the city of Ambriz on January 1, 1963. On January 17, it was claimed that near Tomboco in the Ambrizete district a patrol of the ALNA had engaged a Portuguese Army unit, killing five soldiers and losing two themselves. On January 19, it was claimed that a commando unit of the ALNA attacked a Portuguese patrol near Sombo in the administrative post of Nova Caipemba. They claimed to have killed ten Portuguese. Other releases from the FNLA headquarters indicate armed engagements between the nationalists and Portuguese on May 16, 18, 21, 23, 27, and 30, and June 4 and 6, 1962.

It is not unusual for Portuguese planes flying over rebel-held ter-

[36] See George Houser, "Journey to Rebel Angola," in *Africa Today*, March, 1962.
[37] *Report of the Subcommittee* . . . , A/5286, p. 39.
[38] *Ibid.*, p. 41.
[39] *Angola: Information Bulletin*, January, 1963.

ritory to drop leaflets rather than bombs. Typical is the following leaflet, the contents of which certainly assume the existence of a state of war:

Inhabitants of the Colonato of the Vale do Loge:

Take advantage of the last opportunity given you.
Return to the *colonato* in peace. Your lives are guaranteed to you. Return to your homes. Come to work for your elevation and progress. The Commander of the Troops guarantees your protection. You will be going to take possession of what is yours. . . .
Come in peace. . . . Appear up to the end of the 27th during daylight at the *colonato* by the Toto road.
Come in groups of ten with a white flag.
Surrender weapons as a sign of peace.

The Commander of the Troops,
Abilio Gonçalves Dias,
Infantry Major.

Further evidence about the active status of the revolt is gained from refugees pouring into the Congo. As of early January, 1962, when the special feeding program for Angolan refugees in the Congo ended, the League of Red Cross Societies in Léopoldville reported that 151,200 refugees were on the ration scheme. This, of course, does not include those without ration cards.[40] Through April, 1962, it was estimated that another 20,000 refugees had fled Angola to the Congo.[41] It is generally estimated that there are more than 200,000 Angolan refugees in the Congo.

The reason for the continued exodus of Angolans to the Congo is the large-scale bombing by Portuguese planes in the revolt area. A missionary working among the refugees in the Congo wrote:

Cutting the terrorists off from their supplies of food on the spot is a prime cause of a spate of new refugees crossing during the dry months since May [1962]. This has meant the destruction of food gardens all over the battle area, by fire and bombing. Water sources are suspected of having been contaminated. The operation was designed to prevent the guerrillas from living off the country. The result has been to drive over the frontier those Africans who instead of crossing into the Congo last year lived on in hiding in the forests of Angola.

[40] *Report of the Subcommittee* . . . , A/5286, p. 46.
[41] *Ibid.*, p. 48. (From the report of the U.N. High Commissioner for Refugees as of April 1, 1962.)

The stories which the refugees tell are remarkably similar—how they left their hiding places in the forest because of the bombing and the destruction of their food supply, and walked for days or weeks to get to the border, often being bombed or strafed by Portuguese planes.

The conflict cannot help growing. The Angolan National Liberation Army now has two military bases in the Congo (the one near Thysville was placed at the army's disposal by the Congolese Government in August, 1962). In addition, the reintegration of Katanga into the Congo has opened yet another frontier to the Angolans.

A clear military victory by the nationalists is not likely. But a Portuguese victory is equally unlikely. The war is being run by the nationalists on a shoestring. It is costing the Portuguese virtually all their colonial profits. In fact, the Portuguese authorities are now increasing export taxes on Angolan coffee. Sooner or later, those with large investments in Angola will seek to accommodate themselves to the nationalists. But that is quite another question.

In the end, then, one finds it difficult to disagree with the conclusion reached by the U.N. Subcommittee:

In spite of the uncertainties of the military situation, the Subcommittee has seen no indication of an end to hostilities and is more than ever convinced that the Government of Portugal will not be able to restore peace and order in Angola by military means and repressive measures. . . . Without a political settlement responsive to the aspirations of the Angolan people, the Subcommittee sees no prospect for an early termination of an armed struggle that is bringing nothing but misery and death to the Angolans and Portuguese alike.[42]

[42] *Ibid.*, p. 43.

The Portuguese and Mozambique:
The Past Against the Future*

DOUGLAS L. WHEELER

The Portuguese Historical Dilemma

In order to understand Portuguese Africa today, we must consider several facts of this era: (1) Portugal is a poor, primarily agricultural country with the lowest annual per capita income and the highest illiteracy rate in Western Europe; (2) the government of Portugal is a forty-year-old dictatorship dominated by an economist, Dr. Oliveira Salazar, who was seventy-six in April, 1965; (3) Portugal is the last colonial power in Western Europe with significant commitments to African territories, and she is partially dependent upon revenue from two of her tropical African territories: Angola and Mozambique.

In Portuguese terminology, the colonies are called Overseas Provinces (*Provincias Ultramarinas*); the very term betrays the traditionally emotional and nationalistic attachment of the Portuguese to these areas which were discovered in the late fifteenth century. Nevertheless, the Portuguese territories in Africa were great financial burdens on the national treasury, with little or no public interest or support until the last few decades of the twentieth century. Only after 1930, and the rise to political supremacy of Dr. Salazar, did Angola and Mozambique become profitable possessions.

It would be an oversimplification to state that the Portuguese are wholly agreed on the future of their African territories. A minority in Portugal feels that the cost in blood and treasure to defend the territories from African nationalist insurgency is far too high for poor little Portugal. The great mass of Portuguese are probably indifferent, send their sons to serve their army duty in Angola or Guinea or Mozambique, and go along with the government's campaign to strengthen

* This paper was revised by the author in the spring of 1965.

"national unity." Certain voices urge the creation of a kind of Portuguese "Commonwealth" of autonomous states (in which rule by a white minority would be implicit). The patriots who oppose this path often revive old shibboleths and maintain that if Portugal loses Angola and Mozambique, then Spain may take over Portugal and national independence will be lost. This school, despite the lack of evidence that Spain would do such a thing and the fact that Portuguese prestige in Europe has gained little from African possessions, loyally supports Lisbon's control over Portuguese Africa.[1]

A recent Portuguese book called *Three Paths for the Overseas Policy* contained the following statement: "The union of the various Portuguese provinces is necessary for the preservation of our political independence, and I would go even further to assert that this is necessary for our survival as a people." [2] When it comes to the economic realm, however, the Portuguese attachment to Angola and Mozambique is more realistic and understandable. Revenue from the tropical territories overseas—in spite of an annual outlay of over $120 million for military defense in Africa—is providing the Portuguese economy with a new prosperity. It is only a matter of the last decade, nevertheless, that a bolder attitude toward capital investment by Portuguese businessmen has begun to overshadow the traditional Portuguese penchant for small-scale trading and nonindustrial pursuits. An English economist in 1962 wrote that the loss of the African provinces would be "serious but short of catastrophic" for the home economy.[3]

It is important to realize that Portuguese weaknesses have been political as well as economic. In the political sense, Portugal is still a country of "two nations": a minority concerned with and bearing the responsibility for politics, and the majority, generally less educated (although this is becoming less true), who have little to do with politics. Constitutional government was established in Portugal in the 1820's and was modeled on the British system. Representative government and a two-party system, however, foundered in conditions of frequent bankruptcy, public apathy, and factionalism. There was no democratic tradition to invoke, and a general lack of consensus among the educated elite resulted in either of two extremes: autocracy or anarchy. Government remained the exclusive monopoly of a small

[1] See Douglas L. Wheeler, "Anti-Imperial Traditions in Portugal: Yesterday and Today," *Boston University Graduate Journal*, XII (Spring, 1964), 125–37.

[2] Fernando Pacheco de Amorim, *Tres Caminhos da Politica Ultramarina* (Coimbra, 1962), p. 115.

[3] Richard J. Hammond, *Portugal's African Problem: Some Economic Facets* (New York, Carnegie Endowment for Peace, 1962), p. 36.

oligarchy. Dr. Salazar never tires of reminding his nation, as he did in a speech of February, 1965, that the *only* alternative to his admittedly autocratic system is a discredited state "ravaged" by "anarchy." [4]

Yet the history of Portuguese politics from 1820 to 1926 has a different meaning when written by Portuguese liberals. The Marquis of Sá da Bandeira—patriot, soldier, and liberal statesman during his public life, 1835–75—records that it all might have been different long before the *Estado Novo* established its orthodox historical interpretation. Sá da Bandeira fought a losing battle to implement liberal legislation for Portuguese Africa. In 1873, shortly before his death, he wrote that Portuguese ministries and cabinets turned to authoritarian methods when in difficult circumstances. Even under the two-party system ministers rarely allowed free elections and refused to bear the burden of responsible compromise and the search for public consensus in government. [5] Unfortunately for the future of the Portuguese overseas territories (twenty-two times the size of Portugal), this political tradition has deep roots. Thus it is difficult to assess and to predict the actions of the supposedly "democratic" opposition to the present regime. If Henrique Galvão or other opposition leaders came to power in Portugal or in Portuguese Africa, would they avoid authoritarian government in "difficult" times? And who will determine where "anarchy" ends and democracy begins?

Portugal's historical dilemma is present also in the realm of foreign affairs. The Anglo-Portuguese Alliance is perhaps "Europe's oldest" and dates back to the time of the Crusades. British statesmen and financiers in effect "saved" Angola and Mozambique for Portugal between the years 1890 and 1914, despite the pressures of Cecil Rhodes and Germany; however, Portugal's view of Britain has been schizophrenic: benefactor or greedy enemy. Yet Anglo-Portuguese treaties and the British Navy have protected Portuguese African interests (albeit with lapses) for centuries. The loss of Portuguese India in late 1961, with no British aid forthcoming, was a blow to the alliance and to Portugal's imperial strength. Spain used to support Portugal in Africa, but this has changed since 1961. Recently, the Spanish Am-

4 "Address made by Premier Dr. Antonio de Oliveira Salazar at a Ceremony Installing the Executive Committee of the National Union [the government's official party] in Lisbon, on February 18th" (Portuguese Information and Tourist Office, New York, 1965), p. 2.

5 André Meyrelles, *O Marquez de Sá da Bandeira* (2 vols.; Lisbon, 1875). See also V. de Braganca Cunha, *Eight Centuries of Portuguese Monarchy* (New York, 1911), pp. 206–8. For a view of modern Portugal, see the essay of A. de Oliveira, "Salazar's Portugal," in *Angola: A Symposium, Views of a Revolt* (London, 1962).

bassador in Paris was reported to have said, "Spain does not endorse Portuguese policy in Africa." [6]

Portugal's historical dilemma has been transplanted to Angola and Mozambique. Economics and politics in Portugal and in "their" Africa are of a piece. The heritage of non-Europeans in these territories has been affected by policies of paternalism and conservative traditions. Democracy has a bad name in Lisbon as well as in Luanda and Lourenço Marques.

This is not to say, however, that change is not occurring. Since the 1961 rebellion in Angola, criticism against the regime in Europe and in Africa has been increasing. During 1962–65, in Portugal itself, there has been a good deal of university student agitation and opposition, which was almost unheard of in the previous two decades. Higher taxes to finance defense in Africa are not popular. Although the oligarchy has resented higher income taxes since 1961, the real opposition exists among the youth, intellectuals, and certain laboring groups. The Premier tells the nation in early 1965 that "the war in our Overseas Provinces is finished," but it is clear from daily press reports even in Lisbon that guerrilla operations continue unabated in all three continental provinces in Africa.[7] The opposition in exile has set up headquarters in Brazil and in Algeria and appears, in spite of the abortive *Santa Maria* affair in early 1961, to be gathering some strength.

Mozambique in the Past

Portuguese imperial policy has been characterized by concentration of settlement and trading along coasts and at natural harbors. With scanty manpower and a mercantilist tradition, the Portuguese established coastal rather than hinterland colonies beginning in the late fifteenth century. Thus Mozambique was but a string of garrisons and tiny settlements along the Indian Ocean and up the Zambezi until the late nineteenth century, when expansion inland began in earnest. Except for a small trade in gold, ivory, and slaves, Portuguese activities in Mozambique were only ancillary to imperial effort in India and the East Indies and later Brazil. After the final fall of Mombasa to Arab-

[6] René Pelissier, "Spain's Discreet Decolonization," *Foreign Affairs*, XLIII, No. 3 (April, 1965), 519.

[7] Speech of Dr. Salazar on February 18, 1965, in Lisbon; *Diário de Noticias* (Lisbon), October 10–12, 1964; "Portugal Is Optimistic Over Her Position in Africa," *The New York Times*, March 16, 1965. The Portuguese Defense Ministry announced that 433 Portuguese soldiers were killed in combat from March, 1961, to January 1, 1965. Weekly casualty reports which can be read in the Lisbon press indicate one or two soldiers killed in action in Angola "each week on an average."

Swahili forces in 1729 due to "the gross incompetence of the three commanders concerned," [8] Portugal shifted her interests and efforts south of the Rovuma River, presently the northern boundary with Tanzania. Until 1752, when Mozambique was separated from the Government of Portuguese India, Goa was in fact the capital of the territory, not Mozambique Island; in that year Mozambique became a separate Captaincy-General. For a period, offices in the Mozambique administration were sold to the highest bidder in India.

Until 1897, Mozambique Island was the capital of the fever-ridden province, with fewer than 1,500 Portuguese settlers. Mozambique may have been the "jewel" in Portugal's Indian crown in 1700,[9] but within the context of the Portuguese empire, that province was nearly forgotten in Lisbon. It became a dumping ground for criminals and political exiles from Portugal and Brazil. In fact, Brazil was the darling of the Portuguese economy, but even impoverished Angola overshadowed Mozambique. Brazil became independent of Portugal in 1822, and this greatly weakened Portugal. Portuguese leaders then proposed to develop the largely neglected African territories. Yet reform and development were a long time in coming; in 1849, a document referred to Mozambique as "the most backward of all our possessions." [10]

Geography and climate shape the pattern of administration and settlement. The Mozambique climate was, except for highlands in the extreme north and central interior, worse than coastal Angola. Nearly three-quarters of the province of 302,000 square miles is at an altitude of 2,000 feet or less. More often than not the coastal climate was oppressive, and several governors in the eighteenth century killed themselves out of desperation (and perhaps sheer boredom).[11] In the late sixteenth century, a Bantu tribe swept through the province like a raging fire, but Portuguese administration survived.

In the sixteenth century, the Portuguese traders had replaced the Arab middlemen in the gold and ivory trade. New competitors arrived in the seventeenth century, however. Indian traders (often referred to collectively as Banians) from the southwest coast of India settled in coastal towns. Soon they dominated retail business and itinerant trade

[8] C. R. Boxer and Carlos de Azevedo, *Fort Jesus and the Portuguese in Mombasa* (London, 1960), p. 84.

[9] Eric Axelson, *The Portuguese in Southeast Africa, 1600–1700* (Johannesburg, 1960), p. 195.

[10] "A Instrução Primária em Mozambique de 1840–1849," *Archivos das Colonias* (Lisbon), II, No. 2 (June, 1918), 290–96.

[11] Rocha Martins, *História das Colonias Portugueses* (Lisbon, 1933), p. 257.

in some districts, where their presence annoyed the Portuguese administration. During the 1890's, when the Portuguese were imposing a military administration in the interior, Indians were arrested and even deported for their part in the alcohol and fire-arm traffic and for meddling in tribal politics.[12]

The nineteenth century was the most crucial period for the future of the Portuguese in Mozambique and for the fate of the indigenous peoples. Slavery and slave trade flourished during a good part of the century, carried on mainly by Arabs and Europeans. As a result, agriculture, mining, and industry were neglected. Just as decisive in their effects on Mozambique, however, were two other developments: the Ngoni-Zulu invasion of the southern half of Mozambique after 1819 and the rapid economic development based on mineral exploitation in the Rhodesias and in South Africa.

Sweeping over the hinterland and sporadically attacking the Portuguese coastal settlements was the Shangana invasion, which originated in interclan warfare in Zululand after 1818. Under Chief Soshangane, a refugee army and their families migrated into the Limpopo Valley and gained control of the interior of the region between Delagoa Bay and the Save River; this area became known as Gaza. The Shangana subjugated weaker tribes such as the Tonga, Ndau, and part of the Chopi and terrified the Portuguese. They migrated from place to place frequently, but, after 1880, began to drift southward in response to Portuguese expansion from the Zambezi and to their own interests in grazing lands, cattle, and tribal power. After 1868, the Shangana were also attracted by the new economy and opportunities for employment in South Africa.

The Portuguese did little to expand their control over the interior until the 1890's, when Cecil Rhodes and other British financial interests threatened to buy Mozambique or to drive out forcibly Portuguese administration. During 1894–95, according to one of Portugal's erstwhile "heroes of Africa," Mousinho de Albuquerque, Portugal nearly lost Mozambique.[13] Heavily indebted to foreign financiers and pressed by British activity to the west, the Portuguese decided to make a supreme effort to pacify Mozambique and conquer the Shangana Chieftaincy in Gaza. A rebellion by several petty chiefs in late 1894 gave the administration the excuse it needed to dispatch an expedition of several thousand Europeans to Lourenço Marques in 1895. In

---

[12] Trindade Coelho (ed.), *Dezoito Annos em Africa. Notas e Documentos para a Biographia do Conselheiro José d'Almeida* (Lisbon, 1898), pp. 360–492.

[13] J. Mousinho de Albuquerque, *Moçambique, 1896–1898* (Lisbon, 1913), p. 73.

a disjointed operation of ten months, Portuguese forces managed to defeat Chief Gungunhana (who had had a subsidy from Rhodes's British South Africa Company since 1890) and send him to exile in the Azores Islands in 1896. Thus a new era began in Mozambique, and for the first time the Portuguese controlled the interior and demarcated the frontiers. In 1897 the capital was transferred from Mozambique Island in the extreme north to Lourenço Marques in the extreme south.[14]

It was in the middle of the nineteenth century that the Portuguese and the Boers of Transvaal cemented their relationship, which eventually developed into the modern liaison between the Republic of South Africa (dominated by an Afrikaans-speaking minority) and Portugal. In the 1850's and 1860's, Portugal negotiated treaties with the independent Transvaal Republic on frontier locations, mutual defense plans, and transportation development. For much of that century, these two peoples had a powerful enemy in common who threatened their independence: Great Britain. As the Portuguese began to appreciate the strategic and economic importance of the port in Delagoa Bay, perhaps the best natural harbor on the coast of East Africa, other economic interests also came to value it. In the 1840's, the Boers negotiated unsuccessfully to purchase Lourenço Marques, and in the 1880's and 1890's Cecil Rhodes did the same. Delagoa Bay became an international *cause célèbre* since it was the most convenient port for landlocked Transvaal and her mineral wealth. When the railroad from Lourenço Marques to Pretoria was finished, in 1895, southern Mozambique was irrevocably welded to the economic future of South Africa as a strategic nexus. Thus both territories shared a future: Portuguese African migrant labor worked in South African mines and beefed up the labor force, while South Africa used Portuguese transport facilities to export her products. Both governments signed a number of agreements regulating labor migration and traffic.[15]

Mozambique's economy became highly dependent upon the surrounding white-dominated territories after 1895. The proximity of Rhodesia and South Africa has greatly influenced Portuguese policy in economics and in African affairs. Only recently has the highly artificial economy depending on African migrant labor and customs revenues begun to show signs of developing independent agriculture and light industry.

[14] See Douglas Wheeler, "Gungunhana," in Norman R. Bennett, *Eastern African Biographies* (Boston, 1966).

[15] James Duffy, *Portuguese Africa* (Cambridge, Mass., 1959), pp. 170–72.

The Peoples and Their Problems

In 1965, the population of Mozambique was estimated to be just under 7 million. The African population, the great majority, numbered about 6.5 million, while the European population, overwhelmingly Portuguese, accounted for about 130,000. In the last few decades, Portugal has encouraged European emigration to Mozambique. Colonizers in the nineteenth century hoped to create in southeast Africa "another Brazil," a multiracial society where the color line would eventually be eliminated. Yet the mixed population of Mozambique is estimated to be only 30,000 in number, some 10,000 fewer than in Angola. Although there is some intermarriage between Africans and Portuguese, it is quite insignificant—in the past twenty years, Portuguese immigrants have come with their wives and families from Portugal, Madeira, or the Cape Verdes.

The increase in the Portuguese population in Mozambique has been spectacular, although miscegenation is still not much in evidence. Lourenço Marques developed from a shantytown of 700 in 1864 to a "showcase" metropolis of 184,000 (counting suburbs) in 1964.[16] The following figures indicate the growth of white settlement in the province: 18,000 in 1932; 27,500 in 1940; 48,000 in 1950; 67,000 in 1955; 85,000 in 1960; and 130,000 in 1965.[17]

The non-European population of Mozambique is far more varied than that of Angola. There is a considerable Arab-Swahili population concentrated north of the Zambezi and along the coast to Cape Delgado. The Makua, Makonde, and Lomwe peoples are predominant in the north, while the Tonga, Chopi, and Ngoni (Zulu, Xhosa, and Swazi) are concentrated in the south. There are small minorities of East Indians and Chinese who are settled chiefly on the coast as businessmen. During 1962, about 10,000 of the East Indians were deported to India by order of the Portuguese Government in retaliation for India's conquest of the Portuguese enclaves of Goa, Damão, and Diu in December, 1961.

Portuguese is spoken throughout Mozambique and is the official language in education and government. The government has been careful to emphasize the teaching of Portuguese at all levels of education, but several Bantu tongues and Swahili (in the north) are spoken widely by Africans. In October, 1963, it was reported that a

[16] Volkmar Wentzel, "Moçambique: Land of the Good People," *National Geographic Magazine*, CXXVI, No. 2 (August, 1964), 199.
[17] James Duffy, *Portugal in Africa* (Cambridge, Mass., 1962), p. 19.

university had been established for about 300 students in Lourenço
Marques, but little is known of its racial composition.

Demography in Mozambique is affected by heavy African migration to Rhodesia, Malawi, Tanzania, and South Africa. To pay their
taxes, to earn enough to marry, to earn their fortunes, Africans have
emigrated to outlying English-speaking territories since the 1860's.
The English traveler Elton wrote in about 1870 that in southern
Mozambique Africans knew that "the English pay for labour." [18]
This population movement increased over the years. The Portuguese
authorities viewed it with mixed emotions: On the one hand, they
realized it created a labor shortage in the province, while on the
other, Africans who returned with English currency could be taxed
for state revenue. As early as 1890, Portuguese authorities in Gaza
tried to stem this migration to South Africa and stopped Africans at
the coast.[19] Later, the authorities established regulations with South
Africa to attempt to control the labor migration. The estimates of
the numbers migrating, however, are usually quite inaccurate or only
general in nature; a Portuguese report in 1950, for example, estimated
that 500,000 to 2 million people had emigrated from Mozambique
to the bordering territories in recent years.[20] It was noted that the
Tete district on the Zambezi suffered depopulation from "clandestine emigration" into Nyasaland.

There has long been a debate about the effects on Africans of the
emigration tradition. In 1910, one observer wrote of the ill effects of
labor in mines on the Tonga and Chopi in Gaza; thousands returned
home broken in health.[21] A Portuguese priest, Padre Cruz, reviewed
the situation at about the same time. Shiploads of African workers
from as far north as Beira entered the Limpopo River to disembark
and travel overland. English agents from the mines roamed the interior to recruit workers.[22] According to Cruz, 10–20 out of every 100
workers who traveled to the mines never returned. Especially in
southern Mozambique, but also in the north, Africans were attracted
by prospects of earning "the English pound." The rinderpest epidemic which swept away cattle in much of East Africa during 1894–
1900 undermined the economy in Mozambique as well. English currency soon became a chief medium of exchange in Gaza as well as in

[18] Frederick Elton, "A Journey from Delagoa Bay," *Journal of the Royal Geographical Society*, XLII (1872), 1–49.

[19] Coelho, *op. cit.*, p. 264.

[20] Oliveira Boleo, *Moçambique* (Lisbon, 1951), p. 211.

[21] O. W. Barrett, "Impressions of Mozambique," *National Geographic Magazine*, XXI (1910), 807–30.

[22] Daniel da Cruz, *Em Terras de Gaza* (Oporto, 1910), pp. 214–19.

Lourenço Marques. According to Cruz, the "major incentive" for emigration was the desire to earn enough to marry.

Cruz opined that the African movement was beneficial in the long run since Africans returned with money, new ideas, and more incentive to "progress." [23] Emigration, noted the priest, altered the language of the peoples by giving them an opportunity to learn a smattering of English. By the Convention of 1909 (there was a *modus vivendi* in 1901), the Portuguese Government and the South African Government formalized arrangements. South Africa would recruit between 65,000 and 85,000 workers annually for mine work. This recruiting had to take place below 22° S. latitude, or at about the Save River. In return, Portugal was guaranteed a high percentage of the railroad traffic from Pretoria to Lourenço Marques. Though modified since then, this agreement has remained essentially the same. Methods of recruitment, treatment in the mines, and the attitude of the Portuguese Government have been surveyed elsewhere.[24]

According to an estimate in 1961, some 400,000 African adults, nearly all males, leave Mozambique annually to work in outlying areas. This emigration is not only a drain upon the economy and the future development of Mozambique, but acts as one cause of disunity among its peoples. Southern Mozambique has been affected far more than has the north; the Zambezi River has acted as a real dividing line between regions. Significant differences between the northern and southern regions of Mozambique can in part be gauged by noting the differing tax rates for each section. The northernmost districts paid in 1960 a rate of about 90 *escudos* (U.S. $3.25), while the southern districts paid about 300 *escudos* (U.S. $11.50).[25] It is not unreasonable to conclude therefore that the peoples of the south participate in the modern cash economy in greater depth than those of the north.

Another important problem for the south deriving from emigration is the extraordinarily high ratio of women to men in that section, especially noticeable in the vital age group of from fifteen to forty-four. A common ratio is 120–130 women to 100 men (or about 15–20 women more than the average European ratio). Contract labor,

[23] *Ibid.*, pp. 219–21. Between 1904 and 1910, from 52 to 66 per cent of the African labor employed in Transvaal gold and coal mines came from Portuguese East Africa. (Leonard M. Thompson, *The Unification of South Africa, 1902–1910* [Oxford, 1960], p. 498.)

[24] Edwin S. Munger, *Mozambique: Uneasy Today, Uncertain Tomorrow* (American Universities Field Staff Report, 1961).

[25] Antonio de Figueiredo, *Portugal and Its Empire: The Truth* (London, 1961), p. 112.

to use a conservative estimate, is indirectly responsible for nearly 12,000 to 15,000 annual deaths beyond the norm in younger age groups.[26]

The government contract labor system has met criticism from certain private circles in the European population. The Bishop of Beira, Sebastião Soares de Resende, and certain newspapers in the two major towns of Beira and Lourenço Marques have expressed open disapproval of the social effects in African society. They object to what is called "demographic anemia."[27] In 1961, there was a critical food shortage in northern Mozambique that was blamed in part upon the fact that many Mozambicans were diverted from agriculture to migrant jobs. An editorial entitled "Suggestion" in the *Diário de Moçambique* lamented the fact that so many thousands of workers left home to work at the seaport and railroad of Beira. Leaving their families for months, workers lived alone in a community "inn." The writer suggested that family residences be built for these migrant Africans as a healthy alternative to appeal to the family-minded Portuguese society.[28]

The Present and the Future

There is an inescapable unity about the history of Portugal and Portuguese Africa. Are not the reforms of 1965 merely faint echoes of those of the statesmen of 1865? The calm and relative isolation of most of Portuguese Africa was broken in 1961–62 by outbreaks of guerrilla warfare by Portuguese African nationalists, first in northern Angola and then in Portuguese Guinea. It seemed that Mozambique was immune to such trouble, but just in case, the Portuguese dispatched an army of nearly 24,000 to that province to build up a defense.[29] In February, 1964, an advertisement was printed in *The New York Times* by an American agency which created a peaceful even Victorian image:

> African Safari
> Mozambique
> 42,000 Sq. Miles
> Peaceful Competent Natives
> Experienced White Hunters.

[26] See Marvin Harris, *Portugal's African Wards* (New York, 1958), and Rita-Ferreira, "Labor Emigration among the Moçambique Thonga: Comments on a Study by Marvin Harris," *Africa*, XXX (1960), 141–52.

[27] Munger, *op. cit.*, pp. 8–11.

[28] *Diário de Moçambique* (Lourenço Marques), December 3, 1961.

[29] *The New York Times*, September 2, 1964.

Readers of the *National Geographic Magazine* in August, 1964, could read the considered opinion of traveler Volkmar Wentzel, who, after a stay of eight months in the territory, wrote: "I found Mozambique—to all outward appearances, at least—an island of tranquillity." [30] Shortly after this article appeared, during the last week in September, 1964, African nationalist groups (with years of planning and preparation) began to infiltrate the northern Mozambique frontiers with Tanzania and Malawi and to raid Portuguese posts and several towns. The Portuguese press in Lisbon on October 10 reported that five such bands attacked from Tanzania; on October 11, the Governor-General of Mozambique made a significant tour of the extreme north of the province through the towns of Porto Amelia, Moeda, Palma, Ibo, and others in response to the materialized threat. Reports of losses on both sides were quite conflicting, but it was clear that the rebel activity was not on a scale comparable to that which ravaged sections of the Congo District of Angola in March, 1961. Mozambique, described as "one big garrison" several weeks before the first open fighting and sabotage, had now reached a new era in her history.[31]

Who was responsible for these raids, which Dr. Salazar later reported in his speech of February 18, 1965? Most of the African nationalist groups involved are based in Tanzania to the north and have received aid in various forms from Algeria, Ghana, private American sources, and Communist China. The Soviet Union has given radio time to Mozambican students in exile to gather support.[32] As yet, the nationalist movement is not completely unified, but it did effect a coalition of two parties in 1962. Included in the parties are:

UDENAMO (União Democrática Nacional de Moçambique), founded in 1960 among Mozambique workers in Southern Rhodesia, and led by Adelino Gwambe. MANU (Mozambique African National Union), organized in 1960 in northern Mozambique by Mozambique workers in East Africa.

UNAMI (União Nacional Moçambicana de Independencia), organized originally in Malawi among workers from Mozambique and later merged into FRELIMO.

[30] Wentzel, *op. cit.,* p. 200.
[31] *Diário de Notícias* (Lisbon), October 10, 11, 12, 1964.
[32] "Report of Second Annual General Assembly of UNEMO (União Nacional dos Estudantes Moçambicanos–U.S. Section)," *The Mozambican* (printed privately in Bloomington, Indiana), II, No. 1, 34. The Mozambique section of UNEMO, a student group, has been able to use Radio Moscow for Portuguese broadcasts to Africa.

FRELIMO, an amalgamation or coalition, brought about in 1962 chiefly through the efforts and inspiration of Dr. Eduardo C. Mondlane, an American-educated leader. FRELIMO was pledged support by the Organization of African Unity at its meeting in Addis Ababa in May, 1963.

There have been many reports of heavy African migration out of Mozambique to Tanzania; it is difficult to estimate the numbers of these refugees who have settled in camps in southern Tanzania. What part they play in the nationalist raids and infiltrations into northern Mozambique is not clear. The Rovuma River frontier is approximately 500 miles in length and is difficult to patrol due to the climate and topography. Yet the Portuguese buildup during 1961–65 included the construction of landing strips, new roads, and the importation of heavier machinery and equipment. Increased defense training for volunteers and civilian militias accompanied the general preparation, with training for Portuguese of European and African descent alike.[33]

African dissent in Mozambique has not been alone. For the European community in the 1958 elections gave a fairly heavy vote to the opposition candidate, General Humberto Delgado. The regime was startled. In April, 1961, Mozambique white liberals reacted to the Angolan crisis with determination: They addressed a petition to the President of Portugal, Admiral Americo Tomas, and demanded immediate reforms and self-government. They saw the future of Southern Africa as "desperate." [34]

The Portuguese government has reacted to the pressures of the last four years and has put into effect a number of reforms. The system of forced cotton cultivation in practice in sections of Mozambique, along with the *indigenato* system, was reportedly abolished in late 1961 by government decrees. In theory, the Mozambique African would have the same legal rights as the metropolitan Portuguese or the Portuguese settler, or *assimilado*. Education for Africans at the primary and secondary levels was improved, and a certain part of the Portuguese Army garrisoned in Mozambique (and heavily reinforced after 1961) took part in teaching and health services.

That the post-1961 reforms and changes have not been fundamental is clear. Portuguese policy tended to remain inflexible. The independence of neighboring territories Malawi and Tanzania (the Malagasy Republic is a neighbor, too) acted to encourage a greater

33 *The New York Times*, September 2, 1964.
34 Figueiredo, *op. cit.*, p. 118. Figueiredo is a Portuguese living in Britain in exile from his place of birth, Mozambique.

measure of representative government in Mozambique. The Overseas Organic Law of November, 1963, increased the representation in the legislative councils of Portuguese Africa. In Mozambique, there was an increase of five members elected by "organic" groups, or occupational interests, but there was no addition to the directly elected members. Of the twenty-seven elected to the Legco, eleven are Africans, fifteen are Portuguese, and one is from Angola. On the Economic and Social Council, eleven are Africans and five are from Portugal.[35]

The Portuguese administration has placed great importance on economic development in the country and, in particular, on farming schemes. The Limpopo Valley Settlement scheme plans to irrigate and settle European and African families in villages along 50 miles of the fertile valley floor. This valley has attracted populations for centuries—the Shangana from Zululand settled it in the nineteenth century—and the Portuguese are now developing its potential; apparently soil here needs little or no fertilizer. Plans are under way to settle 3,000 families in each of several projects whereby emigrants from Portugal, Madeira, and the Azores will be lent up to 25 acres, implements, cattle, and material and agree to repay the government over a long period.[36]

The geographical position of Mozambique, bordering as it does on two more developed and militarily endowed states (Rhodesia and the Republic of South Africa), has long influenced internal policy and is likely to do so in the future. Beira and Lourenço Marques are the favorite summer seaside resorts of Rhodesians and South Africans. The Portuguese who could afford it and who desired a superior education have sent their offspring to high schools in Rhodesia and South Africa. Furthermore, their economies are intimately tied together. The Portuguese have defense as well as economic agreements with these two states which continue policies of racial segregation and the virtual exclusion of non-Europeans from full political rights.

Edwin Munger suggested in 1961 that Mozambique might face partition by one or more of the four powers on her borders. In some respects, southern Mozambique is more South African than Portuguese. More than once, South African statesmen in the twentieth

[35] United Nations General Assembly, "Territories Under Portuguese Administration," working paper prepared by the Secretariat, A/AC. 109/L. 126, June 9, 1964, pp. 48–49.

[36] Wentzel, *op. cit.*, pp. 200–203. See also Robert Conley, "Lisbon Settles Peasants in Mozambique," *The New York Times*, July 27, 1964; this article appeared at the time of the well-publicized visit to Mozambique of the President of Portugal, Admiral Tomas.

century have considered making Mozambique a part of a South African Federation as a matter of practical policy.[37] The transportation system of the Republic has improved since the original agreements of 1901 and 1909, when such a "federation" scheme was afoot in Transvaal; today Lourenço Marques facilities need further modernization for increasing traffic volume and South Africa is no longer so dependent on Mozambique ports for export. African labor from Mozambique, however, remains vital to the South African economy. A sudden, overwhelming crisis in Mozambique could well bring South African intervention under certain circumstances.

The port of Beira is highly developed. The Rhodesians depend upon the Beira route as the major exodus for their products, although some pass through Transvaal on the South African rail system. Like the South African Government, the Salisbury government acknowledges that it has a "great deal in common" with the Portuguese in Mozambique. Relations between Rhodesia and Mozambique have stepped up since 1961 and the "Angola scare," and it is not unreasonable to assume that Rhodesian troops, if needed, would cooperate with Portuguese units in time of crisis, and perhaps vice versa. It is a moot question whether or not land-locked Rhodesians would someday help themselves to a convenient corridor of Mozambique territory to the coast that would include Beira.[38]

When discussing the future of Mozambique, one can find a myriad of unanswered questions. This Overseas Province of Portugal is still relatively unknown to African specialists and laymen alike; its prehistory and history from 1700 to the present have not been adequately or objectively analyzed. Portugal is historically, economically, and nationally committed to a place in the future of Mozambique. But the small nation cannot afford to defend the territory indefinitely. African nationalists will continue to press for a Mozambique independent of Portuguese supremacy, whether in the form of white-settler government or a Lisbon-run administration. On the other side of the coin, the African political leaders are not solidly united into a mass party that could command a majority in every region of the territory. In one respect, the migrations to the mines of South Africa have discouraged Mozambican regionalism and tribalism: Hundreds of thousands of Africans from different backgrounds experience together a regimented life of migrant labor. As Eduardo Mondlane has described this significant phenomenon: "Mozambican unity was born out of toiling together in the deep, hot, narrow, and dust-ridden

[37] Thompson, *op. cit.*, p. 76.
[38] Munger, *op. cit.*, pp. 13, 15–17.

shafts of the gold, diamond, and coal mines of the Transvaal and Orange Free State." [39] Ironically, this effect was not part of the outcome foreseen by the economists in Lisbon or Lourenço Marques. One factor acting against nationalist success is that the African nations aiding a guerrilla movement in Mozambique are increasingly occupied with their own internal problems.

Because of the shape of the country—a 1,600-mile coastline and the Zambezi River, which cuts it almost in half—Mozambique will be afflicted by regionalism and micronationalism. The economic development and the nature of Portuguese administration have not knit the country into a tight whole. It would seem that the Portuguese language is one important unifying legacy of Portugal's policy. Political analysts such as Dr. Mondlane and Dr. Munger claim that nationalistic movements do cross tribal lines,[40] but the test of political unity is yet to come. Until national movements cross regional and racial lines, until the economies of the north and south are properly balanced, and until the white and black races in Mozambique reach some sort of a consensus about equal political rights for all races, Mozambique will be two or perhaps three nations instead of one. Outstanding European and African leadership and willingness to compromise for the sake of justice are needed to make Mozambique a free and prosperous society. It is tragic that the leaders of both of the "two nations," the Portuguese and the Africans, have turned to violence to settle their differences.

The processes of change are under way in Portuguese East Africa. There is room for a bright future in a land that Vasco da Gama called *Terra da Boa Gente*—Land of the Good People.[41] Africans and Portuguese alike have a right to equal opportunities in a multiracial future. A recent Portuguese immigrant in Mozambique stated in 1964: "One has land and hope here." [42] That this hope will favor the 7 million people of Mozambique is uncertain. An astute statesman wrote about Portuguese Africa:

What has happened in these last years and what is now happening in Africa can serve as a lesson to those who still harbor the old illusions and think they can resist the tide that is invading everything. What is needed is not to oppose it, but to enter into it, more along with it, moderate its impetus, and divert it to where it favors our interests instead of letting it

[39] Mondlane, "The Development of Nationalism in Mozambique" (unpublished paper, December 3, 1964), p. 11.
[40] Munger, *op. cit.*, pp. 15–17.
[41] Wentzel, *op. cit.*, p. 197.
[42] *The New York Times*, July 27, 1964.

destroy us. . . . The world today is passing through an enormous transformation; and this is such that it sweeps before it the preconceptions of men and nations, and prepares the future—not for petty vanities, but for the indestructible fraternity of men on earth.[43]

This was written in 1883 by the Minister for the Navy and Overseas Provinces, addressing himself to the Portuguese nation. To this, he might have added in addressing present-day Portugal: *In hoc signo vinces.*

[43] João de Andrade Corvo, *Estudos sobre as Provincias Ultramarinas* (3 vols.; Lisbon, 1883), I, 213–14.

The Struggle for Independence
in Mozambique

EDUARDO C. MONDLANE

The Portuguese always talk of their relationship with Mozambique in terms of having a "500 years' presence" there. It would be more accurate to say that the Portuguese first touched the coast of Mozambique at the end of the fifteenth century; it is one thing to touch a coast and quite another to develop deep roots in a country. When Vasco da Gama landed in Natal, South Africa, in 1497, and later in Inhambane and Sofala, he was groping for a way to India and was not in the least interested in establishing trading posts in East Africa. Only in the sixteenth century did the Portuguese find it necessary to set up posts in Africa to supply food for ships sailing from Lisbon to India, and the first post was located on the island of Mozambique (near the northernmost point of the present-day country), obviously to avoid direct contact with the people on the mainland.

The so-called Portuguese Empire in East Africa, of which Mozambique was supposed to be a part, was in fact composed of Arab city-states scattered throughout the central part of East Africa. When the Arabs began to question the intrusion of the Europeans in the trade with India, they were conquered by the Portuguese. At no time did the Portuguese venture into the interior long enough to establish contact with the indigenous population. Even if one were to admit that the Portuguese were the lords of the East African coast on the basis of having conquered the Arab city-states, it must be pointed out that the area they conquered was the equatorial portion of the coastal strip now known as Kenya, Tanganyika, and the northern portion of present-day Mozambique. The country even derives its name from that small northern island, which originally was the main center of Portuguese control of East Africa.

The Portuguese interpretation of the nation's historical presence in Mozambique is typical of practically all colonial powers, pressed to show cause why they should not yield imperial authority to the indigenous population. It is used by the South African whites and by the Southern Rhodesian whites, who try to connect their first settlement of Southern Rhodesia in 1887 with the arrival of the Dutch settlers in the Cape in 1652.

It was only during the latter half of the nineteenth century that Portugal, like all other European colonial powers, began to engage in imperialist adventures with the intent of conquering as much of the African territory as possible from the indigenous peoples. By that time, however, the largest proportion of the boasted Portuguese Empire in East Africa had already been taken over by the British, the Germans, and the Italians. All that remained in the hands of Portugal were a few northern Mozambican islands, and the Arab city-state of Sofala. Portugal began to claim some trading posts on river estuaries and on the bays of Beira and Lourenço Marques, but only at the very end of the century did she succeed in subduing the African armies under the leadership of various African kings. The Portuguese presence in Mozambique can be counted only from 1898, the year that the last of the African emperors was defeated. Those Mozambicans who continued to resist Portuguese authority either were exterminated or fled to the neighboring countries of South Africa, the Rhodesias, Nyasaland, and the then German East Africa, and in due time became part of the population of those countries.

The Portuguese Government consolidated its position in the rest of the country until it had complete control, but at no time has the acceptance of authority been complete enough to obviate the use of the army or police in order to keep the African people under Portuguese sovereignty. One of the means of ensuring authority was to break up our kingdoms into a multiplicity of chiefdoms, under carefully picked paramount chiefs, petty chiefs, and headmen who were under the direct supervision of Portuguese white administrators, and chiefs of post (*chefes de posto*). These administrators and *chefes de posto* are responsible for seeing that Portuguese law and order are maintained and that every able-bodied African serves Portuguese interests. The African chief is an instrument of the Portuguese Government to carry out its political, economic, and social policies.

The Portuguese argued that they were imposing their authority on the African people because the latter were "primitive." The "civilized" Portuguese certainly had superior technological skills, especially the skill to produce powerful and accurate weapons. The African people began to believe, therefore, that if they learned these techniques they might be able eventually to challenge the Portuguese. Many Africans joined Christian churches and sent their children to Christian mission schools; many thousands of young men risked their lives in the gold, diamond, and coal mines of the Transvaal in order to improve themselves materially. At first the Portuguese Government applauded these efforts, and at times even encouraged them as means by which the African peoples could become "civilized," and thereby accepted into the power structure of the society. But as time went on the Portuguese began to perceive the future political significance of the African interest and began to question the wisdom of the encouragement that they were giving.

There began to develop, for instance, a tendency for white settlers to rediscover the virtue of being "primitive," for, they argued, a "native" is happy and content when he lives by his own tradition; why bother the conscience of the African with new values and needs when he is happy with his own way of life, they would ask. Yet, at the same time, the Portuguese settler wanted the African to be his servant, his laborer on the plantation, and the instrument by which he could profit from the gold and diamonds of South Africa. In short, according to the Portuguese, the African must not develop himself to the point of competing with the white settler, but only to the point of being an effective instrument of material wealth for the white man.

In the late 1930's and early 1940's, Portuguese settlers began a one-sided debate in the state-controlled Portuguese press, arguing that if the white man's authority over the African was to continue, it was not safe to educate the African in all phases of modern science. What the black man needed, they went on, was "spiritual growth" and not material improvement. They insisted that all phases of "native" education should be placed in the hands of the religious institutions, whose main purpose was to convert and not to educate, in the modern sense of the word. The white newspapers of Lourenço Marques and Beira carried letters from white farmers, businessmen, and plantation owners pressing for a change in the educational policies of the colony in line with this idea. At first, many people believed that the Salazar government would not heed these obviously selfish pleas of the white settlers. By the early 1940's, however, it became clear that the Salazar regime not only heeded them, but also negotiated and signed the 1942 Missionary Agreement with the Vatican to hand over all African education in Mozambique, Angola, and so-called Portuguese Guinea to the Roman Catholic missions, while keeping for itself the responsibility for the education of Europeans and Asians. As part of the agreement, Portugal was to give an annual subsidy for maintenance of the school buildings, salaries of the African teachers, and other relevant expenses. At a time when education for the African peoples in most of Africa was expanding, the opportunity for educational

advancement in the Portuguese colonies was curtailed. The Portuguese colonies of Mozambique, Angola, and Guinea are the only
African countries where there are no secondary schools for black people and where the state has completely relinquished the responsibility
of educating the children of the majority of the people to a private
religious organization. Furthermore, the existing rudimentary schools,
or "*escolas de adaptação*," are so poorly subsidized that it is not possible for the Roman Catholic Church to reach more than about 20
per cent of school-age children.

The African is also exploited economically by the Portuguese, who
have constructed a network of labor laws, international labor agreements, and pacts aimed at squeezing the last dime out of the African's
sweat. These laws have put the African in the position of having to
find work on the farms and plantations and in the homes of the Europeans, in the government, in the mines, and in industry within six
months, or face arrest and forced labor, a system cynically called
"*contrato voluntario*" by the Portuguese Government. Under this system, millions of Mozambicans have been forced to take up jobs
within and outside Mozambique at wages much below subsistence
levels, thus allowing the South African mining interests to obtain each
year hundreds of thousands of cheap workers who flock into the gold,
diamond, and coal mines to escape arrest, for they cannot prove to
the Portuguese administrators that working on their own farms and
taking care of their own homesteads is a *bona fide* productive activity.

The international labor agreements between South Africa and Portugal give to Portugal, *inter alia*, payments by the mining companies
of about U.S. $6 in gold bullion per African worker signing the con-
tract; half of four months' worth of the worker's wages; the promise
that 47.8 per cent of the imports-exports of South Africa will be
shipped through the port of Lourenço Marques; the right to hunt
and arrest all Mozambican Africans who may have either run away
from the mines or entered South Africa clandestinely; and the with-
holding of half the wages of all Mozambican workers for about two
years, at the end of which time these wages are handed back to the
workers in Mozambique in Portuguese currency without interest.
Portugal, therefore, receives from gold mining each year estimated
profits exceeding U.S. $10 million simply by controlling the African
labor traffic to and from South Africa. This does not include the
financial benefits accruing to her from the 47.8 per cent of the Witwatersrand imports-exports that must pass through the port of
Lourenço Marques.

Those Africans who had ever had any illusions about the good intentions of Portuguese colonialism could not help waking up to the

facts as they were. They began to see their people becoming gradually poorer as the white people were getting wealthier. The more the black people tried to force themselves into the European system of life, the more stringent the Portuguese laws became. While the Portuguese had been talking earlier about "civilizing" the black man and "assimilating" him when he had attained certain cultural and educational standards, later on they began to restrict the facilities that might have enabled at least a few Africans to get the necessary tools to gain access to the power structure.

The reaction to this situation was the formation by Africans of so-called regional, linguistic, civic, and mutual-aid organizations. Whenever these groups demanded the rights they had lost to the white man, however, they were ruthlessly slapped down by the Portuguese Government. Since the beginning of Pan-African nationalism, these organizations—which helped to develop a national attitude toward Mozambicans—have either died away or given way to an all-Mozambique nationalism. In the earlier part of the century, when Portuguese authoritarianism had not yet crystallized, many African groups that were openly aimed at political emancipation were formed in various parts of the country. The Associação Africana and the Centro Associativo dos Negros de Moçambique were two organizations whose membership tended to reflect the color line between the so-called mulattoes (or *mixtos*) and the indigenous Africans. Later on, however, the Portuguese Government purged these organizations of the more nationalist-minded and planted its own stooges as leaders. These two African associations still exist today, but are either controlled by the government or led by men who do not dare to express their opinions. In any case, they are really not popular organizations because they do not serve the majority of the African peoples. They are at best simply bourgeois social clubs, often called upon to shout their part in the militarized chorus of allegiance to Salazar.

Before I discuss the source and development of the Mozambique Liberation Front, I should like to mention just one other type of crypto-nationalistic organization that made its imprint in Mozambican politics. I am referring to the Associação dos Naturais de Moçambique (Association of Native-born Mozambicans). This organization was established and for a long time (and still, to a great extent) run and supported by white people. In fact, it was meant for Europeans born in Mozambique, and not for Africans or Asians. For a long time, it openly discriminated against the so-called non-Europeans in its membership and services. Only in the last fifteen years, and especially after the rise of independent African states, did it begin to encourage other racial groups to join. In fact, during the mid-

1950's, it developed a policy favoring social integration between the two major racial groups and an autonomous Mozambique that would eventually become independent. The leaders of the organization, realizing the paucity of educated black Africans, launched a scholarship campaign to subsidize the education of promising Africans in secondary, technical, and commercial schools. One of its most outstanding leaders was the son of a former Portuguese governor, José Cabral. At first the government encouraged the efforts of this group, believing that the leaders were interested only in the cultural and social welfare of the African peoples, but when the government began to notice a tendency toward a more genuine Mozambican nationalism it took severe steps, which included arresting all the top leaders of the organization, replacing them with a more fascistic group, and placing the organization under the direct control of the social-welfare division of the government. That was the end of the effectiveness of the Associação dos Naturais de Moçambique as a political channel for a future multiracial Mozambique. In view of the present status of our nationalist movement, one might venture the prediction that the Portuguese people, as a European white group, will regret the emasculation of this organization, for with its demise may have gone all hope for a racially tolerant Mozambique.

Now let us turn to the organizations formed with the clear intent of rallying their people to self-government and independence. The Mozambique Liberation Front, also known as FRELIMO (Frente de Libertação de Moçambique), was formed in June, 1962, out of the merger of several political parties, some of them in exile, others still functioning underground within Mozambique. For security reasons, I shall not say anything about those groups still working within Mozambique, except to mention that they were instrumental in achieving union among all the forces working toward national independence.

The most important of the exiled political parties now fused into FRELIMO are the Mozambique African National Union (MANU) and União Democrática Nacional de Moçambique (UDENAMO). MANU was organized originally by Mozambicans who had been working in Tanganyika, Kenya, and Uganda. Some of the leaders of MANU were involved in the political parties of those countries during the formative periods of their development. When it became clear that the political power in East Africa was to be handed over to the African majority, these Mozambicans felt obliged to concentrate their energies on preparing their own people for independence. This was the case with Matthew Mmole, who was president of MANU. The former secretary-general of MANU, M. M. Mallinga, had been in

East Africa for many years, working in the labor unions of Kenya, Tanganyika, and Uganda. He was the organizing officer for dock workers in Mombasa and cotton workers in Uganda. While in Kenya, he worked with Tom Mboya.

Meanwhile, some of the Mozambicans who were working in either Southern Rhodesia or Nyasaland began to interest themselves in organizing a political body to guide the nationalist aspirations of their fellow citizens from the coast. This was the beginning of UDENAMO, which had its first temporary headquarters in Salisbury, Southern Rhodesia. As long as the Rhodesian Africans were allowed to form parties, Mozambicans continued to carry out their work unhampered. One of the officers of UDENAMO was Adelino Gwambe, who, according to his own account, had been a member of the greatly feared Portuguese secret police force (PIDE) and had been sent by the government of Portugal to spy on his fellow countrymen in Rhodesia. Once there, however, Mr. Gwambe decided to join the nationalists and, in 1959, agreed to go to Dar es Salaam, Tanganyika, to contact members of MANU and try to establish a common front. Mr. Gwambe was warmly received by MANU leaders and taken in as a full member. Later, a conference of nationalist organizations against Portuguese colonialism was held in Rabat. Since most of the members of MANU could not speak Portuguese, they asked Gwambe to attend the conference and represent them. During the conference, Gwambe announced that he was representing both MANU and UDENAMO. For a while, MANU and UDENAMO were the only two Mozambican political parties in East Africa. Later, Baltazar Chagonga, the president of another Mozambican party, also came to Dar es Salaam as representative of a Nyasaland-based group, the Mozambique National Independence Party. Mr. Chagonga was for many years a medical aide in Mozambique, but was forced to retire because of his nationalistic inclinations. When the situation worsened, he left Mozambique and settled for some time in Blantyre, Nyasaland, but since the Portuguese police are free to arrest Mozambicans in Nyasaland, he had to continue on to Tanganyika.

Out of these parties came the Mozambique Liberation Front, the only political party representing the interests of the people of Mozambique. Its formation represents the determination of our people to achieve independence in the shortest time possible. At the conference at which the union was brought about, an *ad hoc* committee was elected and entrusted with the responsibility of carrying on work until the first congress of the new organization was held. I was elected national president; Uria Simango, vice-president; David Mabunda, secretary-general; Matthew Mmole, treasurer; Paul Gumane, deputy secretary-general; and Leo Milas, publicity secretary. Four other people hold supporting positions.

It may be appropriate at this stage to describe my background in the context of my present functions as the president of FRELIMO. I was born in southern Mozambique, in the Gaza district, which lies on both sides of the Limpopo basin. My father was a leader of a section known as Khambane, which is inhabited by the Tsonga peoples. As a boy, I herded cattle, sheep, and goats; it was not until I was ten years old that I began my schooling, first at a local government school, then at a mission school. Having obtained the primary-school certificate—the highest educational achievement allowed an African in Mozambique—I enrolled at an agricultural school to learn dairy farming, which I then taught in the Gaza district. In 1944, I received a scholarship to study in a high school in the northern Transvaal, from which I obtained the Matriculation Certificate of the South African Joint Matriculation Board. In 1948, I entered the Jan H. Hofmeyr School of Social Studies in Johannesburg and soon afterward was offered a private scholarship to Witwatersrand University, where I continued my studies in the social sciences.

In 1949, the Nationalist government, under Dr. Malan, refused to renew my permit as a foreign student: I was a black student in a white university. On my return to Mozambique, the government had me arrested, together with other members of an African students' association which I had organized and which drew its membership from the few African secondary, commercial, and technical school students of Mozambique. The government thought the organization was really a political group camouflaged as a social and academic one. I was questioned for three days and three nights, and a report of the interrogation was sent to Portugal's Attorney General in Lisbon. A few months later, his office issued an analysis of the report, which stated that I had been infected with a Communist virus and with an incipient spirit of black nationalism that should be eliminated as soon as possible before it infected other Africans, especially the young people who were members of my association. Although he could find nothing specific enough to allow him to prefer charges, the Attorney General prescribed that I be put under strict surveillance by the police, and that, if possible, I be given a scholarship to study at a Portuguese university in order to keep me away from the African population and cure me of my intellectual and political proclivities.

By the time the Portuguese Government came through with a scholarship offer, I had already obtained one from the Phelps-Stokes Fund of New York. I entered the University of Lisbon in 1950. As far as I know, I was the first black Mozambican ever registered there.

There were, however, Africans from the other Portuguese colonies—the Cape Verde Islands, Guinea, Angola, and São Tomé—and we joined in promulgating our nationalistic ideas.

A. Agostinho Neto of Angola, already a recognized poet, wrote plaintive sonnets clamoring for freedom for the black man; Mario de Andrade of Angola wrote cultural and sociological essays relating to the African past; and I concentrated on talking at closed meetings of students, faculty members, and some of the more liberal Portuguese, describing Portuguese colonial policies as I knew them in my own Mozambique. As a result of our activities, we were constantly harassed by the PIDE. My room was ransacked practically every month by the police looking for documents, letters, pictures—evidence of my suspect political views. The same applied to Neto, Andrade, and most of the African students at Lisbon.

After one year, feeling that I could not continue my studies under these conditions, I arranged to have my scholarship transferred to Oberlin College in Ohio, from which I was graduated in 1953. I continued my studies at Northwestern University, where I obtained M.A. and Ph.D. degrees in sociology, and, after doing research at Harvard University for a year, I accepted a position as a research officer in the Department of Trusteeship of the United Nations, where I remained for almost five years. As an international civil servant, I was able to visit Mozambique during this time, and when I resigned from the United Nations in the autumn of 1961 to teach at Syracuse University's Maxwell Graduate School, I openly joined the nationalist movement. When Mozambique's neighbor Tanganyika became independent in December, 1961, I immediately arranged for my return to Africa with the purpose of urging Mozambican nationalists to unite. I arrived in Dar es Salaam in June, 1962.

I must mention the part played by several African political leaders in urging all Mozambican politicians to unite. Among these were Julius K. Nyerere, the President of Tanganyika, and Oscar Kambona, Tanganyika's Minister for External Affairs and Defense, who tirelessly supported unity from the outset; also, Kwame Nkrumah, President of Ghana, who, at the Freedom Fighters' Conference in 1962, publicly and privately urged our Mozambique politicians to unite in order to avoid the tragic division that has hurt the cause of freedom in Angola. Practically all African statesmen who had anything to do with Portuguese colonial issues at the international level continually insisted on unity within Mozambique. All of these forces were instrumental in leading us toward the formation of FRELIMO.

Soon after the formation of the Front, a congress was planned for that same year to formulate the main lines of the policy of the new organization and to elect a group of officers to carry out its work. The congress was to meet in Dar es Salaam and bring together representatives of the various political groups of Mozambique exiled in East Africa and of as many groups within Mozambique as could send delegates.

The congress convened at the end of September and was attended by 80 delegates and more than 500 observers from Dar es Salaam, Tanga, Lindi, Morogoro, Songea—cities in Tanganyika where there were more than 100,000 Mozambican workers, including thousands of refugees who had recently arrived from Mozambique. There were also observers from Zanzibar, where more than 30,000 Mozambicans work in the shipping industry and on clover farms and plantations. From Mombasa came several people representing a Mozambican community of more than 20,000 dock workers; a few people came from the Rhodesias and Nyasaland. In sum, the first congress of our party was a representative one.

The FRELIMO Congress examined carefully the current situation in Mozambique and recommended a program for the Central Committee to carry out during the year. During the discussions, the following points were noted: (1) that the people of Mozambique were still under the subjection of Portuguese colonialism, characterized by political, economic, social, and cultural oppression; (2) that the Portuguese Government in Mozambique suppressed the basic freedoms to which modern man is entitled; [1] (3) that the Portuguese Government failed to recognize the primacy of the interests of Mozambicans, and that it opposed the right of the people to determine their own destinies, continuing to insist upon labeling Mozambique as an "overseas province"; and (4) that Portugal, instead of seeking a peaceful solution to the conflict between her and the people of Mozambique, continued to use fascist methods of repression, reinforcing the military and police apparatus by the dispatch of military contingents, massacring innocent people, and imprisoning and torturing people suspected of nationalistic tendencies. (I might add that the latest statistics indicate that there are approximately 30,000 Portuguese soldiers, well equipped with NATO arms, in Mozambique.)

The Congress noted that the reforms that Portugal had recently promulgated were within the framework of the same colonialist spirit that has always typified Portuguese action and were, therefore, unacceptable. It stated that the people of Mozambique were forced to seek effective methods of self-defense and called upon all Mozam-

[1] I am pleased to note that the *Pacem in Terris* encyclical states unequivocally what man's rights are. It can only be hoped that Portugal, with its 97 per cent Catholic population, will begin to see the need for respecting the rights of man.

bican patriots to unite under FRELIMO's banner to fight for the independence of their country. It also called attention to the existence of an alliance among the racist powers of Portugal, South Africa, and the so-called Central African Federation, aided by a multifarious system of economic interests financed in London and New York, and urged all freedom-loving peoples of the world to condemn and act in such a way as to frustrate the inhuman activities of these forces.

The Congress of FRELIMO declared its determination to promote the efficient organization of the struggle of the Mozambican people for national liberation and adopted the following program for the Central Committee: (1) to develop and consolidate the organizational structure of FRELIMO; (2) to develop unity among Mozambicans; (3) to utilize the energies and capabilities of each member of FRELIMO to the fullest; (4) to promote and accelerate the training of cadres; (5) to use every effort to achieve freedom in Mozambique; (6) to develop literacy programs for Mozambican people, creating schools wherever possible; (7) to encourage and support the formation and consolidation of trade unions and students' and women's organizations; (8) to encourage cooperation with nationalist organizations of Angola, Guinea, and Cape Verde; (9) to promote the social and cultural development of Mozambican women; (10) to procure all means of self-defense and prepare the people for every eventuality; (11) to appeal for financial support from organizations that sympathize with the cause of the people of Mozambique; (12) to establish permanent centers of information and propaganda in all parts of the world; and (13) to seek diplomatic, moral, and material help for the cause of freedom in Mozambique, especially from the already independent states of Africa, and from all peace- and freedom-loving countries of the world.

It would be unwise for me to indicate what we are doing to implement those resolutions which have to do with direct action within Mozambique. There are, however, two areas of recommended action —diplomatic action and education—that can be outlined publicly. Since the formation of FRELIMO, diplomatic contacts have been intensified in all parts of the world. We have made certain that our point of view is well understood by those committees of the United Nations which are directly responsible for gathering information on Portuguese colonies. As soon as the meetings of the Congress ended, I flew back to New York to petition the Fourth Committee of the General Assembly (which was discussing Mozambique) to consider our territory. We also intensified our contacts with international conferences in Africa, Asia, and the Americas. At the annual conference of PAFMECSA, which met in Léopoldville, Vice-President Simango of FRELIMO presented a petition on our behalf. We sent a team of five members of the Central Committee to the Moshi conference of the Afro-Asian Solidarity Council to present our case. In the United States, I attended the first American Negro Leadership Conference on Africa, where I presented a background paper on conditions in Mozambique. Our university students in Europe and North America are united in an organization called União Nacional dos Estudantes de Moçambique, which cooperates with FRELIMO in informing people outside of Africa of our case against Portuguese colonialism. We hope that through this knowledge the representatives of the peace-loving peoples of the world will be able to take the proper steps to convince Portugal of the stupidity of her position.

In response to the instructions of the Congress to regard the education of the Mozambican people as a priority matter, the Central Committee has begun a crash program on three levels: university, secondary school, and mass literacy. We have requested scholarships from most of the independent countries of the world for Mozambicans who have had enough education to attend schools above the secondary level. We have also appealed to the United Nations to help us in this respect. As a result, we have received scholarship offers from many countries in Eastern Europe, North and South America, Western Europe, and Asia, and have sent students to the United States, where facilities for both training and transportation have been liberally given by governmental and private bodies; to France, where training, especially in medicine, is being given to several Mozambicans; and to Italy, where Mozambicans are studying law and economics. We have also sent some students to the Soviet Union. Because we have more scholarships offered to us than we can use, we are making plans to develop a crash secondary-school program in Mozambique to prepare students for university entrance. We have already asked private groups in the United States and elsewhere for funds to coordinate the efforts of those educational organizations which are now trying to help us with training facilities. In addition, we would like to prepare literacy programs to reach the millions of our people who are not able to read and write, for we believe that without a literate populace our efforts for a stable, progressive, and peaceful Mozambique cannot succeed. We appeal, therefore, to all those who believe in the effectiveness of these programs to give us whatever help they can afford.

Our struggle against Portuguese colonialism is a formidable one. We will do everything we can to hasten the demise of colonialism in Mozambique, even if it means giving up our own lives. For some time we believed that the people of the world were committed to morality and the rule of law, but as we went forth to present our case to the United Nations, to governments within each country, and to the press of the world, we began to realize that interests other than morality and the merits of our case seem to be more important. For example, we know that the United States and her NATO allies are the paramount sources of military and economic power for Portugal. When we presented the facts at our disposal to the people of the United States, they seemed to fall on deaf ears. Even the press lacked interest in reporting on our plight. Instead, the American people are being fed propaganda through high-powered public-relations firms receiving money from Portugal and through various Anglo-American interests. But the people of Mozambique will appeal to all those who believe in freedom for their help in this struggle against Portuguese colonialism. Our people will not rest until they have gained their independence.

Editors' Postscript

On September 24, 1964, the Mozambican rebellion began in earnest as guerrilla squads crossed over the frontier from Tanzania and attacked Portuguese military installations. In the three weeks following, the Portuguese carried out retaliatory operations, and more than 5,000 refugees fled to Tanzania. Some of the refugees reported the burning of all African dwellings near airstrips that the Portuguese were constructing. On October 11, a Portuguese news agency confirmed reports of the capture of guerrillas—reports that had previously been denied by a spokesman from the Ministry of Foreign Affairs.

On October 20, the London Times reported that an anti-aircraft unit of the Tanzanian army, trained and armed by Russian officers, had been dispatched to the Mozambican border. The next day, the Portuguese Foreign Minister, Dr. Franco Nagueira, claimed that Tanzania was a gigantic base for subversion and demanded international condemnation of Nyerere's government.[1] At the same time, troop reinforcements for Mozambique were dispatched from Portugal.

On November 15, the Times reported 1,000 trained guerrillas poised in Tanzania for attacks on Mozambique. In January, 1965, FRELIMO communiqués issued in Dar es Salaam reported 400 Portuguese soldiers killed and 2 aircraft brought down. These reports were denied by the Portuguese authorities, who admitted only that a military plane had crashed because of "engine trouble."[2]

[1] *Africa Digest*, XII, No. 3 (December, 1964), 77.
[2] *Africa Report*, X, No. 2 (February, 1965), 48.

The seriousness of the situation was reflected by Portuguese reactions in Mozambique. On December 28, 1964, a group of freedom fighters was arrested and charged with offenses against the state. Lusitania, the official Portuguese news agency, claimed that the group had received support from the American Committee on Africa.[3] Reports of a second wave of arrests in January were confirmed by an official of FRELIMO, who claimed that the secret police had cracked a resistance cell with the aid of an informer. There were, however, still 400 guerrillas operating in the country, according to FRELIMO. Meanwhile, the Portuguese Defense Ministry denied reports of an emergency and claimed that a rebel group had been wiped out. On March 12, 1965, however, a Southern Rhodesian military mission arrived in Mozambique to discuss plans for a coordinated defense.

Fighting continued throughout April and May, with victories being claimed by both sides. On May 27, FRELIMO announced that eighty-two Portuguese soldiers had been killed in the seven preceding weeks. Three days later, a Portuguese Army communiqué reported that an underground network of FRELIMO had been broken up.

On June 7, a representative of FRELIMO was heard by the U.N. Special Committee on Colonialism meeting in Dar es Salaam. After hearing reports, Chairman Sory Coulibaly of Mali declared that, in his opinion, the situation in Mozambique was a threat to the peace and security of Africa.

[3] *Africa Digest*, XII, No. 4 (February, 1965), 48.

Discussion

CARLOS GONÇALVES CAMBANDO.   We have heard that there are two major political parties in Angola, but I will say, being Angolan and having been born in Angola (I live in the central part of Angola and have lived also in the south), that this is a miracle of unity of the Angolan people.

Residues of colonialism, which are reflected in different approaches of the population to the achievement of independence, still exist. But the peasants, who constitute 99 per cent of the people, are united. It is to the party of these people that I belong. The Union of the People of Angola, which is the main organization of the FNLA, was founded in 1954. Having the benefit of an independent Congo, where Patrice Lumumba was Prime Minister, we had the support of our brothers in the Congo and were able to organize, to speak, and broadcast from the Congo to the people of Angola.

With the coming of the Congo crisis, we had no way to continue our fight. The main goal of our movement was to fight by all means the Portuguese colonialists. Notwithstanding these and other difficulties, we have been able to maintain this fight, and the stronghold of Portuguese colonialists in Angola is being dismantled. In two years of fighting by women, children, and men, young and old, we have undergone all kinds of suffering. Women are cooperating with our army and children carry messages. This is the union of one people, for one purpose. It has been said that we are but a peasant people, but the peasants have intelligence. It is the intelligence of all these people which we will mobilize to build Angola. It is this intelligence which must be used to serve the people, rather than the people being used to serve the intelligentsia.

Today we are confident of final victory, for we have control of more than one-sixth of the territory in the northern part of our country. We have in our possession two military bases in African countries outside Angola, and very soon we are going to have three. This is an African's answer to those who say there is no African solidarity.

At this point, I would like to call your attention to the dramatic situation of more than 200,000 Angolan people living in the Congo, most of them women and children. They are victims of Portuguese violence only because they desire freedom; they have decided not to go back to their homes until they are free. We have been fighting alone for a long time. Now that people scattered all over the world are concerned with the question of freedom, the question of human, fundamental rights, we think that this is the time for the civilized world to join us in our struggle.

I would finally like to point out the implications of the large amount of aid given Portugal by the big powers. Much of the suffering undergone by my people would not be if Portugal were alone. The Angolan people, like all other people in the world, want nothing more than freedom. The continuation of the war of extermination, the increasing military budget of the Portuguese Government have been made possible only by grants of Western countries. Recently, I read in a magazine that twelve more planes would be delivered to Portugal to help them against the Angolans.

AUGUSTO T. P. BASTOS.   George Houser has given the background of the Angolan problem and situation, and one of my brothers, Carlos Gonçalves Cambando, has explained his feelings about the situation in Angola. I would like to call attention to a fact of concern to us and to all the friends who want to help us to get our freedom and independence: Although all Angolans want to be free, want to be independent of the Portuguese colonial power, our political parties are not united.

What is the reason for this? I would think the major problem of unity is the struggle for leadership. But unity is more important than this struggle; the parties should combine to fight and defeat the enemy, whether it be the Portuguese or any foreign force or any foreign country seeking domination of our people.

My point is that we African nationalist students should have played and now must play a stronger role to solve this problem of unity among our organizations. For we must realize that the youth are the future of any government. We are here in the United States and cannot, therefore, be in the fight in Africa. But as students of history we must realize that the struggle for political leadership must follow, not precede, the unified struggle for independence or else the latter may fail. Here our best service for Angola is to preach the unity of our nationalist leaders. We start by uniting among ourselves—that is, we, Angolan students in America, are Angolans all fighting for freedom from Portugal, and we are not of this party or of that. We might learn from the Algerian students, who, despite party differences, presented a united front for independence.

JOÃO NHAMBIU.   Douglas Wheeler speculated on the possibility of Mozambique's being partitioned. Let me emphasize, however, that, although there are different ethnic groups in Mozambique and although the Portuguese emphasize these differences for their own purposes, people from all parts of Mozambique can and want to work for national unity. In our Union we have students from all over Mozambique who are working together. [*Eduardo Mondlane, following the presentation of his paper, also noted that ethnic differences pointed out by Mr. Wheeler were unimportant.* "I, for instance, am from the south," *Mr. Mondlane said,* "and was elected president of FRELIMO by a congress, 90 per cent of whose members were from the north. I don't speak a word of the languages of the north. I was elected because they felt I was qualified to be one of the leaders. And most of the executive council, elected by the same congress, are from the center and south of Mozambique."]

I also want to refer to the problem of education. Education for Africans in Mozambique is no more than learning the *Ave Maria* in Portuguese, learning the Portuguese law and how to obey it, and learning how to serve the Portuguese well without questioning. The whole educational system is geared to preparing Africans for the forced-labor system. We need help in educating Mozambicans so that they can work toward the independence of our country.

JOSEPH CHICUARRA. The Portuguese came to Africa, pushed us into areas that were arid, nonproductive, and very unhealthy, took the power of governing away from us, and then began to treat us inhumanly. They have forgotten, as have all other white people in Africa, that when they arrived, we fed them and gave them a place to settle. Now, Portugal refuses to give us even freedom to learn. She attempts to limit our movements completely. Be assured, however, that she will not be able to prevent us from getting our freedom.

ZARICA JOHN SAKUPWANYA. I have been surprised to hear U.S. Government officials remark at various times on the high standard of living in Mozambique. I have heard this even from people who have been to Mozambique. These people have a completely distorted picture, and this is because their trips to Mozambique have been under the aegis of the Portuguese Government. It is at a conference such as this that such distortions can be corrected and the true picture of Mozambique and Angola brought to Americans, who will realize then how badly their help is needed.

VI

The Nonviolent Struggle

Passive Resistance in South Africa

OLIVER TAMBO

Oppressed people in South Africa have always associated the history of the United States with the great name of Abraham Lincoln. There was an issue involving human rights in his day—an issue that challenged the principles enshrined in the Declaration of Independence. To the honor of his name, his people, and his country, Abraham Lincoln translated these great principles into concrete action.

The U.S. Government has made some forthright statements of policy in condemnation of such practices as apartheid in South Africa, where black men and women are held in bondage in violation of the principles enunciated in the Universal Declaration of Human Rights. What puzzles and worries Africans, however, is the opposition persistently offered by the White House to any action intended to put an end to this bondage.

In its historical development, "passive resistance" in South Africa has been closely associated with the late Mahatma Gandhi and his philosophy. As early as 1907, he led the Indian community in South Africa in acts of passive resistance. In later years there were further passive-resistance campaigns by the Indian community. Mahatma believed in the effectiveness of what he called the "soul force" in passive resistance. According to him, the suffering experienced in passive resistance inspired a change of heart in the rulers. The African National Congress (ANC), on the other hand, expressly rejected any concepts and methods of struggle that took the form of a self-pitying, arms-folding, and passive reaction to oppressive policies. It felt that nothing short of aggressive pressure from the masses of the people would bring about any change in the political situation in South Africa. As a countermeasure to Mahatma Gandhi's passive resistance, the African National Congress launched, in 1952, the Campaign for the Defiance of Unjust Laws, or the "Defiance Campaign."

Before they were finally defeated and subjugated by sheer force of superior arms, our forefathers had been engaged in many bitter strug-

gles against the white foreign invaders and colonial conquerors, both
Boer and British. With spears and battle-axes their only weapons, and
with shields their sole means of protection against bullets, Africans
fought grimly in defense of their land and their national independence. The armed struggle was carried on intermittently for 127 years.
In the end, however, the Africans were defeated, totally disarmed, and
then shepherded into what are known as reserves. These reserves,
260 in number, are usually in the poorest parts of the country and are
utterly inadequate for their large populations.

But wounds could not be licked indefinitely. If the British and the
Boers, despite the bitterness of a hard-fought war, could come together in a united front against the African people, why could not the
Africans unite and face their common problems and enemy, no longer
as individual and separate tribes but as a united people? The answer
was found on January 8, 1912, when African chiefs, intellectuals,
clergymen, workers, and peasants from every tribe in South Africa
met in Bloemfontein and formed the African National Congress. The
organization turned out to be more than a negative reaction to the
formation of a union of white foreigners and conquerors. It became
the symbol of African unity and gave our people a sense of nationhood that has survived the most determined applications of the policy
of divide-and-rule over a period of more than fifty years. Seeing in this
organization a serious threat to their continued political and economic
domination of the country—an evil force to be fought and destroyed
by all means—the white rulers of South Africa and their successive
governments employed a variety of measures to eradicate it. They intimidated and victimized chiefs, teachers, and governmental employees who supported the organization; they engaged the services of
informers and *agents provocateurs*; they engineered groundless quarrels among members of the organization; and they encouraged the
formation of splinter and opposition groups to confuse the people,
to undermine their struggle for national emancipation, and, in that
way, to perpetuate oppression and exploitation.

At the time of the formation of the ANC, there was no question
of relying on armed force as a means of struggle. Only ten or so years
previously, the Boers had tried that method against the British and
failed. Bambata had resorted to arms in 1906 and also failed. Deputa-
tions, petitions, demonstrations, and conference resolutions were the
order of the day. Besides, the Africans had been forcibly disarmed.
The ANC, therefore, led the people into essentially peaceful and
nonviolent forms of action. It was not unusual for governments of the
pre-apartheid era to take some notice of African demands and hold
out some promise of possible concessions. In some cases, political

pressure in the form of public meetings and protest demonstrations yielded favorable results. Although the over-all political and economic situation of the Africans remained consistently intolerable, there was always hope for securing some redress of grievances through peaceful means. The African was not denied such rights as freedom of assembly, speech, organization, the press, and movement—all of which have since completely vanished.

The pattern of legislation passed by successive governments was distinctly discriminatory against the African people and aimed at establishing and perpetuating a servant-and-master relationship between black and white. Thus, Africans employed by white farmers were treated like serfs and worked from dawn to dusk for a mere pittance; the poor and hunger-stricken inhabitants of the overcrowded and arid reserves were subjected to heavy taxation; and, in the urban areas, Africans were harassed by laws requiring passes and were chased from pillar to post by the police.

During World War II, Hitler became the hero, and Nazism the faith, of hundreds of Afrikaners. The fanaticism of the SS was a virtue to be emulated. As the Jews had been shown their place in Hitler's Germany, so would the Kaffirs in South Africa. But the Africans, heartened by the Allies' promise of a postwar world in which the fundamental rights of all men would be respected, became increasingly impatient with their lot. Institutions such as the Advisory Boards, the Natives' Representative Council, the Transkeian Bunga, and the "Native Parliamentary Representatives"—an insignificant handful of whites representing Africans in the South African Senate and House of Assembly—were all attacked by Africans as dummy bodies, and agitation for their boycott was started. Anti-pass campaigns were launched in urban areas where the Africans were most affected by the pass system, protests against poor housing and low wages mounted, and the rural population resisted government schemes that interfered with their rights to land and that sought to limit their livestock.

The war ended, but repression continued unabated. In 1946, the African mine workers in Johannesburg and the Reef went on strike. The strike was ruthlessly repressed and several Africans were killed. The Natives' Representative Council, a dummy African parliament, which, since its establishment in 1937, had struggled in vain to prevent the enactment of discriminatory legislation, adjourned indefinitely in protest. In the same year, the South African Indians launched a passive-resistance campaign against a law restricting their right to land ownership. In the meantime, the growing African National Congress continued protesting against various forms of segregation. The government, on the other hand, adopted more repressive legislation.

It was in this atmosphere of discontent and expectation that the black cloud of reaction and brutal repression descended on South Africa: Dr. Malan's Nationalist Party seized political power in May, 1948. These were the disciples of Hitler. One year later, the shape of things to come was clear. Laws enacted by previous governments were reinforced with vicious amendments and were vigorously enforced by officials who, for sheer brutality, seemed to have been specially recruited from some prehistoric bush where cruelty was a highly prized virtue. Soon the expression became current among Africans that "The devil has been let loose on this country."

Responding to this new challenge, the ANC adopted in 1949 a "program of action" that stipulated that boycotts, strikes, noncollaboration, and "civil disobedience" would now be used as methods and forms of action in the political struggle. The program contemplated participation by the masses of the people. It did not raise the question of violence versus nonviolence. The appearance of the word "nonviolence" in the political vocabulary of the ANC was a product of the objective conditions under which the program was being put into action. The use of the expression "civil disobedience" in the program was, however, of significance. The ANC was an ordinary political organization that had always used methods of political pressure recognized in a democratic country. These methods had been nonviolent, but there had been no specific declaration of policy excluding violence or positively proclaiming nonviolence. In the course of normal demonstration or other forms of political action, the people could conceivably have been provoked into conduct that amounted to civil disobedience, and this could have happened without a policy decision authorizing such conduct. Why then did the 1949 ANC conference go out of its way to provide for "civil disobedience"?

The force with which apartheid struck at the African masses called for action, and the conference decided to commit the organization to specified drastic forms of action. But the program of action did not define "civil disobedience." Did it mean civil disorder? Mob violence? Rioting? It most certainly did not mean any of these types of conduct. The keynote of the disobedience was to be discipline. The expression "civil disobedience" referred to the deliberate breach, or defiance, of government laws, regulations, and orders. The conference, in interpreting civil disobedience in terms of disciplined and purposeful mass action, emphasized nonviolence. It called for self-control on the part of the people and urged them to withstand acts of provocation by the police, who were obviously anxious for a showdown.

Failure to emphasize the need for discipline would have been a fatal political blunder. Nonviolence was thus a political tactic that could be changed according to the demands of the political situation at any given time.

On May 1, 1950, eighteen Africans were killed by the police during a one-day strike staged as the climax to a provincial campaign for universal adult suffrage. On June 26, 1950, the Africans' first national protest strike was called. The strike was the culmination of a country-wide campaign of protest against the Unlawful Organizations Bill introduced by the government and aimed at stamping out all opposition to its racial and oppressive policies. It was also intended as an act of mourning for the Africans killed on May 1 and earlier in the liberation struggle. The strike was a great success and demonstrated the readiness of the oppressed people for determined political action. The Unlawful Organizations Bill was withdrawn as a result of the protest agitation. (It was later introduced and enacted, with slight textual amendments, as the Suppression of Communism Act.)

The policy of uncompromising apartheid was carried out with vigor, violence, hate, and haste. This has remained the pattern of Nationalist Party rule in South Africa to the present day. The country has been in a state of perpetual political crisis now since 1948. It has been the blackest period in the past sixty years and, for the Africans, the bloodiest since the Boer invasions of the eighteenth and nineteenth centuries. In fifteen short years, hundreds of innocent Africans have been shot dead by the police; many more have been wounded by police gunfire during raids, while under arrest, and while in prison; and many have been beaten to death on white-owned farms. In addition, millions of Africans have been convicted of petty offenses, and the average number sentenced to death annually for what are essentially political offenses has been higher than in any corresponding period since Jan van Riebeeck landed in the country in 1652.

When this gruesome phase in the history of the country began to assume a regular pattern in 1950, numerous protests and demonstrations against government policy were staged by many organizations from every racial group. In one way or another, the various groups and movements representing the vast majority of the population voiced their protest. These groups saw the clear advantage in coordinating the anti-apartheid forces and encouraging joint action against the common enemy. Furthermore, since it was the express aim of the government to enforce sharp racial divisions among the population and to set up separate and possibly hostile racial camps, the very act of cooperation and unity among all opponents of racial discrimination and white domination was in itself an attack on government policy. It was, therefore, of great political and strategic importance for the African National Congress to rally, and to welcome, the support of other oppressed groups and of democratic whites. The South African Indian Congress and the Coloured people's leaders readily accepted a basis for conducting joint campaigns.

At its conference in December, 1951, the ANC decided to launch the Defiance Campaign. The story of this dignified, disciplined, and peaceful campaign is well known. It won many friends for the African cause in South Africa and abroad, and served to focus the attention of influential sectors of world opinion on the South African political scene. Within South Africa, the Defiance Campaign strengthened the liberation movement and set the tone for future action. Although toward the end of the campaign the Africans were provoked into some violence, they had amply demonstrated their capacity for self-discipline and their readiness for militant struggle. This meant that it was possible, without resorting to violence, to force the government into a position in which its policy became unworkable. In the years following 1952, hundreds of leaders were banned from taking part in political activities or attending gatherings. Many were restricted to defined areas while others were banished from their homes. Scores were imprisoned, and meetings and processions were prohibited in many parts of the country. Despite all this, however, and despite the fact that the most influential leaders were cut off from the people, the pressures of mass political action throughout the country continued to rise, compelling the government to fall back on an ever-increasing list of repressive and restrictive laws. It made greater use of the police force, equipping it with a growing pile of arms ranging from locally produced pistols to tanks supplied by Great Britain.

When these measures failed, the government resorted to banning political organizations and placing the whole or parts of the country under a state of emergency. The reaction of the ANC to its banning in 1960 was to announce that it would conduct the liberation struggle underground.

The March, 1961, conference of 1,500 delegates representing 145 organizations, at which Nelson Mandela was the main speaker, was organized largely under illegal conditions. It demonstrated the power of the underground organization and the unity of the people. Following this conference, preparations started for a three-day national strike to commence on May 29, 1961. The strike drew unprecedented support from the mass of the African population and was fully backed by the Indian and Coloured communities. Faced with this tremendous political demonstration—which was a triumphant breakthrough for a liberation movement operating under a cloud of repressive legislative prohibitions and restrictions—the Verwoerd government abandoned the political fight and took to arms. The unarmed demonstrators and would-be strikers were confronted with practically the entire South African Army, fully equipped and ready for war.

Today the oppressors are arming feverishly. In 1963, Parliament passed a peace-time "defense" budget of more than £64 million (approximately U.S. $200 million). The Army, Navy, and Air Force are being further expanded and equipped with additional modern weapons. Military training of men, women, and young people has become a regular feature of organized life in the white section of the South African population. The Minister of Defense boasts that 250,000 white men and women can be put into action at any time. The regular army of 20,000 is increasing by 10,000 men annually and will number 60,000 by 1965. The police force, which numbered 20,000 in 1953, rose to 50,000 by 1962 and is being further increased. It has now been equipped with weapons for "combat duty." Arms factories have been established in South Africa and, recently, Britain and France have become notorious as the leading accomplices in the frantic arms build-up in South Africa, they being the chief suppliers of a substantial range of death-dealing war weapons and military aircraft of various types. The Army build-up and the new Anti-Sabotage Act have completely nullified the strategic value of nonviolence, leaving the African with no alternative but to pursue the goal of freedom and independence by way of taking a "tooth for a tooth" and meeting violence with violence.

It is hardly necessary to make the point that we would rather have avoided this course. But if the South African Hitlerites go berserk and seek to drown the country in innocent human blood before committing suicide after the manner of their revered hero, no one should be surprised that the African should take effective and appropriate steps to defend himself, and, by every method that he considers appropriate, to ensure the successful prosecution of his struggle for liberation. In this context, violence is an extension of, not a substitute for, the forms of political action employed in the past. Its use will be confined to the pursuit of the objective of freedom for the oppressed people.

An intensive policy of soliciting and mobilizing world condemnation of apartheid started shortly after the launching of the Defiance Campaign. Visitors to South Africa—numerous journalists, distinguished authors, leading world personalities, and representatives and members of overseas organizations—were briefed in detail on the tyranny of apartheid. By means of annual memoranda sent by the ANC and the SAIC to the United Nations and by South African delegations attending international conferences, the word "apartheid" spread to many parts of the world. The arrest of African leaders on charges of high treason followed by an appeal by Africans for an international boycott of South African goods further increased world support, and offered people and organizations in different countries an opportunity to give tangible expression to their sympathies for our cause. By 1960, the degree of world interest in South Africa was such that the Sharpeville massacres provoked an explosive and universal barrage of indignant protests. This coldblooded carnage brought the whole of mankind face to face with the essentially inhuman and barbarous nature of apartheid.

Many people and organizations in different countries, notably in Britain, Scandinavia, and the United States, took up the issue, and, since 1960, campaigns have been organized to rally support for the boycott of South African goods and for other economic sanctions. Several governments, particularly the newly independent African states, Asian nations, and the Socialist countries, have supported United Nations resolutions calling for economic sanctions against South Africa. The United States and Great Britain, which, of all the U.N. member-states, have the biggest stake in the South African economy, have, however, consistently and strenuously resisted the move to impose sanctions on South Africa. This has so far made it impossible for the U.N. to employ the only form of peaceful and effective intervention open to it, and has consequently enabled the South African Government to pursue its policies with only limited interference from the outside world. Hence the emergence of violent methods of struggle in South Africa.

It would be wrong to conclude that it is now too late to influence the trend of events in South Africa by way of external pressures. On the contrary, the challenge of the present situation is the greater not only to those who abhor racialism and all that goes by the name of apartheid and white minority rule, but also to those who disapprove of all violence. The sooner South Africa is isolated economically, politically, and culturally, the shorter will be the duration of this, the last and bitterest phase of the struggle for human rights and freedom in Africa.

Editors' Postscript

During the past two years, African nationalists in South Africa have increasingly abandoned hope of nonviolent resistance to the Verwoerd regime. On November 6, 1964, *Vuyisile Mini, Wilson Khayinga, and Zinakile Mkaba of Port Elizabeth were executed. A few months later, it was learned that Washington Bongco, a newspaper vendor from East London, had been secretly executed in February, 1965. Mr. Bongco had been found guilty of being volunteer-in-chief of the regional committee of the ANC, of soliciting funds for the banned organization, and of engaging in acts of sabotage. Their strikes broken up, their leaders arrested and executed, African nationalists have organized underground and resorted to sabotage. Recently, there has been talk of a new phase in the struggle.*

In mid-1963, the South African Government cracked down with arrests and bannings affecting every nonwhite political party in the country. A total of 67,637 Africans—1 out of every 236—were held in jail. The powers of suppression were not sufficient to the task, however, and at the end of May, Parliament passed the infamous General Law Amendment Act. This act authorized the Minister of Justice to detain anyone he wished incommunicado for 90 days, to extend sentences without trial for security offenses, and to punish by death anyone accused of sabotage. Only Mrs. Helen Suzman, the lone representative of the Progressive Party, voted against the bill.

With the powers thus provided, the Nationalist government immediately began a ruthless and effective campaign against every form of serious opposition, arresting virtually all African nationalist leaders. Robert Sobukwe, due to be released from prison in May, was indefinitely detained. Two of the most prominent leaders—Nelson Mandela and Walter Sisulu—were brought to trial on November 25, 1963, along with nine other men and accused of plotting to overthrow the government by revolution. The indictment was soon quashed on the grounds that the state had failed to give the accused sufficient information about the charges against them.

The accused were held, however, and charged again. On April 20, 1964, Mandela took the stand and declared that in 1961 he had concluded that, "without violence there would be no way open to African people to succeed in their struggle against the principle of white supremacy." However, he added that it was the policy of the "Spear of the Nation" (one of the underground sabotage groups) to avoid inflicting injury or loss of life while committing sabotage.

Despite pleas from the U.N. Security Council and countless international and civic organizations throughout the world, the Rivonia trial, as it had come to be known, ended with sentences of life imprisonment for Mandela and Sisulu. On July 9, 1964, the leader of the defense team, attorney Abram Fischer, was arrested under the ninety-day detention clause. Later released so that he could plead a case in

London, he disappeared and, on January 2, 1965, sent word to the Johannesburg Magistrate's Court that he had gone into hiding and would not stand trial. Still, he intended to stay in South Africa because "I believe it is the duty of every true opponent of the government to remain in this country and to oppose its monstrous policy with every means in his power." [1] He has not since been found.

In May, 1964, ex-Chief Albert Luthuli was served with a new five-year banning order which covered church services and prohibited him from visiting even the town of Stanger, four miles from his home. In October, 1964, Wilton Mkwayi, former senior executive member of the ANC and the last known African leader who had not yet been banned, arrested, executed, or had not left the country, was arrested and sentenced to life imprisonment.

On January 11, 1965, the 90-day detention clause was suspended. After detaining 1,095 people, charging 575, and convicting 272, the Government of South Africa was satisfied, for it had virtually crushed all resistance.

Beyond the borders of the Republic, however, from Dar es Salaam to New York, the cause of African freedom in South Africa has continued to be pressed. Dar has become one of the major rendezvous of political refugees from all over Southern Africa, including about 100 ANC and 10 PAC leaders. Both groups receive financial assistance from the Liberation Bureau of the OAU.

The diplomatic offensive in the United Nations also continues. In 1963, the General Assembly established a Special Committee on Apartheid which recommended withdrawing all economic and technical assistance, discouraging private investment, prohibiting immigration to South Africa, denying facilities for South African ships and aircraft, and putting an embargo on arms, ammunition, and petroleum. For the past two years, these suggestions have been debated within and outside the General Assembly. In 1964, the United Nations acted to establish an expert committee on the feasibility of sanctions against South Africa. The committee concluded that although South Africa would not be readily susceptible to economic sanctions, such measures would not be without effect. France did not participate in any of the meetings, while Britain and the United States wrote reservations into the record reflecting their hesitation about any form of economic coercion to effect a change in the racial policies of a sovereign state. These last two countries, it might be noted, account for nearly half the investment in South Africa and average profits of 27 per cent on invested capital.[2]

[1] Africa Digest, XII, No. 5 (April, 1965), 133.
[2] Africa Digest, XI, No. 5 (April, 1964), 149.

On April 17, 1964, an International Conference on Economic Sanctions Against South Africa was convened in London under the chairmanship of Foreign Minister Mongi Slim of Tunisia. The conference concluded that sanctions were both feasible and necessary if racial war was to be avoided in South Africa.[3] They also decided that no leadership could be expected from Great Britain and that the United States must be pressed to undertake this role. Meanwhile the South African economy is booming. Ample credit is available, investment is increasing, and the growth rate is one of the highest in the world, reaching 8.5 per cent in 1963. The volume of trade with most countries—including those of Africa, Asia, and the Soviet bloc—was increased in 1964.

Calls for an embargo on arms and ammunition have met with somewhat more success than those for an embargo on trade. In 1963, the United States voted for a Security Council resolution calling for an embargo on shipment of arms but noted that she did not consider the resolution mandatory. France and Britain abstained and continued sales, the former supplying South Africa with vitally needed Mirage III jet bombers. British Prime Minister Macmillan, concerned with use of the Simonstown naval base, announced that Britain was committed to supplying South Africa with weapons for external defense. The government was widely attacked on this issue as it was noted that Britain still supplied parts for Saracen armed personnel carriers of the type used at Sharpeville, Wasp helicopters, and Buccaneer low-level jet aircraft. Since the Labour Party victory, the British Government has acted more decisively, announcing on November 17, 1964, that all armament shipments would be discontinued. After being threatened by Dr. Verwoerd with revocation of the 1955 agreement permitting use of the Simonstown naval base, Prime Minister Harold Wilson hedged a bit and stated that existing contracts for Buccaneer jets would be fulfilled. Critics pointed out that Simonstown was no longer vital to Britain as supply ships could now perform many of the base's functions. In addition, Freetown in Sierre Leone and Mombasa in Kenya have been suggested as suitable substitutes.

During the past two years, the United States, Sweden, Denmark,

[3] Concerning racial war, the Rand *Daily Mail* quoted Dr. Piet Meyer, head of South African Broadcasting and of the Broederbond, as saying: " 'South Africa will make a decisive contribution to the consolidation of the entire West as a White world united in its struggle against the forces of the Yellow and Black races,' and that once America got over its 'transitional sickness' and took over 'the leadership of the whole White world' the West would be 'very favourably placed to win the racial struggle on a global scale.' " (As recorded in *Africa Digest*, XII, No. 5 [April, 1965], 131.)

Switzerland, Italy, and Canada have all decided to prohibit arms ship-ments to South Africa. These measures have been taken, however, only after South Africa was well on the way to becoming self-suffi-cient militarily. Currently engaged in a military build-up designed to meet every conceivable threat both from within and from outside the country, South Africa has budgeted defense spending at $294 million in 1965, compared with $61.6 million in 1960. The call-up for mili-tary training in 1964 was increased 60 per cent, and it is now reported that some 17,000 draftees are receiving military training annually. In addition, there are rumors that white women will also be called up. In the weapons field, the government is now preparing to manufacture poison gas, jet aircraft, and guided missiles in addition to various light arms. A nuclear reactor is also in operation.

In view of her economic and military strength, it is now believed that South Africa would be most vulnerable to an oil embargo. Since she produces only 5 per cent of her needs and has storage facilities for only a six weeks' supply, a disruption of oil shipments could quickly bring South Africa's vital industries to a grinding halt. Enforcement of such an embargo would probably require a naval blockade, perhaps under U.N. auspices. So far, no major powers have shown signs of seriously considering this possibility. On December 3, 1964, British Prime Minister Harold Wilson declared to the House of Commons that an oil embargo would be equivalent to a declaration of war. The major Western powers are now biding their time pending an Inter-national Court of Justice decision on South West Africa.

Propaganda in the South African Struggle

LEWIS NKOSI

Though it would be difficult to assess its effectiveness with accuracy, propaganda has done a great deal to advance the cause of human freedom in South Africa. It has been a valuable instrument for advising the world of the nature and extent of the African peoples' discontent, and it has helped to educate the African masses to their own potentiality for bringing about changes in the social structure. It has served also to break down the isolationism of the tribes, and to forge a new spirit of African nationhood, embracing both the Sotho and the Nguni tribes.

This paper deals with the role of newspapers, pamphlets, books, songs, and slogans in the nonviolent struggle for human rights in South Africa. Although, in certain cases, evidence exists indicating the effectiveness of propaganda as a weapon in our nonviolent struggle,* nowhere is conclusive proof available as to what extent it has assisted. Generally, its effectiveness can be evaluated by indirect methods—by, say, the response of the masses to certain directives from political organizations where the mass media were either absent or hostile, or by government response in the form of bannings, suppression, and curbs on newspapers, pamphlets, books, and recorded songs containing material of a political nature. It is interesting to note here that even jazz records by militant and politically conscious musicians like Max Roach and Abbey Lincoln have been banned in South Africa.

Newspapers and Modern Political Movements

After the Boer War, the white races in South Africa made the first moves to sink their differences and bring the four provinces together

* The writer does not think that the struggle in South Africa has been entirely nonviolent, nor does he think the nonviolent method is likely to prove effective. The paper deals merely with that phase in which nonviolence was tactically considered a more realistic method of struggle.

into some kind of union. In 1909, the Native Convention, the first of its kind, was held, bringing together politically conscious Africans from all the corners of South Africa to ponder the consequences of a white union in which Africans would have no say whatever. The only nationwide political group existing at this time was Dr. A. Abdurahman's African Political Organization (APO), which consisted largely of Coloured people. Dr. Abdurahman brought out his own newspaper, which clearly reflected the mood of the times. "Our political destiny," said the newspaper editorially, "is in our hands, and we must be prepared to face the fight with grim determination to succeed. . . . Undoubtedly the Coloured and the native races of South Africa hold the strongest weapon in the hands of any class. . . . It may ere too long come about that the necessity will be imposed upon us in every sphere and throughout the whole subcontinent, to refuse to bolster up the economic fabric of the people who refuse us political freedom. That would bring the foolish white politicians to their knees."

The four provinces of South Africa were granted autonomy by Britain in 1910 when they agreed to form a union. That year marked the turning point in the nonwhite struggle for human rights in South Africa, for this Act of Union virtually meant that Britain had handed the nonwhite population over to the tender mercies of a repressive white minority. It is interesting at this stage to reflect that Britain is now being asked to perpetrate what can only be regarded as the same ghastly mistake concerning Southern Rhodesia.

It was about this time that genuinely sophisticated and modern political movements sprang up in South Africa. Significantly, it was also at this time—when the rights of nonwhite people were threatened or under assault and a reactionary wind was blowing through every corner of the land—that black and brown people in South Africa saw the advantages of closer cooperation. The African National Congress was formed in 1912 specifically as a reaction to the hostile Act of Union by the white races of South Africa.

Welcoming this first historic conference of the South African Native Congress on February 24, 1912, the APO newspaper put the case forward with admirable perspicacity:

This is one of the most important events that [has] ever happened in South Africa. . . . The conference has sounded the death knell of the race differences [among Africans] of the past. It has paved the way for a complete understanding between the native races. It has transformed them from a congerie of warring atoms into a united nation voluntarily determining to sink all petty differences. . . . It has changed the whole native outlook.

For the first time in a nonwhite newspaper, we began to capture a real note of sophistication, an unapologetic militancy, and a thinly veiled impatience with the leadership of white liberals: On January 25, 1912, the APO reported: "The Natives' emancipation cannot come about as a result of pastime hobbies of white men, nor from the oft-professed good intentions of our legislators. Their emancipation must be the result of their own efforts and determination. . . . They lead themselves. They must eliminate a good lump of selfishness from their natures by an acceptance of the axiom that 'an injury to one is an injury to all' and act upon it."

One of the founders of the South African Native Congress was an illustrious African scholar, P. Ka I. Seme, a young African lawyer with a B.A. degree from Columbia University who had also studied law in London before his return to South Africa, in 1910. Seme started his own newspaper, *Abantu-Batho*, which was the mouthpiece of the African National Congress for many years. *Abantu-Batho* contained articles written in English, and represented every linguistic group in South Africa. A few of the privately owned African newspapers of the time were later incorporated into *Abantu-Batho*. It did more perhaps than any other organ to break down tribal barriers. It popularized various national slogans at different periods: *Vuka Afrika!* (Wake up, Africa!) and *Mayibuy' Afrika!* (Let Africa come back!).[1]

Since the 1900's, there have been several newspapers and journals that have wielded some influence in the African community, or in the nonwhite community as a whole: the *Ilanga Lase Natal*, which was founded by Dr. John Dube in 1902; the *Bantu World*, which was started in 1932 with white capital and later went on to absorb most of the African papers into a newspaper combine called the Bantu Press; *Inkundla*, which displayed some of the most brilliant journalism in the liberation movement of Southern Africa; and *Umsebenzi* (*The Worker*) and *Inkululeko* (*Freedom*), both mouthpieces of the Communist Party which threw their weight behind the struggle of the African people in South Africa. The Communist papers were most fearless in their support of pass-burning campaigns and the bloody mine workers' strikes of the 1930's, but they suffered from the well-known malady that seems to afflict the Party in most countries: They tended to see the African struggle in South Africa as subordinate to Soviet power politics.

Bantu World has lately been very hostile to the African National Congress and has tried to sabotage its campaigns. *Ilanga* has be-

[1] See Eduard Roux, *Time Longer Than Rope* (London, 1949).

come editorially innocuous. It is sad to see these papers, which were founded by Africans, taken over by white businessmen and turned into the jejune newssheets they are today. *Ilanga*, for instance, will long be remembered in the African community for the profoundly instructive, ceaselessly fighting editorials of Herbert I. Dhlomo, one of the best writers Africa has produced. Another newspaper of influence was *Indian Opinion*, edited by Manilal Gandhi (Mahatma Gandhi's son) up until the time of his death in the early 1950's. Manilal served time in jail for his part in the passive-resistance campaign of 1952. *Drum* magazine, white-owned and edited by Englishman Anthony Sampson, and once one of South Africa's most able and crusading journals, did more to expose social conditions than most magazines in South Africa. Writers like Bloke Modisane, Ezekiel Mphahlele, Henry Nxumalo, and Arthur Maimane were associated with *Drum* at one time or another. It, too, has suffered a severe decline since the days of Anthony Sampson and Sylvester Stein and now seems satisfied with publishing thin, evasive pieces of journalism or articles of mainly criminological interest.

There are two other newspapers which, interestingly, stand on opposite sides of the ideological line and have bitterly attacked each other from time to time, although they have both contributed immensely to the cause of the liberatory struggle in South Africa: *New Age* (which has many aliases) [2] and the liberal weekly journal *Contact*. Few of us who were in South Africa during the Sharpeville tragedy will forget how *Contact* distinguished itself on that occasion by printing the only comprehensive and authoritative eyewitness account of that event. The story was written by an editor of *Drum*, although that venerable journal seemed unable to treat the story on any terms other than timid, superficial ones. Patrick Duncan, the editor of *Contact*, was jailed, "gagged" by government order, and now edits his paper from exile in Basutoland. *New Age* has proved to be an invaluable friend of the ANC. It is difficult to see how various Congress organizations could have reached as many people as they did without *New Age*'s stalwart and fearless support. Although I would not recom-

---

[2] The newspaper first appeared as *The Guardian*, a mouthpiece of the Communist Party, in the 1930's. With the advent of the present Nationalist Party government, it was banned under the Suppression of Communism Act, but the publishers were never given an opportunity to defend themselves in court as they were never formally charged. *The Guardian* then appeared as the *Clarion*, which was refused registration on technical grounds. It then appeared as *Advance*, and was banned in 1954. Then it appeared as *New Age*, and was banned again, late in 1962. It appeared next as *Spark*; this paper ceased publication in March, 1963, when most of its staffers became proscribed writers under the Sabotage Act. The paper has been sold to a new company.

mend *New Age* for an objective report on Cold War politics, I have nothing but praise for the way it has consistently exposed the shocking conditions under which our people live in that godless country, which is more than can be said about many other newspapers that are published purportedly to serve the interests of the nonwhite peoples of South Africa.

The press does not have an easy time in South Africa. Despite the fact that up to now there has been no newspaper censorship,[3] the incitement laws in South Africa have made it sufficiently difficult to support political campaigns directed against the state. This has tended to limit the scope and function of the newspaper during any specific campaign of passive resistance. It is one thing for a newspaper to report that the African National Congress or the Pan-Africanist Congress has set a date upon which it proposes to march to jail in protest against the pass laws; it is quite another thing to urge the masses to support such a campaign.[4]

Another difficulty arises out of the fact that newspaper editors do not—and certainly cannot be asked to—always assume the attitude that they have no other function than that of praising and abetting the actions or the leadership of any single organization. Sometimes editors feel that they have to differ with a decision made by a political organization. Opinion is necessarily divided as to how much newspapers should criticize political organizations in a situation where any political action is better than none. In 1959, Ronald Segal, editor of *Africa South,* decided to publish an article by Julius Lewin meant to debunk the idea that a revolution was around the corner in South Africa. Such an article was not welcome to African political organizations, of course, and was very convenient for the Government of South Africa, which was trying to convince investors that South Africa was safe and that Dr. Verwoerd was really in control. The point is, how does an editor decide when and when not to print a truthful article? Segal wrote: "I hesitated for more than a week before deciding to publish the article. . . . Clearly, a significant function of revolutionary propaganda was to sap confidence, both inside the country and beyond, in the ability of the government to retain control. . . . Yet, clearly, too, a revolutionary leadership that fed off its own propaganda would soon enough fall into a stupor of self-satisfaction."

It is with regard to this kind of dilemma that newspapers have to

[3] The South African Government has placed before Parliament a Publications and Entertainments Bill, which will introduce internal censorship for the first time in the country.

[4] Tom Hopkinson, *In the Fiery Continent* (London, 1962), Chapter 25.

be judged when specific instances of hostility against political campaigns are being discussed. One example that comes to mind is the "general stoppage" by nonwhite workers organized by the ANC in South Africa to coincide with election week, 1958. Almost all the newspapers, except *New Age*, which was more or less the mouthpiece of the ANC, were hostile to or skeptical of the idea of a work stoppage, and wrote editorials to say so. An Africanist wing of the ANC was also violently opposed to the strike and could be charged quite rightly with having helped to split the nonwhite workers into two camps. Their opposition to this strike could have been made known to the masses only by making use of a willing press. When the strike failed, many people in the ANC felt that newspapers—even those published for nonwhites—had been partly responsible for the flop and had to take some of the blame. Stanley Uys, one of the leading political analysts in the country, wrote a post-mortem of the strike for *Africa South* in which he summarized the reasons for its failure. "Clearly, too," Uys wrote, "the ANC's propaganda and other resources were not adequate to cope with the white man's armory of promises, threats and pressure." [5] An interesting summation of the press in South Africa was given by a young African journalist in *The New African*.[6] Referring to the English-language press, the writer said:

> The Press seems to prefer stooges and Advisory Board leaders who have but a small following. Sobukwe, Mandela and Sisulu are seen by Africans not as "agitators," but as some sort of African "Spartacus" battling for their liberation. . . . During the 1957 bus boycott, *The Star* spoke of "responsible native leaders" who wanted to end the boycott, a line which was also followed by almost all the English papers.
>
> On the other hand, the Bantu Press, particularly the daily *World*, is a definite "carbon copy" of the English Press. . . . This paper seems to be at pains to show the Africans that apartheid is not as bad as they think, as there are shopkeepers among the people. . . . *Golden City Post*, on the other hand, seemed to be a paper for the people. Like *Drum*, it used to expose apartheid and bolster the activities of the ANC because that organization favored multiracialism. But nowadays it seems the editors are afraid of offending white supremacy and have followed the line of the *World* by toning down on news to suit the commercial and political views of its proprietors.[7]

[5] Stanley Uys, "The Strike That Failed," *Africa South*, July–September, 1958.

[6] Peter Motsoane, "The Partisan Press," *The New African*, February, 1963.

[7] Additional information about South African newspapers can be found in Eric A. Walker's *A History of South Africa* (London, 1928); Eduard Roux, *op.*

Creative Writing as Propaganda

Presumably, one is not being called upon to make an artistic judgment on creative literature when it is used primarily, as so often happens in South Africa, as an instrument of propaganda. My intention here is not to define a novel, which would be a futile exercise, or to assess the artistic merits of Alan Paton's *Cry, The Beloved Country*, which would be irrelevant to this discussion. What I intend to suggest is that Mr. Paton's work contains the best tracts of propaganda that have ever been sold to an overseas public under the guise of creative fiction, and it is one for which Africans, as underdogs, can be grateful. I know certain people here in America and England whose first awareness of the tragedy of South Africa began with their encounter with Mr. Paton's novel. They were terribly moved by it and, ever since, they have wanted to do something about the unhappy state of affairs in that country. *Cry* clearly stands in relation to the black people of South Africa as *Uncle Tom's Cabin* does to the Negro people of America, and the novel shares more or less the same faults with that other work and stimulates the same kind of controversy.

This novel differs from *The Story of a South African Farm* by Olive Schreiner, certainly the first mature South African novelist to write in English, which did contain some harsh criticism of the treatment of black people by white people in South Africa. Criticism, however, seems incidental to the main purpose of the writer, which is to tell a story, to develop a theme, or to fulfill functions other than those of expressly exhorting the reader to racial tolerance. *Cry* also differs from Nadine Gordimer's *A World of Strangers* or Dan Jacobson's *Evidence of Love*, because, though these novels contain some implicit appeal to racial tolerance and some protest against the atomizing effects of apartheid laws, the writers seem, at bottom, to be motivated by a desire to tell the story first and to protest only secondarily. However, Miss Gordimer's novel is an important and legitimate piece of propaganda in favor of an integrated society in South Africa. The novel sees our tragedy mainly as our failure as a nation to accept the premise that we are indissolubly linked together

---

cit.; Ronald M. Segal, *Into Exile* (London, 1963); Anthony Sampson, *Drum* (London, 1956); Leo Kuper, *Passive Resistance in South Africa* (London, 1956); Alexander Hepple, *Censorship and Press Control in South Africa* (Johannesburg, 1960); Tom Hopkinson, *op. cit.*; and Brian Bunting, *The Story Behind the Non-White Press* (Johannesburg, n.d.).

in a multiracial state. This fact emerges more clearly in *Dilemma*, the recent film based on that novel. The film was shot secretly in the country in 1962 by the Danish producer Henning Carlsen, who persuaded the South African Government that he was there to film the "good" side, or what the government likes to call the "other" side of the picture. The film contains some wonderful jazz by Max Roach and Abbey Lincoln, which makes me feel that the American South and South Africa are lucky to claim the same kind of attention from these talented and committed artists.

To turn to the writing by black South Africans is to turn to prolonged and unrelieved protest writing. I do not feel that I must deal with this subject at length because we have heard about nothing else these last few years, whenever South African writing is discussed. The short stories of writers like Bloke Modisane, Arthur Maimane, Richard Rive, James Matthews, and Ezekiel Mphahlele, to name only a few, all contain some form of protest against social injustice, against the degradation of black by white men, against the African's political inability to change the social structure that forces him to endure social emasculation.

The rage that consumes so many characters in black fiction comes out of this apprehension of the black writer's world as a prison of futility securely enclosed within walls of oppression that cannot be scaled. Because of this social claustrophobia, the writer's vision of his people's full potentiality, not as they are but as they might be in a free society, is severely limited.

But black people have also magnificently endured. In some of the less shrill-toned pieces—for instance, *The Dignity of Begging* by Bloke Modisane or Can Themba's *Marta*—the black writers tell the story of that magnificent survival. These stories may be satirical, gay, or cynical, but they are informed by a feeling of unsurpassable grief turned into bitter strength—turned even into laughter, that liberating irony which underlies the "blues" feeling. Alan Paton's failure to capture this feeling when writing about places like Sophiatown and his tendency to see only dereliction in these places is a source of constant irritation to some of us who lived there.

Though we certainly need propaganda that helps us to expose the appalling social conditions under which our people are forced to live, we also need the propaganda that tells of us as we really are—a people of supreme strength and boundless faith and spiritual authority.

Songs and Slogans

It is when we come, finally, to songs and slogans that we are made sharply aware of the African people's ingenuity in utilizing various forms of communication as vehicles for anti-apartheid propaganda. Since the frontier wars of 1779, songs in South Africa have been used as a powerful medium for propaganda in the struggle for freedom. Eduard Roux reports that, in 1818, Mahana led a Xhosa army that sang crusade songs as it advanced:

> To chase the white men from the earth
> And drive them to the sea,
> The sea that cast them up at first
> For AmaXhosa's curse and bane
> Howls for the progeny she nursed
> To swallow them again.

Of the first African composers who reacted to conquest and disinheritance, Todd Matshikiza, composer of the music for the South African stage musical *King Kong*, had some interesting comments to make in the course of a lecture he gave in England recently: [8]

The proud songs of Southern Africa have been described by someone in a very apt phrase as the songs of the temporary underdog. This description sums up the spirit of a nationalism that has risen since the first white pioneers ventured into the Cape Province and clashed with the AmaXhosa, the first African linguistic group to make frontier and social contact with the white man in the South. Their music in particular shows some of the signs of this early, close contact. Their madrigal is adopted by early African composers and in general a Western musical style utilized by the people in songs expressing anti-Western sentiments, or more precisely anti-white South African ideologies.

The most interesting of these are work songs or chants that bear striking resemblance at times to some U.S. Southern Negro work songs and chants. Most work songs contain some devastating attack on the values of white people, on their exploitation of black people, or on their "enhanced uselessness" when it comes to physical effort, or even to making physical love. I would like to feel that all these sentiments are calculated to incapacitate white people for exercising

[8] This BBC lecture was reprinted in the British magazine *New Society*, December 13, 1962.

oppression over black people, or to make them feel insecure and less impudent; however, some of the themes expressed by these songs constitute the myths that black people believe about white people as a whole.

The following is a favorite work song in South Africa. There are many variations on the words:

> Abalengu ngo-damn
> (White people, be damned!
>   be damned!
> White people, be damned!
>   be damned!)

> or

> Abelungu Ngodoti
> (White people are dirt!
>   are dirt!
> White people are dirt!
>   are dirt!)

Some songs are well-known hymns hastily pressed into service for political propaganda, such as the following one, which substitutes the name of Chief Albert Luthuli, the Nobel Prize–winner, for Jesus:

> I will follow, I will follow Luthuli,
> I will follow, I will follow him,
> I will follow, I'll follow Luthuli,
> Everywhere he leads me I will follow him.

Where organization against the state is difficult and newspaper circulation hampered, songs have taken on the role of the traditional drums. The Security Police might think that the "natives are enjoying themselves," when actually a message of great political import is being passed on through chants and songs. In his BBC lecture, Mr. Matshikiza remarked:

More relevant to the present political struggle is the song of the Pondo tribe in the Transkei. For many years the battle has raged between them and the Government over land, stock limitation, and the demotion of their chiefs. The Transkei has been placed under emergency regulations since 1960, and one recalls how these frowning but quiet men have resorted to the deep forests to meet since organized public protests are banned. Today they answer, not to the magistrates' summons, but to the "Song of the Cattle" that rumbles in deep, guttural tones across the valleys, calling the men to a secret meeting place. The music fascinates, for its long throaty sounds almost croak like a frog, or in some remote and peculiar way are reminiscent of the mountain music of Tiber. But even taken outside of particular grievances, the protest song has not only united the undaunted Xhosa and Pondo diplomats of the "deep south" with the mountain men of the late King Moshoeshoe's northern statesmen, but has also linked the proud Zulu warrior with the more privileged "Coloureds" (people of mixed parentage) in the Western Cape. Under the country's judicial system the African and the "Coloured" have found a bond in common.

The slogans serve more or less the same function as songs, with the difference that they are epigrammatical, pithy, and concentrated. "Freedom in Our Lifetime!," "*Mayebuye Afrika!*" (Come Back, Africa!), and "*Izwe Lethu!*" (The Country Is Ours) are examples. Slogan writing is a veritable profession in South Africa. Many of my friends—most of them students—have been sentenced to jail terms for plastering public buildings with large painted slogans. For instance, one morning Johannesburg woke to find the following slogans, most of them quotes from the Freedom Charter of the Congress Movement, painted on the walls of various public buildings:

> On the Supreme Court building: "Equality Before the Law."
> On the bank building: "The People Shall Share the Wealth
> of the Country."
> On the public library: "The People Ain't Reading."

The last one was cleaned up by the City Council but was soon replaced by "The People Ain't Reading *Yet!*"

Discussion

NDABANINGI SITHOLE.　　Nonviolence is a very important subject. All human beings would like to settle their problems peacefully, but when "peaceful" means that problems cannot be settled, then, of course, other means are resorted to.

Nonviolence is an appeal to the moral conscience. If the "powers that be" have no moral conscience, nonviolence is left without any power whatsoever. Leaders may be committed to nonviolence, but the masses may regard this as an unrealistic approach, overthrow their leaders, and resort to violence. Peaceful strikes, demonstrations, and boycotts are the usual forms of nonviolence, but when soldiers and police attack, then what began as a nonviolent movement becomes a violent movement.

It has been pointed out that nonviolence relies completely on constitutional means. But what constitutional means are available to the 11 million Africans in South Africa who are outside the constitution of the country? You have to have a constitution of your own before you can commit something that may be construed as unconstitutional. In Southern Rhodesia, in South Africa, we do not have constitutional means of getting redress, and therefore nonviolence cannot work.

We know that there are many spiritual, ethical, moral, and humane considerations underlying nonviolence. We realize that basically human beings like to be nonviolent, but times come when they are pushed to a point when they must be violent in order to get their own human rights.

ARTHUR N. L. WINA.　　Nonviolence succeeds or fails depending upon the political environment within which it operates. If the environment is sensitive to human values, then of course there is a greater possibility that nonviolence will succeed. If the powers prevailing are absolutely indifferent to human values or moral precepts, then nonviolence is likely to subject its followers to arrest or even to hanging. We have seen this in Southern Rhodesia. The Southern Rhodesia Government has passed a law that makes it an offense punishable by hanging merely to agitate for freedom of the people. Verwoerd and his type condone no movement that threatens the existing political system.

The success of nonviolence will depend on leadership control. If the followers become impatient with the progress made, believe that leadership is using nonviolence merely as a cover for inaction, or realize that they have no hope whatsoever of achieving their objectives, they will get out of control, overthrow the leadership, and substitute that leadership which speaks their language—namely, violence. Moreover, the success of nonviolence is very much dependent upon international opinion, for if world opinion remains passive and complacent, then the whole basis of nonviolence is undermined and rendered almost useless.

SAUNDERS REDDING.   I would like to say a word about African nationalist propaganda emanating from Dar es Salaam. From the day of its independence, Tanganyika became a haven for the politically disaffected, the hunted and the hated from the southern end of Africa. Tanganyika was favorably located, and its government was known to be ardently anti-oppression. The word got around that anyone with "a dark skin, a tale of woe, and nationalist leanings" could be sure of asylum. Indeed, to say that the government was sympathetic to nationalist causes is to understate. In 1960, Julius Nyerere offered to postpone Tanganyika's independence for a year on the condition that the postponement "would expedite the independence of Kenya and Uganda." And when independence came, the ruling party, the Tanganyika African National Union, welcomed political refugees from Mozambique and Angola, the Federation, South West Africa, and South Africa. Until recently, these various nationalist groups had offices in the headquarters of TANU itself. Now each has its own quarters, and one section of the main street of Dar es Salaam, Independence Avenue, is referred to as Freedom Fighters Square.

The African National Congress published a five-page mimeographed paper in Dar—the *South African Freedom News*—which very effectively straightened the slant of the news from the white South African press. ANC distributed another paper—*New Age*—which was printed in South Africa until it was banned in January, 1963, and which was reputed to be the most outspoken of the nationalist papers. Also, the ANC was supported —as all African nationalist movements are—by *Spearhead*, a monthly. Ably edited by Frene Ginwala, and frequently carrying stories by Nyerere, Mboya, Nkrumah, and Colin Legum, *Spearhead* aims at an intellectual readership and regards itself as the "conscience of African socialism." All of these publications zero in on such vulnerable targets as Roy Welensky, Winston Field, Hendrik Verwoerd, and Charles Swart. In South Africa, it is an offense punishable by five years in prison to have a copy of *South African Freedom News* in one's possession. I have been told that the paper is smuggled into South Africa, and that several hundred people commit this offense weekly.

The possession of a newspaper is not yet declared sabotage in Southern Rhodesia, but now that ZAPU has been banned and its leader forced into exile in Tanganyika, it may soon be. ZAPU already has its own organ, a tabloid that was started in Dar, but it is still not sufficiently sure of itself to go in for the refinements of political arguments and international questions that characterize *Spearhead* or the monthly magazine *Fighting Talk*. *Fighting Talk* is still published in South Africa and, judging by its contributors—for example, Ezekiel Mphahlele and Lewis Nkosi—as well as by its stories, poems, and drawings, is very sophisticated indeed.

Much if not most of the work of two former liberation movements in Mozambique, which united about a year ago to form the Mozambique Liberation Front (FRELIMO), is coordinated in Dar es Salaam. It is no secret that FRELIMO, under the strong leadership of Eduardo Mondlane, has gone beyond propaganda's first stage, which aims at creating a oneness of will, and is ready to take those practical political steps that will lead to independence. FRELIMO has no propaganda organ in Dar, but it does have a publicity secretary, Leo Milas; Dr. Mondlane has ample coverage in the Tanganyikan press. South West Africa's nationalism is represented by two establishments in Dar—the South West African People's Organization and the South West African National Union.

Each of these several nationalist movements concentrates on achieving independence for its own country, and the propaganda of each is designed primarily for that purpose. But necessary to the accomplishment of independence is the willingness of other countries—on both sides of the diplomatic curtain—at least to see it accomplished, if they cannot be persuaded to help in the accomplishment. The South African ANC is by far the most sophisticated, in its approach to winning independence, of the nationalist groups operating in Dar. This may be because the situation in South Africa itself is by far the most stubborn and dangerous, and the greatest menace to the peace of Africa and the world. South African nationalists have had long experience with that situation, and they exploit it in the international press. ANC spokesmen in Dar get the attention of Tass, the Associated Press, and Reuters; and correspondents for the *Christian Science Monitor*, the London *Times*, the London *Observer*, and the *Times* of India have been known to go to Dar from Nairobi to attend an ANC press conference. With considerable financial support from "outside," South African nationalists (and liberals) publish and distribute world-wide the mimeographed bulletin *South Africa* and the first-rate quarterly *Africa South*. African writers from South Africa—Ezekiel Mphahlele, Alex La Guma, and Bloke Modisane—are among the best known of African writers; and the work of Alan Paton, Elspeth Huxley, and Nadine Gordimer —whatever the reaction of black South Africans to it—has certainly not hurt the South African independence movement in the rest of the world. Though the world has not yet seen fit to move effectively against it, the present South African Government gets an astoundingly bad world press. That Chief Albert Luthuli was awarded the Nobel Peace Prize is at least some measure of the success of South Africa's nationalist propaganda.

As independent as each nationalist group is in the pursuit of its own aims, as a whole they do not represent separate and separatist movements. They spring from the same single impulse—which the sooner the rest of the world recognizes, the better—and they are bound together in PAFMECSA, which gives them both mechanical and emotional cohesion. The Pan-Africanist Freedom Movement for East, Central, and South Africa, operating on funds that come from Africa, Europe, and the East, proposes to free the countries of Southern Africa one after another—by nonviolent means if possible. This over-all union also serves as a forum and a clearinghouse for ideas. It organizes ceremonials for visiting nationalist leaders, and its offices are made available to them for press conferences. Though PAFMECSA has no publication of its own, it has taken an important part in establishing a paper, which, when it begins publication, will be run by TANU in the interest of independence movements in all of Southern Africa.

In short, PAFMECSA is Pan-Africa in action, and its members seem in complete agreement with the thirty-year-old declaration of the now defunct African National Congress Youth League: "To unite and to rally the African people . . . on the basis of African nationalism . . . and to work for unity and community between the free African states." As Julius Kiano of Kenya points out, the Pan-Africanist Freedom Movement even envisions the "development of specific principles and moral ideologies which would comprise the fundamental creeds and philosophic content for the emergent African nations."

Whether or not this addition to the intellectual dimensions of Pan-Africanism is politically practicable, it cannot be denied that it has emotional viability for Africa and for those to whom Nyerere once referred as the "homeless sons of Africa" all over the world. And it will have greater viability when the apparatus of propaganda is more precisely geared to the masses of Africans who have yet to be propagandized. For all their dedication to the cause of national independence, leaders in Southern Africa are but limited and mortal men. Only at great sacrifice of their energies and in some instances only at hazard to their personal liberty can Kozonguizi, Tambo, Mboya, Kaunda, and Sithole go constantly to the remotest corners of the continent to carry the message of freedom to those people for whom the printed word has as yet no meaning. It is to be hoped that with Radio Tanganyika free, its propaganda potential will be increasingly realized. Through PAFMECSA and its "Free Northern Rhodesia" offensive, Radio Tanganyika played an important part in Kenneth Kaunda's election campaign. It introduced a "foreign service" beamed to Northern Rhodesia, and carried undiluted United National Independence Party propaganda in Shona, which is the main language of Northern Rhodesia. Although this caused a rumpus with the British-owned Federal Broadcasting Corporation in Lusaka, Radio Tanganyika was not daunted.

VII

The Struggle by Violence

Force: Its Thrust and Prognosis[*]

JOHN A. MARCUM AND
ALLARD K. LOWENSTEIN

Deprived of reasonable hope for peaceful change, Southern Africans are abandoning moral suasion as ineffective. They are resorting increasingly to violence in their efforts to end minority rule.

The tactics of violence are still being evolved and vary greatly from place to place. Angola has been in a state of insurrection for two and a half years, and fighting is under way or reported imminent in the other Portuguese colonies in Africa. Both South Africa and Southern Rhodesia are experiencing heightened government repressions, justified by their governments as necessary to head off revolution. The United Nations Committee on South West Africa has described the situation there as so tense "that only intervention by the United Nations can prevent armed racial conflict."[1]

In the absence of internal collapse in Portugal and of external intervention in South Africa and Southern Rhodesia, the period of violent upheaval may be prolonged. Neither collapse nor intervention now appears likely, and the legacy of European settlement in Southern Africa may consequently be destruction of catastrophic proportions. This prospect will not dissuade Africans from force. Americans fought an extended war for independence that was prompted by grievances that look paltry compared to those now present in Southern Africa.

The Portuguese Colonies

THE ANGOLAN WAR. Angola has become the focal point of the mounting African campaign to end the Portuguese colonial empire.

[*] This paper was revised and updated by the authors as of June, 1965.
[1] United Nations General Assembly, 17th sess., *Report of the Special Committee for South West Africa*, Suppl. no. 12, A/5212 (1962).

Furthermore, the war in progress there since March, 1961, has tended to make it the focal point of the conflict to end European domination throughout Southern Africa.

The União das Populacões de Angola (Union of the People of Angola, UPA) began serious efforts to organize a political underground inside Angola during 1959–60. Impeded by the proscription against political parties in Portuguese Africa, the UPA set up headquarters across the border in the Congo and spread written and oral propaganda as best it could inside Angola. It did this in the hope that a political offensive, coupled with prodding by the United Nations, would lead Portugal, like other colonial powers in Africa, to accede to self-determination. There was an awareness that resort to force might ultimately be necessary, but UPA tracts and pronouncements of that period bear witness to the hope of inducing change without violence. The Portuguese response to organized African political activity, however, was repression; and this response, UPA President Holden Roberto has said, convinced him and his supporters that events in Angola were fated to follow a familiar pattern: nationalist protests, repression, "then a struggle which generally moves through three phases—attacks, guerrilla activity, and war." [2]

Spreading from its original northern base (São Salvador), the UPA had organized by mid-1960 a steady flow of persons and literature between its offices in Matadi, Léopoldville, and Elisabethville, and the interior of Angola. In June, 1960, it sent emissaries to make contact with and distribute tracts among African soldiers of the Portuguese Army stationed in Luanda and Nova Lisboa. Among those influenced by these appeals was João Baptista Traves Pereira, a young Kwanyama-speaking corporal in the Portuguese Army. In 1960, his unit was transferred to the northern frontier as part of the Portuguese effort to seal out influences from the politically turbulent Congo. In August of that year, he escaped into the Congo from his post at Noqui.

After a brief period as a leader of a newly formed UPA youth organization, Baptista was authorized by Roberto to form a Revolutionary Commission from among other Portuguese Army deserters recently arrived in Léopoldville. At its second meeting, the eleven-man commission decided to turn itself into the nucleus of a military force designed to wrest power from the Portuguese. The party approved, and, in January, 1961, it began following night classes

2 Speech by Holden Roberto, in Léopoldville, on March 16, 1963.

conducted by a Tunisian officer serving in the Congo. The commission was scheduled to proceed to Tunisia in March for intensive military training.

But Henrique Galvão's capture of the *Santa Maria* in January upset these leisurely plans. Amid speculation that the ship might be heading for Luanda, crowds of Africans attacked Luanda's prisons, evidently determined to release political prisoners. These attacks occurred on February 4, and during that day and the two days of noisy demonstrations that followed, hundreds of Africans were shot and several thousand arrested. The urban-based Movimento Popular de Libertação de Angola (Popular Movement for the Liberation of Angola, MPLA) played a major role in organizing the Luanda demonstrations, although UPA partisans claim to have been involved also. It is hard to piece together events of the next few weeks, as foreign newsmen were banned and local reporting was rigidly controlled. What is clear, however, is that the cycle of protest and repression spread to the coffee and cotton plantations of Uige-Carmona and Malange. In early March, Baptista sent his military commissioners into Angola to attempt to channel the unrest, and Roberto flew off to New York, where the U.N. Security Council was to discuss the Angolan situation. Workers on the large Primavera Plantation near Madimba, among others, were instructed to strike on March 15. The plantation owner, Señor Reis, fired on the workers as they massed to demand back wages.

Reports that strikes and violence occurred over an extended area during the night of March 14–15 seem to indicate that the UPA had planned protest actions sufficiently widespread and provocative to command international attention during the debate at the U.N. Similar limited violence short of general insurrection, synchronized with discussions at the U.N., it should be recalled, had proved helpful in speeding independence for Morocco and Tunisia. UPA instructions called only for work stoppages and for the destruction of crops, bridges, and buildings; there were specific orders "not to attack persons, but only property,"[3] although army or police reprisals could be met in kind. But profound discontent among Africans produced a more volatile situation than the UPA had anticipated. Instead of limited disorders, there was killing without quarter on both sides. Hundreds of Europeans and thousands of Africans (some estimates run as high as 50,000) died. At this point, the Portuguese appear to have panicked. Planes bearing NATO equipment[4] flew in from Europe and bombed

[3] Instructions as related to Cyrille Adoula, then Congolese Minister of the Interior, by Angolan refugees when he visited the frontier shortly after the uprising began.

[4] An action later protested by the United States.

villages far from the scene of the fighting. This served chiefly to extend considerably the scope of the revolt.

Thus war came to Angola. Nationalist forces ranged over extensive areas in the north, and found themselves unexpectedly in control of deserted towns, roads, and airfields. The Portuguese were surprised and disorganized, but resilient. Bolstered by aircraft acquired from West Germany, they began to drop napalm bombs (many of which bore U.S. Air Force markings), incendiary bombs, and rockets on areas of suspected activity. What military equipment the nationalists had was mostly Portuguese, some stolen by houseboys, some brought over by deserters, some captured in combat. Beyond this, they were obliged to reply with machetes and antiquated hunting guns. The commissioners hurried back to Léopoldville to seek more arms.

Roberto had meanwhile returned from New York to find that he was expected to equip and sustain an unplanned war. He gave the Revolutionary Commission all the weapons that he could immediately procure (seven rifles, two machine guns). With these, the commissioners, now led by Baptista, returned to Angola to organize a guerrilla war. With the approach of the dry season, Portuguese forces had regained a good deal of territory, and the nationalists were generally confined to forests and hills. Refugees now were streaming into the Congo, where they numbered 150,000 by the end of the year.

On June 1, 1961, Roberto named Baptista commander of field operations in northern Angola and settled into directing the daily operations of the militia (Angolan National Liberation Army). A pacifist group led by Jean-Pierre M'Bala broke away from the UPA and formed the Movement for the Defense of Angolan Interests (MDIA). Lisbon dispatched 40,000 troops to Angola,[5] announced the war was over, and set about to snuff it out of the news. The summer of 1961 was a period of retrenchment for the nationalists. The ANLA's ragged, untrained army of perhaps 5,000 men was obliged to pursue a hit-and-run strategy and to elude any decisive battle. Roberto admitted that the ANLA did not have the wherewithal to fortify and hold fixed positions, and that, as a result, it had given up towns held in the early days of the revolt. He predicted, however, that the prevailing calm would "soon end," [6] as indeed it did with the onset of the rains in late autumn.

The project to send a military contingent to North Africa for training was revived. A group of potential officers, selected to represent a balance of ethnic groups and regions, was sent, via Tunisia, for in-

[5] *The Times* (London), November 26, 1962.

[6] Speech made at the Connaissance Conference, at the University of Pennsylvania, in Philadelphia, on December 2, 1961.

combat training with the National Liberation Army of Algeria.[7] The ANLA was operating from relatively secure hideaways, and, in January, 1962, two American observers were able to travel for nearly two weeks over a network of paths in nationalist-held territory in northern Angola.

The Americans walked some 200 miles through forest and elephant grass, across vine bridges and around open-pit animal traps. They found the nationalist zone to be organized into a loosely linked system of self-governing village units. The first sizable shipment of arms from outside was distributed at this time to elements from forty-odd military "sectors." Air-raid whistles, military drills, Protestant hymns and marching songs, passport check points, military runners, grass-hut dispensaries, tattered mission-school syllabuses, skimpy manioc meals, and sporadic encounters with Portuguese patrols—this was life in rebel-held territory,[8] an area then estimated to be 150 miles wide and 200 miles deep in northern Angola.[9] The war had settled into one of attrition.

Rebel dispatches of this period described engagements extending from Sanda Massala in Cabinda to Ucua near Luanda, and claimed a continuing toll of Portuguese soldiers,[10] but neither side could inflict much damage on the other. The nationalists were, however, to sustain two serious blows before the winter of 1962 had ended. On February 6, Baptista was reportedly killed in an attack upon a Portuguese fort near Bembe, and, shortly afterward, Marcos Kassanga, chief of staff of the ANLA, defected. (Kassanga and other southerners [Ovimbundu] charged that Baptista had actually been murdered by Bakongo soldiers loyal to Roberto.)

Perhaps of longer-range significance was the March 27 decision of the Democratic Party of Angola (PDA, formerly ALIAZO) to abandon nonviolence and join the UPA in the Frente de Libertação Nacional de Angola (Angolan National Liberation Front, FNLA). A week later, the FNLA established the Government of the Angolan Republic in Exile (GRAE). One of the major elements among Angolan nationalist exiles, however, the MPLA, did not become associated with either the Front or GRAE.

[7] Subsequently, the MPLA sent some of its supporters to train with the Algerians in Morocco.

[8] Joint press statement by George Houser and John Marcum, on February 7, 1962.

[9] *The Star* (Johannesburg), July 14, 1962, credited the rebels with only "a base of 1,857 square miles of tangled jungle, limestone caves, mountain territory and swamp in which they have established a sort of headquarters."

[10] Communiqués of the Angolan Republic in Exile (GRAE) Ministry of Information.

Meanwhile, in the face of eyewitness testimony and lengthening, if unpublicized, casualty lists, the Portuguese Government acknowledged that fighting persisted. Radio Lisbon announced on March 9, 1962, that Portuguese inability "to completely close the frontier" was caused by the flow of supplies from the Congo that were reaching the "terrorists." The broadcast went on to describe Roberto's leadership of the rebellion as "discredited" and "associated with the idea of failure and incompetence." It suggested that the "management of the subversive war in Angola" would consequently devolve increasingly on the MPLA, which it called an "openly Communist organization." In a broadcast aimed at North American listeners, Radio Lisbon concluded: "The MPLA has the backing of the financial resources of international Communism, together with the instructors, arms, technicians of sabotage, propaganda, and subversive war. The most important thing is that the MPLA is controlled by European brains and is not a purely African organization."

Portuguese authorities also accelerated their military effort. A large airbase was built at Negage in northern Angola, antiguerrilla training was instituted for units of the Portuguese Army, and air attacks were intensified in the rebel-held zone.[11] On June 2, the nationalists announced the return of twenty-four soldiers from eight months of training in North Africa,[12] and, during the summer, a military base was established at Kinkuzu, near Thysville in the Congo, where ANLA officers were to train new recruits. Colonel José Kalundungo, a twenty-eight-year-old Bailundu who had been educated by American Methodist missionaries, was named base commander and chief of staff of the nationalist army. Like his predecessor, Baptista, he came from southern Angola, and was a veteran of the Portuguese Army, from which he deserted in March, 1961.[13]

In late November, a London *Times* correspondent estimated that between 3,000 and 8,000 armed Angolans were "subverting" an area of about 35,000 square miles "hanging like a sack from the northern frontier to within thirty miles of the Luanda-Malanga railway, about one-twentieth of the whole area of Angola." The correspondent put rebel losses at 250 to 400 a month, including killed, prisoners, and civilians who surrendered. He concluded that "but for reinforcements from Thysville, where there is an Angolan training camp for 1,300 guerrillas with Algerian-trained instructors, the suppression of their

11 *The New York Times*, June 3, 1962.
12 *Ibid.*, August 21, 1962, and GRAE Ministry of Information, *Revue de Presse*, No. 13.
13 Other principal officers trained, like Kalundungo, in Algeria were assistant chief of staff Norbert Sengele, Jacinto Isaias Kiela, and Alberto Pires.

revolt would be a matter of time. . . . As things are, guerrillas can be kept fighting indefinitely." [14]

As the war entered its third rainy season, there was some indication that the drift of events might be more hopeful for the nationalists than for the Portuguese. On January 14, 1963, Roberto told newsmen: "Our base in the Congo . . . will permit us within the next few months to send in some five to six thousand men, well-trained and fully equipped, in order to intensify our struggle for liberation." [15] Algeria made available to the FNLA 100 tons of arms and ammunition.[16] The GRAE Ministry of Information announced that the ANLA would open a new training camp in reintegrated Katanga, and continued to report frequent guerrilla engagements, in many of which it was claimed that the Portuguese Army had suffered five to ten casualties. The Nationalist Army began operating from new bases and was reported to have extended its activity to the northeastern frontier region adjacent to Kasongo Lunda of the Congo.[17] The General League of Angolan Workers (LGTA), an affiliate of the International Confederation of Free Trade Unions, cooperating with the FNLA, said it would intensify its activities in "liberated territory" and collaborate with the Army in training a corps of "political commissioners." [18]

Furthermore, the MPLA had entered the military picture. Its headquarters were moved from Conakry to Léopoldville in late 1961, and, in December, 1962, the party was reorganized and placed under the presidency of Dr. Agostinho Neto, a noted African poet and physician who had escaped from Portugal that summer. While Dr. Neto toured Western countries in an effort to broaden international contacts and support, the MPLA's Popular Liberation Army (APLA), led by Manuel Lima, a former officer of the Portuguese Army, carried out a raid into Cabinda on January 20, 1963.[19] The APLA claimed that nineteen Portuguese soldiers were killed in this operation, which was apparently launched from Pointe-Noire in the Congo Republic (Brazzaville).[20] The Portuguese admitted the loss of one man in an attack on the post of Massabi that was "beaten off by our troops." The raiders, according to the Portuguese announcement, left behind a "large number of

[14] *The Times* (London), November 26, 1962.
[15] *Angola Bulletin d'Information* (Tunis), No. 1 (January, 1963).
[16] *Jeune Afrique* (Tunis), No. 113 (December 17–23, 1962).
[17] Correspondence from a Canadian doctor working among Angolan refugees.
[18] *Le Courrier d'Afrique* (Léopoldville), February 23, 1963.
[19] The MPLA had earlier claimed to have a force in the Nambuangongo area of Angola, but this was its first authenticated military action.
[20] MPLA, "Vitoria ou Morte," No. 1 (February 4, 1963).

dead." One of the raiders, Mateus André Suami, defected. He told a press conference at Portuguese Army Headquarters in Luanda on March 2 that he had been trained for three months under Algerian direction in a training camp at Dar Queb Denib, Morocco, but that he had surrendered in Cabinda out of disillusionment with "bandit life." [21]

Unless the MPLA could extend its military activities into Angola proper, its military role would remain peripheral. This aspect of its future, therefore, was greatly dependent on the attitude of the Léopoldville government, which appeared deeply committed to the FNLA-GRAE, so long as Adoula was Premier. Meanwhile, Dr. Neto was reported to have reached an agreement reinforcing MPLA ties with the anti-Salazar opposition in Portugal led by Umberto Delgado.[22] Whether such an alliance, which was alleged to include the Portuguese Communist Party, would affect the MPLA's strength within Angola remained to be seen.

Some nationalist leaders professed to see possible future benefits to their people from the course of events in Angola. National unity, Roberto thought, was being hammered out on the anvil of revolution. "In our case, we have had to suppress regionalism, or tribalism, if you like, in order to save our skins. Perhaps if it had not been for the war, sectional and ethnic divisions might have played a disturbing role for a long time to come." Traditional rivals are fighting side by side, often sacrificing their lives for one another: "This is what produces nationhood, and I think our future tasks will be easier with our people so aware of the necessity of sticking together." [23]

Angolan rebel leaders grew confident that one day they, like the Algerians before them, would negotiate with a European power weary of colonial wars. Their desire for such negotiations was stressed in speeches made in Léopoldville on the second anniversary of the March 15, 1961, rising. Roberto and Vice-Premier Emmanuel Kunzika were joined by Congolese Premier Adoula in calling for peace based upon independence and future cooperation with Portugal.[24] Urging the

[21] "A Provincia de Angola" (Luanda), March 5, 1963.

[22] *The Christian Science Monitor*, March 4, 1963.

[23] Holden Roberto, in his Connaissance speech.

[24] *Le Progrès*, March 18 and 19, 1963. A correspondent for *Le Courrier d'Afrique* (Léopoldville) observed the commemorative ceremonies at the Kinkuzu base. In the issue of March 27, 1963, he described military exercises by "some thousands of determined and disciplined" young soldiers, "bearded in the style of the Algerian maquis." Machine-gun fire, exploding bombs and military chants, a football match, and a speech by Roberto were reported to have been the highlights of the day. Roberto is quoted as having expressed "his faith and firm hope

Portuguese in Angola to show "realism and understanding in order to preserve the future," Roberto said: "With the aid of all men of good will, we want to construct a free Angola where racism, injustice, obscurantism, and forced labor will be banished forever. It is thus clear that the future of the Portuguese living in our country rests in their own hands." [25]

MOZAMBIQUE AND GUINEA-BISSAU. The Algerian victory and the sustained military revolt in Angola have encouraged African nationalists in other Portuguese colonies to turn increasingly toward the use of force.

The first significant effort to build a political organization to challenge Portuguese rule in Mozambique dates from the creation of the Mozambique Liberation Front (FRELIMO), in June, 1962. Dr. Eduardo Mondlane, President of FRELIMO, announced that FRELIMO leaders planned to try diplomatic pressure for some months and then move to "direct action" if it should become "desperately necessary." [26] From the outset, FRELIMO, with headquarters in Dar es Salaam, received support from Tanganyika analogous to that extended by the Congo to the FNLA.

Portuguese authorities, determined not to be caught off guard again, began building military strength in Mozambique soon after the outbreak of hostilities in Angola. A year later, an American newsman reported that Lisbon had "vastly increased its military forces" in Mozambique (from 3,000 to 13,000) and had undertaken the organization of a special civilian volunteer force, new riot police units, and a better intelligence network.[27] At the end of September, 1962, the Johannesburg *Star* reported 30,000 to 50,000 Portuguese troops in Mozambique and intense patrolling of the Tanganyika and Nyasaland borders.[28] The construction of 15 military airfields and of naval-marine commando bases has been speeded.[29] By 1963, the Angolan war and the military buildup in Mozambique were estimated to be costing the Portuguese Government about U.S. $70 million a year.[30]

---

that March 15, 1964, would be commemorated not in the Congo but in the interior of Angola."

[25] Speech in Léopoldville, on March 16, 1963.

[26] *Christian Science Monitor*, March 1, 1963.

[27] Joseph L. Sterne, in the *Baltimore Sun*, April 27, 1962.

[28] This figure, however, was put at closer to 20,000 by Peter Lessing, in the *Christian Science Monitor*, March 19, 1963.

[29] *Christian Science Monitor*, March 1, 1963.

[30] *International Conciliation*, No. 539 (September, 1962), p. 58. GRAE sources estimate that Portugal's direct and indirect military expenditures rose from 17 to about 30 per cent of the state budget between 1961 and 1963. (GRAE Ministry of Information, *Angola Bulletin d'Information* [Léopoldville], No. 1 [1963].)

At the same time, a new contest of force began in the West African colony of Guinea-Bissau. The Conakry-based African Independence Party of Guinea and the Cape Verde Islands (PAIGC), led by Amilcar Cabral, announced that it dominated "vast zones" of the southern part of the 14,000-square-mile territory. The *Christian Science Monitor* (on February 26, 1963) reported an emerging "pattern of sabotage and guerrilla warfare against the authorities of Portuguese Guinea." In Senegal, where a rival Movement for the Liberation of Guinea and the Cape Verde Islands has found little government encouragement, the press credited the PAIGC with launching a major drive to overthrow Portuguese rule. The organ of the Senegalese governing party, *L'Unité Africaine*, belittled the importance of military equipment coming through Conakry, and described PAIGC strategy as that of "isolating certain military posts, cutting communications, and then trying to capture the posts in order to procure arms that are immediately used to equip another sector, where it is possible to proceed in the same manner." [31]

Portugal rushed in reinforcements to bring its troop strength close to 10,000 and denied PAIGC claims that 164 Portuguese soldiers had been killed in guerrilla operations during January and February.[32] There were reports of desertions from the Portuguese expeditionary force,[33] and, in early March, the PAIGC announced the capture of a Portuguese officer, Captain Curto Carreira.[34]

Thus, it was clear by the summer of 1963 that the consequences of continued Portuguese refusal to agree to self-determination in Angola and Mozambique would be protracted and bitter conflict; as long as the Portuguese ruled by force, the Africans would pursue the struggle to force an end to their rule.

POSTSCRIPT. The momentum of the Angolan rebellion reached a high point in mid-1963 when the GRAE was recognized by the Organization for African Unity and most independent African states as the legal government of Angola. The new arms shipments arrived, and increased military activity appeared imminent.

The GRAE apparatus, however, proved unequal to the task of escalation. Its cadre of trained military officers and political administrators

[31] *L'Unité Africaine* (Dakar), No. 37 (March 20, 1963).

[32] *Le Courrier d'Afrique*, March 26, 1963.

[33] *Jeune Afrique*, No. 125 (March 11–17, 1963).

[34] The same communiqué claimed to have put another 150 Portuguese soldiers "out of combat." (PAIGC communiqué, Conakry, March 9, 1963; and *Le Courrier d'Afrique*, March 19, 1963.)

was small. There had been no follow-up after the original group of UPA officers had returned from training by the Algerians. Only the MPLA had continued to send military personnel abroad for training.

Quarrels developed over military strategy. Southern leaders, such as Jonas Savimbi, demanded that a new front be opened along the Katanga border. Roberto agreed in principle, but claimed that the Adoula government would not permit such operations until such time as it had secured its own authority and military position so as to be able to cope with possible Portuguese reprisals, which might include cutting the Benguela railroad. Dissatisfaction with this explanation led to protest, unrest, and defection among Ovimbundu soldiers in the Angolan army. This in turn led to their arrest by Congolese authorities at the request of the GRAE.

The Viriato Cruz wing of the MPLA announced its adhesion to the GRAE in the spring of 1964, but this was followed shortly thereafter by the resignation of Jonas Savimbi and most southern elements. The Agostinho Neto–Mario Andrade wing of the MPLA carried on its operations from Brazzaville, and in late 1964 was given recognition and support by the Liberation Committee of the OAU, thus boosting its position as a competitor of the GRAE. Also, the Soviet Union denounced Roberto and came out in support of the MPLA. Meanwhile, Moise Tshombe had come to power in Léopoldville, where the GRAE —already reduced in scope and starved for arms—now received less cooperation from Congolese authorities and faced a possible further curtailment of military activities. As fortunes faded, tribal animosities, personal quarrels, and ideological differences significantly limited the thrust of the Angolan rebellion.

In Portuguese Guinea, however, PAIGC forces still held considerable areas of the country, and held down important units of the Portuguese Army that were now better equipped and trained for guerrilla warfare than they had been in 1961. In Mozambique, some scattered raids by FRELIMO and other African nationalists had brought the threat of violence to realization by September, 1964.

The situation in early 1965 was as follows: Portugal had made no practical moves toward meeting African and U.N. demands for the progressive implementation of self-government in its African territories. To the contrary, Lisbon had reinforced its military control, and for the time being had managed to contain the African military challenge. Both parties had opted for a military solution. But the long-term ability of the Portuguese to hold out against the tide of African nationalism was likely to be less impressive than their apparent short-term success.

South Africa

TURN TOWARD VIOLENCE. South Africa has known sporadic racial violence for a long time. The transition to planned violence began after the sequence of events climaxed by the Sharpeville shootings on March 21, 1960. It did not gain much momentum, however, until after the strike called for May 31, 1961, failed to induce the government to convoke a multiracial national convention to discuss a new constitution. Thus, the deliberate use of force as a weapon to depose the government is still in its infancy in South Africa.

The Africans' turn toward violence in South Africa has been reluctant and painful. As late as December, 1961, Chief Luthuli was still saying, "We in our situation have chosen the path of nonviolence of our own volition," [35] and refusing to discuss the possibility of abandoning nonviolence, although he was surrounded by opportunities and pressures to do so while in Europe to receive the Nobel Peace Prize.

Witnesses at the 1961 treason trial insisted, under intense cross-examination, that violence was outside the policy of the Congress Alliance, but few could be certain whether this insistence came of conviction, lingering lip service, or legal strategy. Nelson Mandela, a leader of the ANC and one of the chief organizers of the May, 1961, protest strike, commented: "If peaceful protests like these are to be put down by mobilization of the army and the police, then the people might be forced to use other methods of struggle." [36] And ANC leaders abroad—including men with long records of moderation and patience like Oliver Tambo and Robert Resha—began to talk about a "new situation" bordering on "war"; it was now necessary, they said, to use both violence and nonviolence to achieve freedom in the "hope that the world will help us to prevent another Algerian situation arising in our country." [37] By February, Mandela was telling the PAFMECSA conference in Addis Ababa that the policy had been "peaceful struggle" but that "the situation has now radically altered."

Similar thinking began to prevail in other opposition groups. Philip

[35] *Africa Digest*, February, 1962.

[36] Allard K. Lowenstein, *Brutal Mandate* (New York, 1962), p. 214. Mandela had written Sir de Villiers Graaff on the eve of the strike to warn of the implications of any government refusal to call a multiracial convention, and the alternatives became to "talk it out or shoot it out." (*Africa South*, October–December, 1961, p. 22.) In June, 1964, Mandela was sentenced, together with other ANC leaders and one white man, to life imprisonment on charges of, among other things, conspiring to commit sabotage.

[37] *Agence France Presse*, April 12, 1962.

Kgosane—the young PAC leader who in the spring of 1960 had led several thousand silent Africans into and out of Cape Town in South Africa's most striking protest march—announced in London as early as April, 1961: "We are an organization committed to the overthrow of white domination in South Africa. We are not going to preach violence. We think that nonviolence is the best way. But we reserve the right to take whatever action is necessary to defend ourselves." [38]

In December, 1962, Potlako K. Leballo, Acting President of the PAC, told a London press conference that violence should be expected: "The African people recognize that to effect any change in South Africa, the present situation, whereby white South Africa holds the monopoly of military power, must be changed. This can be achieved only by our acquisition of the means of challenging that military power." [39] Leballo had previously announced that PAC, in preparation for "revolution," was establishing four commissions to plan for national security, economic development, education, and legal reform, and that it would be asking Afro-Asian and other friendly states to underwrite a major loan to help "reduce the present military imbalance of power in South Africa." [40] In February, 1963, Nana Mahomo, a member of the PAC Executive Bureau, was reported to have received promises of military aid and training facilities from Premier Ben Bella of Algeria.

The evolution in the thinking of Mandela, Leballo, and other African leaders has been paralleled among opposition leaders of other races. In early 1959, Patrick Duncan, a liberal European who was then editor of *Contact* magazine, warned that violence would mean "devastating wars . . . more terrible than any the continent has yet suffered." [41] A year later, after the Cape Town demonstrations against the pass laws, he could still write that "Africans . . . have seen enough of the power of nonviolence to make them sure that nonviolence has

[38] The "organization" referred to in this statement appears to have been the short-lived South Africa United Front.

Furthermore, veterans of independence movements in other parts of Africa told ANC and PAC representatives that they had not sacrificed enough to get much support elsewhere. "We lost 50,000 of our people before we got freedom. You want it for 500? Come back after you've shown you care—then we can do something," one official of a sympathetic government told a meeting of South African exiles. Even Northern Rhodesia's Kenneth Kaunda, a staunch supporter of nonviolence, viewed Sharpeville as evidence that in South Africa "nonviolence does not pay. If anything, it provides cheap cannon fodder." (*New Africa*, January, 1963.)

[39] *Africa Digest*, December, 1962.

[40] *The Times* (London), October 16, 1962.

[41] *Africa Today*, January–February, 1959.

everything that is necessary for their success in the future." [42] Two years after that, however, Duncan, then in exile in Basutoland, had changed his mind: "Through the unyielding oppressiveness of the apartheid government there is now no chance of a peaceful transition to freedom and democracy. The way to power in South Africa now lies through the use of force. . . . The best, perhaps the only guarantee that a future free South Africa will be non-Communist is that the South African revolution be begun and led to victory by men who are not Communist. Such men exist within South Africa, but they have insufficient arms and money. They must now be given what they need." [43]

Anthony Sampson, astute observer of South African affairs, after visiting South Africa for the first time since Sharpeville, wrote in February, 1963, of a changed atmosphere: "My African friends who before had been talkative and open—often far too much so—were now far more guarded. . . . The atmosphere was much more austere and cautious." He found African politicians given to laconic utterances like, "Wait until 1963, we have our plans," or "The days of nonviolence are over." Conversation, he reported, had turned to sabotage, terrorism, counterterrorism, and civil war.[44]

OBJECTIVES, TACTICS, AND RESOURCES IN THE NEW SITUATION. But if a turn toward violence became inevitable after the repression of the protest campaigns of 1960 and 1961, the shape of the violence—if, indeed, it was to be more than spontaneous outbursts in the townships and reserves—was far from clear. Patrick van Rensburg, one of the ablest younger leaders of the Liberal Party,[45] analyzed the situation in the early months of 1962:

> South Africa has a police force of some twenty thousand whites and thirty thousand Africans, Indians, and Coloureds. The white force is armed with revolvers, sub-machine guns and armored Saracen cars. . . . There is a sizable political branch of the police force. This branch can open mail, tap telephones, and search houses at any time. It has an intricate system of spies. There is a permanent army of some twenty thousand men, armed with all modern weapons, including light artillery.

[42] Ibid., April–May, 1960.
[43] The New Republic, March 9, 1963.
[44] Anthony Sampson, "Johannesburg: Ugly, Brutal, and Dangerous," Show, February, 1963.
[45] Van Rensburg is of Afrikaner lineage and had resigned from the South African Foreign Service in protest against the government's racial policies before becoming active in the Liberal Party. He helped to organize the boycott movement in Britain and is now in exile.

. . . The air force is well equipped with modern fighters, capable of strafing or bombing townships. . . . There is a reserve which trains about three thousand men each year. . . . There are the skietkommandos, whose members practice target-shooting regularly. . . . "Mobile Watches" are being established. . . .

The whole defense force is designed to put down internal rebellion. . . . There will shortly be twelve tank and infantry regiments in strategic parts of the country, equipped with Saracen and Ferret light tanks. South Africa has established her own arms industry, probably in anticipation of an arms embargo. . . . Against this might, how would armed revolution be organized? Where would it obtain armaments? Where would it set up its bases of operation? The African townships? There are large police-stations in each one. . . . Strong detachments of police are poised within minutes of them. . . . There are very few rural areas without substantial white populations. Even the native reserves are well covered by government officials.

Violent revolt in South Africa would be ruthlessly and quickly suppressed.[46]

If the realities have made nonviolence seem futile, or at least inadequate, the same realities cause one to scoff at the possibility of massing sufficient force to overcome the assembled power of a modern heavily armed state. There can be no serious question that South Africa can crush any rebellion if the contest is contained within her borders. Thus, a major objective of planned violence must be to obtain support from abroad and eventually to force an international intervention. Even those who insist that freedom will have to be won primarily by Africans in South Africa work hard to obtain such support. One observer has commented:

No non-European politician, however militant, welcomes the prospect of an extended campaign of violence; the contending forces are too unequal, the inevitable damage too great. But now hope for freedom is focused on the outside world, and indifference there to nonviolence at home has become a powerful incentive to violence: surely *someone* will

[46] Patrick van Rensburg, *Guilty Land* (New York, 1962). Van Rensburg warns, moreover, of the temptation to draw too glib an analogy between South Africa and the operations of European underground groups during periods of Nazi occupation: "How successful can an armed underground be, remembering some of the resistance movements in countries occupied by Germany? The answer is another question. What country with twelve million people was occupied by three million Germans, with ninety out of one hundred of the Germans potential agents of their Reich? What of the pattern of the Algerian underground? But what Morocco and Tunisia lie to the east and west of the Union?"

have to step in if civil war starts. . . . How long can so unequal a struggle go on before outside help is solicited? Independent African states might be the first to send help, but inevitably one group or another will seek assistance from Russia and China.[47]

Two basic approaches may be discerned in the organized violence to date: (1) sabotage and hit-and-run attacks against industrial and communications installations; and (2) popular outbursts, coupled with sporadic killings and bombings. Two illegal organizations, the National Liberation Committee and Umkonto We Sizwe (Zulu for "Spear of the Nation") are known to have functioned as sabotage groups, and one, Poqo (Xhosa for "Pure," "Only," or "We Are Alone"), fell into the second category. There was no cooperation among these groups; they developed acrimonious disputes over tactics, political orientation, racial policy, and competitive approaches to sympathizers in independent Africa and elsewhere.

Poqo was by far the best publicized of the three, thanks in part to the number of people involved in its activities, in part to the dramatic, sometimes brutal nature of these activities, and in part to the government's selection of Poqo as its chief adversary. Poqo was responsible for the riots in the town of Paarl in Cape Province, for the slaying of a pro-government chief, and for the killing of five Europeans in the Transkei. But it is doubtful that these episodes were part of a general plan aimed toward any specific, short-range goals, and it is now clear that the organization was neither strong nor cohesive enough to survive police retaliation.

The Paarl affair occurred on November 22, 1962, when more than a hundred crudely armed Africans marched into town from Mbikweni African Location and attacked a police station in an attempt to free several Africans who had been arrested that day. Five Africans were killed in the ensuing clash, during which stores were burned, windows smashed, and two Europeans hacked to death.[48] Ten weeks later, on February 7, 1963, six Africans were sentenced to death for slaying Chief Gwebindlala Gqoboza, a murder they told the court they had committed under pressure from Poqo.

Then, in mid-March, the one-man Commission of Inquiry into the Paarl riots, Justice Snyman, issued an interim report urging drastic measures to crush Poqo. "I have found," Justice Snyman wrote, "that both Bantu and whites are so terrified of the outrages of the Poqo movement that they are too frightened to give information to the authorities." The political correspondent of the Johannesburg Star

[47] Lowenstein, op. cit., pp. 215–17.
[48] Africa Digest, February, 1963.

(March 23, 1963) summarized the Commission's findings: "Terrorization of Transkei Africans and whites has reached a dangerous level. The longer the reign of fear continues, the more law-abiding Africans will be estranged from the state."

Such reports did not discourage comparisons of Poqo with Mau Mau,[49] although much of what was said about the group was conjecture.[50] For the moment, at least, it served the purpose of both Poqo and the government to encourage tales of Poqo's power and ruthlessness. Poqo's advantage from such publicity was obvious. The government, on the other hand, never doubted it could crush Poqo. But it was convinced that the more terrifying and powerful the reputation of the foe it crushed, the more devastating the psychological blow to all its underground opponents of the regime. By April 6, in fact, "police officers" in Pretoria were already being quoted as "confident" that Poqo had been "smashed," its leaders "captured or on the run," and the rank and file "disorganized." [51] In June, 1963, the Minister of Justice informed Parliament that Poqo had been "knocked out" and that "peace and security" had been restored "throughout the land." [52]

Mr. Justice Snyman found Poqo to be an arm of the banned PAC, and reported that "people who address Poqo gatherings previously addressed PAC gatherings. The entrance and subscription fees are the same. The aims are the same. The division of the work is the same." This was a description that the PAC leadership was quick to endorse. In the December 27, 1962, issue of the Liberal weekly *Contact,*

[49] "Like the Mau Mau, the initiates undergo a series of repulsive rites. Human urine and goat's blood quaffed from kerosene tins supposedly make them invincible. Ashes are rubbed into incisions in the forehead to make them bulletproof. While witch doctors chant *"izwe lethu"* ("our land"), the initiates reply *"inkololeko nqoko"* ("we must be emancipated now"). To create a sense of terror, Poqo members make a ritual of their killings by gouging out the eyes of victims, decapitating them, dousing them with kerosene, then setting them aflame. Mulattoes and Indians are targets of the racist terrorists as well as whites. Not surprisingly Poqo commands more fear than popularity among S.A.'s downtrodden blacks, who are largely illiterate." (*Newsweek,* April 8, 1963.)

[50] There were reports of young Africans recruited "by the score" in Natal and sent by "secret routes" to West Africa for training in guerrilla warfare, and of Poqo schools for judo and unarmed combat techniques organized in African townships southwest of Johannesburg. (*Philadelphia Bulletin,* February 24, 1963.) The organization is said to be divided into two groups—the "general pack" and the "task force." The "general pack" consists mainly of "older men" and those not in good health.

[51] *Star* (Johannesburg), April 6, 1963. And *The New York Times* reported on June 21, 1963, that 3,246 Africans had been arrested as "suspected members" of Poqo, and that 124 members had been found guilty of murder.

[52] *The New York Times,* June 21, 1963.

Leballo, writing as acting head of the PAC, had predicted: "As a result of the ban on the Pan-Africanist Congress which has been powerful in the Cape, there was no doubt that there would emerge a vigorous revolutionary underground movement to take its place. The Poqo organization therefore is a direct manifestation of the helplessness of striving for democratic demands without an open body such as the PAC was before it was banned. The present uprisings in the Cape are only the beginning of a general ferment through South Africa."

Then, on March 25, in an interview at Maseru, Basutoland, Leballo announced that a large-scale uprising would be launched in South Africa during 1963 and that the Pan-Africanist "revolutionary council" was "discussing the time and manner in which action will be launched." "It is imminent," he said.[53]

On the same day, Leballo was quoted as stating that PAC and Poqo were synonymous. He credited the outburst in Paarl and the Transkei killings to "impatient PAC members disobeying orders to wait until instructions were given." [54] He was critical of attempted industrial sabotage, which he described as the work of Communists and the ANC: "Those who embark on sabotage have not got the following for mass action. What are the uses of these isolated explosions?" Poqo's strength, he went on, is its membership, which he estimated at 150,000 men "carefully organized" into 1,000-man "cells." [55]

The Snyman Commission of Inquiry found evidence to support the existence of a plan for a 1963 rising in the testimony of an alleged member of Poqo who is quoted as saying that "on a certain night this year Africans throughout South Africa would rise and kill the whites, cut telephone lines and wreck railway lines. . . . We were told that Sobukwe, in prison since 1960, wanted soldiers who would be ready when he came out of jail. We were also told that the big year was 1963 when the Bantu would get their country." [56]

Meanwhile, the NLC and Spear continued to implement independent campaigns of sabotage. Spear appears to have been composed largely of those sections of the banned ANC willing to use violence, joined by elements of the same European, Indian, and Coloured

[53] The Times (London), March 26, 1963.

[54] Christian Science Monitor, March 26, 1963.

[55] Star (Johannesburg), March 30, 1963. Some supporters of Spear and the NLC discount Leballo's more extreme threats as publicity-inspired, and some go as far as to question the extent of his knowledge, let alone control, of what is going on in Poqo. It has been alleged in these hostile circles that the PAC has merely capitalized shrewdly on the Snyman report.

[56] Leballo, however, has been at pains to dissociate Sobukwe from these plans. "Sobukwe is in jail," he said. "He knows nothing about our plans and activities." (Star, March 30, 1963.)

groups that had cooperated in the Congress Alliance. Nelson Mandela —whose feat in eluding the police for an extended period after "going underground" made him a most celebrated figure—aroused much interest in Spear before his imprisonment. Rumors of a split between pro- and non-Communist factions within Spear, and of further splits among Communist factions, have circulated,[57] and there is evidence of some concern that too close an involvement with Communists might keep Spear from receiving support from some nationalist groups in parts of Africa.[58] On the other hand, there have also been reliable reports of offers of substantial financial assistance from Communist sources.

The NLC eschewed mass participation and sought to avoid publicity. Its membership included socialists, disaffected members of the Liberal Party and of the Congress of Democrats, some Trotskyites, and some persons not known to have been previously involved in politics. A large proportion of the group was white, including a number of demolition experts, and the NLC appears to have been most active in blowing up power installations and other utilities. NLC leadership hoped to recruit "useful" individuals, whatever their former associations, although it was hostile to cooperation with Communists.

It is difficult, under the circumstances, to assess with any assurance just who has done what, but incomplete compilations of incidents indicate that the cumulative result of NLC and Spear activities during 1962–63 was significant. In late October, 1962, the Ministry of Agriculture was bombed. The Manchester *Guardian* of November 10, 1962, reported that twenty-five attempts at sabotage—half of them in Cape Province—had taken place within six weeks, and that twenty-nine telephone lines had been cut and two train derailments attempted in the first week of November.[59]

Despite all this, the life of the average European has not reflected any fundamental change in his position, and he has yet to face the new situation. At this point, in fact, an almost schizophrenic contrast persists for most of the dominant race: The sunny South African way of life as he knows it day by day seems totally unconnected to the prophecies of doom and revolution that inundate him when he

[57] It should be borne in mind that such stories may be the product of the rival organizations. None of the three is reluctant to encourage the idea that the other two are suffering from internal disorders of various kinds.

[58] In this connection, it is interesting to note a report that appeared in *Newsweek* on April 8, 1963: "Ghana's President Kwame Nkrumah is believed to have contributed $70,000 as well as weapons to the terrorist organization [Poqo]."

[59] The Minister of Justice is quoted in the same source as admitting that twenty-three attempts at sabotage had occurred since late September, including seven "petrol bombings" in Port Elizabeth and three in Western Cape.

reads the foreign press. To him, the pleasantness is still the reality. But events of the past three years have forced his government to reappraise "reality." Even the unflagging effort to depict South Africa as stable, happy, and united except for a few "agitators" and "Communists" has wobbled. Minister of Justice B. J. Vorster recently repeated that he and Dr. Verwoerd "had frequently stated South Africa was calm and orderly—perhaps the world's most peaceful country." [60] But Dr. Verwoerd himself was quoted as saying that "nobody will deny that a crisis exists in South Africa," and Sir de Villiers Graaff observed that "for the first time organized murder is being used as a political weapon." [61] Eric Louw's public estimate of the situation in the spring of 1963 was: "We live in difficult times and the outlook is perhaps a bit darker than people think. I do not wish to sound unduly pessimistic, but we are, in its fullest sense, involved in a cold war." [62]

Budget figures and new laws may indicate the degree of official alarm even more graphically than official pronouncements: Military expenditures have been quadrupled since 1960, and the effort to stamp out sabotage has produced laws that the International Committee of Jurists stated have reduced the liberty of the citizen "to a degree not surpassed by the most extreme dictatorship of the Left or the Right." [63] The budget for national defense rose from $61.6 million in 1960 to $168 million by 1962–63, and is headed toward $220 million for the fiscal year 1963–64. [64] In June, 1962, the Minister of Defense announced that South Africa could mobilize more than 250,000 men on short notice. The police force was revamped to be "ready at all times for action to ensure internal security, while heavily armed police are on a 24-hour standby footing. In Pretoria, 2,000 home-guard recruits were mobilized last month. Women's pistol clubs are now practicing daily. In Cape Town, wives of ministers are taking

[60] *Star* (Johannesburg), March 30, 1963.
[61] *The Times* (London), March 27, 1963.
[62] *Christian Science Monitor*, March 29, 1963.
[63] *Report of the International Committee of Jurists*, June, 1962. Under the provisions of the so-called Sabotage Act, for example, such things as painting antigovernment slogans on walls, striking for higher wages, and even trespassing can be construed as acts of, or encouraging, sabotage, and are thus punishable by death. To date, at least two Poqo members have been sentenced to death under these provisions, and a substantial number of persons, European as well as African, have been sentenced to five years of "house arrest." Persons thus sentenced may be prohibited from leaving their place of residence and from having visitors other than a doctor for medical purposes. In January, 1965, the "ninety-day clause," which permitted indefinite detention without charge and solitary confinement for successive ninety-day periods, was suspended; it is still on the books, however, and may be reinvoked at the discretion of the Minister of Justice.
[64] *Star* (Johannesburg), March 23, 1963.

rifle lessons, and in Johannesburg, a Sherman tank on display outside the National War Museum was taken down from its plinth because it had only 100 miles on the clock and might be needed." [65]

While leader of the Labour Party in Britain, Harold Wilson, among others, has proposed an embargo on arms for South Africa. Such suggestions provoked indignation from the South African Government and a rallying-round-the-flag by some Europeans normally critical of the government. "To suggest that the Republic should be cut off from all arms supplies," the Johannesburg *Star* said in a lead editorial, "is utterly pointless. A defenseless South Africa would be the prey of continental and international gangsters and be reduced to chaos." [66] In any case, the government has been moving to reduce its dependence on overseas supplies. In January, 1963, £10 million was contracted for the construction of three munitions factories in South Africa.[67]

The government would have preferred to explain its military preparations as a response to the threat of external attack, presumably from independent African states or Russia. "All this planning is done with emphasis on defense against outside aggression," [68] the Minister of Defense, J. J. Fouche, has said. It has been particularly important to maintain this explanation overseas, where the image South Africa seeks to project might be impaired if its government seemed obliged to undertake intensive armament to protect itself against its own people. Yet Defense Minister Fouche is reported also to have said in December, 1959, "You must not think we are arming against an external army—we are not. We are arming to shoot down the black masses." [69]

It seems fair to assume, from the nature of the equipment sought and of the training planned, that both internal and external factors have entered into the government's calculations. But heavy priority seems to rest on the concern over internal revolt.

NEIGHBORING TERRITORIES AND INTERNATIONAL COMPLICATIONS. The situations in South West Africa, Southern Rhodesia, and the High Commission Territories are developing along lines that will affect the course of affairs in the Republic, and vice versa. It is possible that each of these three situations might provoke a broader explosion, or induce a general intervention, before events in South Africa itself are likely to do so. Each, then, contains the possibility of influencing decisively the future of South Africa.

[65] *Newsweek*, April 8, 1963.
[66] *Star*, March 23, 1963.
[67] *Ibid.*, January 25, 1963.
[68] *Africa Digest*, March 21, 1963.
[69] M. L. Piliso, *Imperialist Rule in South Africa* (Cairo, n.d.).

If the International Court, in the case now before it, should find that South Africa has violated the terms of her mandate in South West Africa, efforts to implement the ruling might elicit South African defiance. (The Republic has ignored all General Assembly resolutions of censure passed thus far, but a decision from The Hague carries the full weight of international law.) Clarence Randall, a prominent American businessman who toured South Africa in 1962 as a guest of the South Africa Foundation, became convinced from discussions there that the South African Government would resist any United Nations intervention. If the U.N. should try to intervene, his "prominent" informants intimated, South Africa "would take over South West Africa at once by military means and ignore the United Nations." If this should happen, he concluded, "the whole rule of law in international relationships would be at stake." [70]

There have been no known incidents of organized violence in South West Africa to date; African protests are still couched in nonviolent terms. Should activity in Angola move southward, however, it could conceivably spill across the frontier, especially as the Ovambo tribe lives on both the Angolan and South West African sides.

The victory of Winston Field's Rhodesian Front, the dismantling of the Central African Federation, and Ian Smith's overwhelming sweep of the May, 1965, elections have confronted Africans in Rhodesia with the fact of white minority rule for an indefinite period. The Southern Rhodesian Government is demanding immediate independence from Britain and is likely to proclaim itself independent with or without British consent. If such a development occurs, an African government-in-exile is, sooner or later, likely to appear, and in the face of international sanctions, the Smith government may well have to turn to South Africa for financial and military support.[71] If South Africa should agree to help, a showdown throughout Southern Africa might be at hand sooner than is generally expected.

Even if South Africa avoids such a total commitment, it would be difficult indeed to confine the Rhodesian crisis to Rhodesia, should it devolve into bitter racial fighting. It is, therefore, worth noting the observations of two journalists, one in Rhodesia, the other in London. The correspondent of the *Washington Daily News* wrote from Salisbury on March 27, 1963: "This reporter has been assured by dedicated and thoughtful men on both sides of the fearful battleline drawn here

[70] *Sunday Times* (Cape Town), January 26, 1963.
[71] Dr. Verwoerd and Sir Roy Welensky, former Prime Minister of the short-lived Central African Federation, conferred for several days in South Africa in the spring of 1963.

between black Africans and white Europeans that Rhodesia's future will have to be proved by blood." And Sidney Gruson of *The New York Times* reported from London on April 8, 1963:

> An increasing sense of helplessness is evident among many politicians and members of Parliament, particularly Conservatives. There is almost a resigned acceptance of the prospect of violence [in Rhodesia]. The phrase "another Algeria" is heard with increasing frequency. . . .
>
> Reports to London from Salisbury, the colony's capital, say that relations between whites and Negroes are deteriorating every day the situation goes unsolved. The possibility that Southern Rhodesia will proclaim its independence and defend it by force, or that it will seek incorporation into neighboring South Africa, is being discussed here. The latter step is generally ruled out, but no one here would be surprised if South Africa extended large-scale economic help if Mr. Field declared Southern Rhodesia independent.

Basutoland, Bechuanaland, and Swaziland are likely to attain full self-government within the next few years.[72] All have become havens for South African refugees, and one or more may develop into enclaves from which nationalist undergrounds operate in South Africa. Basutoland has come to the special attention of the South African Government in this connection, in view of the 400-mile common frontier and of the PAC headquarters, which functioned actively for a time in Maseru. The potential awkwardness of this situation is obvious, perhaps above all for the British, who could be caught between South African Government pressures and strong African emotions. The recent Leballo interview there is believed to have been the first occasion on which violent overthrow of the South African Government has been advocated publicly in one of the Protectorates. The Johannesburg *Star* (March 30, 1963), under the headline "Leballo Action Raises Issue of Basutoland," summarized the situation as follows:

> The British Government allows political refugees to stay in Basutoland almost indefinitely on the understanding that their temporary-residence permits remain in force if they keep out of Basutoland politics and do not try to embarrass the administration. The main question facing both governments is whether Basutoland is to be used as a springboard for attacks on South Africa. This is the professed aim of independent Africa as well as of Mr. Ntsu Mokhehle, leader of the Basutoland National Congress.

[72] Since this was written, all three have achieved some degree of self-government.

A South African decision to seal off the Basuto border [73] could produce a Berlin-style situation, but both Britain and South Africa will do everything possible to avoid such an impasse.[74]

What is new about the South African situation is that the violence there is now *planned*. What the United States and the United Kingdom do or do not do about the situation now is likely to shape the course of events for a long time to come. And what distinguishes South Africa from other potentially explosive areas are the long-range worldwide implications of a racial war at the foot of Africa.

Postscript

Since this paper was originally prepared, the South African Government has moved swiftly to discourage and discredit opposition. The year-long Rivonia trial, which ended in June, 1964, removed the ANC's most vigorous leadership: Nelson Mandela, Walter Sisulu, and Govan Mbeki are now serving life sentences on Robben Island, the nonwhite prison in Cape Town Harbor. Also in June, Nobel Prizewinner Albert Luthuli was served with a second five-year banning order restricting him to a tiny area of the eastern Cape. In Cape Town and Pretoria, trials of young white and Coloured opponents of the regime (most of them university students) continued through the summer and fall of 1964. These trials served to deter students from political opposition and the advocacy of violence, and to illustrate the government's sophistication in intelligence and police techniques.

Public opinion in the Republic began to move more solidly behind Dr. Verwoerd after the Rivonia revelations of organized attempts at sabotage. Then, on July 25, 1964, a bomb was exploded in the main concourse of the Johannesburg railroad station, injuring several and killing an elderly white woman. John Harris, a young teacher and Liberal Party member, was tried for the murder and subsequently executed, on April 1, 1965. This highly publicized trial, along with the revelations in the Pretoria trials that other members of the Liberal Party had been involved in the first stages of planning sabotage, did much damage to the public image of Alan Paton's party, although the

[73] Basutoland is surrounded by South Africa, and her economy is especially vulnerable. South African police have maintained posts on the main routes to Basutoland for some time. It is now necessary to have travel documents to travel between South Africa and the Protectorates.

[74] Basutoland's independence apparently will not alter its determination to "coexist" with South Africa. *The New York Times*, May 15, 1965, reported that Chief Jonathan Leabua, Prime Minister of Basutoland, would seek closer cooperation with the Republic.

Liberals' policy has been and continues to be one of change through nonviolent means.

A great many arrests of white, Coloured, and Indian opponents of the regime were made during the summer of 1964. These were climaxed by the trial of thirteen Johannesburg residents under the Suppression of Communism Act on the following charges: that between May 12, 1962, and July, 1964, these defendants were members of the Communist Party of South Africa; that within this period, defendants "took part in acts calculated to further the aims of Communism"; and that "their common purpose was to replace the present government of the Republic of South Africa with a dictatorship of the working class." Abram Fischer, chief advocate in the Rivonia defense team and a self-admitted Communist, was the leading defendant; others included journalists, teachers, trade-unionists, and a doctor. Fischer jumped bail in March, 1965, and is thought still to be inside the Republic. The other defendants received sentences of two to five years in April, 1965.

An important aspect of several of the trials was the extent to which the government succeeded in getting some of the accused to give evidence for the state. The trials revealed the security measures taken by these opposition groups as hopelessly inadequate in the face of government agents, one of whom had in fact been a member of a Johannesburg group for several years.

In sum, the day of effective amateur resistance in South Africa has passed. Since 1960, and with increasing alacrity in the past year, English-speaking South African whites have joined the *laager*, giving at least a qualified support to the Verwoerd regime. For the moment, the government has good reason to be confident—a confidence illustrated by the suspension on January 11, 1965, of the "ninety-day clause."

Counterthrust and Prognosis

SUPPORTERS OF CONTINUED EUROPEAN RULE. Admiral Vasco Lopes Alves, then Portuguese Minister of Overseas Provinces, visited South Africa in 1959. He chose the occasion of this visit to remark: "We are accomplishing a parallel task in our territories, and if Western civilization is threatened on this continent, South Africa and Portugal should work together." [75] Since official Portuguese and South African policies are theoretically at opposite poles—forced assimilation versus forced separation—it may not be unfair to conclude that this "parallel task" is the preservation of European rule. Thus, contradictory pro-

[75] George W. Shepherd, *The Politics of African Nationalism* (New York, 1962), p. 115.

nouncements about the color bar can blend into a common defense of the Southern African *status quo*. The enemy, at least, is the same: change.

And in this context, it is logical (and inevitable) that the two governments have coordinated their policies whenever possible, and have worked to slow the southward push of African nationalism in regions like Katanga and Southern Rhodesia. Indeed, as the pressures for change mount, so do the pressures for closer cooperation against it. Sooner or later, this spiral could lead Portugal and South Africa into military alliance and increasing economic interdependence.

Soon after the outbreak of the Angolan rebellion, in July, 1961, South African Minister of Defense J. J. Fouche visited Lisbon. No formal treaty was announced, but new forms of collaboration soon became evident, and reports of "secret agreements" gained wide circulation. South Africa has undertaken to patrol the 900-mile frontier between Angola and South West Africa, and the Portuguese have hired South African contractors to construct a $160 million, 3,000-mile road network in southern Angola for purposes of "military strategy." [76]

Cooperation among Portuguese, South African, and Rhodesian police has been evidenced in the arrest and extradition of African students and others who have left their homelands without proper papers. Students from Angola and Mozambique have been arrested and returned to Portuguese jails by agents of PIDE operating in the Rhodesias. Southern Rhodesian police have delivered "illegal immigrants" back to South African authorities, and the latter are reported to be making vigorous efforts to close down the "underground railroad" that has helped African nationalists to get to refugee camps in Dar es Salaam [77] and elsewhere in independent Africa.

These same governments also extended material and moral support to the secessionist movement in Katanga—a practice reciprocated by the Tshombe regime, which closed down the UPA's Elisabethville headquarters [78] and, according to reports from visitors to the area, permitted the Portuguese to operate an airfield for surveillance of the Angolan-Katangese frontier. South African and Southern Rhodesian mercenaries and military goods enjoyed uninhibited passage across the Northern Rhodesian (now Zambian) frontier during the period of secession, and Katangese officials paid visits to Southern Rhodesia and South Africa.

[76] *Star* (Johannesburg), September 29, 1962.

[77] *Ibid.*, March 16, 1963.

[78] UPA leaders claim that the Elisabethville office had distributed 4,000 party cards before it was shut down and its officials turned over to Portuguese authorities.

An indication of the extent of the aid received by Tshombe from the three governments is contained in a dispatch from Associated Press correspondent Adrian Porter, in which he described the arrival in Kolwezi of a train from Lobito, Angola, loaded with arms, ammunition, and gasoline. Porter, writing during Tshombe's last stand, quoted a Katangese "cabinet source" as saying that Portuguese administrators in Angola had been giving "every assistance" in the fight against the United Nations.[79] After the collapse of the secession, Katangese mercenaries were given asylum in Angola, a state of affairs that Premier Adoula has announced he intends to bring before the United Nations as representing a continuing threat to his government.[80]

Portuguese–South African economic cooperation also increased substantially. Portugal is now seeking development capital for her territories, and has opened a Luso-South African Chamber of Commerce and Industry in Johannesburg.[81] South African Airways is planning to use Luanda and Lisbon to replace African airports now closed to its London flights. And a major involvement of South African economic strength and industrial skill in the affairs of her neighbors may be presaged in a report published in a leading news magazine: "South Africa will go into the foreign aid business in a big way—but with an important proviso: the aid will go to other white-supremacist countries in Africa. The Portuguese colonies of Angola and Mozambique have already begun to get South African money. Southern Rhodesia is next on the list." [82]

It is pertinent here to note some of the continuing props provided by Britain and America despite the distaste proclaimed by both governments for South African and Portuguese racial policies. There are at least peripheral military entanglements with South Africa, including the holding of joint naval exercises, the use of naval facilities at Simonstown by Great Britain, and the use of a missile-tracking station by the United States. The military involvement with Portugal is more extensive and a great deal more complex, in view of Portugal's membership in NATO and of the desire of the Pentagon to continue to have American bases in the Azores and in Spain. The official American position has been that military aid for Portugal is not to be used in Angola, but the provision is not one easily enforced, and, with the opening of discussions concerning the renewal of the leases on the Azores bases, there has seemed to be little inclination on the part of

[79] *Washington Star*, January 6, 1963.
[80] Speech of March 16, 1963.
[81] *Noticias* (Lourenço Marques), January 30, 1963.
[82] *Newsweek*, March 11, 1963.

the U.S. Government to press the point. In fact, in January, 1963, at a time when air power had become the most effective Portuguese weapon against nationalist forces in Angola, the United States announced that it would send twelve T-37C planes to help train Portuguese aviators.[83]

Its alliance with Spain permits Portugal to send a large portion of its military forces overseas. The two governments have long been close. Dr. Salazar's aid to General Franco was exceeded only by Hitler's and Mussolini's during the Spanish Civil War.[84] The Spanish Government periodically reiterates its solidarity with the Portuguese in their colonial troubles.[85] Substantial units of the Spanish Army are stationed at Badajoz, near the Portuguese frontier, whence, many leaders of the Spanish and Portuguese oppositions are convinced, they would rush to the aid of Dr. Salazar in the event of need.[86] The Iberian Pact, signed in 1943, provides for such a contingency.[87] African nationalists have not yet capitalized on the fact that efforts to topple dictatorships at home can weaken them in remote outposts, and that to overthrow such a dictator could obviate the need for inch-by-inch progress in his overseas territories.

The closeness of U.S. and U.K. economic ties with South Africa is indicated by the extent of private American and British investment in industry and mining, which totals some $2.5 billion and $700 million respectively. Some 200 American corporations operate in South Africa; many disavow any intent to endorse apartheid,[88] but see no obligation to oppose it and suggest it is up to the State Department to say whether it is considered against the national interest to invest further in South Africa. The State Department refuses, in turn, to comment directly on the private sector, although at least some of its officials discreetly encourage continued investment, apparently on the

[83] *Hispanic American Report* (Stanford University), January, 1963.

[84] Hugh Thomas, *The Spanish Civil War* (New York, 1961), pp. 634–35.

[85] See, for example, General Franco's speech welcoming Admiral Americo Thomaz, President of Portugal, to Madrid on November 22, 1961, in which Franco eulogized the Portuguese "work of civilization," said he was "sure" it would "overcome" certain "nationalist exaltations," and hailed the "heroic daily act of military defense in Angola."

[86] Correspondence from leaders of Spanish and Portuguese opposition groups in Paris, Madrid, and New York, 1962–63.

[87] *Hispanic American Report*, February, 1963.

[88] Many contribute funds, however, to an organization called the South Africa Foundation, which follows a line close to that of the United Party. Some insist that they try privately to persuade the South African Government to modify its policies, but the over-all purpose and impact of the Foundation has been to further an image of South Africa as a stable, content society with some flaws best worked out without "outside interference."

assumption that prosperity will ease racial tensions and that industrial growth and closer international ties will tend to modify Afrikaner Nationalism.

It remains to be noted that many Americans either approve of South Africa's racial policies or do not consider such policies relevant so long as the South African Government is "anti-Communist." [89] American businessmen visiting the Republic are often inclined, by courtesy or conviction, to comment favorably on what they have seen. The head of the USIA program in South Africa, in the troubled spring of 1961, praised the South African Government "for the steadfast manner in which it opposes Communism," and said "America and South Africa must stand closely together against the Communist danger." [90] Such expressions of support are received with particular enthusiasm by the South African Government and its followers.

OPPONENTS OF CONTINUED EUROPEAN RULE. Opponents as well as supporters of continued European domination have been driven together by events since 1960, but efforts to form united fronts have not been notably successful.[91] Even short-run agreements have been difficult to achieve in movements that lack the means and opportunity to resolve democratically profound differences over questions of co-

[89] For example, Senator Allen J. Ellender of Louisiana; the Legislature of the State of Mississippi; and Anthony Harrigan, Associate Editor of the Charleston, S. C., *News & Courier*. Mr. Harrigan has put this viewpoint forcefully:

> South Africa is . . . openly and totally committed to the cause of Western civilization. . . . [It is] the United States' best and only true friend on the African continent. . . . When the United States votes [at the U.N.] with the Communist bloc and neutralist nations against the interests of South Africa, the United States votes against its own security. . . . Stirring enmity against South Africa is the No. 1 African objective of the Communists. In all likelihood, it is the only nation in Africa that has a destiny as a major power. The reasons are clear: a European population with high standards of education . . . a free press, established parliamentary government, and a vigorous national way of life steeped in the values of the Christian religion.

Afrikaner Nationalists who have participated in exchange and other programs in the U.S. often claim subsequently that once they had "explained" South African race policies to Americans they found widespread approval. The South African budget for "information services" in the U.S. and other Western countries was increased by 50 per cent during the fiscal year 1963. In 1965, the South African Government Information Service ran a series of full-page advertisements in *The Washington Post* and *The New York Times* which elucidated the official experiment in "Bantu self-government," the Transkei. The Government Tourist Bureau maintains offices in both New York and Los Angeles.

[90] Lowenstein, *op. cit.*, p. 236.

[91] For example, the dissolved South African United Front, the Conference of Nationalist Organizations of Portuguese Africa (CONCP), and the Angolan National Liberation Front.

operation with Communists and/or with whites, and the question of violence. Nor are tribal rivalries, lingering historical antipathies, language barriers, great distances, and the problem of infiltration and police harassment overcome quickly.

Some assistance to the African cause has been provided by friendly neighbors: for Angola by the Congo; for Mozambique by Tanganyika; for Guinea-Bissau by Guinea-Conakry; and, in lesser measure, for Swaziland by both African and Communist countries, including Algeria, Ghana, the United Arab Republic, Czechoslovakia, Cuba, and China. Financial assistance has come from some of these last-named countries as well as from Liberia, Ethiopia, Nigeria, and East Germany, among others. Competition between Pan-Africanism and Communist influence lingers and recurs.

The United Nations has provided considerable moral support. The thirty-two African votes, often buttressed by the Asian, Latin, and Communist blocs, have done much to increase international concern and to arouse public opinion about the situation in Southern Africa. To date, resolutions reflecting aroused opinion have been of little practical value, for South Africa has ignored them all, but increased hope for international action has been provided by the contentious proceedings brought by Ethiopia and Liberia against South Africa in the International Court of Justice. Should the court rule go against South Africa, the problem of enforcement would present the world community with a unique and critical challenge.

The Afro-Asian Solidarity Committee and the All-African Peoples' Conference have also provided forums for attacks on European hegemony. The regional Pan-African Freedom Movement for East, Central and Southern Africa (PAFMECSA),[92] meeting in Léopoldville in December, 1962, called for implementation of the sanctions voted against South Africa by the Seventeenth Session of the U.N. General Assembly, and proposed a number of specific measures for collective action. The Léopoldville declaration urged African states and organizations to regard "countries which continue to supply arms to South Africa and maintain normal trade and State relations" as "unfriendly and hostile." [93] Furthermore, it called upon African governments and nationalist movements in countries bordering South Africa "to take vigorous steps to ensure the effective withdrawal of their nations' serving as cheap labour for the South African mines and farms," a proposal, which, if carried out, would affect hundreds of thousands of Mozambicans, Nyasas, Basutos, and others who work in South Africa.

[92] Tanganyika, Uganda, Ethiopia, Somalia, the Congo, Burundi, and Rwanda belong to this organization.
[93] *Tanganyika Standard* (Dar es Salaam), January 3, 1963.

The implications of such a move for the economies of all the territories involved, however, make the implementation of this particular suggestion a dim prospect indeed. PAFMECSA called upon its member states and other African territories to expel Portuguese nationals from their territory, and to sever diplomatic relations with Portugal. "If Portugal does not grant independence [to her African possessions] before the end of 1963," this resolution declares, "PAFMECSA must set up machinery immediately to give financial and material aid to the freedom fighters in these territories and the refugees outside." [94]

But it is to be noted that many African states still enjoy profitable trade relations with Angola or South Africa, or both. And even if African solidarity should be achieved in the matter of a trade boycott, recent experience indicates the futility of economic pressures that Great Britain and the United States, South Africa's first and second trading partners respectively, refuse to support.

Meanwhile, bitterness proliferates in Southern Africa, and lines between the races harden. If there is an explosion, it will be because the world outside, and especially the United States, permitted nonviolence to fail. If the thrust is anti-Western, it will be because the present white governments sustained themselves by Western indulgence. If it is antiwhite, it will be because an official white racism has infected an entire society and because white men failed for so many years to oppose convincingly that which is antiblack. As the situation is developing, both things are likely to happen. Nothing within Southern Africa itself can change the somber prognosis.

[94] This in fact was done by the Organization for African Unity when in 1963 it created the African Liberation Committee to help all such African liberation movements.

Discussion

EDUARDO C. MONDLANE.   Conditions in the Portuguese territories make for violence. To understand the Portuguese machinery for suppressing Africans' political rights is to appreciate the inevitability of violence. One part of the machinery is composed of uniformed police and plainclothes men. The international police of Portugal, PIDE, closely resemble the Hitler- and Mussolini-type police. The police are everywhere. They are black and white, but mostly white. The police recruited among weak, poor, and immoral Africans have been bought to report what their fellow Africans are doing.

Today there are thousands upon thousands in prison, many of them in Mozambique, the more important being sent to Portugal for imprisonment. In Mozambique, there have been massacres of Africans who demonstrated or protested or tried to make representations against actions of the administration. For example, in northern Mozambique, more than 250 people were shot by the police after they had demonstrated against conditions on plantations. In short, Portuguese police reaction is similar to that of South Africa's at Sharpeville.

There is a feeling, especially in the United States, that violence is perpetrated only when the underdog acts, but when the top dog continually suppresses the people, shooting and killing them, such action is not supposed to be violence.

People here in the United States ask: Are there any chances of violence in South Africa? What do they mean? There is already violence in South Africa. Sharpeville is only one case in several hundred. Perhaps this dual standard by which the fact of violence is judged arises in part because white Americans have believed for many, many years that black people are a different breed of humans and are not expected to react as other human beings. But let me assure these people that when the whites shoot us, beat us, trample us under their boots, we will react. It is, therefore, inevitable in Portuguese territory that Africans should begin shooting back.

There are one or two ways to stop violence: There are three major powers in the world that can prevent violence in those territories in Portuguese Africa that are not now engaged in fighting. The most important of these countries is the United States of America. If the United States wanted to, she could prevent Portugal from engaging in further violence against Africans. Documents in the U.S. Department of Defense attest that, in the decade 1951–61, the United States provided Portugal with $500 million worth of weapons. These weapons are supposed to be used in NATO forces to fight some possible attack from Communists. But we happen to know that Portugal is not interested in fighting any Communists. Indeed, Portugal lately tried to make a pact of friendship with the major Communist state in the world, considered to be the arch enemy of the United States. That power is sympathetic with the freedom of Africa.

The point is that the United States has, in ten years, given a half-billion dollars in weapons to Portugal, is encouraging Portugal to suppress the people of Africa—the people of Mozambique and Angola and so-called Portuguese Guinea. It is only when this encouragement is stopped that violence can stop in these territories.

Then there is the United Kingdom. We are hoping that the situation will not worsen in Southern Rhodesia faster than the events can quicken in Britain that might bring about a more humane government. Some of us have great respect for Harold Wilson and his party. We do not think they are altogether holy, but we think they take a saner attitude toward the problem in Southern Rhodesia. But the present British Government is completely in cahoots with big money. It cannot move even when, as in Southern Africa today, the moral issues glare and the legal situation is clear. Just recently, I met one of the former prime ministers of Southern Rhodesia in New York. I asked him whether there is, in the present constitution of Southern Rhodesia, any basis upon which the whites can declare independence without British assent. And he said, "No. I must be frank, there isn't." Moreover, the British during the time of the Mau Mau rebellion fought in Kenya to maintain themselves as a colonial power. Why should they not fight in Southern Rhodesia if the Boers try to infiltrate and support Mr. Field and Mr. Welensky?

The Africans can and will do only one thing, and that is to follow the spirit of freedom that is sweeping our continent. We will continue to press for more action through the associated states of Africa. This concerted action, I hope, will encourage union among African states for the salvation of Africa. But we welcome aid from our friends elsewhere, everywhere. If America wants to join in this list of friends of Africa, let her demonstrate it now; otherwise, we are going to accept friendship from wherever it comes, from people who desire freedom for Africa.

F. Jariretundu Kozonguizi.   All of a sudden, we Africans have become champions of violence and have gone to great lengths to show that violence is necessary in Southern Africa. Violence has always been necessary in Southern Africa. What has been lacking is the means essential to the successful prosecution of the struggle.

What were the missing essentials? First, for any struggle to be successful, there must be unity. But so far what has been the situation in Southern Africa, excepting Rhodesia and Nyasaland? It has been that while proclaiming from platforms that we stand for African liberation, many of us have nevertheless been active in dividing Africans. Secondly, there must be means; people must have arms to fight. You cannot tell people to engage in violence without giving them arms. There is no use in talking about violence when the people are stopped from getting the means to carry out violence.

MORLEY NKOSI.   I was a committee member of the regional Pan-African Conference from its inception and later became Vice-President of the Pan-African Congress until it was banned in 1960. I was in the Union of South Africa throughout the state of emergency.

I will begin by saying that violence must be discussed in the context of the region or country under consideration. It is not the intention of Africans to advocate violence for the sake of violence. That would be outright irresponsibility. All other possible avenues have been explored. Unfortunately, none of the nonviolent ones have been found effective.

Force is an extension of all the possible nonviolent avenues that have been tried and have failed; thus, force is a logical sequence in the progression of trying to obtain certain objectives. Force and nonviolence are interdependent.

Violence in Southern Africa does not originate with the Africans. There is a general tendency to ascribe violence to Africans as if Africans were peculiarly and particularly disposed to violence. The truth is that violence by Africans is a reaction to force or extreme provocation visited upon them by others. It has heretofore been exclusively the legal prerogative of the police and armed forces of South Africa. Limited disorder and peaceful political demonstrations by Africans and nonwhites have always been confronted with tear gas and machine guns. Sharpeville was a unique example of the zeal to kill Africans. It is now crystal-clear to all Africans that a recurrence of Sharpeville would be absolutely disastrous; it would result in a systematic annihilation of Africans.

It is important to observe the fanatic preparation the government has been making since Sharpeville to meet what it has called "any eventuality." Planes, fighters, and helicopters are being bought, and ammunition factories are being increased in number and production capacity. Most whites, including women and children, have been urged to join shooting clubs. Shooting, then, has been generated by the South African Government, which has herded most whites into one group and the Africans into another.

Factors that go to make South Africa what it presently is, especially in terms of military power, are its importance as a member of the Western orbit and its economic wealth. In scrutinizing only these two factors, one is dazed by the complicity of democratic nations. Whether they regard their support of the present South African Government as sound diplomacy or whether their position denotes complete insensitivity to respect for human rights, I do not know. What is clear is that they do not to any degree regard themselves as responsible for the present suffering of South African indigenous people. Yet, it is quite obvious that aid to South Africa, be it economic, political, or military, is a direct stab in the back to the African people.

Poqo, an organization sponsored by the Pan-African Congress, is a direct manifestation of the frustration of Africans in South Africa. There is no better explanation for it.

It is clear to us that our task is not one to be taken lightly. We know we are embarking on a very dangerous campaign, but we have one goal: We have to build a nation, and none but ourselves can do it. Sharpeville was horrible, but we learned from it. We learned, for instance, that strong as the South African Government is, there are vulnerable spots in its armor.

VIII

National and International
Action: Its Impact

U.S. Policy in Southern Africa *

VICTOR C. FERKISS

American policy toward Southern Africa is an extension of American policy toward Africa generally—an essentially negative policy reflecting the belief that the United States has only limited particular interests in Africa, and that its general interest consists in minimizing conflicts and reconciling conflicting parties in order to maximize political and economic stability. American policy has been, and is, a search for means of avoiding choices that will alienate significant elements in African life. This policy is predicated on the belief that the real interests of all major elements in African politics are compatible with those of the United States, and that the United States should attempt to remain on friendly terms with all. Therefore, the United States has shifted its position on particular issues only when it became obvious that its existing policy created more enmity on the part of one party to a conflict than it created sympathy on the part of another. The United States has sought to avoid direct involvement in conflicts and has intervened on a major scale only in the Congo, where it became evident that no viable solution was likely without such intervention. As a result, U.S. policy has had, with the important exception of the Congo, little discernible impact on the course of events in Southern Africa.

It is important at the outset of any discussion of American policy in Southern Africa to recognize the basic guidelines of American policy toward Africa as a whole in order to see how they condition specific policies relating to specific areas. Two equally erroneous generalizations can be made: One is that American interests are or have been identified with the continuation of colonialism or of white supremacy. The other is that American interests are or could be identical with those of the African revolution. The United States is concerned with the creation in Africa of economically viable states, sufficiently re-

* This paper was revised by the author in the spring of 1965.

sponsive to popular will to be politically stable over the long run, and as favorably disposed toward the American position vis-à-vis the Communist world as a realistic appraisal of their own interests makes possible. If the peoples of Africa had been content with the perpetuation of the colonial order, the United States would have had no reason, as a matter of national policy, not to be content with it also. If the peoples of Africa are sufficiently discontented with the old colonial order to overthrow it, the United States has no interest in perpetuating it.

Changes in U.S. policy toward Africa or any part of it are not, therefore, changes in basic aims. They are essentially reflections of changes in the estimate of the U.S. Government and people of the direction of events in Africa, changes in their estimates of the strength of the forces that American policy must take into account if its basic aims are to be fulfilled. As President Kennedy once stated, the first aim of any American foreign policy must be to serve our national interest.

This is not to say that American policy statements in favor of racial and political equality and human freedom are hypocritical. The United States would, in fact, prefer to see basic human freedoms extended to all people throughout the world, including those in the Soviet Union and in China. Only in such a world, it is assumed, can peace and freedom be completely secure. But free elections in the Soviet Union are a low-priority aim for American foreign policy at present as compared with the problem of our basic power relationship to the U.S.S.R. In other areas of the world, such as Africa, it is sometimes possible for our ultimate moral aims to have a somewhat higher priority as instrumental means for creating the stability and good relations we desire.

The nature of American policy toward Africa was well characterized by Professor Hans Morgenthau as far back as 1953, when he said:

> The United States has in Africa no specific political or military interests. As in other parts of the world, American interests in Africa are a by-product, as it were, of the East-West struggle.
>
> The over-all American interest in the containment of Communism requires political stability in Africa.

Fashionable rhetoric may have changed since then, but the statement still holds true. However, as Morgenthau himself points out, stability does not necessarily mean maintaining the *status quo*. Regimes such as that of the Republic of South Africa may be inherently unstable because of their denial of political expression to the overwhelming majority of the population. Indeed, Morgenthau argues, our African policies have too often put the interests of the colonial powers above our own and have tended to put our short-run interests ahead of our long-run interests.

The past decade has witnessed the slow process by which the United States has come to the realization that stability and African nationalism are not necessarily incompatible, that it is better to accept the inevitable gracefully, and that, although it is in the American interest to avoid choosing between conflicting forces whenever possible, our interest is best served by choosing the side that is going to win. This acceptance of reality was intensified by the Kennedy Administration. It is important to recognize, however, that the graceful acceptance of virtual *faits accomplis* is not the same as having an impact upon the course of events. It is the reaction of an observer rather than of a participant. It would be difficult to point to any action taken by the United States during the decade 1950–60 that affected the struggle of Africans for independence in any significant way.

This circumstance is partly due to the fact that the major arena for American policy implementation with regard to Africa has been and is the United Nations. Assistant Secretary of State G. Mennen Williams said in May, 1961: "It is no longer possible to avoid choices on such difficult problems as Algeria and Angola. The United Nations forces an opinion for concrete action from us on every conceivable issue. . . . The United Nations forces us to carry out a duty, to make decisions, which we might otherwise be tempted to avoid."

If one studies the history of the United States in the United Nations, one discerns a policy on colonial issues that gradually shifts in the direction of a more general approval of anticolonialism at the rhetorical level. In 1957, the United States voted against a watered-down, Soviet-sponsored anticolonialism resolution that passed 45–14, with 16 abstentions. In December, 1960, the United States abstained on an Afro-Asian–sponsored anticolonial resolution that passed 89–0. Finally, in December, 1962, the United States voted for an anti-colonial resolution that passed 101–0, with 4 abstentions. But the fact that the United States now votes for such declarations of principle does not affect the fact that it also votes against putting any teeth in these resolutions in so far as action on the part of the U.N. or its member countries is concerned. Anticolonialism is virtually a dead issue at the level of principle. That the U.S. anticolonial position is not inconsistent with the fact that, according to the State Department's own calculations, the United States voted with a majority of its NATO allies on every one of twenty colonial issues to come before the Seventeenth Session of the General Assembly suggests that such a policy is unlikely to have much impact.

American policy toward Africa generally is designed to blur conflicts of interest within Africa rather than to resolve them, and this applies to the policy toward Southern Africa as well. The end is the same, but the protagonists are new. The problem is no longer one of the relationship of indigenous African populations to overseas metropoles, but of the relationship of the races within a country to one another. This is true even of Angola, with its still increasing white-settler population, and, though it is little recognized in American policy, it is true of the Congo as well. Sir Roy Welensky has spoken of Southern Africa as being divided from the rest of Africa by an imaginary line "north of which the concept of a multiracial society will not predominate but south of which the concept of a multiracial society will be the rule rather than the exception." To African nationalists this is the concept of the white redoubt, behind which white domination is to persist under the guise of so-called multi-racialism.

The United States does not officially recognize the concept of the white redoubt as a frame of reference for policy-making. Nonetheless, it is obvious that the policy problems facing us in Southern Africa are different in kind from those we have previously faced elsewhere on the continent. Now the problem of American foreign policy is no longer the need to choose between European military allies and African nations aspiring to independence, but the necessity of choosing between a country's majority and minority groups with their widely divergent interests and values.

Even if the American moral position were not based upon a definition of democracy that combines majority rule with minority rights, the United States would still be ambivalent in its attitude toward developments in Southern Africa. It is ambivalent not because it views the Southern Rhodesian settlers or the South African whites as valuable allies in the Cold War (it does not), or because Americans have investments in these areas, or because the mineral resources of these countries may be of strategic importance. It is ambivalent because, while it favors the extension of political rights to the nonwhite majority, it is fearful that a sudden worsening of the conditions under which the white minority lives would touch off civil war and lead to economic chaos. Even though the nonwhite inhabitants are regarded as probably well able to run the economy without the whites, it is feared that there would not be much economy to run after a racial civil war. Hence the American emphasis on "harmony" and "accommodation" between the races.

Let us now turn to the American record and the statements of American leaders relating to particular situations in Southern Africa in order to see what general positions emerge.

The Congo

In the Congo, as has been stated, the United States was forced by circumstances to depart from its cherished policy of nonintervention, but the exception only proves the rule. U.S. policy for the Congo was simple: It sought to bring about the emergence of an economically and politically viable state, free from Communist domination, able eventually to stabilize itself on the basis of its own resources and capabilities. To that end, the United States rejected the claims of Katanga and other areas to self-determination. Luckily the concept of self-determination could be dismissed as inapplicable in Katanga on the grounds that the unity of the Congo had been universally accepted in the international community, that it had been tacitly accepted by Katangan leaders and populations in the period prior to independence, and that Tshombe had no clear mandate from the population of Katanga for secession.

In pursuing this policy, the United States supported the original resolutions establishing the U.N. presence in the Congo for the purpose of replacing Belgian troops and restoring law and order. It supported Secretary General Dag Hammarskjöld in his attempt to limit the role of the United Nations to these purposes in the face of pressure from various African and non-African nations to make the U.N. forces the arm of the central Congolese Government, thus to assert the authority of the central government in resolving the internal political conflict. Events in the Congo forced alterations in this policy. The dispute over control of the central Congolese Government itself forced the United States to take sides, and, in so doing, the United States had a major impact upon the course of events. By various means, the United States supported the authority of President Kasavubu against Premier Lumumba and his followers. In November, 1960, the United States pushed a resolution through the General Assembly accepting Kasavubu as the legitimate head of state and seating his delegation in the United Nations. This led to a struggle between the United States and certain African nations, particularly the Casablanca powers, which were supported by the Soviet bloc. By December, 1960, an impasse had been reached. An American- and British-sponsored resolution supporting the Secretary General's policy and calling for a conference of Congolese leaders under Kasavubu's chairmanship failed to obtain the necessary two-thirds majority in the Assembly, and a countermotion calling for the liberation of Lumumba also failed. Several African states and the Soviet

Union recognized the Gizenga regime in Stanleyville as the legitimate central government.

The struggle continued through February, 1961. Several African states threatened to withdraw their troops, and the United States fought off a Ghanaian move for what amounted to a U.N. trusteeship for the Congo, but supported the strengthening of the U.N. mandate to bring order to the Congo, as well as a Security Council resolution calling for the evacuation of all foreign military personnel.

The primary role of the United States in the U.N. Congo operation must be stressed. Britain, to a limited extent, followed the United States. France under De Gaulle dismissed the whole U.N. effort, indeed the U.N. itself, as worthless nonsense. Belgium fought extension of the U.N.'s role. A change in the position of the United States made possible a change in the role of the U.N. The death of Hammarskjöld and his replacement as Secretary General by the less cautious U Thant of Burma, plus new evidence of Tshombe's basic unwillingness to cooperate with the U.N., and of the costs of such noncooperation, caused the United States in November, 1961, to change its line, partly from fear that U.N. failure to end secession would lead the central Congolese Government to seek help elsewhere. The United States supported, over British and French opposition, a Security Council measure to authorize the U.N. to use force to arrest and expel the mercenaries who were the military mainstay of Katanga. But the United States did not share the general disdain for Tshombe as a traitor to the cause of African freedom. By its actions it indicated that it viewed him as a valuable leader who could maintain order in at least part of Katanga (the most important part) and who had the confidence of the white elements—whose presence, it was assumed, was necessary if Katanga was to be of value in the future in the building of an economically sound Congo. The United States, therefore, continued to seek a peaceful resolution of the struggle on any terms that would preserve the juridical unity of the Congo and give the central government the revenues it required to survive.

To this end, it sought to conciliate rival leaders. U.S. Ambassador Edmund A. Gullion arranged and participated in a meeting between Premier Adoula and President Tshombe in December, 1961. But the continued evasiveness of Tshombe made the U.S. position less and less tenable. In February, 1962, Premier Adoula visited Washington and was promised, by President Kennedy himself, American support for reunification. The United States continued to support U.N. and central government pressure on Katanga, short of direct assault, despite some bitter domestic opposition and the misgivings of important elements in Great Britain. When, finally, the U.N.—almost at the end of its political and economic rope—was able to take advantage of Katangese provocation to destroy the Katangan military position, Katanga proved to be a "paper tiger" in the showdown. The United States gave this measure its support and joined in the general sigh of relief at Tshombe's downfall.

It is not too much of an exaggeration to say that the situation in the Congo in mid-1963 was largely the creation of the United States. Despite opposition or grudging support from its NATO allies, and despite the opposition of the Soviet Union and various African states, it brought about a unified Congo under a government meeting its specifications of moderation. Behind the scenes, Belgian personnel were quietly returning, and the United States could be counted on to assure their retention, on the assumption that their technical services are a necessary element in an economically and politically stable Congo. Confronted with the alternative of a Katanga in control of interests tied in with Welensky and the Portuguese, and face to face with an ardently anti-European and possibly Soviet-leaning government in Léopoldville, the United States succeeded in using the U.N. to create a regime in the Congo that we regard as most conducive to stability. Though neither involved in nor pleased by Tshombe's replacement of Adoula as Premier after the U.N. withdrawal in 1964, the United States gave Tshombe some practical assistance and its full moral support in his efforts to maintain a unified, moderate, and pro-Western regime in the Congo, even at the cost of alienating many important African nationalist leaders and forces. In every sense, the impact and continued influence of the United States have been greater in the Congo than anywhere else in Africa.

Angola

The difficulties of the United Nations in the Congo were such as to strain its resources to the utmost and even, it seemed, to threaten its very existence. Without extraordinary financial assistance from the United States, the U.N. Congo operation would almost certainly have been doomed to failure. Contemplation of the possibility of a similar U.N. role in Angola and/or South West Africa—to say nothing of Southern Rhodesia and/or the Republic of South Africa—is enough to send shudders down the spines of U.S. officialdom. The United States has therefore sought to minimize conflicts in these areas by means of persuasion, either on its own or through the United Nations.

In the United Nations in recent years the United States has consistently condemned the Portuguese position on Angola, but has been loath to approve action designed to force a change in that position. In March, 1961, the United States supported an unsuccessful Security Council motion by Ceylon, Liberia, and the United Arab Republic stating that the Angolan situation posed a threat to the peace. For this action, the United States was roundly condemned by Portuguese Premier Salazar for allegedly aiding the cause of Communism. The United States supported putting the Angola resolution on the Assembly agenda and voted for the successful Assembly resolution in April. In June, the United States supported the Security Council motion asking Portugal to "desist from repressive measures."

The United States, however, has never endorsed wholeheartedly the aims of either nationalist movement in Angola. In January, 1962, Ambassador Adlai Stevenson told the Assembly that the United States stands for peaceful change and that it respects the right of the Portuguese to preserve order. It wished the people of Angola to be able to choose their future status for themselves and therefore preferred "self-determination" to "independence" as a goal. It has prohibited the use of NATO arms by Portugal in suppressing the rebellion. (U.S. delegate Jonathan Bingham has said the United States accepted the word of the Portuguese that they had not violated this prohibition, and the United States has offered economic aid to Portugal to underwrite possible reforms in Angola.) The emphasis of United States policy on Angola is, therefore, on peaceful change. Stevenson roundly condemned the notion that the United Nations could tolerate, much less use, force to effect political change. There is, he put it, no room for a "double standard." All war is outlawed: Anticolonial war threatens the U.N. and world order just as much as any other kind.

The United States seeks to effect change through conciliation, to keep U.N. action on this level, and to minimize antagonism toward Portugal. It looks with favor on what it believes to be a change of attitude by the Portuguese toward their African territories occasioned by U.N. action. It was in accordance with this position that the United States opposed the proposal of the Special Commission on Colonialism that the Security Council call for sanctions against Portugal if it did not free Mozambique. And, while the United States supported the January, 1962, Afro-Asian resolution that Portuguese refusal of self-determination threatened world peace and security, it did so only after securing the passage of amendments that deleted the specification of independence as a goal and of U.N. measures to be taken against Portugal. The United States voted against a separate motion condemning Portuguese "repression" in Angola.

In December, 1962, the nature of the American position was again indicated. The United States proposed that a study committee be sent to Angola and Mozambique. It withdrew the motion after a Moroccan protest that it was unacceptable to key African and Asian nations. On a final Assembly resolution asking immediate independence for all Portuguese territories, the United States was one of seven dissenters. What is noteworthy is that the original U.S. proposal was written in consultation with Portugal and voluntarily withdrawn after Moroccan objection, coupled with a Moroccan tribute to American motives. The United States is clearly and openly seeking to act as an honest broker between possibly irreconcilable forces. So far, she seems to retain credit on both sides for her good intentions.

Whether U.S. actions have slowed or hastened the progress toward Angolan independence is another question. There seems little evidence of Portuguese willingness to extend greater freedom to the inhabitants of its African territories, despite continued U.S. professions of optimism. On the other hand, there is little evidence that U.N. actions to date would have much effect either. Sanctions lacking American and Western European support would be meaningless. The general U.S. position that sanctions are ineffective because they will not be observed is, of course, a self-fulfilling prediction.

South West Africa

American policy on the question of South West Africa is motivated less by any positive concept of what the future might hold for that territory than by U.S. inability to accept the Republic of South Africa's legal position on the question and by our desire to stay in line with the determination of independent African states to settle this long-festering issue. The intransigence of the South African Government has placed the United States in an almost impossible position, given the American desire to see Southern African questions resolved without resort to force.

Originally, the United States was willing to have South West Africa partitioned between South Africa and a new U.N. trust territory. Recently, the American stand has hardened, but the United States is still unwilling to see the United Nations take specific action. In December, 1960, an African resolution calling for an on-the-spot investigation and the preparation of proposals for internal self-government leading to complete independence "as soon as possible" passed the Assembly 18–0. Fifteen countries, including the United States, abstained, on the grounds that the situation represented no threat to the peace and that, in any case, the investigation was bound to be fruitless. The withdrawal of South Africa from the Commonwealth and a new administration in Washington resulted in a stiffening of American policy. In November, 1961, Mr. Bingham told the General Assembly that the people of South West Africa must be able to aspire to self-determination. In December, 1962, the United States voted affirmatively in a 98–0 U.N. Assembly vote condemning the actions of South Africa in the territory, but only after the United States was unsuccessful in an attempt to substitute the wording "deeply deplores" for "condemns."

If one accepts the premise that U.N. expressions of concern have inhibited the Republic government from going any further in integrating the territory with the Republic, then U.S. support has contributed to this result. If, on the other hand, one is convinced that decisive U.N. action, sanctions, or even military intervention is necessary to resolve this situation, then the American position has hindered a resolution. However, it is becoming increasingly apparent to the United States that some kind of forceful intervention in South West Africa on the part of the independent African states is likely in the not-too-distant future. The United States would probably feel compelled to support U.N. Assembly approval of such action and, in any event, would be unable to prevent it. For these reasons, the United States is presently engaged in an almost desperate attempt to convince the South African Government that further yielding to U.N. pressures for reform and change in South West Africa is absolutely necessary if major political and military conflict over the future of the territory is to be prevented.

Multiracialism

The most difficult policy issues facing the United States are those involving Rhodesia and the Republic of South Africa itself. Conflicts between white minority and black majority within the so-called multiracial territories raise questions that cannot be resolved as simply as those arising out of conflicts between indigenous populations and overseas metropoles. The unyielding attitudes of settler diehards in Rhodesia and of the Nationalists in the Republic of South Africa inevitably lead to a rise of extremist antiwhite feeling among black nationalists, making it difficult for the United States to implement its traditional policy of conciliation. At the same time, the inherent moral ambiguity of American policy is becoming increasingly evident. The moral problems stem basically from the underlying conflict between democratic and liberal values, the difficulty of reconciling majority rule and minority rights. The United States, it is clear, is coming to accept the notion of majority rule in Southern Africa. Increasingly, self-determination is defined not only as independence from the metropole but as a government of the people's own choice.

Assistant Secretary of State for African Affairs G. Mennen Williams has defined self-determination as the "universally recognized principle which asserts the right of people to determine the kind of government under which they want to live. It is the principle underlying change without violence in stable democratic societies." This statement—a typical formulation—implies majority rule. Ambassador Stevenson, speaking in the June, 1962, General Assembly debate on Southern Rhodesia, was even more explicit. "The United States," he said, "supports and has worked steadily for an orderly and rapid decolonization in Africa. . . . Obviously the people of Southern Rhodesia are entitled to share in that process. The objective is progressive liberalization of the franchise in the direction of universal adult suffrage, so as to permit true self-determination for all of the people." American spokesmen have criticized the Republic of South Africa for minority rule, noting that there "the consent of the vast majority counts for little."

Thus black rule is regarded as inevitable. But there must also be, in the words of American spokesmen, protection of the "just rights of minorities." Even Secretary Williams warns against the dangers to the common good of an "understandable but overreaching zeal for reform." What does this mean? It means that the United States is opposed to racial discrimination regardless of what race it is directed against and that it believes that stability and economic progress in Southern Africa depend to a crucial degree on the cooperation of the whites now resident there.

Most African nationalist leaders are quick to deny that if their cause were victorious, they would reverse the present situation and institute racial discrimination against the white minority. But the possibility of such discrimination is not the real problem. The plain fact is that the white minority enjoys a higher standard of living in large part because of the color bar. To destroy the color bar—even without instituting one in reverse—would go far toward destroying white standards of living in absolute as well as in relative terms, especially among the less educated and less well-to-do whites. In addition, there would inevitably be a long period in which those whites whose economic status was not dependent on the color bar would continue to be better off than most nonwhites. The temptation of political leaders to appease the black electorate by such egalitarian legislation as highly progressive income taxes and so forth would be hard to resist. Such legislation need not mention race to have the effect of falling most heavily on the white majority.

Thus, there is a real basis for the fear of most whites of government by the black majority. It does little good to say, as Secretary Williams did recently: "The Europeans who feel that the Africans have an antiwhite attitude are misguided, as far as I'm concerned. In fact, there is so little animosity among Africans that I am always pleasantly surprised on my visits to Africa." The problem goes deeper. The paradox of the multiracial territories, South Africa especially, is that it might be possible for the nonwhites to maintain them as economically and politically stable entities without the help of the white community, but that unless change in the relative status of the races takes place slowly, violent white reaction to change could easily result in a struggle that might totally destroy the economies of these countries.

The aim of the United States, therefore, is change in the direction of racial equality at a pace fast enough to keep the black majority from resorting to disruptive violence but not so fast that the white minority feels it worth while to resort to violence to protect its position.

The Central African Federation

In the former Central African Federation, the United States was able to avoid a direct confrontation with the racial problem by following the British lead. We accepted the "multiracial" pretensions of the Federation at face value when it was formed and have provided over $36 million in aid to this area. We have mirrored British disappointment with events and, with Britain, have accepted the independence of Malawi and Zambia. The American policy position in this area has had virtually no impact, being slightly behind that of leading elements in Britain in adjusting to events. The United States has supported the British position that, while Southern Rhodesia (now known simply as Rhodesia) is a self-governing territory whose internal affairs Britain cannot control, the United Kingdom must be allowed a primary role in persuading Rhodesia to do the right thing and must be allowed time in which to make such persuasion effective. The U.S. attitude is that Britain is acting in good faith and should not be harassed by the U.N. In May, 1962, the United States opposed at several levels a report of the Special Committee of Seventeen on Colonialism, which asked for immediate independence for Northern Rhodesia—although it welcomed Northern Rhodesia's ultimate accession to independence as free Zambia. The United States has asked Britain to hang on to such control as it has over Rhodesia until Britain has completed its job there. In June, 1962, it opposed U.N. action on a resolution asking the United Kingdom to provide a new constitution based on "one man, one vote" to supersede the recently adopted one, on the grounds that Britain still needed time to persuade the Rhodesian Government to liberalize its policies. The resolution passed the General Assembly 73–1, with the United States among 27 abstainees.

Rhodesia is clearly an instance where the United States has been happy to avoid taking a stand. The relation of Britain to Rhodesia has made this possible. But what if British policy fails? It is not inconceivable that the diehard settler group in Salisbury headed by Ian Smith might declare independence. Would the United States recognize such a government? Indications are that it would again follow the British lead. Suppose, as is not unlikely, African states refused to recognize such a state, violence was triggered, and U.N. intervention became a possibility. There is little reason to believe that the United States has a policy for such a contingency. It has chosen to be optimistic over the future of race relations in the area, though certain statements of Secretary Williams have been somewhat less so. But U.S. optimism or pessimism is clearly a reaction to events over which it feels it can have little influence. U.S. policy in this whole area has had no significant impact.

The Republic of South Africa

The most important issue in Southern Africa is the future of the Republic of South Africa. An industrial giant by African standards, it could play a major role in African development if it were not at odds with the African revolution. The dominance within its population of the Afrikaners, a group that has no overseas homeland to return to, makes the peaceful surrender of their present special status particularly difficult and their physical removal without bloodshed impossible. It is possible that the white settlers of Rhodesia could be inundated as a political force and squeezed out as individuals without a major upheaval. Not so the South Africans. It is not easy to refute the gloomy predictions of such Americans as Chester Bowles, who as far back as 1956 spoke of "an inevitable explosion," or of such liberal white South Africans as Patrick van Rensburg and Patrick Duncan, who see civil war as the necessary outcome of the present situation.

American policy has been to seek to persuade South Africa to bow to world opinion by abolishing apartheid and moving toward greater political rights for its nonwhite citizens. Characteristically, the United States has not tried to formulate precisely what the ultimate political goal in South Africa should be. Given the fear of the possible results of majority rule that torments the white community of South Africa and the fact that universal adult suffrage is increasingly the demand of local nonwhites, American policy statements about the necessity for peaceful accommodation between the races seem more and more like empty generalizations to both sides.

It is only recently, however, that even such generalizations as these have been uttered. In 1952, the United States opposed creation of a U.N. commission to study the racial situation in the then Union on the ground that South Africa's racial policies were a purely domestic matter. The United States attacked racialism in the Union at the same time as it deplored the commission's activities. In 1955, the United States voted against continuing the commission, thus contributing to the failure to secure the required two-thirds vote for its perpetuation.

The United States began voting for General Assembly resolutions condemning apartheid in 1957. In March, 1960, the United States promptly and vigorously condemned the massacre at Sharpeville, and the next month voted in the Security Council to condemn apartheid as a danger to world peace. That fall, the United States voted for an Assembly measure asking all member states to consider the "separate and collective action" open to them under the Charter to induce South Africa to change its policies. The following April, the United States again voted to condemn apartheid and supported a measure calling upon South Africa to negotiate with Pakistan and India about the status of the Asian minority in the Union. But, in October, 1961, the United States was one of several nations that did not participate in the Assembly's condemnation of South African delegate Eric Louw for an allegedly racialist speech, on the grounds that free speech and orderly U.N. procedure were endangered.

During the seventeenth Assembly session, lines hardened and the U.S. position on South Africa began to diverge once more from that of leading African nationalists. U.S. delegate Plimpton, speaking in opposition to a defeated Soviet resolution, told the Special Political Committee in October, 1962, that the United States was continuing to urge South Africa to abandon apartheid and that it would continue not to supply arms that could be used to enforce apartheid. U.N. action, he continued, should be limited to reaffirming its earlier condemnation of apartheid, calling upon South Africa to abandon it, making world opinion on the subject known, asking members individually to seek to persuade South Africa to change its course, and setting up a Security Council watch on the situation. Sanctions were undesirable, he held, because they would not be implemented and thus would not be effective. There is no short-cut to change, he contended, and South Africa must not be ostracized but kept within the world community if persuasion is to be effective. In November, 1962, the General Assembly voted a strong resolution of censure against South Africa by a margin of 67–17 (with 23 abstentions), which called for sanctions, the breaking of diplomatic relations, and expulsion from the United Nations. The United States voted against the measure.

What influence has the United States had on the situation in South Africa? American actions in the United Nations have undoubtedly added to the realization of white South Africans that world public opinion is increasingly against them. But what effect has this realization had upon the South African Government's policy? Measures taken by the South African Government to reduce certain tensions—such as the relaxation of the liquor laws—are clearly a calculated attempt to divert Africans from political demands by amelioration of unimportant but particularly annoying aspects of the general pattern of discrimination. Creation of Bantustans proceeds. Indeed, it could be argued that the obvious reluctance of the United States to support U.N. measures with teeth in them has encouraged the South African Government to believe that it can continue its current racial policies with impunity. The increase of American investment in South Africa—a development fully consistent with the stated American policy of maximizing contact between South Africa and the rest of the world—serves to confirm further the South African Government's belief that U.S. condemnation of apartheid is purely a verbal gesture. At the same time, American policy spurs the belief of many nonwhites that amelioration cannot come otherwise than by violence. Thus U.S. policy, which has as its goal the conciliation of conflicting elements, may have the effect of driving them further apart and precipitating the very explosion it seeks to prevent.

In summary, U.S. policy seems to have had only marginal effect on developments in Southern Africa. The United States has moved gradually in the direction of support of the ultimate aims of African nationalists, especially where, unlike the case in South Africa, these aims are clearly stated and appear to be generally accepted by the African population. At the same time, the United States has steadfastly opposed using the U.N. as a lever to force change in the direction of implementation of these aims. Indeed, in many cases, U.S.

attitudes have caused the watering-down of proposals to assure U.S. support.

The United States has striven for a U.N. policy paralleling its own, which, in the words of Secretary Williams, is that "the essential question in obtaining a peaceful resolution of Africa's problems will have to be decided by the African and European communities themselves. . . . But our policy in Africa is to assist in the attainment of harmony among all the continent's peoples in whatever ways we can." In other words, outsiders may seek to persuade and conciliate; they can do no more. This stand is based in part on a principled aversion to interfering in the domestic affairs of others unless American security is considered to be threatened directly. But it also stems from a feeling of impotence, a belief that there is little the United States can do to influence directly events in Southern Africa, especially in the Republic.

Is this conviction justified? American firms did much to ease the color bar in Zambia. Why cannot United States economic influence be brought to bear elsewhere? The United States is one of South Africa's most important customers, and has more than half a billion dollars invested in the area. The plain truth seems to be that there is a desire on the part of U.S. policy-makers to let sleeping dogs lie for fear that the American business community would, if brought into the fray, side openly with the South African Government. A more active American policy against apartheid might also increase racial tensions in the United States. It would almost certainly precipitate a major struggle between the executive branch and powerful elements in Congress and the press, beside which the controversy over U.S. Congo policy would seem paltry.

At a time when the problems of Latin America increasingly dominate the public and official mind, and influential groups such as the Clay Committee advocate what amounts to a downgrading of Africa as an area of American responsibility, it seems unlikely that a more vigorous policy—which might be blamed for a struggle in which American financial interests were threatened—is about to be undertaken. Our present policy is almost certain to continue much as in the past, changing only in response to initiatives outside American control.

Is American policy toward Southern Africa a failure? From the point of view of the African nationalist, yes. But, of course, this policy was not designed to serve his interests. What about the interests of the United States in a stable and prosperous Africa? Here an answer is more difficult. To date, the United States has lost little by temporizing on the issue of how rapidly other areas of Africa ought to become independent. Today, the independent African states are reasonably well disposed, even toward their former colonial masters —a reconciliation that has come about largely without American efforts.

Southern Africa, however, presents a more difficult and somber picture. This is particularly true of Rhodesia and of the Republic. Here reconciliation may be impossible. U.S. attempts to make it possible may only prolong the period of stress and make the final outcome more explosive. If this occurs, the United States, unless it changes its policies, will find itself unready. There is little evidence that we have decided which way to lean if we must choose between irreconcilables. To make such a choice public in advance might undercut hopes of performing successfully in the role of conciliator. Apparently, the government has paid little attention to the need for contingency planning for this area. If a peaceful resolution of the problems of Southern Africa proves impossible, the United States cannot avoid being drawn into the crisis, just as it has been in the Congo. To continue to opt for flexibility is one thing, to be totally unprepared for the crisis if it comes is quite another. The inability of American policy-makers to face the realities in Southern Africa threatens the interests of the United States and of Africans alike.

Editors' Postscript

U.S. policy in the Congo during the last two years has shattered the myth that American interests in Africa are limited. As soon as Communist intervention became a possibility, the United States acted swiftly and with force. In Southern Africa, however, the threat of Soviet or Chinese intervention remains remote and America seems still to be content with the aims of minimizing conflict and maximizing economic stability.

A similar policy was followed in the Congo up to mid-1964 in the form of support for Prime Minister Adoula's attempts to establish some central control over the country. A revolt that had broken out in Kwilu province in January, 1964, however, spread throughout the eastern part of the country and by May had become a serious threat to Congolese unity. On May 6, 1964, the People's Daily of Peking declared the revolt to be an "armed struggle of the Congolese people against United States imperialism and its lackeys. . . . It is now impossible for the Congo to achieve national liberation through socalled parliamentary methods, but only through armed struggle." [1]

[1] Quoted in *Africa Report*, IX, No. 6 (June, 1964), 14.

Faced with virtual disintegration of the country, President Kasa-vubu, in late June, invited Moise Tshombe to return from Spain and to form a government. Tshombe's plans for dealing with revolt and disintegration were simple: He recruited white mercenary soldiers, chiefly from South Africa and Southern Rhodesia, and re-European-ized the civil service.

By late summer of 1964, there were reports that some of the rebel leaders had received training and financial support from China and the Soviet Union. In August, the United States decided to make a definite military commitment to the Tshombe government. Trans-port planes, helicopters, and a "small number" of B-26 bombers were sent to the Congo, although Americans were prohibited from par-ticipation in combat missions. Cuban refugee pilots flew many mis-sions, however.

By November, 1964, the mercenaries, Cuban pilots, and the Armée National Congolaise (ANC) had turned the tide of battle. In the panic of defeat, the rebels announced, on November 16, that they were about to execute Dr. Paul Carlson, an American medical mis-sionary accused of spying, but that his fate was negotiable. Secretary of State Dean Rusk asked Prime Minister Jomo Kenyatta, chairman of the OAU's ad hoc committee on the Congo, to intercede on be-half of Dr. Carlson, and the execution was postponed for several days. Kenyatta, the U.S. Government, and other Western nations appealed for four days to the rebels to allow the Red Cross into Stanleyville. Rebel head Christophe Gbenye, however, was determined to gain something in return for the safety of Dr. Carlson and the others. On November 22, he sent Thomas Kanza, Foreign Minister of the rebel regime, to Nairobi for talks with the U.S. Ambassador to Kenya, William Attwood. Kanza's price was clear—halt the ANC advance on Stanleyville. The discussions ended after one day, with Ambassador Attwood denouncing Kanza's proposal as blackmail and totally un-acceptable. At the same time, Radio Stanleyville announced that the hostages would be killed if the city were attacked.

Meanwhile, the United States had a few days before flown 600 Belgian paratroopers to Ascension Island and then to the Kamina staging base in the Congo. On November 24, these paratroopers were dropped on Stanleyville. A few minutes before they landed, Dr. Carlson and a number of other hostages were killed.

The next day, Prime Minister Kenyatta announced with regret:

As chairman of the OAU commission on the Congo, I had repeatedly appealed to both Léopoldville and Stanleyville authorities to stop all hostilities. . . . These appeals were ignored. . . . When my intervention was formally sought, on behalf of civilian prisoners of many nationalities, I made it clear to representatives of appealing nations that my efforts would be wholly jeopardized if any unilateral action were taken.[2]

For the next few days, American aircraft continued to drop Belgian paratroopers at various points to rescue white hostages. The final results of the operation were 1,700 saved, 80 killed, and 44 wounded.

Although the United States stressed that the purpose of the rescue mission was humanitarian rather than military, most African nations saw it as part of the Tshombe-mercenary drive to crush the Congo rebellion. A twenty-two-nation complaint was lodged in the U.N. Security Council, with particularly bitter complaints on the part of the U.A.R., Algeria, Kenya, the Central African Republic, Congo (Brazzaville), Burundi, Ghana, Guinea, and Tanzania. On December 30, the Council adopted a compromise resolution calling for an end to foreign intervention, a cease-fire, withdrawal of all mercenaries, and OAU efforts to help the Congo achieve a national conciliation.

In March, 1965, America and Belgium agreed to continue military aid to the Congo. Although the rebellion has been all but crushed, white mercenaries still remain. There are some reports that their number is being reduced by allowing their contracts to expire.

U.S. policy in Southern Africa still remains largely one of biding time, minimizing conflict, and encouraging accommodation. For the most part, the United States has refused to vote against her ally Portugal in the United Nations. In the debates on resolutions, however, she has usually supported the efforts of the Secretary General to arrange talks between Portuguese and African leaders and has urged solution through dialogue. Recently, however, on June 10, 1965, the United States voted against a Security Council resolution requesting NATO countries to refrain from sending arms to Portugal.

In U.N. debates on Southern Rhodesia, the United States has continually declared her confidence in the United Kingdom's efforts to use all available influence to broaden the franchise and to eliminate racial discrimination. Yet the United States has refrained from positive support of most resolutions concerning Rhodesia on the grounds that they fail to take into account the real limitations on Britain's power to effect a change in the situation. In April, 1965, the United States firmly declared that she would not recognize a Rhodesian unilateral declaration of independence and emphasized that

[2] *Africa Report*, X, No. 1 (January, 1965), 24.

the Rhodesian Government could not lightly ignore the warnings of the United Kingdom or its own businessmen concerning the diplomatic and economic isolation that would follow a UDI.

Regarding the Republic of South Africa, U.S. policy has stiffened in the past two years. On August 7, 1963, the United States voted for a Security Council resolution that strongly deprecated the racial policies of South Africa and requested all states to cease the sale and shipment of arms and ammunition to that country. In the preceding debate, Ambassador Adlai Stevenson announced that the United States would stop the sale of all military equipment by the end of the year. Yet Mr. Stevenson also argued that economic and diplomatic sanctions would only promote intransigence and discourage a dialogue between the Government of South Africa and its African population.

On December 4, the United States supported a Security Council resolution calling on states not to supply South Africa with material for the manufacture of arms or ammunition. However, the United States abstained on a paragraph that called for the boycott of all South African goods and was subsequently deleted after failing to obtain the required seven votes.

An American embargo on arms to South Africa became effective January 1, 1964. A government representative announced that artillery, shell and rifle equipment, jigs, presses, and casting machines fell under the provisions of the U.N. resolution, but that petroleum did not. So far, the United States has withheld support from all efforts to institute an embargo on the oil so vital to the Republic of South Africa.

U.N. Civilian Operations in the Congo

GODFREY K. J. AMACHREE

Unlike the political and military activities of the United Nations in the Congo, its technical-assistance activities have received very little publicity. The object of this paper will be to describe these activities.

In his memorandum of August 11, 1960, Secretary General Dag Hammarskjöld stated that the Security Council conceived of the civil and military aspects of the Congo operations as interrelated. The United Nations did not, therefore, limit its activities to peacekeeping operations, but endeavored to ensure the maintenance of a minimum of basic public services. This aim meant giving the Congolese Government all help necessary to avoid a complete breakdown of law and order. The United Nations technical-assistance setup, otherwise known as Civilian Operations, is responsible for this aspect of U.N. assistance to the Congo.

Object and Scope of Civilian Operations

In the first progress report to the Secretary General from his special representative in the Congo, the object and scope of Civilian Operations were described thus:

> To give a fair and accurate picture of the meaning of United Nations civil operations in the Congo, one would have to begin by describing the extent to which the country's normal facilities were disrupted and by listing the services which would not be functioning save for the presence of the United Nations. There was an immediate and country-wide breakdown in the regular commercial arrangements for distributing food, to the point where people in some parts of the Congo must now rely for their main sustenance on food supplies distributed from Léopoldville by the United Nations. There was, at the same time, the threat of a major breakdown in the maintenance of water supply and sanitation facilities. Without the services of World Health Organization personnel, who

arrived within two days of the plea for help, these facilities might have failed. There is a more recent ominous threat of a smallpox and plague epidemic, and disquieting reports are being received of an increased number of malaria and filariasis cases.

With the voluntary departure of European personnel incident to independence, there was virtually no trained staff to supervise the operation of telephone, telegraph, telex and radio transmission installations, and these facilities are in operation today only because of the presence of a large United Nations International Telecommunication Union team. Likewise, air traffic control services were deteriorating with the departure of technicians from a very large number of airports. Today, adequate servicing of flights can only be assured at the three airports where United Nations advisers, controllers and radio technicians are based. If there were not any meteorologists assigned by the United Nations to the country—there are five—there would be absolutely no meteorological protection for planes.

Civilian Operations followed the pattern of normal U.N. technical assistance, but went beyond the concept of the usual organization of technical assistance in other countries. For the first time in the history of the United Nations, the organization and its specialized agencies planned a combined operation on a scale described as "unprecedented." The cooperation of the specialized agencies was specially requested by the Security Council in its resolution of July 22, 1960. The FAO, ICAO, ILO, ITU, UNESCO, UNICEF, UPU, WHO, and WMO are, as a result, actively engaged in civilian operations in the Congo. The Special Fund and the Technical Assistance Board have also participated in the operations. The head of the operations reported directly to the Under Secretary in charge of Congo Civilian Operations.

Each agency appointed its local representative in the Congo, who remained in the regular relationship to his agency and under its authority. The Secretary General of the United Nations in turn appointed all local representatives as consultants and members of a consultative group. This group consisted of the Chief of Civilian Operations, who was the Chairman, and the heads of the specialized agencies in the Congo, as well as other United Nations senior staff responsible for United Nations projects. The group met regularly to deal with problems affecting the operations. The consultants maintained very close liaison with Congolese ministers.

The experts, technicians, and other staff serving in the Congo were recruited from 47 different countries. There were some 1,200 such experts and technicians in the Congo during 1962.

Financing of Civilian Operations: The Congo Fund

The Security Council did not specifically indicate the source from which the operations were to be financed. The General Assembly adopted a resolution on September 16, 1962, calling on "all member governments for urgent voluntary contributions to a United Nations Fund for the Congo." It was the aim of Dag Hammarskjöld to establish a Congo Fund of $100 million. (For the actual contributions, see Table I.)

The Fund was to be used under U.N. control and in consultation with the Central Government of the Congo. It was administered separately from the main U.N. budget (ONUC budget) for other operations in the Congo. Contributions to the Congo Fund were voluntary, and many members have made none, although a few of the noncontributors have given bilateral assistance to the Congo. Compared with their contributions to the Expanded Program of Technical Assistance of the Special Fund, the Congo Fund contributions of some countries have been very small. One adverse condition has been that subscribers to the Congo Fund are not obliged to renew their contributions. Except for the United States, countries making large contributions in 1960 failed to renew their pledges.

There have been other sources of funds for Civilian Operations:

(1) The Congolese Government has contributed a total of $4,566,-355 (292,246,720 Congolese francs) to meet local currency payments.

(2) ONUC budget reimburses Civilian Operations for the costs of certain projects of benefit to the military ($1 million in 1962 for airport and telecommunications services). The salaries of a number of the staff employed by Civilian Operations are borne by the ONUC budget. Moreover, the transport facilities of ONUC have been made available to Civilian Operations for the transportation of food and equipment. The total contribution of the ONUC budget to the Civilian Operations in 1962 was about $72,000.

(3) UNICEF contributed $1 million during 1960 and 1961 for relief operations.

(4) A $5 million U.S. grant was made to the Congo in August, 1960, through the United Nations prior to the existence of the Congo Fund. The money was used for the import-support program.

(5) A Congo Famine Relief Fund was established in February, 1961, in response to appeals made by the Secretary General to relieve famine conditions in Kasai and Kivu. Donations were also made to the Congo through the League of Red Cross Societies. Approximately $7 million was received.

TABLE I

Contributions to the Congo Fund, in Dollars

(as of December 31, 1962)

Country	Total Pledged	Received during 1960–61	Received during 1962
Australia	750,000	750,000	—
Cambodia	4,040	2,040	2,000
Canada	1,000,000	1,000,000	—
Denmark	600,000	600,000	—
West Germany	3,000,000	3,000,000	—
Haiti	2,000	—	—
India	105,000	105,000	—
Iran	25,000	—	—
Ireland	25,000	25,000	—
Liberia	250,000	83,333	7,923
Morocco	39,526	—	—
Netherlands [a]	499,262	346,196	153,066
New Zealand	280,000	280,000	—
Nigeria	10,052	—	10,052
Norway	490,616	490,616	—
Philippines	10,000	—	—
Sweden	1,391,304	1,391,304	—
Tunisia	10,000	—	—
United Kingdom	3,000,000	3,000,000	—
United States	27,950,000 [b]	22,950,000	15,000,000 [b] (10,000,000) [c]
TOTAL	$39,441,800	$34,023,489	$15,173,041

[a] The Netherlands pledged a maximum of $1 million subject to the condition that the contributions must not exceed 1.01 per cent of the total pledges.

[b] Total U.S. payments toward U.N. economic assistance to the Congo up to December 31, 1962, amounted to $80.95 million, broken down as follows: (1) $5 million paid to the Congo Government in August, 1960 (prior to the existence of the Congo Fund), for import support under the terms of an agreement of August 23, 1960, between the United Nations and the Republic of the Congo; (2) $22.95 million credited to the Congo Fund in 1960–61, of which $10 million was for technical assistance and $12.95 million was for import support; and (3) $53 million paid in 1962, of which $5 million was credited to the Congo Fund for technical assistance and $48 million to a Special Trust Fund for import support in 1962.

[c] Transferred to the Special Trust Fund account.

The voluntary contributions to the U.N. Fund for the Congo were, according to the General Assembly resolution, "to be used . . . for the purpose of rendering the fullest possible assistance" to the Congo. It is necessary to distinguish two types of activities to which the Fund has been applied. One is technical assistance to the Republic of the Congo in the form of experts, fellowships, and equipment for training purposes; the other is financial support from an import program of essential goods and commodities.

Technical Assistance

Technical assistance is being rendered to the Congo in agriculture, communications, transportation, meteorology, education, finance, economics, health, justice, labor, cooperatives, mining, public administration, police training, public works, and social welfare.

The cost of the technical-assistance program between August, 1960, and December, 1962, amounted to $18,170,000. Eighty per cent of the funds available for technical assistance is spent on the salaries of experts and technicians. Their number grew from 200 at the end of 1960 to about 1,200 at the end of 1962. As an illustration of the acute personnel problem facing the civil service of the Congo, it may be mentioned that the pre-independence Congolese budget provided for about 10,000 Belgian technicians and experts. Of the 8,000 or so Belgians employed in the Congolese civil service before independence, only 2,500 stayed in the service after independence. Of this number, 1,100 were in Katanga and 1,400 in the Central Government.

The training of Congolese was immediately imperative. Apart from in-service training programs, fellowships in various fields of learning are awarded annually to selected Congolese for training abroad. For 1961–62, more than $1.8 million was spent for technical assistance.

During its first year of Civilian Operations and up to the end of 1961, U.N. experts organized a large number of courses of short duration for Congolese technicians and civil servants. In all, 959 Congolese participated in short-term training courses (less than 6 months) that terminated in 1961, and 2,417 in such courses that terminated in 1962, while 836 were following such courses at the end of 1962 and 3,000 teachers were receiving short-term refresher training on the job. The courses covered the whole range of government activity. However, increasing emphasis was being placed on longer-term courses as more elaborate training institutions could be developed. Thus, while only 70 participants completed courses lasting from 7 to 12 months in 1961, 243 did so in 1962 and 429 were following such courses at the end of 1962. The corresponding figures for courses lasting over a year were 30, 40, and 1,341. This last figure included 310 students at the National School of Law and Administration, 400 at the Léopoldville Police School, 120 at the National Institute for Building and Public Works, and 196 at the National Pedagogical Institute (for training of secondary-school teachers).

The United Nations has performed three functions in regard to the training of Congolese outside the Congo. In certain instances, U.N. officials have been responsible for the selection of students and for administrative matters connected with the placement of Congolese at overseas institutions. (See Table II.) In other cases, they have assisted the Congolese Government in negotiating bilateral agreements for the award of fellowships. Fellowship awards have also been made from the Congo Fund. In 1962, 214 fellowships were awarded.

TABLE II

Placement of Congolese at Overseas Institutions, 1960–61

Country	No. of Students	Field
France	40	General administration
	68	Medicine
United States	20	ICA programs in customs, local administration, fiscal administration
	11	ICA program in private-firm management
Tunisia	7	General administration
Germany	35	Telecommunications, engineering
Israel	8	Agriculture, community development
Switzerland	8	Teaching
Luxembourg	10	ICA program in police training

A special effort is being made by UNESCO to reform the system of education that the Congolese inherited from the Belgians. It is often stated that before independence more than 60 per cent of Congolese children of school age were attending primary schools. The truth, however, is that only 30 per cent of the children continue their primary education for more than four years. Many of the primary schools offered only two years of study. The result was that only 152 Congolese children had completed their secondary-school education at the time of independence. The population of the Congo is about 14 million.

UNESCO had to develop and adapt the secondary and primary school systems, establish institutions of higher learning, and undertake teacher-training programs. (Proposals for the reform of the secondary and primary education have been accepted by the Congolese Government.) With funds from the U.N., UNESCO has been able to recruit 560 secondary-school teachers from 27 countries. The drive to increase the number of Congolese with secondary school education will, in the next few years, yield the desired results. Already, enrollment in secondary schools has increased more than 100 per cent.

The Import-Support Program

The import-support program constituted one of the main activities of the Congo Fund. When the Congo attained independence, the country had enough foreign assets to meet essential import requirements. Pursuant to an agreement signed on August 23, 1960, between the government of the Congo and the United Nations, the U.N. made a grant of $5 million to the Congo. This afforded the Congolese treasury counterpart funds, in Congolese francs, and enabled the government to meet its internal financial commitments.

The deterioration of law and order that followed soon after independence badly affected the Congo's export trade, and very little foreign exchange was earned. Maintaining the flow of essential imports at a time when foreign-exchange proceeds were on the decline resulted in a drain on the exchange resources of the country. In May, 1961, it became obvious that the flow of essential imports could no longer be maintained unless foreign exchange was made available to the Congo. The United Nations made an immediate grant of $10 million and set up an import-support program. The operation of the import-support program is governed by the terms of an agreement entered into on June 12, 1961, by the government of the Congo and the United Nations.

The import-support program serves three purposes: (1) It ensures the maintenance of imports at the level required to stimulate agricultural and industrial production in order to meet the internal consumption requirements and to make a surplus available for the export market; (2) it combats foreign-payments difficulties and checks inflationary trends by preventing a shortage of essential consumer goods (it was expected that an inflow of essential imports would prevent a sharp rise of retail prices); and (3) it provides the government of the Congo with counterpart funds with which to finance essential public expenditures and reduce the budgetary deficit.

In July, 1961, a team of International Monetary Fund experts were, by the terms of the June 12 agreement, assigned the task of preparing a program of essential import requirements for the Congo. The program has been implemented by the release of foreign currency as and when available, in successive remittances, either from the Congo Fund ($10 million) or from special contributions by donor countries. The June 12 agreement provided that foreign currency granted to the Congo should be deposited in a special account with a bank in the donor country in the name of the Monetary Council, the Congolese institution responsible for central banking activities. Withdrawals from the account are subject to the joint signatures of United Nations and Monetary Council representatives.

The counterpart funds derived from sales of foreign currency to Congolese importers are deposited in a special account opened with the Monetary Council in the name of the Republic of the Congo. Withdrawals from this account are also subject to the joint signatures of representatives of the Congolese Government and the United Nations. The June 12 agreement stipulates that the counterpart funds are to be channeled through the Congolese treasury and are to be used for "emergency requirements" and for budgetary support. There was an estimated balance of 600 million Congolese francs in counterpart funds in 1963, and a further 2 billion Congolese francs were expected from future foreign-exchange transactions.

This account of the work of the U.N. Civilian Operations in the Congo is not intended to be exhaustive. No reference, for example, has been made to the work being done by U.N. experts in economic rehabilitation and police training. The Congolese Government is growing more and more to rely on such experts and technicians for help and advice. Thus, the continuing success of the operations will depend on the attitude of the contributing countries.

Editors' Postscript

In 1964, the United Nations program of technical cooperation in the Congo consisted of 22 projects, 570 experts, 800 high-school teachers, and 400 police. Together, these provided the base for such essential services as the judiciary, law enforcement, public works, civil aviation, communications, public health, and education. Substantial contingents came from Nigeria, France, Haiti, Greece, Switzerland, the United Kingdom, Italy, Belgium, Spain, Lebanon, and Canada.

The total cost of operations was $17 million, of which the Congo government provided 40 per cent. The U.S. contributed $4 million, while the United Kingdom and Canada gave $500,000 each. Outstanding achievements of the 1964 operations included a nearly balanced budget and the construction of roads, schools, and hospitals.

Discussion

ALEX QUAISON-SACKEY.   In commenting on South West Africa, I suggested that we should decide whether the problems of Southern Africa should be resolved peacefully or violently. The consensus so far has been that they should be resolved by violence in national action. However, I advocate international action. In my view, international action can go hand in hand with national action, whether that national action be peaceful or violent.

One must emphasize here that there are areas in Southern Africa where strong international action is required. In Southern Rhodesia, for example, without U.N. prodding supported by United States action, we might find ourselves facing another South African situation. Godfrey Amachree has said that the United States is waiting to see what the United Kingdom will do in South Africa. I do not think that is a wise policy. The United States and the United Kingdom should listen to the leaders of this area, such as Nkomo and Sithole, and to African delegations, such as my own, that not only have a vital interest in the continent but know the facts. If they will listen to us, they will be able to evolve a policy that is in the interest of peace and harmony.

The United States also has a responsibility in the cases of Angola and Mozambique. The Africans in the United Nations have felt very strongly about the Portuguese claim that their colonies in Africa are extensions of Portugal. We have never subscribed to this claim, and the United States has moved slowly toward our viewpoint. What the United States has not done, however, is to persuade Portugal that no part of Africa can be an extension of Europe.

One way that international action could help in avoiding violence would be to control the shipments of arms to South Africa by the United States and the United Kingdom. If violence breaks out in Southern Rhodesia or South Africa, it cannot be confined to those territories, and is, therefore, a threat to international peace and security. Hence international action may be the alternative to the civil violence so often prophesied for Southern Africa.

WILLIAM E. MORAN, JR.   [*Dean Moran voiced agreement with Dr. Ferkiss' analysis of U.S. policy in Africa, but suggested that all countries— African, European, or American—base their policy on "national interest" as they see it at the particular time and in the particular circumstances.*] What I am leading up to is that many of the problems we have been discussing here in this conference are really international problems, quite probably beyond the capacity of the means of any national state except in terms of that state's own limited national interest. These are problems of the international or universal common good, whereas states are interested primarily in the common good of their own people. [*But Dean Moran seriously questioned whether the existing international organizations could in these times serve the end sought by Ambassador Quaison-Sackey and others. He cited that portion of Pope John's "Pacem in Terris" Encyclical which raised precisely this doubt.*]

ROBERT I. ROTBERG. [*Dr. Rotberg took a different view. He rejected the view of those who maintain that the United States should not be expected to take the initiative in this area. Moreover, he rather unqualifiedly postulated that diplomatic pressure on the United Kingdom and economic pressure on Southern Rhodesia by the United States could prevent the granting of independence to Southern Rhodesia so long as the resultant government would necessarily be a white one.*]

EDUARDO C. MONDLANE. [*Mr. Mondlane expressed the view that national self-interest was too narrowly conceived by the prior speakers.*] Is, for instance, the United States acting in its own national self-interest when it maintains its relationships with Portugal to the detriment of Portugal's African colonies, even though it is a certainty that within a few years Africans will control their own lands? Will the U.S. Government then find itself desperately trying to court the very African nationalists whom now they are ignoring? We now see the United States "scrambling" in West and East Africa in order to erase the last ten years' equivocation.

IX

Problems of Adjustment and Independence

Theories of Multiracialism:
Problems of Political Equality

ARTHUR N. L. WINA

The ten-year-old Federation of Rhodesia and Nyasaland—unable to survive the urges of the African people toward freedom, democracy, and economic opportunity—was finally pronounced dead in March, 1963. Those of us present in London for this momentous event could not help feeling overwhelmed by the significance of Britain's granting Northern Rhodesia the right to secede.

The Federation of Rhodesia and Nyasaland foundered on the rocks of racialism and the monumental bluff behind which its leaders in Central Africa were conducting its affairs. The objective of these leaders was to create a society in which white would lead black for the next 200 years in a forced apprenticeship relation; the objective of the Africans was their immediate elevation to full citizenship of the country, with all the rights and responsibilities of citizenship. The proponents of the Federation strived for economic domination by the European over the African by means of differentials in wage scales based on race, differentials in advancement opportunities in favor of those with white skin, and utilization of arable and accessible Crown land areas by European farmers while Africans were pushed into reserves remote from markets and poorly served with communication and other facilities. These are the measures that killed federation, and these are the conditions and sufferings that inspired Kenneth Kaunda and many of us in Central Africa to fight the Federation until it was buried. Upon its ruins we hope to build something noble, human, and democratic, existing as separate states for the present, but surely at some future date joining to unite the whole of Africa. The Federation is one more theory of multiracialism that has failed, as all of them will fail, based as they are on a system of racial domination openly declared or secretly practiced.

Political equality and equality of opportunity are the dominant issues in Southern Africa today. There is, in that part of the continent, a vivacious, enterprising population of indigenous Africans as politically inspired as are Africans in other parts of Africa by the strong wave of nationalism that has swept the continent since the end of World War II. Also in the same area is a relatively small proportion of persons of European and Asian stock. Of an approximate population of 30 million in Southern Africa, Europeans represent a little more than 11 per cent. It is easy to see why the problems of equality are invariably cloaked in racial terms, as they were not in the racially homogeneous situations of Rousseau's France or John Stuart Mill's England.

In Southern Africa, theories of multiracialism have been the main political planks in the platforms of almost all political parties. That is to say, debate in almost all political discussions has revolved around the "right" type of political relations that should exist between black and white, and, to a lesser extent, among black, white, and Asian. This debate engenders, certainly in South Africa and Southern Rhodesia, passions on both sides similar in intensity to those between the peoples of the Communist and non-Communist worlds. Apart from the tendencies of immigrant races to exploit indigenous resources, there is, among the Europeans, the deeper feeling of insecurity and entrenched privilege, so aptly described by John Gaunt, Minister of Industries in Southern Rhodesia's Rhodesian Front Government, when he said: "What we have, we hold."

In Northern Rhodesia's Copperbelt, where, before the formation of an African government, only Europeans were entitled to do certain skilled jobs, and in South Africa, where this same practice has statutory backing, the design of Europeans to entrench and enshrine their privileged status is clear. Politically, the main objective in creating the Central African Federation was to establish a superstructure above territorial governments. The Federation thus would be the final depository of white power whatever constitutional changes took place at the territorial level that might otherwise result in some form of African control. And, of course, the South African situation clearly and nakedly sets out to achieve through apartheid what the white Rhodesians sought and now have failed to achieve through the sophistry of the Federation.

The limited nature of economic opportunities open to Africans where European settlers control the political and economic opportunities must inevitably give rise to pressures from Africans to force their way into the "garden of Eden." Low wages, poor housing conditions, poor educational opportunities, and limited opportunities for advancement in commerce, industry, and government resulting from

European control of the machinery of state could not but increase the pressures from below. The African urge for independence and freedom from European domination is pregnant with emotion.

A number of ideas, theories, and policies, purportedly intended to solve this problem, have been advanced or formulated. One well-known theory that has been advertised, and discredited, world-wide, is South Africa's apartheid. The system of apartheid attempts to contain African political and economic aspirations and to preserve European privilege by political dictatorship. It seeks to guarantee not only that the African is separated from the European, but that he is made to feel inferior. It has been argued that it is possible to provide equal, if not identical, opportunities in both segments of South African society by community-development schemes in African areas, by land-improvement schemes, by expansion of Bantu educational facilities, and by the institution of semi-independent status in such African areas as the Transkei and Pondoland. The fact of the matter is, however, that ultimate political and economic control under this system must always reside in the white areas, where Parliament, banks, industries, and educational and other national institutions are established. South Africa would not lay claim to incorporation of the protectorates of Basutoland and Swaziland if her policy were separate and equal development of the European and African segments of her nation, nor would she be hanging on to South West Africa in defiance of all international opinion and law.

A second theory that also became government policy, and that is now dead, is the so-called theory of partnership, which has two variations. In its honest and serious form, it was originally advanced by Sir John Moffatt of the Northern Rhodesian Legislative Assembly some years ago. It was intended to ensure that where Europeans and Africans reside in one territory in significant numbers, neither should be permitted to dominate the other by virtue of one's superiority in numbers or the other's superiority in skills and technological advancement. Sir John had in mind Northern Rhodesia, where European domination was increasingly and alarmingly frustrating the legitimate aspirations of Africans. Reference to domination through superiority in numbers was intended to mollify those Europeans who had made Northern Rhodesia their home, and who, although well disposed toward Africans, were nevertheless concerned lest their security and rights be swept away by a democratically elected African government.

Moffat's theory was not only too idealistic; it ignored reality. The eventual subordination of one group to the other was inevitable. Also, the strains and frictions generated by internal forces would spell chaos within the system on purely political grounds. Could anyone imagine that anywhere in Africa the indigenous people, who in the case of Northern Rhodesia outnumbered the immigrant community by 40 to 1, would forever live under such an artificial and forced equilibrium? With all the good intentions of the supporters of such a system, one cannot help describing them as wishful thinkers, because one cannot maintain for long, even by force, any system that does not rest on the broad support of all elements in the country. The partnership theory was rendered even more dubious by interpretations of it by such men as Sir Roy Welensky and Lord Malvern, who saw in it a good cover for their own political ambitions. To them, the theory was no more than a working relationship between a senior partner, the European, and a junior partner, the African. In one revealing and now classic phrase, the theory of partnership was said to mean only the partnership that "exists between the rider and the horse."

In its political application, therefore, partnership has proved to be synonymous with apartheid, the only difference being that the former conceals the patent reality of the latter. As practiced by European politicians in Central Africa, it meant European domination in all spheres of life. The "responsible citizens" always referred to the Europeans; "public opinion" meant European opinion; "people of all races" meant Europeans and a few African stooges; the "civilized standards" meant European standards; "national prosperity" meant European prosperity; and so on. The Federation of Rhodesia and Nyasaland came into being as an institution to preserve this "partnership" between black and white with all the coercive forces of a modern state at its disposal.

In the former Belgian Congo, and in former French West Africa and French Equatorial Africa, a political and, generally speaking, theoretical foundation of colonial rule was based on another myth of multiracialism: association, assimilation, or the myth of the *assimilados* or of the *evolués*, call it what you may. Implicit in all of these theories was the assumption that black Africans could be assimilated and turned into black Belgians or black Frenchmen or black Portuguese. The implementation of this policy varied somewhat from territory to territory, especially from empire to empire. Special privileges were accorded to the *evolué*, the "elect," the aspirant to French culture and tastes. France trained Africans from her empire in French institutions, and graduated them with political, economic, and a limited degree of social acceptance into French society. The "black Frenchman" was made a deputy, and, in one outstanding case, a cabinet minister in Paris. The idea in its early stages was, of course, motivated by a combination of humanitarian and economic considerations

—humanitarian because the "primitive native," as the term went, had no chance of making his way in the "civilized" world unless he made it through the gates of French culture and tradition, and economic because the intention was to integrate the most productive countries of *Afrique Noire* into the industrial economy of France in an interdependent relationship. It worked in the sense that it opened the way for Africans to make their entry into French culture, something which was, and I understand still is, considered by the French to be the best in the whole world. The system foundered partly because African nationalism does not recognize, nor is it vulnerable to, imperialism of any type, be it cultural, political, economic, or ideological. It foundered especially because Africans were deeply impressed by France's history of revolution: by the French Revolution, the fall of the Bastille, the 1848 Revolution, and, more recently, the Algerian conflagration. It was only a question of time before the Africans, in another revolution, used French language, French culture, and French methods to break up French colonialism. Sékou Touré became the hero and initiator of the struggle when, in 1958, he defied De Gaulle's intentions by opting out of the French Community, only to be followed later by all the territories of France's African empire.

The theories of assimilation and association subserved subjugation, not multiracialism. The French failed in Africa because these theories did not provide sufficient recognition to the human and natural desire of people to govern themselves on the basis of self-determination or to enter into associated or federated relationship with other peoples or territories on the basis of consent. Portuguese "assimilation" is doomed for the same reasons.

After a cursory review of unsuccessful theories of multiracialism, the question as to whether there is a workable one arises. My answer is that there is none. Such a theory is called for only if one accepts the premise that there is an inevitable clash of interests in a society of different communities, even when the individuals of these communities enjoy the same treatment before the law. I and the political party to which I belong neither accept nor recognize such a clash as inevitable. Kenneth Kaunda, leader of my party and at the moment Minister of Local Government and Social Welfare in the Coalition Government of Northern Rhodesia, has come out with a "negative" theory in order to satisfy those who think such a theory is necessary. He has rightly called this theory nonracialism. We evolved a theory of nonracialism because we were operating in an environment polluted by people who had made racialism the main theme of our political life. Whatever political party one belonged to, one had to take some position on the question of race, though to do so was repugnant to African concepts of humanism.

Mr. Kaunda has often said that one is born black, green, white, or yellow not by one's choice at all. Thus there can be no question of providing a special position in society for Europeans; contrarily, there can be no question of victimizing them in favor of the Africans. Those who decide to make their home in a territory and contribute, however insignificantly, to the national cause must be accorded identical treatment before the law. We realize that our people have been victims of racial discrimination and have suffered wrongs—especially after the establishment of the Federation of Rhodesia and Nyasaland. We realize that it is sometimes in the nature of human beings to retaliate and to derive some satisfaction, albeit base, from revenge. We realize that after a period of suppressive rule and discriminatory practices the temptation to make the "other chap" go through what one has had to endure from his hands is great. But with it all, we are determined, whatever the temptations and however temporarily justifiable the opposite course may seem, to uphold our concepts of humanism and nonracialism. This problem is primarily one of leadership.

Leadership in the transformation from white domination to democracy must be exceptionally honest and brave. It must be prepared and capable of leading, not merely of responding, to the unrealistic pressures from below. It must be prepared to get its policies understood and accepted by the masses of the people. It must clearly and vigorously show that it is doing those things which the majority of the people are crying for and which are legitimately their right. Leadership must also be aware that there are vested interests and remnants of the old regime that can make transformation difficult; these should be won over if possible. These elements may exercise a significant though temporary control over certain resources, skills, and techniques. In most cases, they are also human and will respond and adjust themselves. In Northern Rhodesia, there is a clear indication that this is the case. But leadership must impress them with its integrity and honesty of purpose and not go out of its way to pacify them. In the long run, and this seems to me to be the acid test of leadership, the people must feel that work is going on to meet their legitimate wants and aspirations as rapidly as circumstances permit.

One cannot end a discussion of multiracialism without a passing reference to the position of the Negro in the United States. Unlike Southern Africa, the southern part of the United States is governed by the U.S. Constitution and the Bill of Rights, which guarantee the rights of the citizen. In spite of these guarantees, and in spite of the clearly recognized determination of the Federal Government of the United States to implement these noble ideals, large sections of the Negro community in America are still denied their basic human rights. I can only say here that the more delay there is in according every American citizen the enjoyment of his rights, the more the moral prestige of the United States as a world leader will continue to be impaired. It is not necessary here to delve into the problems of race in the United States. It is important, however, to remind the people of the United States that as more and more of Africa is liberated, Americans who resist integration will increasingly impair America's image in Africa.

Editors' Postscript

Zambia, under the leadership of Prime Minister Kenneth Kaunda, has become the major laboratory of nonracialism in Southern Africa. Faced with an increasing number of racial incidents since independence, Kaunda has firmly warned both whites and blacks against racial attacks. To reinforce the Prime Minister's warning, the Zambia Parliament passed an Insults Bill that makes it an offense punishable by imprisonment to insult a person because of his race.

The white-dominated countries south of Zambia, though, have continued developing along clearly marked racial lines. Only in Portuguese Africa have there been signs that, at least, the theoretical and legal underpinnings of racialism are eroding. Recent reforms in the Organic Law, which defined Portugal's relationship with her overseas territories, have enlarged the scope of local and municipal government. Moreover, the status of assimilado was abolished in 1961. Theoretically, there is universal suffrage for all who are either literate, taxpayers, or heads of families. Approximately 90 per cent of the Africans are still classified as illiterate, however, and the reforms have not resulted in an appreciable increase in the number of African voters.

In Rhodesia, a mild form of apartheid, known as "communal development," is advocated by Ian Smith's Rhodesian Front Party. The Smith regime, however, is saddled with a constitution negotiated with Britain in 1961 that favors eventual incorporation of Africans into the economic and political life of the country and provides for a gradual increase in the African vote.

Sir Edgar Whitehead, leader of the opposition Rhodesia National Party (RNP), spoke of an African majority in fifteen years during the 1962 elections. The RNP merged with Sir Roy Welensky's newly created Rhodesia Party in August, 1964, and formulated a program of mild reform. Although unwilling to make changes in the exclusive

"A Roll" franchise,[1] the Rhodesia Party called for the addition of more Africans to the "B Roll," gradual repeal of the discriminatory Land Apportionment Act, prohibition of segregation in public places, and a society based on equal opportunity and advancement according to merit. Left to itself, declared Welensky, Rhodesia could be relied upon to work out a "reasonable method and timetable" for the transfer of power to the still backward population.

A few months later, however, Welensky left politics because of an operation and Whitehead was replaced by the more conservative David Butler. Since then, the Rhodesia Party has emphasized economic policy and, like the opposition United Party in South Africa, has dropped all pretense of offering an alternative on political and racial issues.

Ian Smith, meanwhile, has come down hard on all attempts to loosen Rhodesia's racially structured society. His Rhodesia Front Party explicitly favors development of racial communities, regards the 1961 constitution as too radical, and opposes all attempts to weaken discriminatory legislation. Rather, the party intends to erode African nationalism through constitutional amendments that would make tribal chiefs eligible for seats in Parliament and make tribal courts responsible for all African complaints.

The underlying attitude of Rhodesian Front leaders toward the African is revealed in a secret document put out by the party and quoted in Africa Digest: "Africans have 'since recorded time an unfortunate ability to become subject to any other race or, failing that, a despotism of their own kind.' " [2]

In the Republic of South Africa, two racialist doctrines vie with each other for supremacy. The Afrikaner-based Nationalist Party favors a policy of separate development through the creation of black Bantustans, while those who realize the need for cheap African labor in white industry advocate the old tradition of baaskaap—out and out white supremacy.

To stem the flow of Africans into white urban areas—a movement

---

[1] The election rolls stood as follows in 1964:

A Roll	Europeans	89,278	
	Africans	2,263	
	Asians	1,231	
	Coloureds	1,308	Total 94,080
B Roll	Europeans	608	
	Africans	10,466	
	Asians	114	
	Coloureds	176	Total 11,364

[2] Africa Digest, XII, No. 2 (October, 1964), 42.

that was undermining the whole Bantustan policy—the Nationalist Government in 1964, passed the Bantu Laws Amendment Act. Deemed the toughest apartheid measure in fifteen years, this act reduces 7 million Africans outside the reserves to mere units in a vast and fluid labor pool. It provides for a network of labor bureaus to control the influx of Africans into white areas according to the amount of labor requested by industry. If an African loses his job, he automatically loses his right to remain in a white area, even if he was born there and has lived there all his life.

Critics among the opposition United Party, and industrialists, emphasized that the bill would seriously inhibit the growth of a black bourgeoisie—the most reliable bulwark against revolution and economic upheaval.

Prime Minister Verwoerd's determination to stand in the face of massive social and economic forces began to prove a losing battle in 1964 as a serious labor shortage in urban areas developed. Consequently, the government was forced into the embarrassing situation of filling normally white jobs in the post office, hospitals, and building trades with Africans and Coloureds. Leaders of industry called more and more for the training of nonwhites to fill skilled and semi-skilled positions.

At the same time, plans to relocate industry on the borders of the Transkei have not worked, as private enterprise has proved reluctant to build factories in what it considers unprofitable locations. Finally, new government studies have suggested that even with the creation of Bantustans, the black-white ratio in urban areas would still be three and a half to one in the year 2000. Increasingly, there are signs that Verwoerd is giving up plans for separate development and returning to a policy of baaskaap. In March, 1965, for example, Dr. P. J. Riekart, Minister of Planning, announced that the government wanted nonwhites to contribute their skills to the nation's economy. Under-the-counter relaxations in the industrial color bar are reported increasing. There are no signs, though, that Africans are to be brought into the mainstream of social and political life.

Finally, there is still talk of partition, with the Cape—up to somewhere beyond Port Elizabeth—Southern Transvaal, and the Orange Free State forming a white South Africa; and with Natal, Zululand, Transkei, part of the Eastern Cape, and the whole of the Eastern, Northern, and Western Transvaal to form an independent African nation.

Problems of Administration
in the Republic of the Congo [1]

JAMES T. HARRIS, JR.

Legal Background

The history of Congolese administration is the application of the Belgian administrative law to the Congo. Belgian concepts and practice of administrative law are in their main lines derived from French administrative law. Historically, the twenty-year period between the beginning and end of the French domination of Belgium (1794–1814) coincides with the elaboration of the Napoleonic Code in France. This code, which concerns the civil law, was also adopted by the Belgians. With certain major exceptions (i.e., the Belgian insistence on the competence of civil courts in litigation involving administrative acts),[2] the Belgians borrowed the French juxtaposition of administrative law to civil law. The law presently in force in the Congo is the Fundamental Law of May 19, 1960, passed by the Belgian Parliament and accepted by the Congolese Government pending the elaboration and passage of the Congo's constitution.

Unfortunately, the Fundamental Law does not clarify one of the basic questions affecting Congolese political life generally and the administrative apparatus in particular: the choice of a federal or unitary type of government. The law has some elements of both types of government. Federal characteristics include: (1) division of powers between the central government and the provinces (Articles 219, 220, 221); (2) recognition of the provinces' right to elaborate their own constitutions (Article 160); (3) granting to provincial bodies legislative authority as well as an autonomous executive authority; (4) the provincial assemblies' election of the central government's senate of four-

---

[1] This paper was prepared for the conference, but not presented as the author was unable to attend.

[2] Michel Rougevin-Baville, "Cours de Droit administrative" (unpublished manuscript, January, 1963).

teen senators from each province; and (5) creation of the Chamber of Conflicts within the constitutional court to rule on disputes between provinces and the central government.

Unitary aspects include: (1) the importance of the matters reserved for the powers of the central government; (2) the minute detail with which provincial functions are proscribed by the law; (3) controls built in by the establishment of state commissioners appointed by and representing the central government; and (4) absence of financial provisions, which, in effect, makes the provinces largely dependent on the central government.

The ambiguity of legal texts on the question of federalism, however, has had the ultimate effect of proliferating provincial political entities and attendant administrative personnel. (In August, 1960, there were 105,000 state-employed workers under contract; the Ministry of Public Services estimates that at the beginning of 1962 there were almost 300,000 workers under contract to the state.) [3] Furthermore, the laws governing the civil service have been the subject of great debate and political maneuvers in the Congo since the beginning of July, 1960, when the mass exodus of Belgian functionaries provided the new republic with the excuse to yield to the mounting pressures of Congolese civil servants to appoint them immediately to the highest administrative posts.

In an ordinance decreed in April, 1961, the grades and salaries of civil-service workers were transposed according to a new scale. An employee could be named to a grade corresponding to his current functions, even though he had been originally appointed to a lower grade. Protests against this ordinance in the private sector and among labor unions have impeded the government's implementation of it—only transpositions of the top two grades had been executed by mid-1962 —and there is small likelihood that further steps will be taken to implement it until political circumstances permit a stable government and the application of the new constitution.

The Social Environment of Administration in the Congo

In the Congo, as in all other countries, the administration of government is influenced by the economic, political, and social setting. This truism must be stated in view of the hue and cry from self-righteous foreign observers who seem to believe that the malaise of

[3] *Etudes Congolaises*, II, Nos. 5, 8. This figure is highly misleading since a large number of so-called civil servants employed since June, 1960, have never been paid, and the status as well as the physical whereabouts of many is in question.

administration in the Congo is the result of some special evil genius possessed by the Congolese that neutralizes or corrupts all efforts to help. We have all seen some of the consequences of the historic patterns of colonial rule, and noted the anomalies that stem from an administrative operation fitted to serve the peculiar interests (mostly economic) of the metropolitan powers. There are, however, completely indigenous factors that have affected and will for a long while affect the form and substance of Congolese administrative institutions.

ETHNIC PARTICULARISMS. It is commonplace to walk into a particular department or bureau of the central government and find that all or nearly all of the employees are of a common ethnic background. In many cases, the tendency is reinforced because the reputation of a particular bureau as being a Mongo, or Baluba, or Bakongo "stronghold" discourages applicants of other ethnic origins. In some cases, even though the personnel officer may make an honest effort to recruit outside his own tribal group, he may find few or no applicants, since it is assumed that he will naturally favor his own. And so, normally, he will.

To understand the terrible pressures on an otherwise conscientious and hard-working civil servant, an American has only to recall the days of Curley in Boston or Hague in Jersey City. It takes a man of extraordinary courage—both physical and moral—to withstand the importuning of his tribal (often village) brothers. There are a large number of political refugees and those seeking relief from the stagnant rural economies in the metropolitan centers these days. Soon after they arrive, they seek out the "big brother" who has made good. His place in the administrative hierarchy does not deter them: Mail clerk or minister, he is expected to help.[4]

The Western observer who finds himself vexed with the weakness and venality of the civil servant who gives in to this family and tribal pressure must imagine how it feels to expose himself to the undying enmity of the people of *his* village, the curses of the *féticheurs*, and the certain knowledge that he is almost alone in resisting this type of pressure. Furthermore, in the absence of enough trained talent to

[4] Class distinctions are without significance. Urban Congo is as thoroughly classless as any Marxist could hope. There are financial or political distinctions, but neither carries any discernible class-consciousness. One reason, of course, is the newness of it all. The Belgian-built handful of "upper-class" Africans, mostly civil servants and a sprinkling of businessmen, slid quickly into oblivion soon after July, 1960. Another reason for the relative absence of class distinctions is that the criteria tend to be somewhat ephemeral. Clerk today, president tomorrow; labor leader today, prime minister tomorrow; unemployed chauffeur today, senator tomorrow. On Saturday, everyone may be unemployed again.

fill the vacancies in government, the question becomes less a choice between a qualified person and a nonqualified one, and more a choice between two relatively incompetent candidates. To favor a brother in such circumstances is, therefore, tempting, even for an honest administrator.

It is undoubtedly true that tribal rivalry and hostility have been exacerbated by certain colonial policies. The Belgians were peculiarly ill-equipped to help reduce tribal conflict—even had they wished to—since their own "tribal war" between the Flemings and the Walloons was transplanted in all important respects to the Congo, including the administration, and not excluding the missions.

The history of tribal conflicts and warfare in the Congo is not substantially different from the tribal dissensions past and present in Europe, Asia, and elsewhere in Africa. There is nothing in the nature of things that fixes their perpetuity. Enlightenment and strong central authority will no doubt reduce them to the same manageable proportions as in other African nations and on other continents. For the moment, tribal conflicts feed on the generally disturbed political conditions, increasing economic distress, and the consistent failure of central government authority to make itself felt in the interior.

DISORGANIZATION OF TRADITIONAL LIFE. Even before the cataclysmic changes wrought by the sudden independence of the Belgian Congo, the intrusions of nineteenth- and twentieth-century living brought by the colonizers would have been enough to provide years of work for intelligent and devoted social workers and researchers. The Belgians were not unaware of the necessity of providing the minimum elements for the transition from a tribal conglomeration to a modern society, and the attention they paid to the problems of minimizing the conflict between the two was reasonably conscientious and farsighted. At the lowest administrative levels, tribal authorities were incorporated through councils into both the administrative and judicial structures. The administration of government affairs at this level was divided between the customary authorities and representatives of the government. Customary law was respected up to the point where the conflict with modern civil, commercial, and legal requirements made it seem intolerable.

Nonetheless, the erosion of tribal customs by such factors as a money economy, the Christian concept of marriage, compulsory education, education of women, professional prostitution, the acquisitive spirit, and individualism started a process of disintegration, displacement, and disorientation that only a Herculean effort might have moderated and controlled. The Belgians were not temperamentally or otherwise equipped to exert this effort. The training of an elite was discarded as an invitation to trouble. Down to a surprisingly low level, every aspect of economic, social, and political life was controlled, managed, and supervised by Belgians. The Congolese could learn about social management mostly by osmosis.

The exodus of young men to the mines of the east and to the industries of the west created social strains in the villages they left as well as in the urban centers to which they flocked. Most of these problems are too typical and well known to be detailed here. What seems to be peculiarly Congolese about them is the relative absence of violent eruption in situations that probably would have undone other societies. It is still difficult to find a parallel to the fact that with 60,000–80,000 unemployed in bulging Léopoldville (total population estimated at 600,000–700,000), spiraling inflation, and political disorganization, there has been no more violence than has occurred thus far. There are ominous signs, however, that the boiling point may be reached soon—juvenile gangs roaming the native quarters, increasing numbers of armed robberies and assaults, rocketing prostitution, and louder and more vindictive criticism of the "politicians."

Another unique factor in the Congo is the size of the administrative machine compared with the talent available to man it. Clearly, the most drastic reduction in force based on the most reasonable estimates of real needs would still leave an enormous gap to be filled. The social implications are evident in pressures on administrators, especially the enormous economic pressures. Soon after being appointed to their jobs, a great number of these harried men found themselves saddled not only with their immediate families, but with a host of relations and hangers-on who expected to be fed and housed until they "got on their feet." It is a depressing and debilitating experience for the men with jobs to see their salary at the end of each month completely devoured by these peripheral but inescapable obligations.

It is not astonishing, therefore, that these men, hardly trained in the techniques, let alone the ethics, of the civil service, are prey for the hundreds of big and little "con" men who need a signature quickly on a document of dubious legality, or a customs official with convenient lapses of sight and memory, or a licensing officer who makes his laws on the spot, or a sanitation inspector who counts francs better than microbes, or a rent-control official who needs a house for the ten people he cannot accommodate in his own home. It is not difficult to persuade the policeman who makes $50 a month (when he is paid), and must spend all that and more on food and rent alone, to look in the other direction. In sum, the massive and fairly universal corruption within the administration is, in part, due to a massive social disorganization.

The changing situation of women also has its administrative repercussions. The import of the system of concubinage into the big city means that the economic support of the one or more additional households is no longer a village-shared responsibility but the unique charge of the man who feels this indispensable need.[5] No one who has spent more than two weeks at the seat of the central government can be unaware of the intricate pattern of relationships that obtain between men of high office with various "women of the town." In many ways, one would have to go back to the courts of the French kings to find fitting parallels.

What can the civil servant with intellectual pretensions do to enlarge his horizons? Where can he find the stimuli for expanding his knowledge in his field? What provides him the moral support and courage needed to stay honest and efficient in a cynical environment? The common meeting place of administrators on all levels, of workers, and of officials of the private sector is the beer garden—a social institution whose importance is hard to overestimate. The quantities of beer consumed are staggering, but more important is the fact that the activity in the beer garden takes the place of just about all other possible types of social and cultural activities. If you do not go to a beer garden or the movie houses, there is hardly any place to go.[6]

It must also be noted that the missionaries have by no means sufficiently reoriented themselves to respond to the needs of the post-independence situation. Many of the special primary and secondary schools have manfully tried to continue to teach to a predominantly Congolese student body what was being taught to a predominantly European student body before 1960. Their perseverance is to be admired, although much of their energy is misdirected. Nothing similar to the approach of the activist American and European church to the social problems of its communicants can be reported. In all fairness, it may be said that new, younger, and more liberal missionaries are still laboring under the handicaps of the mixed

[5] The author knows of a minister who supported at least forty persons from his salary. Ten to fifteen persons for a married man and three to five for a single man are conservative estimates of the average burden. The family allowance system of salary calculations is often no help since the "dependents" are frequently outside the terms of the law.

[6] Europeans are, for the most part, in the same position. Cultural life nurtured by the Belgians can hardly be considered rich, and as yet only the feeblest efforts have been made in this direction by the post-independence European community.

legacy of cynicism and pietism bequeathed by their predecessors. It will take time and more dynamic effort to eradicate from Congolese memory the dominant belief that the church played a significant role in the implantation and formation of the peculiar colonial expression that was the Belgian Congo.

In any event, there is in the young republic virtually no influential source of intellectual, ethical, and cultural stimulation and standard-setting. As has been seen, not even a strong nationalist party has yet crystallized in the Congo. The danger of this situation is obvious. There is already a restless and increasingly articulate yearning for something or someone to fill the gap. A political party that must do all this alone can hardly escape a totalitarian orientation if it has power as well. The best that can be hoped for is that in the near future sufficient training, education, and ethical principles can be implanted in the younger generation to ensure that the totalitarian movement may be at least restrained by men and women who have some values and notions about human rights and freedom, social and economic justice, and individual decency—values they will want to insist upon and defend.

The Political Climate and Its Effect on Administration

There is hardly any way of talking about administration in the Congo without first describing the political phenomena that created and sustained it. We have seen in examining the historical origin of the laws governing the administrative structure that there is no document describing how these laws have been applied since 1960. It is, therefore, a fact that the political situation has created what, in fact, exists.

In the first place, the Belgian administrators who worked until early July, 1960, had already served notice to the Belgian Government that they would stay in the Congo only on conditions that were intolerable to their Congolese colleagues: special indemnities, educational allowances, guarantees of physical protection, and so on. At the same time, the Congolese civil servants organized in the Association du Personnel Indigène du Congo (APIC) began to demand more and more vigorously the total replacement of Belgian functionaries by Congolese. The demands of the APIC became more urgent and strident as independence approached.

During the round-table discussions in Belgium, Patrice Lumumba and his colleagues, in response to African demands to "Africanize" the civil service, supported a resolution that would place Belgian civil servants under the authority of the Congolese Government. A misunderstanding of the meaning of Africanization caused wide discontent among the clerks as well as in the army. These circumstances, the Belgian Government's ill-timed offer to reintegrate its Congo civil servants into the metropolitan service, and some violence that had already broken out in certain areas of the Congo, precipitated the mass exodus of Belgians that was almost complete by the end of July. Only about 1,500 Belgians were left.

From July, 1960, until January 17, 1961, serious attention could not be given to the reform and organization of the civil service. The struggle for power by the Lumumbist and anti-Lumumbist forces totally disrupted political life in the Congo. The political details of this period have been elaborated in many other works, but it should be noted that it was during this period that the politicization of the administration took root; the contending forces were from all political persuasions. During this period, too, an almost universal cynicism developed among civil servants as hundreds of employees were taken on with little to recommend them other than their tribal or political allegiances. In addition, the practice of building larger and more highly paid political staffs within the administration developed.

One of the most important political phenomena of the period was, of course, the action of the United Nations. The installation of U.N. technicians within the administration had a braking effect on the deterioration of recruitment and selection.

Today, the government does not have sufficient power to command a reorganization of the civil service. This is in large part due to the utter lack of appreciation, by both governmental and parliamentary authorities, of the meaning and importance of a public administration free, at least in the middle and lower working levels, of political intervention. Politics in the administration is personal. The major consideration of nearly all decisions is: Whom does it help or hurt among my friends and enemies? Action based on the concept of national interest is rare.

Successive Congolese governments since June, 1960, have all been plagued by a problem of immense political proportions: The announcement of political programs has in most cases been received with frank incredulity and sentiments bordering on contempt. The reaction is a combination of the usual cynicism attending any politician's promises for further action and the certain knowledge that each of the successive programs will be sabotaged by disrupted and chaotic administration. It is instructive, for example, to compare the programs of Patrice Lumumba with those of Premier Cyrille Adoula to see how many of the original projects are still to be realized. Moreover, each successive government has avowed its determination to reorganize the public services and to take quick and drastic action to train personnel and to import technicians and specialists on administration. In point of fact, Lumumba as well as his successors lacked sufficient power to come to grips with the entrenched interests of the army of clerks waiting at the trough. The appetites of the clerks whetted by the activities and propaganda of the APIC before and after independence, the need to place a larger number of these clerks in important posts just to keep things going, and the understandable popular pressure to see Africans in high places are all factors that still require skillful and sophisticated policies to accommodate, courage to suppress where they are incompatible with national interests, and force to eliminate where they are obstructive or rebellious.

The commissioners-general who succeeded Lumumba's government had a clear vision of the urgency of administrative reform, as witnessed by their supporting the creation of the National School of Law and Administration, but they lacked sufficient cohesiveness and authority to impose their will much beyond the initial stages. Since their mandate was provisional and always in litigation, particular pressure groups and ambitious individuals within the administration found it easy to circumvent attempts to instill the notions of competence and national interest within the administrative hierarchy.

Finally, during the interim Ileo governments and in the Adoula government, the top echelons of state and provincial administration became swollen with a proliferation of political appointees: 140 ministers, 20 secretaries of state; 40 *chefs du cabinet, chefs du cabinet adjoints,* and *secrétaires particuliers;* 420 *attachés du cabinet;* 140 *attachés de presse;* and almost 600 clerks. This inundation has had a demoralizing effect on the administration, and has been complicated by the shifts in the central government, resulting in the replacement of ministers and their cabinets.

How the Administration Works

THE MINISTER. As previously indicated, administration in the Congo is, for the most part, still based on the colonial model, which, in turn, was metropolitan in concept and practice and rooted in the French tradition with Belgian modifications. Many of the weaknesses noted below are also common to the models on which the Congo system is patterned.

At the top of the administrative pyramid is the minister, who in himself has no juridical personality, but is an agent of the state charged with the administration of an ensemble of functions and services in a given area. At the same time, the minister is a member of the government participating in collective decisions bearing on the national interests. He is also a politician who must be a liaison between the parliament and the people, and between the people and his administration. The role of a minister in both Belgian and French practice (a role filled by the Governor General of the Congo when it was under Belgian rule, and the director of the eight principal services including health, education, justice, and social affairs) is central to the whole administrative conception and operation. He must represent the state; he must have the authority and power over all who work within the ministry; he must have the authority to regulate the operation of his ministry by special decrees and regulations; and he must administer funds put at his disposal.

The absence of political power and prestige at the level of President and Premier, the lack of training and background, and the presence of tribal allegiance and political pressures have combined to make it all but impossible to man the ministerial posts with properly qualified persons. In addition, the political instability in the Congo has occasioned so many reshufflings within the government that even the best talent is thwarted. There were twenty-seven ministers in the Lumumba government; at present, there are nineteen. The number of secretaries of state has varied from seven to fifteen. The constant shifting of functions from ministry to ministry as ministries were dissolved or created has made it impossible to develop coherence, consistency, and continuity in ministerial programs and policies.[7] Since many of the ministers are also members of Parliament, their political activities have consumed so much of their time that their responsibilities in the administration, when not left to competent subordinates, have suffered badly. Finally, the threat of replacement occasions harried premiers to regroup their forces in an effort to find a stable combination, and has paralyzed ministerial initiative for much of the time since June, 1960.

THE ORGANIZATION OF MINISTRIES. Since the Fundamental Law does not prescribe the structure or organization of the ministries, the present practice has grown out of the post-independence models based more or less on Belgian ministerial organization. The basic organization includes the ministerial "cabinet," the secretary-general, the *directions*, *sections*, and *bureaux*.

Each minister appoints the members of his cabinet: These include a *chef du cabinet*, a *secrétaire particulier*, one or more *attachés*, and, often, special counselors. There are no statutory requirements what-

[7] The Fundamental Law is silent on the number of ministries or the manner in which ministries shall be created or dissolved.

soever for these persons, and the minister has a free hand in choosing them from within or outside the administration. Subsidiary personnel include a *chef du cabinet adjoint*, a *secrétaire du cabinet*, and two to four clerical persons. Therefore, each of the nineteen ministers of the central government has an average staff of fourteen persons. The functions of the cabinet are to examine the dossiers presented to the minister and recommend the decisions to be taken, to treat all matters that the minister intends to hold for personal decisions, and to assure the minister that his "politics" reigns over the administration that has the advantage of being permanent. There is, of course, the classic conflict between the "political" personnel and the "administration."

The weight of the minister and the way in which he directs the ministry depend on his own force of personality and competence as well as on the quality of the cabinet. In the Congo, it is almost universally true that the cabinet is inferior in power and prestige to the administration supposedly at the minister's service. The reasons are not hard to find. First of all, it is a rare phenomenon when tribal and/or political predilections coincide with experience and competence in the minister's choice of cabinet personnel. Thus, the cabinet is often technically inferior to administrative personnel. Secondly, many of the minister's choices are younger men who have earned their reward in the political arenas of the past three or four years. They are often many years younger than their administrative counterparts. In the Congo, as in other African and traditional societies, age has its own prestige quite aside from wisdom and experience. It is not unusual to find the "older hands" in the administration contemptuous of the "younger boys" in the cabinet.

Unfortunately, this contempt may express itself in almost complete sabotage of the minister's policy or program, especially since the political and other preoccupations of the minister preclude his giving detailed attention to all but a few of the highest priority items. Even matters in which a minister has publicly expressed concern have been effectively sabotaged by administrators who have had years of practice in "losing files," not being able to find vital elements of documentation for completing a dossier, discovering important "legal" objections to the minister's planned course of action. It is all too clear, therefore, that unless the minister has had the good fortune to find, and the good sense to appoint, men with sufficient knowledge and experience to prevail over their administrative counterparts, he is essentially at the mercy of the "old hands."

But it is also true that the cabinets have the tendency to politicize affairs and to substitute themselves for the administration when they can get away with it. Instances are not uncommon of a ministerial decision having been implemented by cabinet personnel circumventing the administration—even to the point of securing funds by direct arrangement with the Minister of Finance and his "cabinet," who in turn deal directly with the budget controllers and the treasurer.

The head of the minister's administrative service is the secretary general, who must normally initial and note all correspondence, memorandums, and so on, submitted for the minister's signature, and who coordinates and supervises the entire administrative operation of the ministry. In addition to his over-all coordinating role, the secretary general often has a staff of his own for certain services directly allocated to him (i.e., general administrative services, mail, certain study services). At the moment, there are under the secretary general a certain number of *directions* headed by a *directeur-chef du service*. Each of these *directions* is subdivided into *sections* headed by a *sous-directeur–chef du service*. Each *section* is further divided into *bureaux* topped by a *chef du bureau adjoint*, under whom fall a variable number of subalternate clerical personnel. (See Figure 1.)

Strictly speaking, this system requires an adherence to the lines of authority for decision-making so that any matter must be treated at five levels before reaching the cabinet of the minister, and at possibly three levels within the cabinet before the minister's signature can be affixed. After signature, the matter redescends the pyramid before being sent out. Under the best circumstances, this is a rigid and cumbersome system. Under conditions in the Congo, particularly at the middle levels, it is nothing less than elephantine. The reputed advantage of guaranteeing control and unity of action presumes a degree of dynamism and competence on the part of departmental heads that is unrealistic in the Congo context.

LOCAL ADMINISTRATION OF CENTRAL GOVERNMENT POLICY. According to law, the minister has two means of assuring the execution of his policies at the provincial level. He may delegate them to provincial assistants, or he may create state services within the provinces directly responsible to the state commissioner, who is in turn directly responsible to the minister. This latter procedure is known as "exterior services." In theory, the exterior services are the direct responsibility of the central government, and all costs are imputed to its budget. The distinction, in fact, between the exterior services of the central government and the general provincial administration is far from clear. The turbulent period since 1960 has witnessed a complete confusion of powers and responsibilities in this as well as in other areas.

In some cases, the provincial authorities have illegally assumed responsibility for exterior services such as the administration of justice,

Figure 1. Organizational Chart of the Ministry of Health [a]

Minister of Public Health

Cabinet
Secretary
Press Service
Legal Service

Secretary General

Health Service for Agronautics
Health Service for the Army
Administrative Secretary

First Direction Administrative organization	Second Direction Pharmaceutics	Third Direction Medical laboratories	Fourth Direction Health service	Fifth Direction Medical training	Sixth Direction Mechanical and electrical appliances in medicine
First Section Medical legislation and administration of personnel (2 bureaux)	First Section Pharmaceutical laboratory	First Section Clinical analyses	First Section Epidemical hygiene and public salubrity (3 bureaux)	First Section Administration and programs (2 bureaux)	First Section Mechanical techniques (4 bureaux)
Second Section Budget, accounting (2 bureaux)	Second Section Supply (5 bureaux)	Second Section Chemical analyses and toxicology	Second Section Medico-social "mixture"	Second Section Maintenance and accounting for I.E.M.	Second Section Woods
	Third Section Price fixing and control of pharmacies (2 bureaux)				

Second Direction
Ministry of Public Function
(January, 1963)

a Reprinted from Rougevin-Baville, op. cit.

customs, internal security, and, upon occasion, even military services. These conditions have obtained—or still obtain—in provinces other than Katanga, which, of course, set up its own government on the pretext of its independence. The central government has lacked the means to enforce its will at the provincial level although nearly all provincial employees are paid by the central government—if they are paid at all. The administrative situation, which was serious even under the former organization of six provinces, has become unmanageable with the addition of seventeen provinces.

Apart from these formal lines of administration, there has been pressure to create special consultative organs that, in theory, can provide the minister with specialized advice. However, although the Fundamental Law prescribes a special constitutional court, as well as special councils at national and regional levels for economic and social affairs, a higher labor council, and a council of higher education, none of these has ever been convoked. Some half-dozen other special councils and commissions have been created by ministerial ordinances and *arrêtés* in areas such as civil service, personnel, labor and medical problems, interior transport, and secondary education reform. The general experience to date has been disappointing, and this device, which can be enormously helpful in providing expertise without upsetting the hierarchy, has not been exploited by the government except recently at the level of the Premier's office, where a bureau of economic coordination with sweeping responsibilities and wide consultative scope has been established. This is an attempt on the part of Adoula to fill the vacuum left by many of his ministers. Needless to say, the opposition to this measure is strong and continuing. It will require all of the Premier's considerable charm and power of persuasion to make it stick.

The Local Administration

Before independence, the six provinces of the Congo were simply subdivisions of the colony. The governor was a civil servant with extended power, to be sure, but he administered under the central direction of the Governor General in Léopoldville. The provinces had no funds or civil service of their own. The Fundamental Law bestowed a juridical personality on the provinces, which were increased to sixteen on April 27, 1962. (The law delimited only two of the provinces; the remaining fourteen are yet to be defined, and there are still several important undetermined areas that will undoubtedly be made into at least seven additional provinces.) Thus, as public collectivities, they acquired these characteristics plus a number of specific powers and functions. Powers not specifically assigned to the province or the central government can be claimed by either. The process of reclamation is subject, however, to the provision that in case of conflict the text supported by the central government is valid and effective until the conflict is settled (presumably by the constitutional court).

There is a sense in which a detailed examination of provincial administration is like trying to get close to a mirage—the closer you get, the greater your realization that it does not exist. Offices are staffed, salaries are paid, there is some correspondence, but . . . Not the least of the problems of administering the provinces is the absence of certain knowledge of what they are and who lives in them, a situation that has occasioned not only administrative confusion but much disorder and bloodshed. Even if the Congolese legislators discover the error of creating more new provinces, they will have difficulty in correcting the situation since the present law permits their creation, although suppression of provinces is the sole prerogative of the constituent body.

In order to bring some kind of uniformity into provincial administration, a meeting of provincial presidents was held in October, 1962, to lay down a certain number of ground rules, including limiting the number of ministers to seven, their cabinet members to five, and their employees to fifty. Unfortunately, some provinces were already well beyond these limits, and the decisions of the meeting were not binding on the participants.

Another source of administrative anarchy at the provincial level is the silence of the Fundamental Law on the respective financial powers of the central government and the provinces. Thus, viewed from the financial aspect, the provinces operate as annexes of the state. Billions of francs were lost through graft, theft, or error as a result of a system which from July, 1960, until May, 1962, permitted the provinces to make unlimited withdrawals on local holdings of the Central Bank (Conseil Monétaire). These withdrawals were often made with no supporting documents ever having been forwarded to Léopoldville. Then, in May, 1962, provinces were obliged to establish budgets according to rules laid down in the Fundamental Law listing receipts and expenses and categorizing items under each heading. In the budget submission for 1963, for example, one province submitted a budget providing for receipts of 200 million francs and expenses of 2 billion—the difference, of course, to be made up by central government subsidies. Without sufficient qualified administrative personnel, the collection of fines, rents, personal income taxes, and so on, is handled quite inadequately.

ADMINISTRATION BELOW THE PROVINCIAL LEVEL. Although the provinces were given authority to reorganize themselves according to provincial constitutions, only the province of Kasai has so acted; the rest continue to be administered under pre-independence legislation. It must also be borne in mind that since 1960 hardly any of these administrative structures have been in working order.

The provinces are subdivided into territories, *chefferies*, sections, and centers. The key man in local administration is the territorial administrator. He controls the circumscription of the *chefferies*, sections, and centers in his territory; census-taking; collection of taxes; [8] and certain technical functions such as preventive health measures, approval of work orders, and determination of local routes and roads. The police as well as army units in the territory are at his disposal and he acts as police judge, with power to incarcerate offenders for a maximum of one month.

It is clear that the training and selection of territorial administrators and their immediate staff should be the focal point of any development program whether for improving the social and economic life of the interior, or for making rational progress in improving the administrative hierarchy. Unfortunately, the disruption of life has been most keenly felt at the territorial level. It is here that the murderous outbreaks of tribal warfare have discouraged any real measure of improvement. Many of the students in various administrative training programs feel that work at this level, vital though it is, is not worth the risk. Consequently, until the police and/or military branches of the state are sufficiently organized and disciplined to provide security for men working in territorial administration, there is little hope for important progress.

Although it is impossible to give a detailed description of the administration of the *chefferies*, sections, and centers, it should be pointed out that these were the felicitous creations of the Belgian administration. Their major purpose was to involve the people at the lowest rural levels in the process of regulating their affairs, and at the same time to create a bridge between the needs and desires based on traditional life and those of modern political administrative life. It remains a task of future governments to perfect these levels of administration by giving them some kind of statutory existence with at least limited authority and responsibility and some small financial resources on a more regular basis. Furthermore, the territorial administrator should be provided with sufficient personnel to deal more

[8] Taxes may be paid in kind and/or labor, instead of in specie, if the territorial administrator determines this to be in the general interest.

intimately with these levels, which are at the heart of rural development.

The Role of the United Nations in the Administration

In commenting on the role of the United Nations and its specialized agencies, one must first appreciate the enormous handicap under which the U.N. attempted to fulfill its mission in the Congo, which began in 1960. Political considerations seemed to dictate that all technical aid, including the hundreds of technicians, should be channeled through the U.N. The objective needs were almost incalculable in terms of money, men, and materials. The complete breakdown of the national machinery was imminent and civil war was a constant threat. As if this were not enough, the political mandate of the U.N.—and its military implications—soon became a matter of bitter dispute in Léopoldville and in New York. In Léopoldville, Congolese suspected the U.N. of political preference for the enemy (the enemy being the constellation of political personalities and parties one did not like), while New York was the locus of big-power arguments that had little immediate relationship to the Congo reality. The U.N. action was mounted, therefore, in a climate that was suspicious, when not downright hostile, both in the Congo and outside.

It is small wonder then that recruitment of the needed technicians was difficult and that many recruits were not up to the task. It was inevitable also that there would be overstaffing, duplication of effort, empire-building, and all the other failures normal in building so quickly something so large and important. A major fault, however, which can be attributed to a less pardonable mistake in judgment and conception was the implanting of the notion that resulted, by the end of 1961, in a kind of paragovernmental apparatus, working more often than not in spite of, or even against, the interests of Congolese administrators. The only excuse is that it was the easy way out. Happily, however, since 1962 there has been a noticeable shift of emphasis and a determined policy to place U.N. administrators alongside their Congolese colleagues and at the service of the Congolese in such a way as to maximize the benefits of their expertise and provide the "in-service training" that is a crucial task for U.N. personnel.

The U.N. has been instrumental in creating, staffing, and financing nearly all the post-independence institutions for the training of primary and secondary school teachers, and for providing police, public works, postal and communication cadres, labor specialists, and meteorological, health, and aviation personnel. Most important, through its invaluable aid to the National School of Law and Administration, the

U.N. has been a prime force in the creation of an institution designed to meet short-term as well as long-range needs in training magistrates and civil servants. This institution, along with the University of Lovanium and the many foreign colleges and universities that are now training Congolese for public service, represents the real hope for the future. The importance of the U.N. presence in maintaining these establishments for the immediate future cannot be overestimated. With all its obvious faults, the U.N. has been able to ensure a minimum respect for honest and efficient administration in the institutions it supports and for which it provides technicians.

It can be hoped that when its operation in the Congo is reduced, the U.N. will have acquired sufficient experience to pinpoint the strategic areas where its aid is pivotal. It seems likely that a formula will have to be devised to determine lines of authority and control. This will undoubtedly be feasible when the Congolese Government has achieved a greater measure of stability and authority.

Conclusion

The essence of Western administrative experience can surely provide guideposts and a frame of reference for the construction of an administrative apparatus in the Congo responsive to the special needs and genius of the Congolese people. This experience must, however, be put in the hands of Congolese who understand the frames of reference but who have not lost touch with the fabric of their own societies. This is the task of higher education in general, as well as the unique task of those who are training administrators.

The United Nations still represents the best hope in solving the most important problem of technical assistance to the Congo. It seems reasonable to hope that once the U.N. is relieved of the tremendous burden of maintaining and servicing its military personnel and installation, it may turn full attention to a more refined recruitment program for its civilian operation. This recruitment will be immeasurably easier if the Congo Government can be made to face up to the realities of the present administrative chaos, and give authority and responsibility to good men. The U.N. executive-training program offers such an opportunity, and both the U.N. and the Congo could benefit greatly from its effective utilization.

Unilateral action on the part of the governments willing to aid the Congo should not be ruled out as an effective channel for aid and development programs, but a prudent and chastened national leadership in the Congo will probably want to avoid a situation in which it risks becoming too dependent on a single source of aid, human or material, be it from Brussels, Paris, Washington, or Moscow. Selecting foreign technicians to aid the young republic is extraordinarily difficult, but crucial. Problems of language and previous cultural exposure will doubtless orient the choice for the immediate future, but steps presently under way to push accelerated language programs and to make English a compulsory second language at a certain level will enlarge the area of choice for bringing in technicians and for training Congolese abroad.

It may be hoped that aid not channeled through the U.N. will be coordinated to a great extent by the assisting nations themselves. It is imperative, however, that the Congolese Government develop its own planning and coordinating organization to influence the type of aid that may be proffered and to make the wisest and most effective use of it. (It is common knowledge that in the latter part of 1960 and up until the fall of 1962 there was an undignified international race to snatch up young Congolese for training abroad. Aside from the disruption of secondary education as a result of removing some of the best student incentive, the chosen youngsters were often totally lacking in the maturity and orientation required for successful foreign study. The obvious and tragic results can be seen in the cafés of Brussels and Paris; in the Congolese diplomatic missions in the United States, where these unfortunate young men go for help; and in the streets and bistros of Léopoldville, where many of the unsuccessful returnees exchange their bittersweet remembrances of paradise lost.)

The errors of the past three years notwithstanding, the central problem of the Congolese administration is still the appalling lack of adequately trained personnel. No amount of money, foreign technicians, or plans can replace the desperate need to train Congolese to man the posts of the crumbling and cumbersome machinery at all levels.

Nothing in this paper should be permitted to obscure the fact that there are in the Congolese administration dozens of capable, honest, and hard-working civil servants. This observer is continuously surprised in his contacts with the administration by the number of sharp, energetic young men who are there and working hard. Young graduates of secondary schools and a few from higher institutions of learning both in the Congo and abroad are constantly trying to perfect their knowledge and skills. There are also many older men who, during the Belgian control, absorbed knowledge and skill well beyond the level for which they were paid. The sad fact is that these civil servants, surrounded by persons who are less worthy of public confidence, are isolated and have no means of communication and interaction among themselves. One can hope that before too long changes in the over-all political environment will permit the grouping of some of the fine and talented public servants in some fashion that will enable them to find mutual encouragement and moral force to help the nation move more quickly along the path to a viable and prosperous independence.

This paper has been designed to illustrate the historical strengths and weaknesses of the administration, the present stagnation, and the possibilities for future reform. Despite the grim situation as of this writing, the author remains optimistic about the future. The Congolese are a warm, congenial people. They are relatively quick learners and have their fair share of honest, hard-working folk. There are signs of genuine intellectual ferment, artistic consciousness and taste, and public concern about government and leadership. The present confusion, corruption, and selfishness at high levels is not deeply rooted. The political amateurishness is the inevitable consequence of colonial policy, but lessons are being learned. Most independent African nations learned these lessons at the expense of the metropolitan power. The accident of history and Belgian confusion imposes the burden of these expensive lessons on the Congolese (and the international community), but the burden need not be accepted as permanent. One of the best hopes of breaking the vicious circle that characterizes the present impasse in Congolese political life is the rapid formation of a reasonably effective civil service.

Finally, let us not be deluded into thinking that civil service in the English, French, German, or American sense is what will obtain in the Congo. An effective administrative organization buttressed by law and institutional practice against unwarranted political intrusion may still have to take into account, for example, tribal allegiances and the problem of the extended family.

It is a touchstone of National School of Law and Administration policy that intelligent and sensitive Congolese administrative trainees should learn not only how but why French administrative courts work for the French, and why the career service works for the British, so that, in time, these students of administration may be capable of devising their own adaptations and creating their own apparatus.

Editors' Postscript

Ethnic and regional sentiments, together with political considerations, led to a breakup of the Congo's six provinces into twenty-one units plus a Federal District of Léopoldville on June 25, 1963. Six of the provinces are ethnically homogeneous (Kongo Central, Kwango,

Cuvette Centrale, Sud-Kasai, Luluabourg, and Lomami), while five others are marginally homogeneous (Moyen Congo, Uele, Kivu Central, Nord-Katanga, and Sankuru). Political homogeneity was a more frequent result, with twelve of the provinces (Kongo Central, Kwango, Kwilu, Cuvette Centrale, Moyen Congo, Kibali-Ituri, Haut Congo, Nord-Kivu, Sud-Kasai, Luluabourg, Sankuru, and Lomami) having a single dominant party and two being marginal cases (Nord-Katanga and Katanga Oriental).

The Role of Foreign Private Capital in Africa

F. TAYLOR OSTRANDER

Before considering Southern Africa, in no part of which has the African majority population yet achieved full political rights, it may be instructive to consider the role of foreign private capital in the twenty-five or so independent nations of Africa south of the Sahara and north of the Zambezi.

Although almost all African national leaders express their desire to achieve what they call "African socialism," African statesmen of every political complexion show a remarkably keen desire to do what is necessary to attract foreign private capital and to have it go to work to help develop their countries' economic potential. Apparently, African leaders are not aware that these two aims seem contradictory to many. I, for one, do not find them so. It seems to me that most Africans understand "African socialism" in pragmatic not doctrinaire terms to mean that the public interest comes first, that they wish to see national purposes achieved; it means an affirmation of loyalty to the greater good of the greater number. I do not believe that most African leaders find anything inconsistent between their desire to achieve African socialism and their desire to attract foreign private investment.

Private enterprise—that is, African private enterprise—flourishes almost everywhere in independent Africa. Native entrepreneurs, shopkeepers, and petty tradesmen thrive. Anyone who has seen the trading spirit, the enterprise system that has grown up among the population of the Lagos area of Nigeria would not doubt for an instant the thriving future of African private enterprise. I would predict that any African political leader who attempts to interfere seriously with these African small-scale but widespread private economic activities will fail resoundingly and speedily.

What of foreign private investment? One of the outstanding features of Africa today is that practically every independent state in tropical Africa is actively seeking foreign private capital.

The efforts of Nigerian statesmen in this regard have been seen at first hand during their numerous travels throughout the United States. The Nigerian Six-Year Development Plan assumed foreign private investment totaling about $100 million a year for the period, as compared with about $150 million a year of foreign aid from official sources. Perhaps even more remarkable evidence of this universal effort to attract foreign private capital were the missions that Sékou Touré's government sent from Guinea to the United States in 1962. First came a Trade and Finance Mission consisting of several ministers and the President of the Central Bank. Then, a month later, came a second mission of private Guinean entrepreneurs to seek American capital for small-scale joint ventures. And then a U.S. Trade Fair in Conakry.

In the fall of 1962, I heard a prominent African leader speak to representatives of New York's financial community at a small meeting on Wall Street. He was frankly worried about the negative publicity his country had received in investing circles in London and New York from exaggerated newspaper reports, and he was determined to improve his country's name. He said, "As we look back today on the utterances made in the course of our revolutionary struggle for independence, we shudder. . . . Now, we all feel responsibility."

Northern Rhodesia (now Zambia) has just emerged from the traditional status of a Southern African colonial territory into a full-scale African government. In the fall of 1962, the United National Independence Party (UNIP), the leading African nationalist party—headed by Kenneth Kaunda—was fighting to come to political power in that rich country of tropical Africa. UNIP issued an election manifesto that contained the following statements:

A conducive climate for private capital shall be created so that both public and private sectors shall support each other in our struggle for a "take-off into sustained growth." . . . One of the objectives of economic policy is to encourage and attract capital from abroad and stimulate domestic investment . . . to achieve a technologically and industrially mature economy, to increase the rate of capital accumulation, to gear up the economy through drastic fiscal and monetary measures so best to accumulate the savings, . . . and to maintain a stable price policy. . . . We believe that nationalization of the mines would lead to political and economic upheavals and uncertainties to investors abroad, but a proper fiscal policy and some control over dividends leaving the country are visualized. . . . The representative government will encourage prospecting of minerals, . . . foreign capital should have access to the country provided that there are no political strings attached. Proper guarantees shall be given to foreign investors . . . but a firm hand shall be exercised to counteract private monopolistic tendencies. . . . In international trade it will be necessary to encourage foreign investment to meet the needs of expanding economy.

Those statements are not going to make Kaunda's future Minister of Finance in Zambia shudder for their wildness!

Similar documentation in one form or another could be given for virtually every African country. Indeed, if one stops to think for a moment, it will be readily apparent that nothing could be more natural than for African leaders who have achieved full responsibility for their national destinies to want foreign capital. The word "undeveloped" means capital-shy. They cannot, within the foreseeable future, produce their own capital in the amounts needed to accelerate their internal economic growth. Even in order to begin the process of economic growth and to begin to stimulate internal capital creation, they are desperately dependent on capital from the outside world. Thus it is that the leaders of African states are actively "beating the bushes" for any sources of foreign capital they can manage to interest in their countries. *They* have to fulfill the promises of rapid economic betterment that they made at the time of independence. *They* are realists, not dogmatists.

There are not many places in this rapidly developing world where capital is in surplus. There is anything but a surplus of capital that can be interested in taking the risks and dealing with the uncertainties of going out into distant, newly independent Africa. There are only two sources to which the countries of Africa can look for foreign capital to assist in their development. They can look either to the industrialized West or to the semi-industrialized East. Capital is a great deal scarcer in the East today than it is in the West, and this will be the case for a long time. Most of the capital for Africa's economic development has come, and will have to come, from the West. Much of it will be private capital, since private capital can, of course, originate only in the West.

I would contend that private capital will leave considerably greater freedom of action and freedom from outside stipulations and control, fewer "strings," than public capital—whether the outside public capital comes from Western governments or from Eastern governments or from intergovernmental sources. Sékou Touré found out that the risks of outside official intervention are greater in taking aid from the East than in taking public capital of Western origin. Certainly, the aid that France continues to pour into the independent countries that were created out of the former French colonial empire in Africa is not without its strings—one of the principal strings being that it is aimed to keep out other foreign capital, whether public or private, Western or Eastern.

The stipulations that accompany capital assistance from American official sources are of an entirely different nature. The U.S. Government has a long record of using its influence to open up markets not only to its own trade and investment but to all commerce in general. Similarly, the diplomatic stipulations that may accompany American aid, and that may increasingly accompany it if the recommendations of the Clay Committee are accepted, are stipulations designed to assist countries in meeting and solving their own economic problems. True, they may not accord with the political objectives of one or another political party, and some political parties, like small boys, exhibit a strong distaste for the medicine that is intended to cure their country's ills.

But private capital does not go into independent Africa with any stipulations of this order. Private capital seeks only to be assured that its position will not be discriminated against or subjected to retroactive legislation or treated without due respect for contracts legitimately entered into or without due regard for that basic economic doctrine—"Don't kill the goose that lays the 'copper' egg." Private capital would not dare stipulate today how a government should handle its over-all fiscal problems or solve its balance-of-payments dilemmas.

Many African leaders, highly conscious of their desire to avoid involvement with outside "power blocs," have expressed their preference for capital that comes to them from intergovernmental sources. It should be realized, of course, that almost all available intergovernmental capital is Western in origin. The Soviets are not members of the World Bank or the International Development Association. Only a few U.N. agencies such as the Special Fund bring together capital resources from the West and the East, and they deal in very small amounts. The World Bank and IDA obtain their sizable resources from subscriptions from non-Soviet bloc governments that make up their membership and, in the case of the World Bank, from the Western capital markets in which it floats its bonds. It is also well known that the World Bank makes its own stipulations when granting outside resources to countries, and these stipulations are in many cases more demanding than those outlined by individual governments. Nevertheless, many states prefer the national anonymity of multilateral prescriptions to prescriptions offered by individual countries.

Most leaders of independent African countries know that they have little to fear from private foreign investment. Indeed, today the shoe is on the other foot. Even the newest political sovereignties give early and unmistakable evidence that they know they have superior power over private enterprise, even over large-scale, long-established private enterprise. The power to tax, the power of exchange control, the police power in the background—these give modern states great control over private enterprise, and particularly over foreign private enterprise. Today, many problems of development are caused by intemperate or hasty misuse of just these powers of political sovereignty.

Nationalization of foreign private investment is one of the actions that can profoundly injure the self-interest of developing countries. The leaders of African states should understand that private foreign capital can serve their interests better than any nationalized enterprise. The essential economic rationale of private investment is its superior efficiency. As a test of profits in considering feasibility, as a means of organizing money, men, technology, and physical resources to achieve stated goals with a minimum of waste, as a means of recruiting technical skills and managerial talents, as a means of avoiding the overloading of limited numbers of indigenous administrative personnel, or, finally, but by no means least important, as a means of creating a larger stream of gross profits than bureaucratic enterprise ever could, and thus automatically of providing a broader basis for transfer of a fair share of profits directly into national budgets as freely disposable tax revenues—in all these ways, the superior efficiency of direct foreign private investment can bring many unique benefits to developing countries. Most African national leaders obviously realize this because there have been very few and only isolated cases of self-defeating treatment of private foreign capital in all the twenty-five or so countries of free Africa.

Indeed, there is some danger that African leaders may have an exaggerated view of the amount of foreign private investment that they will be able to attract by creating a climate of laws, regulations, and attitudes favorable to foreign investment, by their investment offices overseas, by their attractive investment brochures, and by their public assurances to private investors. There is a danger that some of these national leaders will begin to feel "let down," will begin to wonder about the efficacy of the climate they have created, and thus will begin to have doubts about private investment as a whole. As one observer said not long ago: "The impression conveyed by some of the American fundamentalist apostles of free enterprise is that unlimited quantities of private capital can be hired at low cost by any country that passes good investment laws. The present danger is that Americans may have oversold the product—minimizing its cost and exaggerating its supply." As I see it, this reflects a fundamental misconception on the part of some Africans *and* some Americans of the proper role of private investment in economic development.

It just is not appropriate to consider private capital for many of the needs of Africa at the present stage of its development effort. Private capital is not going to go into roads or ports or harbors; it will not go into schools and hospitals and clinics; it will not go into training institutions; it is very unlikely to go into electrical power generation or railroads or on any substantial scale into agricultural credit. Those development needs are going to have to be met by public effort and public capital, in considerable part by public capital from outside— hopefully, and inevitably in large part, from the West.

It must be recognized that it is not a function of private business to go abroad in order to assist in development. In other words, private investors do not ordinarily go abroad merely in order to identify themselves and their capital with the aspirations of a foreign people. Private investors will not go into Africa solely in response to moral or patriotic exhortations to share in Africa's economic development. Nor is it the role of private businessmen to make up for the difficulties of our own aid administrators in selling their programs to Congress and the American people.

I hold that there is no basis for private business to go into Africa or anywhere unless its own feasibility projections indicate that it can make a profit there, a profit that takes into account the risks and the alternative opportunities that exist. For private capital to do anything else does no credit to the enterprise system.

I do not mean to imply, however, that outside capital, American capital, does not have very special social responsibilities when it does decide on legitimate business grounds to go into developing nations. Indeed, the way these social responsibilities are handled when investments are made in the undeveloped world will determine to a large extent the future for private investment in those areas.

American firms that do go into developing nations must participate in providing leadership for economic development in the widest sense. It is vital that American firms going into Africa, either to do business there or to invest there, so conduct themselves as to be the best possible ambassadors for the United States and for our American concept of how to do business and how to treat individual human beings with dignity.

Former Assistant Secretary of State for Africa, now Ambassador to South Africa, The Honorable Joseph Satterthwaite, spoke on this point at a meeting of the African Affairs Society of America in New York several years ago. He asked that American businessmen interested in Africa "see the importance of conforming in their foreign operations to the image which we are trying to project abroad of the United States." I am fond of calling this the "Satterthwaite doctrine." It is a very important point.

Nevertheless, the amount of foreign private capital going into small- or medium-scale projects in Africa will not begin to be very significant for some time to come—especially in the case of American capital. Africa is too far away, the uncertainties are too great, the unknowns are too foreboding, the costs of supervision too high. Indeed, at this stage of economic development in most parts of Africa, one can add that even the opportunities for such investments are too infrequent.

The further economic development goes—based primarily on public capital—the greater will be the opportunities for outside and inside private investment. One of the surest ways of getting to that point is for the United States and other Western governments to put adequate resources, *public* resources, to the task of development in Africa. In my opinion, the United States will not be able to discharge its responsibilities for strengthening the security of free Africa if the amount of aid granted to the many nations of that continent is as unrealistically low as was recommended by the Clay Committee.

Thus, the opportunity for private capital in small- or medium-scale projects in Africa will be limited by the pace of over-all economic development. Private capital should, however, always be able to provide for the large-scale extractive projects. No matter what the political orientation of an African government—short of its being an outright Soviet satellite—it will usually be willing to negotiate an acceptable contract with private interests to open up large-scale extractive projects that will obviously contribute in a major way to development. If both sides have something to sell and something to buy, it is possible to conclude an agreement. No matter how unusual the partnership, no matter how hardboiled the negotiations, if the two sides have something to sell and something to buy, it is usually possible to conclude an agreement.

On their part, all foreign private investors and businessmen dealing with Africa will have to accustom themselves to working in states that are pragmatically welcoming them to come in to assist in the development of African socialism. This is the same as saying that they will be investing or operating in countries that are using governmental powers to meet public aims. Public purpose pervades the new nations' economic policies and determines the ordering of priorities among different objectives of public policy. For, when any nation sets its course toward accelerated economic growth, it means a higher-than-usual degree of public purpose and a correspondingly increased degree of governmental intervention in the economy. In nations with little or no accumulated savings, a high degree of directed public purpose means a high degree of use of public funds.

Thus, much private investment going into Africa is going to find itself associating with public-development organizations and in partnership with equity capital of public origin. The experts in this new science of economic development know this. Some investors, American investors, obviously know it and are willing to live with it. Some leaders of industry know this. At the 1961 International Industrial Conference in San Francisco, Lord Franks (then Sir Oliver Franks, Chairman of Lloyds Bank) said:

> It will not forward the course of private enterprise to indulge in endless and unremitting guerrilla warfare against all manifestations of government activity. . . . There are things the state should do and things that are the province of private enterprise. It is not possible to draw a boundary—valid for all times and places. We are talking of practical affairs, not metaphysical dogmas.

At the same conference, Edgar Kaiser, President of Kaiser Industries, said:

> The characteristics which have made private enterprise an enduring and productive economic force have not changed. What has changed is the recognition that private enterprise alone cannot do the job. . . . The name tag of an economic system is increasingly less important than the dignity and development of the individual.

These are masterful statements of good sense. They give a clear answer to those "fundamentalist apostles of private enterprise" who seek to export their slogans to countries whose situations they do not understand. But I am sure that neither these two men nor I would want to see the developing nations do themselves the harm of tipping the balance against private enterprise and investment, indigenous or foreign, where it is available and can do the job.

President Kennedy, in a message to Congress on the foreign-aid program in April, 1963, forcefully described the unique role of the businessman in development:

Economic and social growth cannot be accomplished by governments alone. The effective participation of an enlightened U.S. businessman, especially in partnership with private interests in the developing country, brings not only his investment but his technological and management skills into the process of development. His successful participation in turn helps create that climate of confidence which is so critical in attracting and holding vital external and internal capital.

This is an appropriate point to come back to the role of foreign capital in Southern Africa, where the majority of the indigenous population has not yet achieved full political rights. The role of all foreign investment in Southern Africa is no doubt destined to come increasingly under the same spotlight of international attention that is now focusing political interest on this area.

Political tension, both open and suppressed, drastically alters the climate in which business is done and economic development sought. It sometimes takes quite a long time for the economics of tension to become apparent. The momentum of economic progress is a powerful force, especially in relatively advanced economies such as Rhodesia and South Africa—where at least the European-dominated money economy is truly advanced. Imposition of exchange controls in a system that permits of efficient administration of such controls—as is the case in those countries—further staves off recognition of the economic results of political tension.

In looking over academic and governmental discussions of the problems of economic development, I am struck by the relative hopefulness of such discussions; but much of the subject matter usually discussed these days under the heading of economic development is not applicable at this stage of history in Southern Africa. Economic development in Southern Africa deals with the economics of disturbed economies. Is there ground for much hopefulness in the politico-economic climate of Southern Africa today? Economic development means investment, yet in the states of Southern Africa capital has been in flight or is subject to exchange controls. I doubt that growth can be self-sustaining in a self-defeating political environment.

In all of Southern Africa, the Northern Rhodesians are closest to overcoming their problems and beginning to move ahead again, even though there are still major steps to be achieved. In a talk to a group of security analysts in New York in April, 1961, I made the following statement about Northern Rhodesia:

When the Europeans in the Federation accept the inevitable and prepare to move realistically, we believe that the stage will be set for a most promising partnership of foreign capital and native resources in the Copperbelt of Rhodesia. The government of that area will have a ready-made basis of cooperation with outside private capital and through this—and only through this—it will have access to overseas markets on a vast scale for its principal products. With continued high output and sale of copper, the government of that area will continue to be able to put the large legitimate tax revenues from copper production to the benefit of the state. Over the next generation, Rhodesia—with its vast copper resources —can become one of the strongest and richest countries in the new Africa.

The behavior of investors in Northern Rhodesia in the first four months after an African majority government was formed (December, 1962) bore out strongly another statement that I had made, in a talk at the American Association for the Advancement of Science, in New York in December, 1960:

> The imposition of law and order does not act as an incentive to investment when that law and order is imposed by a dominant minority group against the will of a majority of the population. Some element of majority consent is an essential prerequisite for a climate which will attract private investment.

As the tension over the future of Northern Rhodesia began to lessen, the interest of outside investors began to rise. The economic future looks more propitious under government by consent than under government by imposed "law and order."

In those parts of Southern Africa still subject to the economics of tension, there are some special problems faced by foreign investors today.

Whether to invest, to reinvest, or to withdraw is one problem. Instances of new funds from abroad put into new projects in Southern Africa by new investors are not as frequent as sometimes claimed. Some investments are made because of unfamiliarity with the "economics of political tension." In some cases, investors put forward plans and proposals in order to keep a foot in the door, but with no intention of putting up much money until the political situation clears up. (I might add here that some long-term projects may outlast all present political tensions.) The investor in going projects is to some extent "locked in." Mining, for example, requires continuous reinvestment in order to keep up with its inherent depletion. Under exchange controls, reinvestment may be easier than obtaining permission to withdraw larger proportions of earnings, or reinvestment may be inevitable if transfer of funds is denied or if compulsory investment in government securities is to be avoided.

When a country is under strong outside condemnation for its policies, investors in that country are frequently admonished to "withdraw their capital," and they may be subjected to serious criticism if they do not. Now, capital cannot be withdrawn from a mine or a factory; all that can be done is to sell assets to someone else. Under the conditions we are discussing, this means selling at "fire sale" prices, handing capital assets over to the new buyers as bargains. That hardly achieves what the critics want, especially as in many cases the new buyers may be more committed to the political policies under criticism than the original investors were.

One of the knottiest problems faced by investors in Southern Africa today is how to handle corporate relationships with existing governments while a transfer of power to new hands is a possibility. The problem can be put this way: No corporation can afford to "bite the hand that taxes it." This is particularly true where that hand has the extraordinary powers or the authoritarian outlook that often accompanies efforts to resist rising political pressures from indigenous peoples.

One of the most delicate tasks of business diplomacy concerns its efforts to be neutral toward forces that might be the governmental authorities after a transfer of power to indigenous people has occurred. This is a question of "not biting the hand that now taxes— even while preparing not to be bitten by the hand that is going to tax"! Perhaps no corporation can achieve this dual task satisfactorily, but any responsible corporation in a situation of political tension and potential political transfer must try to make some such effort.

A related problem grows out of the legislative requirements of governments that impose severe limitations on what in modern American industrial practice would be considered normal and acceptable procedures. No one is likely to argue that it would be desirable, if it were feasible, to transfer the structure of South African mining legislation to the mining industry in the United States. I refer here to the system of semiofficial recruitment of workers from rural reserves to work in mines on short-term contracts, to live in controlled compounds without their families, with wages and facilities under government control, strikes and labor organizations forbidden, and training and advancement strictly limited. Yet, if American management participates in mining in South Africa, or in South West Africa, it must abide by this system. In times of political tension, this system and the governments that decree it—as well as the corporations that operate under it—come under criticism and attack. How to live with this situation is one of the practical nondevelopmental problems of American investors in Southern Africa.

Those who criticize American investment in such situations must acknowledge that American economic participation in white-dominated societies gives employment to Africans, develops the economic resources of the country for the benefit of all its inhabitants, and provides a stronger basis for a future that may be based on consent of all the people. In fact, the presence of American or other outside investors can sometimes result in improvement and modernization of industrial conditions that would not have been achieved by national investors alone. One outstanding case of this was the breaking of the industrial color bar in the copper-mining industry in Northern Rhodesia, in 1955. Neither the local government of the territory nor the Federal Government in Salisbury nor the British Government in London was prepared to tackle this matter and to take the risks of opposing the powerful European (white) mineworkers' union. It was the determination of outside investors that forced the issue to a successful conclusion. This kind of outside pressure is far less feasible in situations that are more authoritarian than Northern Rhodesia was.

In the frozen political situation that exists in Southern Africa today, any new investment—foreign or domestic, enthusiastic or reluctant—has an important leverage. Investment increases the scope and modernity of the economic structure. Thus, it increases the likelihood of a change in archaic political and racial theories. The same thing is true in the American South—as has been amply demonstrated. In Southern Africa, a new investment means more urbanized African laborers; it means a wider extension of the African's knowledge of modern economic processes and industrial skills and habits; it means an increased flow of wages going into African pockets and an extension of the African market for the goods produced by other firms—some of whose owners may still imagine it is in their interest to support theories that would restrict the development of African consumption. Any new investment takes Southern Africa one further step along the road which cannot be squared with the doctrines and practices of apartheid.

It is a fact that our government in Washington has never instructed American investors not to invest in Southern Africa. For example, the U.S. Government neither encourages nor discourages investment in the Republic of South Africa. When businessmen visit the Departments of Commerce and State to inquire about a possible investment in the Republic, they are provided with an evaluation of economic conditions in the country and are helped to find the answers to their specific economic problems. I believe that U.S. officials also consider it essential that potential investors be made aware of the political situation in the Republic, for it is my understanding that, as with economic matters, the government believes that businessmen should be acquainted with all of the available facts. The decision to invest or not to invest, of course, is made by the potential investor himself, and U.S. officials refrain from making direct recommendations.

I would like to stress that it is not a proper role for private business to try to make up for what some groups believe to be the indecisions or other shortcomings of governments, or to engage in its own foreign policy by, for example, taking steps to impose private economic sanctions where official sanctions have not been legislated.

Finally, I want to discuss some current myths concerning outside investors in Southern Africa. It is alleged in some quarters: (1) that there is a conspiracy that binds together all the mining concerns of Central and Southern Africa; (2) that the mechanism of this conspiracy is a system of "interlocking directorates"; (3) that these concerns are in control of the states in which they operate; and (4) that apartheid in its various forms is a deliberate tool of these mining companies, used to exploit cheap labor for the companies' own selfish advantage.

These myths are naïve and misleading and not in accord with the facts of either international finance or international mining or with the facts of national or international politics affecting racial problems. They have, however, gained a limited currency recently, in places where they can do great damage to the West. Certain widely circulated charts compiled from the pages of a standard reference volume, Skinner's *Mining Yearbook*, containing information that has been available to the public for the past twenty or thirty years, show what is called a "system of interlocking directorates in the mineral industry of Africa south of the equator."

Of course, this is nothing but a new form of guilt by association. When allegations of this type were perpetrated by Senator Joseph McCarthy, the Left was the usual victim. Now, a doctrinaire assault on the mineral industry and Western capitalism has been constructed on the same basis of guilt by association, set out as a pseudo-scientific methodology though without analytical documentation.

These allegations seem so persuasive to many new statesmen of Africa and Asia, as well as to some elements in England and America, that they are accepted by some without questioning or without challenging the assumptions on which they are based. Naturally, the Soviet-bloc nations have eagerly taken up this bonanza handed to them with the imprimatur of the West. These allegations were referred to, directly or indirectly, in dozens of instances in the discussions at the United Nations' Fourth Committee during 1962–63.

It will be hard to undo the harm that has been done, and the extent to which these myths come to be believed will be highly pertinent to whether mineral resources are permitted to be developed in some countries. If African statesmen or politicians believe these myths, it can jeopardize their own economic development by making them unwilling to receive foreign private capital on terms that will be acceptable. Of course, the only alternative will be to turn to the East—where the new nations will be able to find real conspiratorial interlocking directorates and direct political intervention hidden behind the supplying of capital and skills.

In mining, mixed participations in ownership often arise from the existence of multiple claims to prospecting areas. More often, they arise from the sharing of risks, which are so great in mining. Sometimes they arise from combining resources of various types and from various sources—technical skills from one source, financial resources from another. Sometimes they result from the necessity of marshaling from several sources the huge amounts of capital required for mineral development. And because there is a relatively small number of mining firms in the world with the resources of talent and money to undertake large-scale mineral development, there is a tendency for some of the same firms to appear in various combinations in these mixed ventures. When minority interests in companies result from any of the above factors, there will, of course, be minority representation on the boards of directors.

Now it is obvious that if diverse interests join in any single venture, they will find permanent expression in diverse representation on boards of directors. We all know that in many cases this is a source of weakness, not of strength, but it has to be lived with. Indeed, many directors sit on boards not to "interlock," but just in order to represent separate interests and separate points of view. They are watchdogs, not conspirators.

There is no conspiratorial single brain, no single financial octopus that could control the governments of all the countries of Southern Africa, nor does any individual mining company control any individual country.

As for the allegation that mining enterprises want to keep indigenous peoples politically repressed in order to provide themselves with cheap labor, it should be recognized that modern industrialists do not by preference employ ignorant, illiterate, backward people just because their wages are low. Otherwise, one could not explain the massive expenditure of effort and money on training programs in the Copperbelt and in other mining industries in Southern Africa. Modern industry has learned that there is no better asset than a highly productive work force, earning the good wages that go with high productivity. And those who deal with national economics know that the only way to expand the production and sale of industrial products is to expand the incomes of those who will ultimately buy these goods.

The last of those myths is that the attitude of international mining concerns is the decisive factor in the survival of white supremacy in those parts of Southern Africa where minority populations still hold dominant political power. I am in no position to speak for all the individual mining companies that operate in Southern Africa on the question of whether the present system, sometimes loosely referred to as "white supremacy," should continue or not. I know that there is no unanimity among the various companies, and I doubt that there is unanimity of view on this subject among the members of many boards of directors. I know that the record will show that my company, American Metal Climax, Inc., and our associated company, Rhodesian Selection Trust Ltd., believe firmly in economic and political advancement for Africans. But individual corporate and personal views on this matter are beside the question.

What can a mining company do to change a political pattern that has been adopted by an electorate and is supported as a matter of major political purpose by a determined government? If all the mining companies in the white-governed areas of Southern Africa had a unanimous desire to end the system of "white supremacy," it would not lie in their power to do so. Corporations have to live with whatever political system is in control. Sometimes their managements approve of these political systems, sometimes they do not. There is little they can do about it. The policy of most corporations is to stick to their business in the hope that those who determine political policy in a country will allow them to produce, to give employment, to make profits, and to pay their taxes. These facts are overlooked by those who claim that a particular political system depends upon the support of mining companies or on private investment generally.

Capital and the Congo*

ALVIN W. WOLFE

Prefatory note: This paper is printed essentially as it was presented to the conference in April, 1963. The re-entry of Moise Tshombe, replacing Cyrille Adoula as Prime Minister of the Congo, has not invalidated anything in the paper. In fact, subsequent events may help the reader to appreciate even more one point of the paper—that any government beholden to foreign powers, public or private, is certain to generate considerable opposition within its own territory and will thus be unable to organize for self-sustaining growth. Since this paper was written, the United States and Belgium (under American prodding) have involved themselves more directly in the Congo, beginning with technical military assistance, then arms, planes, and pilots, and finally the well-publicized paratroop attacks on Stanleyville and Paulis that ensured the defeat of the anti-Tshombe forces in that area. The only action of the Tshombe government aimed at changing the system of external control over capital was the decree of November 29, 1964, dissolving the Comité Spécial du Katanga and declaring that all its rights and properties became the rights and properties of the Democratic Republic of the Congo. No real consequences have flowed from this declaration, and even through 1965 there has been no real change in the administration of any of the operating companies.

The Congo is one of the largest of the African nations in territory, being eighty times the size of Belgium and one-third the size of the United States. Its boundaries enclose land that is varied, so that, unlike some African nations, the products on which its economy depends are diverse. The tropical forests on either side of the equator produce for export bananas, cacao, coffee, palm oil, palm kernels, rubber, and timber. The higher lands produce coffee, cotton, fibers,

* This paper was revised and updated by the author in the spring of 1965.

and pyrethrum. And from beneath the surface of the earth are extracted cobalt, copper, gold, manganese, silver, tin, tungsten, uranium, and zinc, as well as the nonmetallic minerals, coal and diamonds. Not only has the Congo a near-monopoly on the production of industrial diamonds, it is also the major African producer of cobalt, silver, tin, tungsten, and zinc.

Although the Congo is by no means densely populated, its 13 million inhabitants make it one of the larger African nations in population. As a labor force, however, this population does not show high productivity, per capita national income being well under $100. While this is not an accurate measure of what one man can produce in a year, it still suggests something less than full commitment of this resource to commercial production. Actually, fewer than half the adult male population have been actively engaged in the money economy—that is, working in productive enterprises other than traditional agriculture. One can imagine what the Congo would do if the potential labor force were fully employed. As a consequence of the paucity of technical and professional personnel among the African population, most positions requiring such training have been filled in the past by non-Africans recruited from Europe, largely from Belgium, at costs that far exceed those for comparable personnel in Europe. Fernand Bézy, economist at Lovanium University, found that Belgian personnel in the Congo cost their employers approximately three times as much as comparable personnel in Belgium.[1] In 1957, the 115,000 Europeans in the Congo had a per capita income of $2,791, while the 13 million native Congolese had a per capita income of $42.[2]

The Congo has had the benefit, more than most African nations, of considerable capital investment, both public and private. Much of this is in the mining industry, as a consequence of which productivity per man has been rising rapidly in this sector, which produces more than 20 per cent of the national product, yet employs less than 10 per cent of the labor force. The value of the product per African worker was, in 1957, $812 in the tin industry, $3,820 in the industrial diamond industry, and $19,210 in the manganese industry, the variation correlating directly with the amount of capitalization, according to Bézy.[3] The important role of capital in the economy is suggested when one observes the 149 per cent increase in production in the mining industry in the years 1950–57, during which time the number of workers actually decreased. In manufacturing, production

[1] *Problèmes Structurels de l'Economie Congolaise* (Louvain, 1957), p. 186.
[2] *Ibid.*, p. 212.
[3] *Ibid.*, p. 197.

increased by 256 per cent, while the number of workers declined.[4] During the same period, capital investment in the total economy increased by almost $2.5 billion, capital formation running at the rate of 30 per cent of gross national product.[5]

W. W. Rostow, observing the Congo economy of 1951, cited it as one that lacked only the third condition for the take-off to sustained growth.[6] So healthy was the economy, that the remarkable growth referred to above was accomplished almost entirely from internal sources, external borrowing accounting for less than 10 per cent of the cumulative capital formation from 1950 to 1957.[7] Actually, it could well be argued that the Congo's economic growth has always been financed "internally," for it is unlikely that capital imports have over the years exceeded the export to Europe of dividends, salaries, and other benefits. Fernand Bézy concluded a study of economic development of the Congo prior to independence on an optimistic note: "What is important is that the conditions seem satisfied now for development to proceed by indigenous forces." [8]

Such a summary review might justify a prediction of continued growth for the Congolese economy. With ample natural resources and labor supply, especially as education proceeds, and with ample capital sources, organized in the production of mineral and agricultural goods for which the world demand is stable or growing, the Congo ought to be in the forefront of developing societies, whether independent or not. But there is something wrong with the picture these statistics present. They tell us how the economy grew, but they do not tell us why. Investigating the situation more thoroughly, identifying the concatenation of circumstances that made for such a high rate of capital formation before independence, we shall understand that the future may be something quite other than a mere projection of the past, and we may even be in a position to say what that future will be. Our approach to this task ought, it seems to me, to be guided more by the integrated perspective of anthropology, which prepares us to deal with relationships among all the institutions of social systems, rather than the narrower perspective of economics, whose perfect analytical models tend, unfortunately, to blind one to factors that may be crucial in some systems.

[4] *Ibid.*, p. 196.
[5] United Nations, Department of Economic and Social Affairs, *Economic Survey of Africa Since 1950*, E/CN. 14/28 (1959).
[6] *The Stages of Economic Growth* (London and New York, 1960), p. 45.
[7] United Nations, Department of Economic and Social Affairs, *Economic Survey.* . . .
[8] "Belgian Congo," in Adamantios Pepelasis *et al.* (eds.), *Economic Development* (New York, 1962), p. 214.

The Congo economy did not develop by chance, or by the unfettered operation of producers and consumers in a free market. Rather, its development was guided—or cajoled, pushed, forced—by two strong hands quite deliberately controlled so that they worked for the most part with perfect coordination. One of the two hands was the government: first that of the Congo Free State under Leopold II, from 1885 to 1908, then the Belgian colonial government from 1909 to 1960. The other hand was the big private investor, primarily in the mining industry but with fingers extended into all sectors. All nerves, arteries, and veins led toward Europe, where resided the crucial tissues of heart and brain. From its very beginnings up to the excitement of the year 1960, this system has seen government in business and business in government.

Surely it was not chance that brought President Chester Arthur of the United States to recognize Leopold's private business enterprise, the International Association of the Congo, as a "friendly power" in 1884. This act made a government out of a business. It was a business free of governmental control, and a government that derived its power from its capital, not its people. With skillful diplomacy and considerable force, the chairman of the board and head of state staked out his estate in the interior of Africa, making sure that he got what was necessary to make the state a profitable concern. He kept control over access to the sea at the mouth of the Congo River in dealing with Portugal and France. He was able to keep a finger of land jutting down into the Copperbelt of Rhodesia, by then claimed by the British South Africa Company, by promising a third of its wealth to another company in which Rhodes also had major interests, the Katanga Company. It was here, in the mining industry of Katanga, that business and government were indistinguishable and that little was left to chance, or free enterprise, either in the beginning or in recent years, when it became necessary to turn some sort of government over to those who had been governed.

Because it is so important for an understanding of how economic development was fostered on such a grand scale, we must go in some detail into the relations between government and business in the Congo under colonial rule. Much more than any other government in Africa, the Congo Government has participated in what has been called the "private sector" of the economy through direct investment in common and preferred shares, in bonds, and in loans to business firms. While this portfolio has been carried regularly in the assets column of the government balance sheet, it is of course difficult to determine its precise value at any time because the shares are in such blocs that they could not be put on the market without depressing the price. Professor J. Wertz, in the semiofficial *Encyclopédie du Congo Belge*, estimated its total value as of June 30, 1952, at 11.96 billion francs (U.S. $240 million). *Etudes Congolaises* reports its value as of January, 1960, at from 32 to 38 billion francs (U.S. $640 to $760 million). Some part of this, a relatively minor part, consists of investment in public bodies, such as cities and the Office de Transport, which is a parastate organ. These figures do not, however, include regular public investment in roads and such. This government investment in business enterprise had been growing steadily as the whole economy developed, and, at the same time, the revenue to the state increased just as the revenue to private shareholders was increasing. In 1940, the portfolio of the Belgian Congo brought into the treasury 122,751,535.53 francs (approximately $2.46 million), but by 1951 it brought into that treasury 344,791,062.40 francs (approximately $6.9 million), and by 1959 it yielded 1,198,000,000 francs (approximately $24 million). Income from business investments, then, accounted for something like 7 per cent of total government receipts.[9]

The most precise information available in 1963 on the constitution of this investment portfolio was a report in *Etudes Congolaises* on the situation as of December 31, 1959, just six months prior to independence.[10] Sixty-three firms in which the government owned shares are listed, although the value of these holdings is not estimated. This same source lists twenty corporations in which the government has, or had, 50 per cent or more of the shares, or a majority of the voting rights. These are, or were, just prior to independence:

Banque Centrale du Congo Belge et du Ruanda-Urundi
Union Nationale des Transports Fluviaux (Unatra)
Société des Chemins de Fer Vicinaux du Congo (Vicicongo)
Compagnie des Chemins de Fer Katanga-Dilolo-Léopoldville (KDL)
Société des Transports en Commun de Léopoldville (TCL)
Société Anonyme Belge d'Exploitation de la Navigation Aerienne (Sabena)
Société des Forces Hydro-Electriques du Bas-Congo
Société des Forces Hydro-Electriques de l'Est de la Colonie
Société Minière du Kasai
Compagnie Minière du Congo Belge

[9] Sources: J. Wertz, "Organisation Financière du Congo Belge et du Ruanda-Urundi," in *L'Encyclopédie du Congo Belge* (Brussels, 1953); Banque Centrale du Congo Belge et du Ruanda-Urundi, *Rapport 1959* (Brussels, 1960); "Quelques Notes sur le Contentieux Belgo-Congolais," *Etudes Congolaises*, II, No. 5 (1962), 42ff.

[10] *Etudes Congolaises, loc. cit.*, pp. 104–9.

Société des Mines d'Or de Kilo-Moto
Compagnie Minière du Congo Occidental (Cominoc)
Société Minière du Congo Septentrional (Sominfor)
Société Minière du Nepoko (Mineko)
Société Minière du Luebo
Office des Produits Agricoles
Office du Café Robusta
Office des Produits Agricoles de Stanleyville
Société Internationale Forestière et Minière du Congo (Forminière)
Comité Spécial du Katanga (CSK)

The real prize in the government portfolio was the two-thirds share in the Comité Spécial du Katanga (CSK). The other third was held by the Compagnie du Katanga, in which the government also held shares, though not a controlling proportion. The CSK, to which the Congo Government had the right to appoint two-thirds of the members, held about 25 per cent of the shares of that revenue-producing giant Union Minière du Haut Katanga, which itself has scores of subsidiaries. To give some notion of the significance of Union Minière to the Congo portfolio, it can be pointed out that of the 1951 revenue produced by that portfolio, almost two-thirds was from Union Minière alone—$4.14 million of the $6.9 million. In addition to the dividends, CSK gets a royalty, two-thirds of which goes to the state, amounting to a sum equivalent to 10 per cent of all dividends distributed over and above a certain total. In 1951, the government received approximately $1.38 million under this rubric. Furthermore, Union Minière pays to the state taxes of several kinds. Of course, the private investor in CSK (Compagnie du Katanga, controlled by the Société Générale de Belgique) also benefited handsomely, as did the direct investors in Union Minière. And its profits permitted the growth of Union Minière to be self-financed. By 1959, Union Minière was able to distribute profits of $54 million, which meant dividends and royalties to the Congo Government alone in the amount of $11.5 million in that year, more than double what it had received in 1951. It should be clear that whatever the government could do to help Union Minière and the other mining companies to increase their profits would benefit the government in two ways: first, it would increase the government's revenue; second, it would make the Congo economy show up well in terms of economic growth.

How did the government help? Two methods stand out clearly. First, the government, under Belgian control, holding the power that stock ownership in corporations gives, regularly yielded that power of management to the Belgian businessmen who represented private financial interests and not necessarily the Congolese public interest. For example, the government's control of the CSK gave it the statutory right to name the president of the board of directors of Union Minière; nevertheless, that powerful office always went to a director of the Société Générale de Belgique, which owned directly only a fraction of the voting shares. Similarly, Forminière, a huge operation in Kasai before its collapse in 1962, was managed as if it were a subsidiary of the Société Générale even though the government of the Congo owned 55 per cent of the shares while the Société Générale held a scant 5 per cent.[11] In such ways, the directors of the Société Générale de Belgique came to control a much larger segment of Congo industry than their risk, in terms of actual capital investment, warranted. In consequence, this Belgian company is in a stronger position than its investment warrants in the supranational system of mining enterprises that involves such giants as Tanganyika Concessions, Rhodesian Selection Trust, De Beers Consolidated Mines, Anglo-American Corporation of South Africa, and the British South Africa Company.

What this means internationally, in the mineral industry especially, has been treated in other works and cannot be discussed fully here.[12]

The other outstanding way in which the government of the Belgian Congo used its power to aid private business interests and thereby make the Congo a profitable enterprise was fairly complicated, though it can be stated simply. The government forced the Congolese to invest their labor in the system. As Fernand Bézy put it in his study of the Congo economy: "In effect, the development of the economy of the Congo has been financed by the forced savings of the workers and, in a more general manner, by the local proprietors. In addition, the economic policy has permitted this phenomenon to take place and to persist by keeping agricultural prices artificially low in order to avoid an increase in the cost of living which would entail a raise in wages." [13]

Only in the beginning was it necessary for the government to use, or to permit the companies to use, labor acquired by direct application of force. Early collections of ivory and rubber illustrate that approach only too well. After World War I, the Belgian Government acquired

[11] For more particulars, see Pierre Joye and Rosine Lewin, *Les Trusts au Congo* (Brussels, 1961), especially pp. 217, 227, and 279–88. See also *Morphologie des Groupes Financiers* (Brussels, 1962), and various editions of the *Mining Yearbook* (London).

[12] See Alvin W. Wolfe, "The Team Rules Mining in Southern Africa," *Toward Freedom*, January, 1962.

[13] "Belgian Congo," p. 213.

control of the densely populated territory of Ruanda-Urundi, which could supply large numbers of workers for the Congo plantations and mines at relatively little cost.

By the 1930's, the administrative system was firmly enough established over the whole of the Congo to control population movement and ensure tax collection on a per capita basis. This permitted the inauguration by the government of a rigidly enforced system of native agriculture that had extremely important consequences. By encouraging, under penalty of imprisonment and whipping, each adult male not otherwise profitably employed to raise on a specified plot of ground a specified cash crop—rice, cotton, peanuts, and others—which could then be sold to a specified "private" buyer, for example, to the Société d'Elevage et de Culture au Congo, or Compagnie Cotonnière Congolaise, at a specified price, the government could see to it, first, that each Congolese had the means to pay the tax in money; second, that growth of the money sector of the economy was fostered; and third, that agricultural production was high enough to feed and clothe those workers removed from the subsistence economy without raising agricultural prices.

Congolese laborers were remunerated, at minimums established by the government, in money and in subsistence goods. The lower the agricultural prices could be maintained, the better could the Congolese workers' subsistence needs be taken care of by the paternal company while the company could operate at a level of profit that would permit, first, a high rate of reinvestment, and second, a high rate of dividends in which, of course, the government shared. The agricultural prices, enforced by the government, were established by a joint committee of government and agricultural company representatives. This is but another instance of the close coalition between the two, and really the only two, segments of what we have been calling the "economy of the Congo."

As an illustration of how this operates, we might take the Compagnie Cotonnière Congolaise, owned primarily by the same Belgian financial corporation mentioned previously in connection with most mining operations, the Société Générale de Belgique. The Belgian Congo Government participated also, at least up to 1960, by owning more than 17,000 shares. The government recognized Cotonco, as the company is popularly known, as having the monopoly rights to all cotton grown under the government's forced agriculture program in the northern parts of the colony, in the provinces of Equateur and Orientale (Stanleyville). The price the company would pay the Congolese farmer was, of course, established by the company and the government. Needless to say, the operation was profitable to the company, and to its parent Société Générale de Belgique, just as were the operations of its other affiliates, whether in mining, in power, in transportation, or in foodstuffs. Needless to say, the operation was important for the economic growth of the Congo economy, contributing more than may be apparent to the maintenance of a favorable balance of trade and a favorable balance of payments.

The foregoing demonstration of the close cooperation between the Belgian colonial government and the predominantly Belgian private business firms is introduced into this paper not to tar the Belgians, after the fact, with the brush of harsh imperial exploitation, but to identify those conditions which fostered, over many years, a high rate of growth for the Congo economy. Our problem is to predict, if at all possible, whether the "Congo economy" will be viable in the years ahead. In order to attempt that, we must understand what made it viable in years past. Now, we must inquire what, among these conditions, has changed and what effect such change ought to have on the economy of the Congo under a political regime that has Congolese occupying governmental positions.

Conditions began to change with the first awareness on the part of some Belgians in about 1956 that the Congo would have to become politically independent. Some civil disobedience and violence in the Congo in 1959 preceded the sudden announcement that the Congolese would be granted their independence in 1960. Then, of course, the events that followed independence—the mutinies, the secessions, the strikes, the violence, the involvement of the United Nations and the United States—resulted in such chaos that many observers of the scene, even after the reintegration of the dissident provinces in 1963, feel predictions ought not now be made. It will be argued here, however, that at least two major changes are of such magnitude that the narrow and rocky path of the future can be identified even through the smoke raised by internal and international crises that may give the illusion that all depends on chance and on personalities. These two changes are: first, the significant weakening of the government, a result that would have occurred in the process of transfer from colonial to independent status even without the secessions and mutinies; second, the relatively greater isolation of an economic system that had never been in any full sense a "national economy," though economists, for lack of appropriate concepts, tended to treat it as such. Though theoretically more important, this second change is much more complicated and more difficult to argue. For that reason, and because the first, the weakening of the government, may well be sufficient basis to predict cessation of growth, and probably inviability, for the Congo economy, it will be discussed first.

More than any other such transition in Africa, the Congo changed from a political system in which all power derived from above or outside the society, to a political system in which the government derived, or was supposed to derive, its power from the will of the governed. In all the other territories that have achieved independence, and even in those which have not, there were institutionalized means for the expression of will and, frequently, for the making of decisions by the population, even though the metropolitan state was recognized as the ultimate source of power. In the Congo, until the last few years preceding independence, there were virtually no legal means of expressing opposition, no free labor unions, political parties, or even traditional communities. The government was in no way dependent on the support of the population. The decision-makers and administrators consisted wholly of outsiders. For appointment, they depended on the Belgian Government. For operating revenue, they depended heavily on the taxes, royalties, and dividends received from the European-operated firms. As we have seen, the mutual aid between the European corporations and the government was such that no opposition was felt from this quarter, the only other potential source of power in the situation. Here was, then, an *unusually strong government*, relative to the population.

The Congolese, for their part, were so intimidated—and so disorganized—that the government could maintain firm control without expending great sums on enforcement. As recently as 1953, when the author was in the Congo, one young European agent, with rank equivalent to a noncommissioned officer in the Belgian Army, could maintain a tolerable sort of order over a rural population of more than 30,000 Congolese with no more than a submachine gun, a motorcycle, and 6 or 7 Congolese policemen armed only with clubs. Even his itinerant prison was self-financing, in a sense, for the prisoners were used for public works. Obvious as it was to the local villagers that they could at any time overpower him, it was also certain that swift retribution would come in the form of the Force Publique, or the paratroops, against which their unarmed villages were helpless. In 1953, the government boasted that Léopoldville, a teeming, booming city, had fewer policemen than any other city of comparable size.

Now, a government democratically elected, a government of Congolese men, could not intimidate the masses of Congolese as the Belgians had done, especially since on the eve of independence there arose scores of organized power cliques with rapidly shifting alignments. At the least, a Congolese government would have to have the support of *some* Congolese. At the very least, a Congolese government that would be as strong as the colonial government would need much more in the way of enforcement, and where would it get the revenue for such a task?

The logical source for increased revenue would be those same big companies which had financed the colonial government. Here, however, lies a myriad of obstacles. Some disinvestment had begun as early as 1956, at the mere prospect of greater Congolese participation. Most of that early "flight of capital" was probably made up of savings of private persons and smaller enterprises, but by 1959 even the Société Générale de Belgique showed its concern and perhaps its intention by causing Union Minière to declare a larger dividend than usual, and just before independence the Compagnie du Katanga petitioned to withdraw its shares from, and hence effectively to dissolve, the CSK, through which the government had had the potential, for sixty years past, to influence Union Minière by naming directors to its board.[14] It was clear, then, even before independence, that the European financiers were either not going to cooperate with the Congolese Government or were preparing to charge a higher price for their cooperation than they had under the previous system. In short, financial structures were being arranged so that the new government would be in a weaker position vis-à-vis European businessmen than was the case under Belgian administration.

It must be recalled that under the old regime, a sort of balance of power was possible between business and government, partly because, politically, the Congo Government was a branch of the much more powerful Belgian Government. Under the independent system, the Congo Government, supposedly deriving its power from the governed, who are economically impotent, is a weak government at best.

The test came quickly, in July, 1960, when the Banque Centrale, under European administration and with deposits guaranteed by the Belgian Banque Nationale, refused to advance to the elected government the funds the government felt it needed to pay the Force Publique in the hope that this might satisfy the mutineers. The July secession of Katanga and South Kasai—in which provinces are found Union Minière, with most of its affiliates, and Miba, producing more than 70 per cent of the world's industrial diamonds—constituted, of course, a blow to the financial structure of the state, already considerably weakened by the dissolution of the CSK and by the withdrawal, during the previous year, of $100 million of private capital even while the public debt of the Congo had been rising steadily during the process of financing a major economic development plan, conceived by the Belgians in 1948. By legal maneuvering, the Congo Govern-

[14] See Joye and Lewin, op. cit.; and Morphologie des Groupes Financiers.

ment was deprived temporarily, at least, of the voting rights in virtually all those "private" corporations in which it held shares.[15]

The Belgian Government has a legitimate concern about the integrity of the Congo and its viability, for the Belgian state stands as guarantor for most of the Congo public debt. Thus, whereas in the colonial era the interests of that government and the major private companies in the Congo were wedded, conditions are now such that certain companies may benefit from events that are detrimental not only to the Congo Government but to the Belgian Government.[16] This is not the place to discuss the entire Katanga affair, but it is important to know that neither the Société Générale de Belgique, Tanganyika Concessions Limited, nor the Katanga Company speak or act for the state of Belgium. Actually, the secession of Katanga put the Belgian Government in a most difficult position.

To return to the basic problem the independent Congo faces, we recall that in so far as the government is elected by universal suffrage it is dependent on considerable support of the Congolese population, but in so far as it must have revenue to operate it is dependent on the European-controlled business firms. The relatively small direct contribution of the African population to governmental revenue can be appreciated when one knows that the *impôt africain*—the tax that encouraged Congolese participation in the money economy and the only direct tax paid by the overwhelming majority of Africans— netted only about $7 million, even in 1959, the last full year of Belgian rule. By contrast, the revenue from the stock portfolio in that year was $22 million; revenue from the income tax, which applies to Europeans and corporations, amounted to $70 million; and income from customs and excise duties, paid predominantly by Europeans rather than Africans, due to the grossly uneven distribution of purchasing power, amounted to more than $100 million.

One might be tempted to interpret as a stabilizing mechanism this peculiar balance of forces under which an independent government would have to operate. If the government of the Congo is dependent on the popular support of Congolese, it cannot move too far from expressing "the will of the Congolese nation"; on the other hand, so long as it is dependent for its revenues on the foreign-controlled business enterprises, it cannot move too far from a position expressing the interests of capital investors. To the average American, and possibly

15 *Etudes Congolaises, loc. cit.*, pp. 42–44.

16 For instance, the Katanga secession. If Katanga had successfully seceded without assuming responsibility for any part of the Congo's public debts, Katanga and companies operating wholly in Katanga would have benefited while the Congo and Belgium would have suffered.

the average European as well, such a situation suggests a moderate "middle-of-the-road" government that ought to be positively valued. Given, however, the structure of the Congo economy and polity, and taking into account that the remarkable growth of the Congo economy in the past was achieved with the very active participation of a strong government, it is perhaps more valid to interpret this peculiar balance as one that places the government between two essentially opposed forces capable of tossing the much weakened government in a stormy political sea. In such a situation, no Congolese government will be able to act decisively in matters that have a direct bearing on the development of an economy that, despite its apparent self-sufficiency, is woefully lacking in local capital and in the means to increase local savings. Virtually the only indigenous capital is that held by government, and that capital was built up, as was the foreign private capital, during a period when the colonial government could apply firm controls on labor and prices. What can a weak government do?

One of the first things the new Congo Government almost had to do was to meet the demands of the soldiers of the Force Publique for higher salaries. Later, it granted salary increases to most government personnel. Within a year of independence most clerical salaries had tripled. The general desire for more money in the pocket, and a serious diminution of production of many necessities, combined with other factors beyond the control of the government to bring about serious inflation. According to the price index calculated by an economic research unit at Lovanium University, the price level had doubled in the first two years of independence.[17] The skyrocketing costs of government accompanied by serious reduction of revenue created conditions favorable to even more inflation. If the colonial government's ability to keep the Congolese cost of living, and therefore wages, at low levels was important in maintaining the profitability of capital investment prior to 1960, the new government's inability to control these factors now makes unlikely any increase of investment. The huge deficits in the public accounts are not simply temporary; they are not due only to the secession of Katanga. Expenditures are up because of inflation, but also because certain public needs, such as higher education and the maintenance of legislative bodies, simply have to be met. It is unlikely that expenditures will recede; therefore, it is essential that revenue shall increase if there is to be any kind of political stability that might make economic development possible. What can produce the necessary revenue?

[17] *Etudes Congolaises*, III, No. 8 (1962), 17–26.

We noted earlier that the Belgian-enforced agricultural program served to increase the supply of foods and fibers locally produced at a relatively cheap price. The present government, dependent as it is on Congolese support, can no longer enforce so effectively this program. The seriousness of the breakdown is seen in production figures. The 1961 cotton crop amounted to a mere 20,000 tons, as against an average of more than 50,000 tons annually in the six preceding years. Rice production, equally dependent on government pressure on individual Congolese villagers, dropped to 54,000 tons in the year 1961 from an average of almost 175,000 tons in preceding years. That these declines are due primarily to collapse of the government's agricultural program and not to breakdown of the commercial economy or the transportation system seems demonstrated by comparison with figures for rubber and palm oil, export items produced primarily on European-operated plantations. Rubber production was hardly affected by the events of independence, for the exports of rubber in both 1960 and 1961 amounted to more than 35,000 tons, very close to the average in the four preceding years. The Congo exported, through the port of Matadi, in 1961, 153,000 tons of palm oil, only slightly below the annual average of 170,000 tons in the four preceding years.[18]

Caught between the need for popular support and the need for revenue that only the foreign-owned corporations can now supply, any government of the Republic of the Congo is unstable. A further difficulty, from this point of view, derives from the fact that the government of 1962–63 was able to bring back under its jurisdiction the major mining firms only through the intervention of the United Nations, the United States, and finally, Belgium. In the process, dependence on these additional external elements increased. In order to train and maintain the vastly enlarged military and police forces now necessary simply to keep the Congo integrated—for which is required much more revenue than was produced under much better circumstances—American and Belgian technical and financial assistance was accepted. Any government so beholden to foreign powers is certain to generate considerable opposition within its own nation. Obviously, under these circumstances, little attention can be given to the problems of organizing for genuinely "self-sustaining growth," an undertaking fraught with difficulties even for nations much more efficiently organized than the Congo.

It is appropriate now to consider the second of those two major changes that bear so heavily on the economic future of the Congo— referred to above as "the relatively greater isolation of an economic

[18] The figures for production and export are all taken from *Main Congo Agricultural Products, Annual Review* (Antwerp, 1961).

system which had never been in any full sense a 'national economy.' "

Politically, the Congo was always an adjunct to the Belgian state system, even though it had, constitutionally, a *personnalité unique*. Economically, it was an adjunct to the Western industrial system. Almost wholly devoid of private indigenous capital, and lacking any internal capital market, its capitalization depended ultimately on the world financial markets. Even though most financing was from re-invested profits, the decisions regarding reinvestment and dividend distribution were made with an eye to the world money market. Internal demand for goods produced by the commercial sector of the economy was so low in relation to production capability that more than 60 per cent of the product was intended for sale abroad. On the other hand, the needs of the commercial sector were such that almost 40 per cent of the disposable goods were imported.[19]

The point is simply that the "Congo economy" (and I call attention to the quotation marks) is so tightly integrated with other national economies that it seems unrealistic to view anything as the "Congo economy." All the factors of production, including entrepreneurship, depend in important ways on outsiders. Patterns of internal distribution, as we have seen, were not the result of free interplay in a market but were heavily controlled by a government whose power derived from the outside. The major market for the goods produced in the Congo was the world market, upon which internal Congo forces had virtually no effect.

Another vitally important way in which economic institutions in the Congo are far from independent is seen when one analyzes the mineral industry of Southern Africa as a whole.[20] The mining firms in the Congo, the single most important sector of the "Congo economy," are integrated with not only the parent firms in Belgium, but with other mining firms in Southern Africa, on which depend the "economies" of the Rhodesias, Angola, South West Africa, and the Republic of South Africa. Not merely do they participate in the same world capital market, and in the same market for the sale of their minerals, but they participate in a common system of production through functional agreements, formal and informal, and through interlocking directorates that ensure the sharing of information among

[19] Bézy, "Belgian Congo," p. 203.
[20] See Wolfe, "The Team Rules Mining in Southern Africa," *Toward Freedom*, January, 1962; Wolfe, "The African Mineral Industry and Its Significance for Anthropological Theory," unpublished paper presented to 61st Annual Meeting of the American Anthropological Association, 1962; and Wolfe, "The African Mineral Industry: Evolution of a Supranational Level of Integration," *Social Problems*, Fall, 1963.

all firms. Similarly, the transportation network which most of these firms use and have interest in is an international one that necessitates a certain economic integration.

For all the foregoing reasons, we should question whether there is any but a spurious statistical validity in the concept of a unique Congo economy. So much does every aspect of the commerce of the Congo depend on other economic systems that predictions cannot possibly be made from a study of internal economic resources and their organization. The Congo itself was certainly not at the point of "take-off to sustained growth." The forces that produced statistics indicating such growth were generated and controlled by institutions external to Congo society. The events of 1960, somewhat euphemistically called "the achievement of independence," changed the social and political structure of the Congo so markedly as to weaken those forces significantly. To the extent that the economic units in the Congo become isolated from the total Western industrial economic system—by the rupture of the political bonds with Belgium, by the straining of the bonds which made for close collaboration between European firms and the Congo Government—the economic statistics will show considerably less potential for growth. On the other hand, to the extent that such bonds remain intact, political independence has very little meaning. The dilemma of the Congo would appear to be this: The welfare of the Congolese is dependent upon an international industrial system in which they participate without having, even through their own government, any significant voice. Perhaps realistic analysis would reveal that this is the dilemma of all Africans, and a dilemma they share with many other peoples in both East and West—the dilemma of those who strive for political independence in isolated state structures even while economic realities necessitate interdependence.

Discussion

ALVIN W. WOLFE. Mr. Ostrander may find it surprising when I begin by saying that there is much in his paper with which I agree. This does not include, however, his criticism of what he calls the "myth" of the supranational integration of the mining industry in Southern Africa.

The subject of this session is "Problems of Adjustment and Independence." Yet each paper presented has focused on economic development after independence—as if the achievement of independence required no "adjustment." African leaders at this conference have all spoken with strong feeling of the failure of nonviolent means in Southern Africa and have left us no doubt that they are now *adjusting* for the use of violence as a means of achieving independence. The Africans, having been told again and again that "they have nothing to invest in the situation but themselves," seem quite ready to buy independence with their lives. I would strongly urge that before they move to full-scale violence, they investigate the possibility that they can deal in mineral futures.

If there is validity in my observations about the organization of the mining industry in Southern Africa, and I certainly believe there is, it should be possible for the African leaders to communicate to the mining industry that the future of the industry will be much brighter if the industry suffers a slight loss now in helping to bring down white supremacy than it will be if African independence must be achieved by the long hard road of guerrilla-type war. Three things the mining companies can do for the Africans, three things they *must* do are: (1) to put economic pressure on the colonial and white-supremacist governments, one by one if necessary; (2) to inform the U.S. and British governments of their intention so as to permit these to take proper action; and (3) to provide financial and other support for governments-in-exile.

That these actions by the mining companies would be expensive to them is certain, but not nearly so expensive as years of economic stagnation consequent upon a lengthy and violent war. In fact, with certain agreements to share the burden, the companies who lose most in the economic squeeze could be reimbursed by those which gain most. Portugal could be encouraged to cease its violent actions, and Angola could be handed over to its own population very shortly and in good order, if the Benguela Railway were not used and if Diamang diamonds were not put on the market. In the meantime, Tanganyika Concessions Limited and the Société Générale de Belgique could make it up by increased activity in the Congo.

But before such action is attempted, one must be sure of success. What is required is a careful analysis of what kind of integration exists in Southern Africa: How interdependent are these territories? How interdependent are these companies? How interdependent are the companies and the territories? And how much does the European industrial system depend on the African mineral resources?

If we become too enthusiastic about violence now, or too enthusiastic about profits now, we may miss the last opportunity to establish a social system so organized politically and economically that both Africans and Europeans may live and prosper in the long term.

This is what the panel should have been discussing—the adjustment to independence. I am sorry that my works have been so maligned by representatives of the mining companies, because my message would be good for them as well. It is my desire to see as much freedom as possible come to Africa with a minimum of violence, and with the stage prepared for economic development.

M. W. KANYAMA CHIUME.   In our part of the world, the problems of adjustment after independence are really the problems of the adjustment of the white man after independence. The white man must reconcile himself to being a mere citizen demanding no more rights than a citizen can expect in a state and prepared to perform the duties that a state expects from its citizens. If the white man accepts this condition, there is absolutely no worry at all, for the African, as we have indicated, is not anti-white, to use the American expression, but is against the system of domination of one man by the other. If the white man is not prepared to adjust himself to this situation after independence, then of course he has the opportunity of going to another part of the world where his snobbishness can be tolerated. If he is incapable of removing himself, the African governments certainly are capable of removing him from the African territory.

As far as capital is concerned, there is no worry. In spite of all that you have read in the papers, the Africans or the African governments are not against capital, but they are asking capital to behave in exactly the same way as they are asking the individual white man to behave—that is, to recognize that on a black continent the black man must rule himself and that Africans cannot tolerate any other masters. As long as capital is prepared to behave in this manner, capital has absolutely no worry at all.

I think I will be failing in my duty if I do not say that in other parts of Central Africa capital has misbehaved. In the near past, it must be remembered, two companies subsidized Welensky and the Federal Government over a long period. Now, that type of behavior cannot be tolerated in Africa. The mineral companies in the Congo promoted and sustained a type of rule that Africa after independence cannot tolerate. The African has no intention, as has been suggested in many statements, of confiscating the property of investors. Africa needs capital, either from foreign investors or from foreign governments.

GODFREY K. J. AMACHREE.   Professor Wolfe's account of the Congolese economy is a gloomy one indeed. I am not an economist, but I would like to question the economic theory Professor Wolfe has propounded. We at the U.N. do not think of the Congo in terms of the past. We are beyond the stage of merely criticizing the Belgians; we think of a newly independent African state that requires international help in planning for the future.

Is the Congo in any different position than the other African countries were in at the time of independence? The other countries tackled their economic problems and so will the Congo. It is a simple action to put an end to control by international cartels. It is true that when this action is first undertaken the economy of the country probably suffers, but recovery soon occurs.

There are, nonetheless, many problems to be solved in the Congo. It is a vast, rich area with nine different frontiers. But for the timely intervention of the United Nations, the Congo might have been the cause of a third world war.

Katanga is still a problem. The central government's general amnesty allowed many to remain in power in that province and in the central Parliament. These people have continued to engage in intrigues and plots. The Katangese *gendarmerie*, which was supposed to give up its arms, take the oath of allegiance, and be incorporated into the national army, has escaped into the bushes; it has been impossible to collect all of its arms. There is still suspicion in Katanga of the central government's intentions, and suspicion in the rest of the Congo of the intentions of Tshombe and his former ministers. This means that a mobile international force is needed that can be moved from place to place in order to ensure continued security. The United Nations, however, is having difficulty in obtaining funds from its member nations for these troops. Also, there is some disagreement among U.N. members as to the procedure to be followed in assisting in the training of the Congolese National Army, the Air Force, and the Navy. This training is going on to some extent now, but it must be done on a larger scale for, as many of us have come to realize, it is the United Nations' duty before it withdraws to aid the army in developing discipline and leadership and to aid the government in maintaining law and order.

Unless the United Nations' activities in the Congo are allowed to continue, the lives lost and the time and effort and money spent will have been for naught. Although I have the bias of a representative of the United Nations, I believe that with the proper leadership and international assistance, the Congo can be almost entirely independent of foreign aid within a year.

X

Nationalist Movements
and Pan-Africanism

Possible Political Unities: The Thrust of Labor Movements in Pan-Africanism *

COLIN LEGUM

The Field and the Problems

The area covered by this paper extends from South Africa to Ethiopia and Somalia; it includes the three High Commission Territories (Basutoland, Bechuanaland, and Swaziland), South West Africa, Zambia, Rhodesia, Malawi, Rwanda, Burundi, the Congo (Léopoldville), Angola and Mozambique, Kenya, Uganda, and Tanganyika, and the islands of Zanzibar and Mauritius—twenty territories in all.

Eleven of the twenty territories under discussion are independent: Ethiopia, Somalia, the Congo, Tanzania (Tanganyika and Zanzibar), Uganda, Rwanda, Burundi, Zambia, Malawi, and South Africa. (South Africa's "independence" is not, however, accepted by the Pan-African movements.) Mauritius has self-government, and the three High Commission Territories are in the process of establishing representative forms of government. The remaining five countries—South Africa, South West Africa, Rhodesia, Angola, and Mozambique—have neither representative governments nor any likelihood of getting them in the near future.

Relationships between the labor movements and the political movements are the cause of strenuous controversy in several of these territories. This produces strains within the individual nationalist movements as well as in the Pan-African movements. Out of eighteen significant labor movements in PAFMECSA-affiliated territories, ten are members of the ICFTU (International Confederation of Free Trade Unions), five of AATUF (All-African Trade Union Federation), two of the WFTU (World Federation of Trade Unions), and one of the IFCTU (International Federation of Christian Trade Unions). These alignments raise two questions related to the theme

* This paper was revised and updated by the author in the spring of 1965.

of this conference: (1) What contribution can the forces of Pan-Africanism make to the struggle for liberation in Southern Africa? and (2), How effectively can Pan-Africanist leaders act when, no longer engaged in fighting the common enemy of imperialism, they come to implement their ideas for achieving Africa's unity? Although this paper does not attempt direct answers to these questions, it offers material that might contribute to a meaningful discussion of them.

Trade Unions: Nationalism and Pan-Africanism

The trade-union movements in East, Central, and Southern Africa have inevitably become involved both in the nationalist struggle for liberation and in the Pan-African movement for wider unity. Every trade-union center in this region holds the view that a single Pan-African trade-union movement should be established "to unite the workers of Africa." They have supported the motions favoring this proposal taken at every AAPO (All-African Peoples' Organization) conference since 1958. Two difficulties, however, have stood in the way of agreement: (1) the sponsorship of AATUF, and (2) the autonomy of national trade-union centers.

The problem of autonomy is often misunderstood; as a result, the impression has gained ground that the dispute between African labor leaders is over the question of belonging either to a Pan-African movement or to an existing labor international. But the real argument is not about whether or not to belong to AATUF, WFTU, ICFTU, or IFCTU. It is about the right of each national trade-union center to make its own decisions on all questions, including those of affiliation.

Several attempts have been made to find a compromise—e.g., a proposal that AATUF should itself be affiliated with labor internationals, or that individual trade unions should be allowed to join their respective internationals (e.g., the International Seamen's Union, International Miners' Federation, and so on). But these attempts have always foundered on the conflict of principle about the autonomy of national trade-union centers in all matters, including that of external affiliations. This struggle, however, has in practice turned out to be between the affiliates of AATUF and of the ICFTU, and this has obscured the real issues. Early in 1963, all the trade-union centers in Kenya, Uganda, and Tanganyika decided to end their ICFTU affiliation and agreed to discuss a new basis for an AATUF type of organization.

The WFTU has stopped canvassing directly for African affiliates, preferring to work with and through the AATUF. The IFCTU still has a few affiliates, the only one in Central, East, or Southern Africa being the Union des Travailleurs Congolais. This is the present line-up: The Kenya Federation of Labour has been in the forefront of the fight for the right to retain labor's links with any international of its choosing. The KFL's choice has always been the ICFTU. Uganda's TUC is also a strong ICFTU affiliate. This applies also to Mauritius and to two of the three main labor centers in the Congo—the Fédération Générale des Travailleurs du Congo, once led by former Premier Cyrille Adoula; and the Confédération des Syndicats Libres. The third Congo center is an affiliate of the IFCTU; and there is a small WFTU affiliate that has no significant strength.

Members of the ICFTU that are not in any particular way dedicated to its cause include the Tanganyika Federation of Labour, the Confederation of Somali Labour, the Malawi Congress of Labour in Nyasaland, and the Southern Rhodesian African Trade Union Congress. They remain members because they see no reason in principle why they should not, and because they resent the high-handed demand for disaffiliation by AATUF leaders. But there are pro-AATUF elements in all these centers, and there is no reason to believe that sooner or later their views might not prevail.[1]

Two centers that have disaffiliated from the ICFTU to join AATUF since the Casablanca meeting are the Zanzibar and Pemba Federation of Labour and the United Trade Union Congress of Northern Rhodesia. There are trade unions but no national centers in Swaziland and Bechuanaland, but tiny Basutoland has three—all of them small, militant, and changeable. At the last reckoning two were affiliated with AATUF, and one with WFTU. Ethiopia has no effective unions yet; the government introduced, in 1962, the first labor legislation allowing the right to associate in trade unions.

Immediately after the formation of AATUF, a rash of splinter unions grew up in the ICFTU-affiliated territories, encouraged and in some cases financed by AATUF. This challenge was a conscious policy announced by Ghana's John Tettegah after the AATUF conference, when he declared "total war" on the ICFTU unions. ("We shall isolate them and enter their countries and form AATUF unions there.") None of these splinter unions has come to anything. The policy of patiently converting established unions has clearly turned out to be more profitable than trying to fight them.

The African labor movement in South Africa must be treated as a special case, partly because of the relatively large European working-class and the highly developed industrial society, partly because of

[1] In 1964, AATUF was formally launched as an independent trade-union organization following a conference held in Bamako.

government legislation and practice designed to control and restrict African trade unionism, and partly because there are competing nationalist movements. Until recently, the only ICFTU affiliate was the South African Congress of Trade Unions (SACTU), which is closely associated with the African National Congress (ANC), and includes African and a few white unions. Relations with the ICFTU deteriorated when SACTU began to show strong sympathies for AATUF, and especially when it sent delegates to the WFTU conference in Accra. The South African Trade Union Congress (SATUC), until recently an all-white body, has recently begun to accept nonwhite associates largely to qualify for affiliation with the ICFTU. Thirdly, there is the Federation of Free African Trade Unions of South Africa (known as FAFATUSA), which has links with the Pan African Congress; it, too, is now asking for ICFTU affiliation on the grounds that its all-African membership is the most representative in the country.

But important though these Pan-African groupings are, they are probably only an indicator of the attitudes of the labor leaders; the practical results are often very small. Of greater concern at the moment is the question of relations between the trade unions and the governments or the nationalist parties. East and Southern Africa have a fairly conscious tradition of free or independent trade unionism. It is interesting, for example, that one of the objectives expressed in the original PAFMECA Charter was to "press for the recognition of full trade union rights in every country in Africa"; while another resolution at its first conference at Mwanza emphasized that "trade unions should not be under the control of any political party." This view of unionism is an article of faith with the unions in ICFTU and is encouraged by them.

Nevertheless, the trade unions and the nationalist parties work closely together during the struggle for independence, particularly since trade-union members are generally also members of the nationalist movement. Moreover, the harder the struggle the more difficult it becomes to separate political from industrial issues; this is particularly true in South Africa, where the African is by law denied industrial and other economic rights. This situation has given rise to the question of whether it would not be more efficient for the unions and the nationalist parties to pool their resources in a single nationalist movement and agree to serve under a united command instead of acting independently.

In answer to this question, one of Southern Rhodesia's top trade-union leaders said the unions and the party clearly should work in the closest possible accord, especially since it has become increasingly clear that one of the strongest cards in nationalist hands is the strike weapon and other industrial action. Nevertheless, he warned: "We must keep our roles clear. If the party wants to call a strike for political reasons, they are very welcome to do so after consulting us. *But it must be they who call it. Not us.* The workers must be quite clear that they are responding to a political and not to a union call. Only in this way can the unions preserve their essential industrial functions without becoming a political tool to be used someday for non-nationalist political ends."

This view would be supported by many of the present leaders in Kenya, Uganda, the Congo, and, probably, Somalia. A totally different attitude is adopted by the Tanganyika Government. In its view, the labor movement and the nationalist party are inseparably bound together in the liberation struggle; after independence, the trade unions become the industrial arm of the governing party. This view is justified on the ground that the government, built with the support of the workers, is the workers' party. Organized labor, therefore, need no longer think in terms of a struggle *against* the government; the struggle should be seen as being alongside the government against their common enemies. Sympathetic critics of this Tanganyika view (which is also that of Ghana, Guinea, and Mali) regard it as a justification for a simple pragmatic need in Tanganyika—that of pooling everyone's efforts to get the country moving economically, and of preventing a small group of organized workers from ransoming the country for an unfairly large slice of the national cake. Malawi also associated the governing party with the trade unions. It, too, is poor and desperately underdeveloped; like Tanganyika, its primary national purpose is to pull itself up by its own bootstraps.

These two different views on the relations between government and the unions distinguish the policies of Kenya and Tanganyika, two of the important nucleus members of PAFMECSA. In 1962, the Tanganyika Government passed its new labor legislation making strikes illegal unless prescribed arbitration procedures had first been exhausted—providing, in other words, for compulsory arbitration. Some months later, two labor leaders were rusticated for actively organizing among sisal-plantation workers industrial opposition to labor legislation. They were apprehended shortly after a wave of strikes had badly shaken the economy. The government felt that it must have overriding powers in industrial matters to ensure the implementation of its economic policy. But there is no indication that these powers will be used in an arbitrary or harsh manner: On the contrary, the trade unions are consulted on every measure that concerns them as fully as they were before the government assumed these powers. The leaders who were briefly rusticated had, in fact, behaved in a highly provocative manner by actively encouraging opposition to legislation they had themselves previously supported.

About the same time as Tanganyika was being hit by strikes, Kenya was going through a similar experience. But the Kenya Government, after hinting at compulsory arbitration, adopted a different solution. It introduced an Industrial Relations Charter, the first of its kind in Africa. It is not a legal document, but represents a kind of pact between workers and employers signed by their representatives in the presence of (and under the signature of) the Minister of Labour. The Charter does no more than set out the ideal behavior and attitude of organized labor and employers toward each other and pledges both sides to try to live up to it. The Charter has also won approval in Uganda. The labor ministers in both Kenya and Uganda, as well as both labor and management, see the Charter as a real alternative to the type of legislation that Tanganyika has introduced. They hope to persuade Tanganyika to opt for the Charter instead.

How do the various union centers line up on this issue? The Zanzibar unions are associated with the party at present in power, but are not dominated by it. The same is also true of the Zambia and Rhodesian trade-union centers, which work closely, and on the whole happily, with UNIP (United National Independence Party) and ZAPU (Zimbabwe African Peoples' Union) respectively. The labor movement in South Africa is deeply divided over its support for the rival nationalist parties and on their attitudes to racial questions. The Somalia unions are associated with, but not tied to, the ruling party. All the Congo unions are independent; even Mr. Adoula's former union does not hesitate to criticize him or his government. The unions of Malawi and Tanganyika ally themselves closely with government policy; those of Kenya and Uganda stand militantly for the right to independent action and free collective bargaining.

Economic as well as political circumstances in each territory appear to affect the relations between the unions and the governments. The movements—trade union as well as political—have had the chance to watch developments in West Africa. On the whole, they have reacted against too much government control and have produced a sensitivity to autocratic methods that often finds its first expression in the trade unions. In East Africa, there is a greater and deeper awareness of the problems and experience of neighboring territories than there was in West Africa, which (at least in the former British territories) lacked the experience of semifederal institutions. The trade-union centers in Uganda and Kenya are already talking of the formation of East Africa unions for joint negotiations with employers and governments.

Pan-African Freedom Movement of East, Central, and Southern Africa

ORIGINS AND GROWTH. PAFMECSA began as a regional unit of the All-African Peoples Organization. It did not set itself up as a rival to any existing organization. Its major role was that of coordinator of policies in its region. This did not save PAFMECSA from being accused of separatist or regionalist tendencies. Nor did PAFMECSA refuse to speak up when it felt impelled to do so—even at the risk of being considered "deviationist."

In this and other ways, PAFMECSA came to acquire a personality of its own. It developed half a dozen distinguishing features. It was the first regional organization to succeed in holding together all the territorial units within its immediate sphere of interest. Indeed, it grew considerably beyond the boundaries originally set for it. It grew in influence when none of its original members had achieved independence. Its core membership managed to retain, reform, and expand the nucleus of a unifying institution—the East African Common Services Organization (EACSO). This achievement is all the more remarkable since it called for actual sacrifices—first from Tanganyika and later from Uganda, both of which agreed to share their sovereign power with their nonindependent neighbors. Nor were these only moral sacrifices; they entailed, if not actual economic loss, at least the loss of policy-making powers normally reserved to sovereign states. PAFMECSA operated where the problems of multiracial societies exist in addition to the ordinary colonial situation, and this raised special problems both for PAFMECSA and for many of its affiliates, which have to concern themselves with questions both of principle and of tactics in handling the problems of mixed communities. It marks the first attempt to associate on equal terms the governments of already independent states with nationalist movements still engaged in their own liberation struggles. Finally, PAFMECSA brought together states with totally different governments and attitudes (e.g., Ethiopia and Tanganyika), and some with deeply conflicting interests (Ethiopia, Somalia, and Kenya).

All this was to PAFMECSA's credit. But there was a negative side as well: (1) In the early stage, before the Zanzibar revolution in January, 1964, there had been the estrangement of the Zanzibar Nationalist Party, and a tolerance of anti-Arab sentiment among some of PAFMECSA's affiliates. (2) Initial support for the Mwami of Rwanda and his exile movement (UNAR) made relations with the republican government of Rwanda difficult; this support was later dropped. (3) The intense rivalry between KANU and KADU in Kenya was carried over into PAFMECSA despite attempts to avoid doing so. (4) Once Somalia, with its well-known Greater Somalia aspirations, was admitted into membership, no firm initiative was taken to allay the Somali irredentist problems in Ethiopia and especially in the Northern Frontier District of Kenya. (5) Relations between PAFMECSA and the AAPO were allowed to deteriorate.

Despite a great lack of resources, both financial and manpower, PAFMECSA went from strength to strength until the decision was taken to dissolve it, in October, 1963. Organizationally and financially, it was the weakest of all the major Pan-African organizations. It had no doctrine of its own, beyond the doctrine of pursuing the shared Pan-African ideal of unity. It published no literature. It had hardly any full-time staff. Its modest headquarters in Dar es Salaam could hardly be described as a beehive of activity. Yet, in the four and a half years of its existence, it went further along the road toward creating a regional federation in Africa than any other Pan-African organization.

POLICIES AND ORGANIZATION, 1958. From the start PAFMECA (Pan-African Freedom Movement of East and Central Africa) embraced two basic Pan-African principles: support for the liberation struggle against colonialism and commitment to the creation of a wider unity of African states. Historically, it is important to recall that PAFMECA's first conference (Mwanza, Tanganyika, September 16–18, 1958) was held three months before the first All-African Peoples' Conference (AAPC) (Accra, December, 1958). But the idea of forming a regional organization for East and Central Africa originated in Accra. Julius Nyerere and other East and Central African leaders had discussed it with Kwame Nkrumah and the late George Padmore at the first-anniversary celebrations of the independence of Ghana, in March, 1958. Although Dr. Nyerere was from the beginning the moving spirit in the formation of PAFMECA, he worked in close cooperation with leaders of the nationalist movements in Kenya, Zanzibar, and Uganda.

Five territories were represented at the Mwanza conference to launch PAFMECA: Tanganyika, Uganda, Kenya, Zanzibar, and Nyasaland. Both the Kenya Federation of Labour and the Tanganyika Labour Federation were represented, in addition to these territories' political movements. Kenya's representation was provided by the African Elected Members Organization of the Legislative Council.

(The split between KANU and KADU later destroyed AEMO.) Uganda was poorly represented: The nationalist congress was split into several parts, and the leading role was played by E. M. K. Mulira's unrepresentative Progressive Party. Nyasaland was the only Central African country represented, although the others had also been invited.

The points on the agenda illustrate the major problems that PAFMECA felt it faced at its inception: coordination of policy and tactics of the nationalist movements in East and Central Africa; eradication of tribalism; harnessing the forces of traditionalism for political struggles; problems of non-Africanism. One of the resolutions called for the establishment of common political principles and economic patterns in all the territories concerned. The immediate target was formulated in the slogan "Colonialism must go."

The question of federation was raised: Should the territories remain permanently separate or should they federate? If the latter, when and how? The conference resolved that "the question of East African Federation is irrelevant and does not arise at this time." The reason for that decision was that as independence dates had not yet been set for any of the territories concerned, federation could not be spoken of in meaningful terms. It could arise only with self-government.

PAFMECA's first constitution set itself five aims and objects: (1) to foster the spirit of Pan-Africanism in order to rid East and Central African territories of imperialism, white supremacy, economic exploitation, and social degradation by stepped-up nationalist activities to attain self-government and establish parliamentary forms; (2) to coordinate nationalist programs, tactics, projects, and efforts for the speedy liberation of the said territories; (3) to assist in the establishment and organization of united nationalist movements in African territories through political education, periodic conferences, encouragement of interterritorial African endeavors in all fields, and by any other means that this organization may determine; (4) to establish a joint East and Central African Freedom Fund; and (5) to champion nonviolence in the African nationalist struggles for freedom and prosperity.

Membership was open to all nationalist, labor, and cooperative organizations "which accept and conform to the policy of Pan-Africanism and the liberation of Africa." Sectional or splinter groups (these were not defined) would not be eligible for membership. The organizational structure provided for an annual general meeting in August of every year, a Coordinating Freedom Council (CFC) to act as the governing body, and Territorial Freedom Committees (these were never created). Dar es Salaam was chosen as the headquarters; almost automatically, Tanganyika began to fulfill the role of a "leader country."

PAFMECA's first two practical tasks were to try to coordinate the factional groups in Uganda's national movement, and to mediate between the two rival parties in Zanzibar. The Uganda initiative met with little initial success; the task in Zanzibar was made impossibly difficult by the fact that TANU (Tanganyika African National Union) was openly supporting the ASP (Afro-Shirazi Party) against the ZNP (Zanzibar National Party), labeled an "Arab" party.

PAFMECA AND THE AAPC, 1958. PAFMECA was the only regional group represented at the first AAPO conference, in Accra in December, 1958. Its representative, Dr. J. Gikonyo Kiano, had been instructed to raise six points: (1) the need for a Pan-African freedom movement; (2) representation for such a movement at the U.N.; (3) democratization of all independent African states; (4) creation of a freedom fund; (5) instructions to independent African states to "take positive action" in the U.N. and all its agencies in the Commonwealth of Nations and elsewhere "on all matters affecting the freedom of the African people"; and (6) breaking down of the "present iron curtain surrounding some colonial states" (a reference to the Belgian and Portuguese territories).

Dr. Kiano's address to the Accra conference, delivered in PAFMECA's name, conveys the spirit of its founders:

> We believe in the moral and right power of nonviolence—but not in the idea of turning the other cheek. . . . Our struggle is . . . prompted not by negative emotions of hate or bitterness but by the positive dedication to the ideals of freedom under African democratic governments. Whoever is against the idea of Africa being ruled by Africans should hear this: The ports are open and ships available for such enemies of African freedom to pack up and quit Africa! . . . Those not with us are against us. We cannot have faith in those major and minor powers who profess democracy in general terms but who, when it comes to specific issues, such as the liberation of Algeria, the smashing of the settlers' powers in East and Central Africa, the emancipation of our brothers and sisters enslaved in the iron curtain colonies of Angola and Mozambique, either abstain or vote with the imperialists in the United Nations. America, Soviet Union, United Kingdom, France and Belgium, Spain and Portugal, hear this: Africans do not believe you when you say you believe in democracy and human freedom. Your actions or abstentions speak louder than words! And they contradict what you say.

Two important decisions affecting the relationship between PAFMECA and the AAPO were taken at the Accra meeting: PAFMECA should function as a regional organization within the framework of the AAPO, and its sphere of interest should include not only the territories of East and Central Africa but also the then Belgian Congo and Ruanda-Urundi. But its sphere of influence did not include Southern Africa or the Horn of Africa.

TRIBALISM AND TRADITIONALISM, SCHISMS, NON-AFRICANS: 1959–60. PAFMECA's first Coordinating Freedom Council was held in Zanzibar in April, 1959. It was a deliberate move to try to conciliate the two rival parties, but it failed. Its second conference (September 8–12, 1959) could not be held in Uganda because of a ban by the colonial administration; it was held instead at Moshi in Tanganyika. Nyasaland was not represented on this occasion, but there were for the first time representatives from the Congo (Léopoldville) and Rwanda. (UNAR [National Union of Rwanda] was in conflict with the Belgian administration and with PARMEHUTU, and was seeking external support.) In welcoming them, the conference passed a resolution hoping that "all nationalist movements in the Congo will respond positively to become full members of the organization." It expressed concern over the "apparent existence of tribal feelings," and condemned "tribalism wherever it may exist." One of the themes developed by Dr. Nyerere in his opening address was the integration of different communities into the new societies: "We would like to see in all these PAFMECA countries that a citizen is a citizen irrespective of color, irrespective of religion. . . . We are not fighting here for the color black. If all these countries of ours were inhabited by black pigs do you think we would be fighting here? We are fighting for human beings." The Moshi conference met at a time when Kenya, Nyasaland, Southern Rhodesia, and Northern Rhodesia were under a state of emergency, and when certain parts of Uganda were declared disturbed areas. The conference spent much of its time discussing these problems. It demanded liberty for Kenyatta and Banda. A second major question was the threatening split in Kenya's AEMO (African Elected Members Organization) on the eve of round-table talks in London for a new Kenya constitution. Kenya's leaders were urged to maintain the unity of the AEMO and to go forward "with one voice."

PAFMECA, already faced with divisions in two of its associate states (Zanzibar and Uganda), was soon afterward faced with similar divisions in Kenya and Rwanda. In 1960, the AEMO finally split and produced two parties; both retained PAFMECA membership, but their rivalry led to organizational disputes. The problem in Rwanda was complicated by TANU's decision to champion the rights of the exiled Mwami and his party, UNAR, against the dominant Hutu party, PARMEHUTU, which was at first regarded as having been created by the Belgians themselves.

There were difficulties, too, in the relationship between AAPO and PAFMECA. These were due partly to the conflict over the right method of creating AATUF, and partly to the method of work of AAPO's central committee. As AAPO chairman, Tom Mboya was at the center of these controversies. His own relations with Accra and Conakry became increasingly cool. These difficulties came to a head at the second AAPO conference in Tunis (January, 1960), where the delegations from the PAFMECA countries (joined on this occasion by Southern and Northern Rhodesia and by some of the Nigerian delegations) stood together in a challenge against the platform's allocation of speakers' time and handling of resolutions.

Dating from this event, there was a feeling in some AAPO quarters that PAFMECA was becoming "too regionalist" in its attitudes. This view was sternly repudiated by PAFMECA leaders, who insisted that their only concern was with the practice of democracy within the AAPO, to which they still felt loyal.

GROWTH OF THE FEDERAL IDEA: 1960–61. There was a major breakthrough in East Africa in 1961. Tanganyika's independence was set for the end of the year; a successful constitutional conference opened the way for self-government in Uganda; the deadlock in Kenya was finally broken at the celebrated Lancaster House conference presided over by Iain Macleod, then British Colonial Secretary. There was greater confidence among PAFMECA's leaders, and the beginning of an awareness of the difficulties that might arise if the three major territories achieved their independence at different times.

Dr. Nyerere used the opportunity of the second Conference of Independent African States (Addis Ababa, June 14–24, 1960) to make his first public plea for what he called the Federation of East African States:

> In our struggle against imperialism we have emphasized that our strength lies in unity. We have warned ourselves against the dangers of divide and rule. . . . We know that a balkanized Africa, however loudly it might proclaim to the world its independence and all that, will in fact be an easy prey to the forces of new imperialism. . . . The question really is *how* to bring about this unity; and in particular *when*. It is my belief that at least for us in East Africa, the time is *now* and the method

is to *combine the freedom movement and the unity movement into one and the same thing so that both freedom and unity are achieved at the same time.* Somaliland and Somalia have done the nearest thing to what I think we should do in the remaining parts of East Africa.

In other words, Dr. Nyerere was pleading for the suspension of independence for the separate territories until they could emerge jointly as a single federated state, and for political union. He made his offer, unique in the Pan-African struggle, to hold up the impending independence of his own country until the others were ripe to join in the creation of a single unified state. He was attacked from two sides: by nationalistic elements in TANU and by Pan-Africanists who felt that an independent Tanganyika could make a greater contribution to the wider struggle. But he defended his position at the third PAFMECA conference, held at Mbale in Uganda (October 24, 1960), where the original nucleus of members (including Nyasaland) gave general acceptance to the idea of an East African Federation. The question, at last, was no longer thought to be irrelevant. But the details of the proposals were left to be worked out at a special conference held in Nairobi on January 12, 1961, and attended by the heads of organizations affiliated with PAFMECA. This meeting was not a regular meeting of PAFMECA, but was called at the suggestion of Kenneth Kaunda. By this time the affiliates had grown to include UNIP (United National Independence Party, Northern Rhodesia), the NDP (National Democratic Party, Southern Rhodesia), and the Democratic Party (Uganda). Attending the conference were Julius Nyerere, Tom Mboya, Benedicto Kiwanuka (later Premier of Uganda), Joshua Nkomo, and Kenneth Kaunda.

Before them was a twelve-page memorandum on East African Federation entitled "Freedom and Unity," drafted by Dr. Nyerere. It elaborated his arguments in favor of federating before independence. Its main argument was developed against Mr. Kiwanuka's Democratic Party, then the dominant party in Uganda, that "we must put our separate houses in order first," before contemplating federation. Dr. Nyerere continued: "I do not accept this argument. If we were all in chaos it would be silly to add chaos to chaos. . . . But when does one satisfy oneself that our house has been put in order? I say after responsible government. Some of my friends say after independence." The conclusion of the Nairobi meeting was to endorse a resolution "that a Federation of Eastern Africa is politically and economically essential now for the unity and social betterment of the peoples of these countries; that such a Federation can be designed and brought about only by elected and African-controlled governments in Eastern Africa."

But in the end the cause of Nyerere and his supporters was defeated not by arguments but by the pressure of events. British policy (though officially sympathetic to an East African Federation) was not flexible enough to help speed up the timetable for Uganda's and, especially, Kenya's independence. The growth of intense party rivalries in Kenya temporarily changed the tempo of its constitutional advancement and altered the course of its political development. A third factor was the reluctance of the Democratic Party (which formed the Uganda Government in 1961) to commit itself to federation before independence; even more important, though, was the uncompromising opposition of Buganda's traditionalist forces—especially Kabaka Yekka, which became influential through its coalition partnership in Milton Obote's government formed in 1962.

In March, 1961, Tanganyika's date for independence was finally fixed for December of that year. In June, 1961, a conference was held in London to consider the effect of Tanganyika's independence on East Africa. The result was the decision to establish the East African Common Services Organization (EACSO), which will be considered later.

One other development needs recording: At the independence celebrations of Somalia (July 1, 1960), representatives from Mauritius for the first time raised with Nyerere the possibility of their becoming associated with an East African Federation. They have since maintained their interest.

FORCES FOR AND AGAINST FEDERATION. This is perhaps a good moment to break off the narrative account of PAFMECA's development to look a little deeper into the forces operating within the movement. It is easy to identify the supporters of Nyerere's ideas. His two strongest allies were KANU (Kenya African National Union) and the UPC (Uganda People's Congress). The KANU leaders were united on the issue of federation. Although Oginga Odinga had early reservations, these were later withdrawn. Kenyatta's support, once he was at liberty, was wholehearted. So was Milton Obote's (the new Prime Minister of Uganda and leader of the UPC). Although the ASP in Zanzibar was primarily interested in federation with Tanganyika, it supported the idea of an East African Federation as a secondary objective. The ZNP, though by no means opposed to federation, was less openly committed because of its conflicts with TANU on the one hand and with the Kenya parties (over the Coastal Strip) on the other.

The Democratic Party (now Uganda's official opposition) adopted a more equivocal attitude. Its manifesto of April, 1960, declared: "While appreciating the desirability for economic cooperation between Uganda and her neighbors, the Democratic Party is, as a matter of principle, opposed to any imposed type of association, be it political, economic, or otherwise; and it is further opposed to any association in which Uganda will not participate as an equal partner, and whereby other parties or interests are enriched at our expense." The Democratic Party leader, Mr. Kiwanuka, said, in January, 1961:

> We in Uganda are not opposed to the concept of an East African Federation as such, but to its timing. . . . In Uganda we have to solve the complex problems of traditionalism and tribalism before the question of a federation can be resolved. Another factor to be considered in Uganda —and also in Kenya—is the prevailing uncertainty as to who will take the reins of a future independent government in these territories. . . . Things will be still more difficult in the event of Uganda itself adopting a federal instead of a unitary form of constitution. Even so, a "federation within a federation" could be made to work with the cooperation of all concerned. It would be a new experiment not yet tried in any other part of the world, but there is no reason why we should not make it work.

The attitudes of the Central African parties are harder to define. Burdened by their passionate struggle to rid themselves of one unwanted federation, they were understandably hesitant about committing themselves too fully to another. In principle, the idea of a wider federation was, however, accepted by the Malawi Congress in Nyasaland, by UNIP in Northern Rhodesia, and by ZAPU in Southern Rhodesia. Dr. Banda repeatedly spoke in favor of a close association with Tanganyika under the leadership of Nyerere. On May 11, 1961, he declared, "I hope to see the day when Dar es Salaam is the capital of the United States of Central Africa or the Federation of East and Central Africa—whichever is decided upon." Neither UNIP nor ZAPU committed itself without qualification to the idea of joining a wider federation, although the leadership of each party frequently expressed itself in favor of the principle of wider association and particularly in favor of sharing in the work of EACSO.

KADU's relationship with PAFMECA has not been altogether easy. There was a moment, at the time of the Nairobi meeting in 1961, when KADU's leaders bitterly attacked PAFMECA's handling of the conference arrangements. They have always felt somewhat cold-shouldered. But there has never been any doubt about KADU's support in favor of the principle of federation. Its leader, Ronald Ngala, consistently championed it. So did its economics spokesman, P. J. H. Okondo. "During my college days at Cape Town, I preached the idea of an East African Federation among my fellow students," Okondo wrote in *The Guardian* (Manchester, June 13, 1961). "I called it the Federation of Keuta—taking the first letters of the three territories' names. This idea is now gaining ground rapidly among the thinking people of Kenya."

FRELIMO (Mozambique Liberation Front), led by Eduardo Mondlane, was always a strong supporter of the view that a liberated Mozambique should one day become associated with a federation of East and Central African states.

The Mauritius Labour Party, the island's governing party, always took a lively interest in the idea although it did not join PAFMECA. Its hesitation was probably due to uncertainty about the future of the Asian communities in East Africa—an important consideration for a party dominated by Indians.

The hard-core opposition to federation came from the Kabaka Yekka, despite its affiliation with PAFMECA. While this Buganda traditionalist party came so far as to adopt a resolution in favor of EACSO (passed by the Lukike in 1963 in response to a request from Obote), it never disguised its antipathy to the idea of Uganda becoming federated with its neighbors. As the Kabaka Yekka was part of the Uganda Government, it was bound to raise difficulties. There was little evidence of practical support for a federation from any of the dominant parties in Rwanda, Burundi, or the Congo.

PAFMECA BECOMES PAFMECSA: 1962. PAFMECA's influence increased rapidly after Tanganyika's independence, at the end of 1961. As the first independent territory in East Africa, Tanganyika offered a more convenient base for the liberation movements of Central Africa, South Africa, the High Commission Territories, and Mozambique than did the older political capitals of Africa. The tendency of refugees and of liberation leaders to gather in Dar es Salaam and the warm sympathy shown to them by the Tanganyika Government and TANU gave a new significance to PAFMECA's capital, for, although the liberation movements continued to look to the older political capitals (Accra, Conakry, Cairo, and Tunis), they found it more convenient to operate out of Dar es Salaam. They mostly agree that they have never been made to feel that Dar es Salaam was trying to rival other capitals as a political city.

The enthusiasm of the South Africans for Tanganyika was greatly increased by the stand taken by Nyerere in demanding that South Africa be excluded from the Commonwealth. His intervention on that occasion deserves some elaboration as an example of effective Pan-Africanist action.

Late in February, 1961, a few weeks before the Commonwealth prime ministers were due to meet in London to consider, *inter alia,* South Africa's application to retain its membership after becoming a Republic, the South African United Front (which at that time included both the ANC and PAC) decided to lobby the African and Asian Commonwealth prime ministers to vote against South Africa's application. Although the Malayan Prime Minister had taken a strong line against South Africa at the 1960 meeting of Commonwealth prime ministers, there were signs of a weakening resolve on his part. Nor was there any indication that any of the other prime ministers intended to take a strong line. The prime ministers of Nigeria and Sierra Leone were due to take their place for the first time at the conference, and their attitudes were by no means clear. Nor did the United Front missions to the various African and Asian Commonwealth capitals succeed in their efforts to get firm commitments of support. Their impression at that time was that no prime minister was willing to make the first move, although several were ready to be "the first to be second." Although Tanganyika was not yet independent, the United Front had sought Nyerere's intervention. He sent a private communication to the assembling prime ministers in London, and he wrote an article, "Commonwealth Choice: South Africa or Us," for *The Observer* (London, March 12, 1961), in which he said: "We believe that the principles of the Commonwealth would be betrayed by an affirmative answer to South Africa's application for readmission as a Republic. Inevitably, therefore, we are forced to say that to vote for South Africa is to vote us [Tanganyika] out." Those in a good position to judge what happened agree that Nyerere's intervention was a crucial factor in the subsequent events that led to South Africa's withdrawal from the Commonwealth.

During 1961, interest in PAFMECA was shown in a new quarter. After Kenyatta's release, Haile Selassie, Emperor of Ethiopia, invited him to visit Addis Ababa. The Emperor was naturally concerned about the policy a future Kenya Government might follow over the Somali demand for the transfer of the Northern Frontier District in Kenya. He was delighted to find that the Kenyan leaders were determined to resist the demands for the transfer of the NFD for the cause of a Greater Somalia. Wishing to identify Ethiopia more closely with Kenya and its neighbors, the Emperor sought membership in PAFMECA. At that time, the constitution did not allow for affiliation by government.

Ethiopia's interest in PAFMECA deepened Somalia's earlier interest in it. Somalia's economy is closely connected with East Africa's, and Somalia could hope, within PAFMECA, to find a Pan-African solution to its frontier claims. Thus, in 1961, PAFMECA found itself extending from the Horn of Africa all the way to South Africa. It accepted an invitation to hold its fourth conference in Addis Ababa, on February 2–10, 1962.

Five important results were achieved by the Addis Ababa conference. First, by admitting Ethiopia and Somalia to membership, the scope of a possible federation was widened. The Emperor himself committed Ethiopia to this idea. The Somali delegation expressed a similar interest in becoming associated with a wider federation. Second, by accepting affiliations from nationalist organizations in South Africa, South West Africa, and the three High Commission Territories in Southern Africa, it officially drew these movements into its orbit—a decision formally recognized by the change of the name of the organization to the Pan-African Freedom Movement of East, Central, and Southern Africa (PAFMECSA). Third, it established the principle of governments and nationalist movements having equal rights of membership. This was made possible by the adoption of a new constitution allowing membership "to all nationalist organizations and governments which accept the aims and policy of PAFMECSA and are striving for the liberation of Africa." Fourth, for the first time, it turned its attention seriously to the problems of Central and Southern Africa. It set itself a program of priorities: first Northern Rhodesia, second Southern Rhodesia, next Southern Africa and Mozambique. To give special emphasis to its priorities, it chose Kenneth Kaunda of Northern Rhodesia as the first Chairman of PAFMECSA. Fifth, it abandoned its professed support for nonviolence. The new constitution omitted from its Aims and Objects "to champion nonviolence in the African nationalist struggles for freedom and prosperity," proclaiming instead the objective of uniting the people of Eastern, Central, and Southern Africa, "in order to rid these countries of imperialism, white supremacy, exploitation and social degradation by stepped-up nationalist activities to attain self-determination and establish democratic governments for the social and economic well-being of the people."

The presence at the conference of the "Black Pimpernel," Nelson Mandela, one of the outstanding figures in the South African liberation movement, made a strong impression. The possibility of the struggle in South Africa turning to violence began to be accepted as perhaps inevitable. The language of violence was often heard in debate. There was great applause, for example, when John Msonthi, one of the Malawi Congress representatives, said: "Force is bound to be used because it is the only language the imperialists can hear."

On the negative side, the Addis Ababa conference brought two problems to the surface: the relations between PAFMECSA and the AAPO, and a latent hostility to Arabs from certain quarters. The AAPO had sent two delegates to the conference: Secretary General Abdoulaye Diallo and AATUF leader John Tettegah. Although the relationships between the two organizations were thrashed out, they were not entirely clarified. There was a suggestion that PAFMECSA was following a course of its own and was in danger of letting regionalism cloud its continental vision. Nkrumah had warned (June 4, 1962) that "regional associations and territorial groupings can only be other forms of balkanization unless they are conceived within the framework of continental union." That he did not have only the UAM in mind at the time was shown by the fact that Tettegah, at a press conference in Addis Ababa, repeated this warning in almost the same terms, adding: "So long as we remain balkanized, *regionally or territorially*, we shall be at the mercy of colonialism and imperialism."

PAFMECSA in Central Africa and the Congo: 1962. PAF-MECSA played a leading role in helping UNIP to emerge as the strongest party in the October, 1962, elections in Northern Rhodesia and subsequently in helping to consolidate the territory's first predominantly African government (an event that precipitated the final breakup of the Central African Federation and had important repercussions in Katanga and the rest of the Congo). The following episode is one of the most striking examples of the success of a Pan-African enterprise.

The Addis Ababa conference had taken place at a time when Kaunda's party was in serious difficulties brought on by the protracted negotiations to get an acceptable constitution. It was under considerable pressure from Sir Roy Welensky's UFP and from Harry Nkumbula's ANC (supported by Moise Tshombe). There was the risk that UNIP might again be proscribed. Northern Rhodesia itself was in a state of incipient violence. Kaunda's leadership was being seriously challenged because of his unwillingness to abandon negotiations in favor of more militant, or even violent, methods of struggle. In this situation, UNIP's leadership looked to Pan-African support to enable it to do three things: to counteract the influence of the advocates of violence on the party rank and file; to increase the pressure on Britain to agree to a new constitution; and to establish an alternative party headquarters outside Northern Rhodesia in case UNIP was outlawed.

At this decisive stage in the liberation struggle in Northern Rhodesia, UNIP's leadership got considerable support from the Pan-African movement as a whole, but particularly from PAFMECSA. UNIP was given a firm base in Dar es Salaam. PAFMECSA's Freedom Fund (established at the Addis Ababa conference) was devoted exclusively to UNIP's needs at that time. The African Freedom Action Group was set up in Dar es Salaam under the sponsorship of PAFMECSA, TANU, UNIP, and the World Peace Brigade for Nonviolent Action. It planned a nonviolent march into Northern Rhodesia, to take place if UNIP was proscribed or if the constitutional negotiations in London failed again. Although the march, in fact, never did take place, the group's existence was reckoned by those in a position to know to have been of great value in keeping up the morale of UNIP's supporters by holding out the prospect of militant Pan-African action. Finally, PAFMECSA's leaders and several Commonwealth African prime ministers used their influence with the British Government to urge changes in the Northern Rhodesian constitution. When, in the end, changes were made, the new constitution still left UNIP facing an almost impossible task in the elections scheduled for October, 1962. It needed money, transport, and propaganda material. Again, aid came from several Pan-African quarters, not least from PAFMECSA. Tanganyika's radio was used for UNIP's election campaign; election material was printed in Tanganyika and distributed from there; funds were raised.

The elections confirmed UNIP's position of authority. It won 59,648 out of the 76,313 African votes on the Lower Roll; but it emerged with only 14 seats, compared with the UFP's 16 and the ANC's 7 seats. To form the government, it needed an alliance with Nkumbula's ANC. Such an alliance would finally frustrate Sir Roy Welensky's UFP, deprive it of control in Northern Rhodesia (as the Malawi Congress had already done in Nyasaland), and hasten the downfall of the Central African Federation. PAFMECSA came in to help in the negotiations to bring UNIP and ANC together. The main problem was how to disengage the ANC from the arms of Tshombe, to whom it was greatly indebted for support. (The ANC-UFP electoral alliance on the other hand had not survived the elections.) The task of persuading Nkumbula to negotiate with Kaunda was a lot easier than getting him to stick to his arrangements. His own difficulty was how to come to terms with Kaunda (known for his hostility to Katanga secessionism), while at the same time conciliating Tshombe. For Kaunda, too, the situation was tricky: how to get the necessary majority to give Northern Rhodesia its first African government without making concessions to Katanga.

The sequence of events from October to December, 1962, provides an interesting example of the interplay of Pan-African forces.

PAFMECSA sent an executive member to sound out Tshombe. (This member, a representative from Somalia, was, incidentally, captivated by the Katanga leader.) At the same time, two senior PAFMECSA officials went to Nkumbula: He demanded that either the Katanga government or Tshombe's party CONAKAT, should be allowed to join PAFMECSA. The words were Nkumbula's, but the voice was undoubtedly Tshombe's. The Katanga leader had been quick to seize the importance of the Northern Rhodesian election results. These, he saw, foreshadowed the defeat of his ally, Sir Roy Welensky, and the emergence of a hostile Northern Rhodesia in place of the formerly friendly one that had secured his back door. Tshombe urged Nkumbula to use his bargaining position to secure Kaunda's good will and to get him to use his position as PAFMECSA's chairman to admit Katanga to membership. (These proposals were subsequently raised directly with Kaunda by Tshombe.) Katanga's membership in a Pan-African grouping like PAFMECSA was important to Tshombe because his staunchest friends were beginning to waver. They had recently warned him that unless he could break out of his isolation in Africa, his position could not be held much longer. With nemesis close at hand, Tshombe perhaps felt he had nothing to lose. Even though Kaunda had explicitly told him in a private conversation that Katanga could not be considered for membership, Tshombe nevertheless used the pretext of his meetings with Nkumbula, Kaunda, and the PAFMECSA delegation to claim that he was about to be taken into PAFMECSA. This claim was broadcast over Radio Elisabethville, and assiduously disseminated by the "Katanga Lobby" in Europe, in the United States, and, particularly, in Britain. It is astonishing how widely these reports were believed in financial and diplomatic circles. They became an acute embarrassment to Kaunda and PAFMECSA, and they caused considerable anxiety to the Congo central government (until then an inactive PAFMECSA affiliate). For a time, they were inclined to suspect that an ANC-UNIP coalition might be bought at the cost of Northern Rhodesia's supporting secessionist Katanga, or even that the two might confederate—an idea assiduously promoted by Nkumbula. PAFMECSA's next move was to encourage Nkumbula to accompany Kaunda to London as a joint delegation to the British Government to demand Northern Rhodesia's right of secession from the Federation (a point on which both were agreed). Arrangements were made for Nkumbula to meet Nyerere and Kenyatta en route to London. Both the PAFMECSA leaders welcomed him warmly into the Pan-African fold, but both again confirmed that there could be no question of Katanga joining PAFMECSA. Nevertheless, on his arrival in London, Nkumbula continued to advocate Tshombe's cause while still holding to the coalition agreement. Meanwhile, in London, it was arranged that Kaunda and two PAFMECSA officials (Peter Mbiyu Koinange and Bhoke Munanka) should meet the Congo Foreign Minister, Justin Bomboko, on his way from the U.N. to Léopoldville. It was then that the decision was taken to arrange an urgent meeting of PAFMECSA in Léopoldville, with the primary aim of publicly discounting the reports that PAFMECSA was showing friendship for Katanga. On December 28, the conference opened in Léopoldville with the majority of the leading PAFMECSA figures present. It was the first time that the Congolese leaders themselves had attended a PAFMECSA conference. But by then the die was cast in Katanga; the conference was able to send a message to the U.N. Secretary General giving "unqualified support to action now being taken by U.N. forces in Katanga. . . . We oppose any talk of cease-fire till operation is completed."

Although none of the Congolese leaders committed themselves in any way to joining in a federation with East and Central Africa, the effect of Tshombe's maneuver had been to bring the Congo Government more intimately into the orbit of PAFMECSA's activities.

But the main enterprise survived: The UNIP-ANC coalition government held uneasily together, while Katanga secessionism was being smashed. The British Government accepted the reality of African majority rule in Northern Rhodesia. The right of Northern Rhodesia to secede was conceded; and this brought the end of the Central African Federation in sight.

Looking back now, one can see that the turning point in this major transformation of the Central African situation dates from the moment UNIP was helped to maintain its leadership and organization in February, 1962. From then on it was given sustained help and encouragement until it emerged from the October elections as the dominant political force. What would have happened if UNIP had been left to fight alone, without support from the Pan-African forces at large and PAFMECSA in particular? Its chances of success at that critical point would not have been great.

The preceding account of events shows what is not usually easy to describe: (1) the way in which Pan-Africanism works; (2) the nature of the relationship between nationalist movements and Pan-African organizations; (3) the interdependence of nationalist movements and independent African states; and (4) the dynamic interplay of political forces in present-day Africa.

PAFMECSA, MOZAMBIQUE, AND OTHER SOUTHERN AFRICAN COUNTRIES: 1962. The relationship between PAFMECSA and the liberation movement in Mozambique can only be briefly touched upon. Its role was to succeed in establishing a united liberation front, FRELIMO, in place of the rival groups of UDENAMO (National Democratic Union of Mozambique) and MANU (Mozambique African National Union). This is the first positive example of a Pan-African initiative succeeding in uniting different wings of a liberation movement. It is too early yet to know if FRELIMO's unity will be preserved; but the fact of its achievement, requiring the cooperation both of the Mozambique parties led by Mondlane and of PAF-MECSA's leaders, is important.

However, it was less easy to eliminate rivalries in countries like South Africa and Basutoland, where politics are much more sophisticated and where differences sometimes derive from fundamental disagreements about tactics and principles. The rivalries in Angola, too, are likely to be less tractable than those of Mozambique. Territories offering more reasonable prospects for achieving unified nationalist movements are South West Africa, Bechuanaland, and Swaziland.

TOWARD FEDERATION: THE EAST AFRICAN COMMON SERVICES ORGANIZATION. EACSO is the most advanced interterritorial institution so far developed in Africa. It has the decisive advantage of being financially almost self-supporting, and of operating in a single region. Even so, it remains an imperfect instrument for effective political union or even for federation. Its importance (apart from its services) is that it is a functioning institution around which the forces favoring closer union can coalesce.

EACSO grew in 1961 out of the old East Africa High Commission, established fourteen years before as a colonial-type organization. The High Commission had succeeded in developing the major transport, communication, power, and other essential services under state ownership and interstate control. It also laid the basis for an East African Common Market of 22 million peoples—one of its strongest assets. The East African Common Market exists by virtue of the arrangements that were imposed by the British Government when it had complete responsibility for the East African territories. To some extent, the High Commission had management responsibilities over the operation of the Common Market, and had responsibility also for economic and industrial coordination. The EACSO Constitution specifically excluded any responsibility for control or management of the Common Market Currency and Economic Development Coordination. The Constitution provides that EACSO shall offer machinery for the coordination of any matters of mutual interest to the participating territories, including economic matters. This machinery has been fully exploited, the most important case being the use of the EACSO machinery for the proposed negotiations with the European Common Market.

Although EACSO has no economic control over the territories, the recent appointment of an EACSO Economic Adviser, after consultation with the territorial governments, is already beginning to have the result of bringing the territories closer together in the planning of economic development and in the taking of joint action on fiscal and currency matters related to the proposed Central Bank.

The position therefore is that the East African Common Market exists, but only by the common consent and agreement of the three governments that operate through the adoption of common tax, external tariff, and excise measures in their annual budgets and through their common Currency Board. There is a legacy of common legislation on all fiscal, commercial, and industrial matters. EACSO's role in this field is to collect income-and-company-tax revenue and customs-and-excise-duty revenue in accordance with rates fixed in the territorial budgets (which are the same), and transmit the proceeds to the governments, after deducting collecting expenses and the amounts that should go into the distributable pool fund. EACSO also has some commerce-and-industrial-coordination functions but not extensive ones. It controls two self-contained, self-financing services: the East African Railways and Harbours and the Posts and Telegraphs. It controls a further twenty nonself-contained services, ranging from civil aviation to statistics.

But EACSO has no economic or fixed control over the three territories. It has not yet established a common economic policy, although steps have been taken in this direction. In the past, strong feelings had grown up in Tanganyika and Uganda that an unfair share of the cake was going to Kenya. This feeling has made for suspicion about federation in some quarters.

Another hopeful factor in the growth of the federation idea was the ready willingness shown by all three territorial governments in March, 1963, to entrust EACSO's staff with responsibility for preparing the case presented by the East African Common Market to the European Economic Community. Although the interests of the three territories are by no means equally affected by the policies of the EEC, they responded to each other's needs; a joint delegation presented the case for East Africa in Brussels.

THE PRESENT POSITION IN EACSO. EACSO has only three members at present—Kenya, Uganda, and Tanganyika. Its constitution allows Zanzibar to share in the use of its common services. Since the merging of Zanzibar with Tanganyika as Tanzania, they will hold a joint membership.

Ethiopia sent a team of senior representatives to study the work of EACSO; Somalia, though it agreed to send a similar delegation, has not yet done so. Both have sent observers to a meeting of EACSO's Central Legislative Assembly. Full membership has been offered in principle to both these countries. Mauritius sent representatives for discussions with both PAFMECSA and EACSO. There has been no attempt by any of the other PAFMECSA territories to join EACSO.

THE PROBLEMS FACING EACSO. In earlier sections, there has been some discussion of the likely areas of support and opposition to the idea that EACSO should be turned into a fully operative federal organization or political union. The major obstacle lies with Uganda's traditionalist forces, especially the Kabaka Yekka. There are also strong reservations by some elements in the Democratic Party. Uganda, while willing to accept an EACSO kind of association, is by no means unanimous on the value of a wider federation: There is strong feeling in Uganda that her own internal problems must be solved first. This, however, is not the view of Prime Minister Milton Obote, who is anxious to see the rapid growth of a wider East African Federation. Although this remains his attitude, the economic nationalist forces in Uganda have forced him to hold his hand.

In the case of Mauritius, the only serious possible difficulty would be if its government felt the Asian communities of East Africa were not being given fair treatment.

Ethiopia's adherence, potentially important because of the contribution an expanded home economy could make to the size of the Common Market, would raise practical problems. It is hard to see Ethiopia fitting into the transport and communications services already established or integrating its services with those of EACSO. The relative lack of economic development in Ethiopia and the nature of its present government could produce difficulties when the time comes to discuss effective unification.

Somalia's membership would be a much easier affair were it not for the disputes over the right of Somali peoples in Kenya and Ethiopia to join in a Greater Somalia. Theoretically, a Pan-African framework should provide the ideal solution for the Somalia land problems; but so long as the governments of both Ethiopia and Kenya hold strongly to the inalienable line of their present frontiers, any thought of easy solutions must be ruled out.

Rwanda and Burundi would both seem to be natural members of EACSO. Their main trade routes have traditionally gone through East Africa; thousands of their migrant workers find employment in Uganda every year. But the possible difficulty to association is the lack of common experience in administration and the language barrier. In Rwanda, too, time will be needed to get over PAFMECSA's earlier support for the party of the exiled Mwami. Another difficulty is the strained relations between Rwanda and Burundi.

The Congo's likely future relations are obscure. Its eastern province, Katanga, forms a natural unit with Zambia. But strong forces pull the Congo toward the Francophone economic unit, the OAC-ME, with whom it has territorial contiguity, language affinity, and elements of common experience in education and administration. There are also forces operating against these pulls—e.g., the economic and political weakness of the OACME territories contiguous to the Congo, differences with the regime of Congo (Brazzaville), and conflicting Belgian and French economic interests. Until the Congo finally achieves a degree of political stability and discovers its authentically representative government, it would be hard to say whether it will accept the pull toward Central and East Africa or toward Equatorial and West Africa.

Of the Portuguese territories, Mozambique is more likely to become associated with its immediate neighbors than with Angola. Mozambique's freedom struggle will be fought with the help of the East and Central African governments, and this will have a binding effect. Angola's future depends largely on the way its own struggle develops, and, to some extent, on the future course of its northern neighbor, the Congo.

Of the three Central African territories, one can expect both Zambia and Malawi to become associated with an EACSO type of organization. Whether either, or both, will be ready to join in a more effective political union is less certain. It would be hard to make any worth-while guesses about the future role of Southern Rhodesia, except that it is likely one day again to move closer to Northern Rhodesia; therefore its future may to some extent be determined by what Northern Rhodesia does. Ultimately, the relationships of all three Central African territories are likely to depend on the kind of political and economic unity the three major East African territories achieve. The present dark uncertainties in Southern Africa rob any guesses of all possible value.

Finally, there is the problem of Kenya—the copestone of the structure. A Kenya in disintegration after independence could set back the whole idea for years; equally, a vigorous, purposeful Kenya could move the whole enterprise forward with great speed. A KANU-dominated government is likely to work more easily with its neighbors than a KADU-dominated government. But even a KADU government would be likely to take a cooperative attitude. A KANU-KADU coalition government, on the other hand, would reflect the weaknesses of a divided Kenya, and it would be hard to say how this would affect the federation; it would probably delay and weaken it.

WHAT KIND OF UNITY? Nowhere in any of the numerous speeches, policy statements, or resolutions produced by PAFMECSA and its leaders does one find the slightest indication of what political and economic institutions they have in mind when they speak of federation. There is only one exception: Nyerere's first memorandum to the second Conference of Independent African States, in 1960 (see page 394). Otherwise, there appears to be almost a deliberate avoidance of any discussion about the kind of unity envisaged. The usual reason given for this apparent lack of planning is that useful discussion must await the independence of the territories principally concerned. There are other more likely reasons. PAFMECSA's leaders were too deeply buried in their own struggles to spend much time thinking out the real problems of unification. However, their practical experience of trying to achieve effective territorial constitutions and administrations will no doubt contribute greatly toward clarifying ideas when the time comes to tackle the question of federation or unification. Another reason is that PAFMECSA's leaders are anxious at this stage not to increase the grounds for objections to unification by being too precise about their objectives. For although there is no public discussion on the possible alternatives, there is no lack of private discussion. Three ideas compete for attention: (1) That progress should come through the gradual transformation of EACSO as a territorially expanding, regional economic institution with strictly limited political powers. This is the pragmatic, functionalist approach. (2) That the need is for a confederation, limited in the first place to the East African territories (Kenya, Uganda, Tanzania), but allowing for associate membership and subsequent widening federation. The territorial units would each retain much of their separate sovereignty. (This would be the limit of KADU, the Uganda Democratic Party, the Zanzibar Nationalist Party, the Malawi Congress, and UNIP.) (3) That the interlinking problems of East Africa demand complete political unification—e.g., Nyerere's 1960 proposal when he cited the unification of the two Somalis as the ideal solution. Unification along these lines would involve the creation of interterritorial national parties. Two possibilities would be the unification of KANU, TANU, UPC, and ASP as one movement.

(In this area of discussion, the relevance of Tanganyika's decision to convert itself into a one-party state naturally arises. Is this a possible pattern for future development? Does it make the task of interterritorial cooperation easier or harder to achieve?) This jostling of private ideas is bound to surface once Kenya gets its independence within the next twelve months. That will be the time of real challenge to the PAFMECSA leaders working for closer association.

PAFMECSA's LEADERSHIP. A word about the PAFMECSA leaders. There is no question about Nyerere's being the pivotal figure; his close colleagues in Tanganyika on the PAFMECSA front are Oscar Kambona, Minister of External Affairs and Defense; Rashidi Kawawa, Deputy President; and Bhoke Munanka, Deputy Secretary General of PAFMECSA. In the early stages of PAFMECA's development, Nyerere's closest collaborators in Kenya were Tom Mboya, Minister of Justice; Dr. J. G. Kiano, Minister of Commerce and Industries; and James Gichuru, Minister of Finance. Since his release, Kenyatta has worked closely with Nyerere. Oginga Odinga, too, has moved into closer association; and Peter Mbiyu Koinange has become Secretary General of PAFMECSA. Among the Uganda leaders, Milton Obote stands out as the leading figure. One has seen growing up within PAFMECSA's organization a triumvirate of East African parties (TANU, KANU, and UPC), and a close grouping of powerful political leaders, the majority of whom hold important government positions. To this group should be added the name of Kenneth Kaunda. As Chairman of PAFMECSA, he came to stand close to the leaders of the triumvirate. The only other Central African leader who played an active role in the organization was Malawi's former Minister of Education, Kanyama Chiume.

But while it is possible to identify this group as constituting a nucleus, it would be wrong to conclude that there has been any deliberate attempt by PAFMECSA either to exclude or reduce the participation of other nationalist movements in East Africa. Both Nyerere and Obote, for example, were at great pains to maintain close relations with the KADU leader, Ronald Ngala. There was never any attempt to organize a countermovement to the present PAFMECSA leadership, and there were no rival groups within its organization.

Problems Facing the Liberation Movements

Every liberation movement in Southern Africa has produced at least two rival parties: ANC and PAC in South Africa; UPA and MPLA in Angola; SWANU and SWAPO in South West Africa; UNIP and ANC in Northern Rhodesia; the Democratic Party and two wings of the Peoples' Party in Bechuanaland; the Democratic Party and no fewer than four wings of the Progressive Party in Swaziland; the BCP, BNP, and the Maramatlou Freedom Party in Basutoland; ZANU and ZAPU in Southern Rhodesia; FRELIMO and UDENAMO in Mozambique, as we have seen, have achieved a unified freedom movement.

The causes and nature of some of these rifts have been discussed in earlier papers; what is relevant here is the extent to which these schisms have prevented effective aid being given by the Pan-African movement to the liberation struggle in Southern Africa. Confronted with competing claims, the majority of independent African states have, on the whole, preferred not to take sides. In many cases "not taking sides" has meant either providing minimal aid or, at any rate, giving considerably less than might otherwise have been expected. There are, however, instances of a choice being made in favor of one movement over its rival. Examples of this are the support for the UPA by the Congo (Léopoldville) and Tunisia; the support for the MPLA by members of the former Casablanca group (at least in principle, if not always in practice), and the support by Ghana for the BCP in Basutoland and the Nquku faction of the SPP in Swaziland. In the case of South Africa and South West Africa, the general tendency has been to avoid making a clear choice between the competing claims. There have been a few notable instances of the rival African political capitals trying to play off one group against the other for the sake of gaining a particularist Pan-African initiative. But, on the whole, this type of maneuver has not been carried very far. The main interest of the typically Pan-Africanist states has been to encourage the unification of the divided political movements (though not of the divided labor movements). Such an attempt was made, for example, by Ghana in calling its conference of Freedom Fighters in Accra (June 4, 1962). "You must forget your theoretical differences and minor political polemics," President Nkrumah told the conference. But this good advice led nowhere. Nor is it likely to do so without proper consideration being given to the often deep ideological and tactical differences that have produced the schismatic movements.

Two questions offer themselves: (1) What practical steps can Pan-Africanists take to help bring about unity? (2) If unity cannot be achieved, will the time come when, at the Pan-African level, decisions will be made to select a single movement for support? [2]

The second question is bound to present itself for more serious consideration in the future than it has in the past. The difficulties of making a choice are enormous. Will support for one party lead to rival Pan-African groupings supporting another? On the other hand, the prospect of allowing the rifts to grow is menacing. Not the least of the dangerous possibilities is that Cold War politics will seriously infiltrate the contest for power, as happened in the Congo. (One also remembers the Spanish Civil War.) There is already considerable evidence that some liberation movements will find greater favor than others with certain Soviet or Western countries.

If the forces of Pan-Africanism fail to stem this danger, the already serious problems in Southern Africa must become much graver; hence the role within the nationalist movements of exclusive groups that owe their greater loyalty to ideologies associated with power politics is clearly relevant to any serious study of this problem.

The Role of the Major Powers

If the leading Western powers could agree to follow a policy of actively opposing the regimes of South Africa, of Southern Rhodesia, and of the Portuguese in Africa, the task of the liberation forces would become much less difficult. Therefore, a primary objective of the nationalist movements must be to look to the independent African states to apply firm pressure on Western countries to change their policies. There is evidence already of how such pressure has changed the direction of the policies of some of the Western countries. The intervention by the Afro-Asian members of the Commonwealth of Nations that resulted in South Africa's withdrawal from the Commonwealth is one clear example of how such pressure has worked. There are other examples. A change in Western policy would also greatly diminish the dangers of Cold War politics in the struggles of the liberation movements.

The role of the Communist countries is much more straightforward. They give full encouragement to the liberation movements but generally choose to support one party in each country. The compli-

[2] When the OAU established its National Liberation Committee in 1963, it tried at first to do just this; but although it managed for a time to achieve limited success in Angola, Mozambique, and South West Africa, these efforts did not last, and the committee was compelled to recast its ideas.

cating factor in the roles of the Russians and the Chinese is that they support Communist parties inside Southern Africa as well as the "national liberation movement." The relationship between these Communist groups and the nationalist movements can, and does, produce a strong element of divisiveness in the liberation struggle. (The experience of the FLN in Algeria with the Algerian Communist Party—both during the liberation struggle and after independence— is a good example of the problems that face the nationalist movements.)

CONCLUSIONS. Seven major factors will determine the effectiveness of the thrust by the nationalist and Pan-African movements against the five territories of Southern Africa still under white minority rule: (1) how quickly newly independent states can consolidate power within their own frontiers; (2) how effectively the ideas for a wider unity of states in East and Central Africa can be implemented, and how well they can be correlated with the continental movement for unity; (3) how much agreement can be obtained at a Pan-African level in providing effective support for the liberation movements; (4) how much success there will be for the efforts either to eliminate altogether or to minimize the conflicts between liberation movements operating in the same territory; (5) how successful the Pan-African elements will be in winning control inside territorial liberation movements and preventing them from becoming nationalistic; (6) how effectively Cold War politics, and other external rivalries, can be excluded from operating through the liberation movements; and (7) how successful the efforts will be to persuade Western countries to change those aspects of their policies which are harmful to the liberation struggle.

Postscript

This concluding section has been written just two years after the completion of the original paper. In the intervening years, significant political changes occurred in East and Central Africa. Kenya, Nyasaland (Malawi), and Northern Rhodesia (Zambia) achieved their independence; Zanzibar was first swept by revolution and then drawn into union with Tanganyika to form the Republic of Tanzania. The secessionist state Katanga belongs to the past, and Tshombe has switched his role from that of a separatist leader to that of the unifying Premier of the Congo Central Government. Somalia was brought to the verge of open hostilities with Kenya and Ethiopia. The first shots of a violent liberatory struggle were fired in Mozambique.

PAFMECSA itself went into limbo to comply with the Organization of African Unity's requirement of its members that regional political organizations should be dissolved. And, finally, all that now remains of the promise that an East African Federation should come with the independence of Kenya is unfulfilled hopes. The consummation of this ideal in the foreseeable future is not rated very high. Even the ability of EACSO to survive in its present form is now in question.

These dismal results were not unexpected; they were in fact predicted by President Nyerere in his 1960 statements, in which he warned that all might be lost unless federation preceded the separate independence of the East African states. "To those people who would wait until the countries are separately independent I say that they do not know human nature. You must rule out the question of federation after we take our seats as sovereign states in the United Nations." [3]

Even so, the gap between success and failure was a narrow one. On June 5, 1963, the leaders of Kenya, Uganda, and Tanganyika met in Nairobi and issued a "Declaration of Federation by the Governments of East Africa" in which they proclaimed these intentions:

We, the leaders of the people and Governments of East Africa . . . pledge ourselves to the political federation of East Africa. Our meeting today is motivated by the spirit of Pan-Africanism and not by mere selfish regional interests. For some years we have worked together in the PAFMECSA where we have accepted common objectives and ideas and created the essential spirit of unity between ourselves and among our people. We are happy that with KANU's victory in the Kenya elections we now have in the three East African countries governments which are fully committed to genuine African nationalism and Pan-African unity. The East African High Commission and its successor the Common Services Organization have taught us the value of links in the economic field. . . . Thus the value of working together has been adequately demonstrated in the EACSO and in the Common Market, but the scope for further joint action remains wide. We are convinced that the time has now come to create . . . [a] central political authority. A working party is being established which will prepare a framework of a draft constitution for the Federation of East Africa. It will report back to a full Conference of East African Governments. In its work it will consult with the three Governments and with their consent may co-opt constitutional or other experts. The EACSO will be associated with these deliberations.

[3] *The Times* (London), November 5, 1960.

The Working Party was set up and, in fact, reached unanimous agreement on all major issues. In the words of Tanganyika's Foreign Minister, Mr. Oscar Kambona:

> In view of what has subsequently occurred, I wish to make it clear that the members of the Working Party reached unanimous agreement at this meeting on all major issues. We were able to give the lawyers instructions about the type of Federation constitution we thought should be established in East Africa. These instructions covered the disposition of executive power in the Federal Government, the composition of the Legislature and the division of power between a Senate, representing the principle of equality, and a House of Representatives elected on a popular vote. We were also able to tell the lawyers that we were in favor of a strong federation and, in the light of this recommendation, indicate to them in broad outline how legislative power should be divided between the Federation and its constituent states. We also agreed on the site of the Federal capital.[4]

But by the time the heads of government met again, this time in Kampala on June 29–30, the picture had changed dramatically. The Uganda delegation announced that they could no longer be bound by previous decisions. Disagreement was over the disposition of the executive power in the federation and the relationship between the Senate and the House of Representatives. Uganda now took the view that the powers of the Senate should at least be equal to those of the House of Representatives. Kenya and Tanganyika jointly agreed that if so much power were given to the Senate (based as it was on the principle of state equality), the states would overshadow and weaken the federal center.

Subsequent discussions in the Working Party widened the gulf between Uganda and the other two states, especially when the former added to its objections that external affairs and citizenship should be regarded as exclusively federal subjects. The implications of these reservations were described by Mr. Kambona:

> If each constituent state in the Federation was to retain control over external affairs and be separately represented in the United Nations, how could the international personality of the Federation be identified in the eyes of the world? And how could the ordinary man in East Africa regard the new Federation as the focus of his political loyalty? These questions were never answered by our friends from Uganda.[5]

[4] Statement to the Tanzania Assembly, June 23, 1964.
[5] *Ibid.*

It was soon to become clear that Uganda was not only concerned about questions affecting its national entity, but that the forces of economic nationalism were beginning to gain the upper hand inside Premier Obote's camp. The first shot in this cause was fired with the demand that each of the states should retain its right to raise its own external capital.

By the time the Working Party came to hold its next meeting in Nairobi, on July 15, the members could agree on only one point: that the differences between Uganda and the others were of a kind that called into question the whole conception of federation. Nevertheless, efforts at salvage continued with a further meeting of the Working Party in Dar Es Salaam on August 9 and 10; this time Zanzibar for the first time joined in the discussions. But, by then, relations between Tanganyika and Uganda were ruffled, with some Ugandans more and more inclined to argue that the Tanganyikans, as the poorest members of the community, stood to gain most from the deal, and were, therefore, motivated less by Pan-African idealism than by self-interest. Such arguments from Uganda's economic nationalists were strengthened by two other contentions. First, that the influence of the African voice in the U.N. depended on having as many votes as possible; hence East Africa should keep its three seats (or four, if Zanzibar were included) instead of reducing it to one. Second, that the OAU Charter was against regional federations. This latter point (which is wholly inaccurate) reflected the views of President Nkrumah —whose opposition to PAFMECSA's role has been previously noted, and who openly and strenuously intervened against the formation of an East African federation as inimical to ultimate African political unity.

When the heads of government met in Nairobi on January 14, 1964, it was merely to confirm the inevitable. Dr. Obote explained the political difficulties he was facing at home over the proposed federation, and urged that it would be more helpful to concentrate first on the economic aspects of closer association. They concluded: "It was agreed that there were certain problems connected with economic development which need to be sorted out urgently for the harmonious development of all three states, and Ministers or Directors in charge of economic planning should meet to examine and advise on these problems."

At the next meeting, held in Kampala on March 17, Tanganyika raised the question of the East African common market, explaining its dissatisfaction with the existing arrangements. This view confirmed some Ugandans in their suspicion that Tanganyika was interested in federation primarily because of its own economic interests. Relations had become so strained that nothing further could be usefully discussed. An attempt to deal with these deteriorating relations was made by the three heads of government at Nairobi on April 10. Some progress was made in at least clearing the air and in saving EACSO by accepting the justice of the claims that had been put forward by Tanganyika at the previous Kampala meeting.

The climax to this discouraging round of talks came at the final meeting of the Working Party in Kampala on May 30, when in response to a direct question from Mr. Kambona as to whether they thought that political federation was not feasible, the leader of the Uganda delegation, Felix Onama, confirmed that that indeed was their view.

Since that time, federation has remained a lively political issue, but no further efforts have been made to revive it as an immediately practical idea. The merging of Tanganyika and Zanzibar is the one positive step toward unification that has been taken, and President Nyerere is on record as saying that while he still hoped for federation with the other two East African countries, if that were not possible he would consider union with Kenya alone. For their part, President Kenyatta and Premier Obote have kept the door open to a resumption of negotiations when conditions are more propitious; both appear to feel the need for enough time to enable each of the states to overcome its internal problems.

But if there was little encouragement to be gained from the talks on political federation, developments toward greater economic cooperation were perhaps more fruitful. On June 17, the EACSO partners signed the Kampala Agreement on Economic Cooperation, which provides for: (1) higher output of an important range of goods in Tanganyika, with a corresponding reduction in imports; (2) exclusive rights for the United Republic in the manufacture of a further range of industrial goods for the whole East African market; (3) a temporary quota system for use in redressing trade imbalances between surplus and deficit countries; (4) increased purchases of United Republic products by Kenya and Uganda; (5) close consideration of the whole question of the future allocation of industry in East Africa by a committee of experts.

In accordance with the provision of the agreement, moves are being made which will reduce the annual trade imbalance between Tanzania and Kenya by 24 per cent. At the same time, the agreement accords Tanzania exclusive rights in the future development and operation in East Africa in respect of: (a) assembly and manufacture of Land Rovers; (b) truck assembly and manufacture (Tanzania to have rights for at least one type); (c) radio assembly and manufacture; (d) motor vehicle tires and tubes.

There has also been agreement to establish a joint East African shipping line. On the negative side of functional cooperation, there has been the failure to consolidate the growth of an integrated East African university and the unwillingness to establish a joint defense system.

What of the other former PAFMECSA members? Somalia and Ethiopia both expressed a continuing interest in a possible federation when the first meeting was held in Nairobi in June, 1963. Malawi and Zambia were kept fully informed throughout the negotiations. But Malawi's relations with Tanzania deteriorated sharply after the rupture in Banda's government toward the end of 1964, when he accused President Nyerere of giving support to his former ministers in their alleged efforts to overthrow his government. Relations with Zambia, however, have developed along more promising lines. The three East African governments have expressed a joint interest in seeing the fruition of a plan to build a railway line from Zambia through Tanzania to be linked to the East African railways and harbors system.

Discussion

ARNOLD BEICHMAN.   Peter Tobias, at the recent Kampala Confederation of Trade Unions Conference, said: "The greatest argument of the newly independent states in Africa is that once the national movement takes over, the Federal Trade Union as a free institution ceases to exist." I do not subscribe to that view. The right of free trade unions in Africa to exist and function was never questioned by African leaders during the colonial period. The trade unions in Africa had their martyrs who were killed in the struggle for freedom and trade unionism. The real question is what happens after independence not only to the free trade union, but to all institutions that we regard as bearing on the questions of freedom: freedom of the press, religion, and so on.

There are those authorities who seek to justify continuously what is happening in Africa. I personally do not see very much difference between the dictatorship of Duvalier in Haiti and things that are happening in Africa today. If one opposes Duvalier, I am sure you know what will happen. We used to hear a great deal about how the people of Hungary, East Germany, and Poland espoused freedom by risking their lives, and we should not deny that right in Africa after independence. Africa will have to develop a multiparty system, which today, in a sense, is not permitted. The African personality is no different from any other personality and it can only wither if we endow would-be dictators with stature and nobility and keep silent in the name of understanding and sympathy for the problem of the poor dictators. My sympathy is with the people, and I think Africa will rise or fall not merely by the amount of economic or financial subsidies from abroad or by the genius of its leaders, but by the power with which it enlists the African masses behind the struggle to make the word "freedom" a living entity and not a shabby slogan that some people in Africa would rather forget.

[EDDISON ZVOBGO, A. N. L. WINA, H. E. ALEX QUAISON-SACKEY, *and* THE REVEREND NDABANINGI SITHOLE *took sharp issue with Arnold Beichman's remarks. Each of them expressed regret that more time could not have been given both for Colin Legum to develop his paper and for them, as discussants, to speak more on the issue of the Pan-African unities. As African leaders, each felt impelled to use the few moments allotted to rebut Mr. Beichman.*]

EDDISON ZVOBGO.   [*Mr. Zvobgo said that African nationalist leaders had no argument with that premise of the ICFTU stating that trade-union movements should remain apart from and outside the control of nationalist political parties.*] What African nationalism does dispute, however, is the existence of trade unions that are affiliated with other international organizations and that use that affiliation to bifurcate, disrupt, and pervert the nationalist cause. The allegation that after independence the trade-union movements that have worked very hard to achieve freedom are necessarily oppressed and suppressed by nationalist parties is an exaggeration because one should recognize that in most of the African states where our economies are not yet diversified, every man and woman is a worker. Our nationalist parties are in essence workers' parties, and to establish a separate and challenging organization which may not in all essentials cooperate with the nationalist party is to create a new instrument that challenges and seeks to divert the nationalist energies from the very serious struggle against unemployment, against nationalist development and the consolidation of our newly won independence.

ARTHUR N. L. WINA.   I do not know how often we are going to have to repeat and repeat again that you cannot try and discover the minute particles of Western democracy in Africa. I say this because I am a bit disappointed, not unexpectedly, that Mr. Beichman should say that what is going on in Africa is one more form of dictatorship no different in any way from the dictatorship of Latin America or the dictatorships of Hitler and Mussolini.

If there were any country in Africa where people were forced against their will to maintain one party, then I would say that there is a grain of truth in that statement. But the truth of the matter is that in any country in Africa, political parties are free to organize but political parties themselves realize that you can get elected to power only if you enjoy public support. The facts of the matter are that in Ghana the public support is enjoyed by the CPP, in Tanganyika by TANU, in Northern Rhodesia by UNIP, in Nyasaland by the Malawi Congress, in Zimbabwe by ZAPU. And I can go on and on from one country to another and confirm our premise that it is not the political leadership that is forcing masses to join those parties to the exclusion of other organizations; it is the choice of the people that produces the one-party system in African countries. [As to the freedom of trade unions, Mr. Wina confirmed Mr. Zvobgo's analysis that, since Africa is a country of workers, the people identify their political leaders as being, if you will, the leaders in their struggle for better working conditions.]

ALEX QUAISON-SACKEY.   [Ambassador Quaison-Sackey thought that Mr. Beichman had raised issues that could be argued ad infinitum, but he considered Mr. Wina's answer to them sufficient. He then addressed himself to Mr. Legum's paper.] I am a strong believer in African unity. Anything and everything happening in Southern Africa, in East Africa, in PAFMECSA, indeed in any place in Africa, can be realistically and intelligently appraised only within the framework of African unity.

NDABANINGI SITHOLE.   [The last speaker at the conference suggested that basic erroneous concepts of African political heritage and thinking are pervasive. He cited Lord Hailey's work in which it was said that "self-

determination is a concept that was not born in the African world but was born in the Western world." Sithole said that this left the impression that the struggle in Africa for freedom arises out of an African emulation of the white man. He disagreed with this impression.] Those who live very close to nature know that the principle of self-determination is inherent in every living and moving thing. If you get hold of a chicken, for instance, you see it struggling, trying to get out of your grip so that it might exercise self-determination in the open air. So this principle for which the peoples of Africa are struggling is inherently human; it is as natural for people as for animals to try to pursue self-determination. I remember a comment that was made some time back that the black people of Southern Africa do not want to be ruled by other Africans, they want to be ruled by the white man. Then we said in our argument that if you are perfectly sure that the black man wants to be ruled by the white people, why don't you give them the vote so that they may vote for you? We were quite satisfied that the very fact that the white people were refusing to give the black masses the vote was sufficient proof that they knew that the black man did not want to be ruled by anybody except by himself.

Notes on the Contributors

GODFREY K. J. AMACHREE, formerly Solicitor General of Nigeria, was until recently U.N. Under Secretary for the Department of Trusteeship and Non-Self-Governing Territories. He has also served as Under Secretary in charge of U.N. Civilian Operations in the Congo.

BRIAN BASSINGTHWAIGHT, a South West African, is a student at Syracuse University. He has also studied at Lincoln University under a U.N. grant.

AUGUSTO T. P. BASTOS, an Angolan, has studied at the University of Lisbon and the School of Foreign Service at Georgetown University.

ARNOLD BEICHMAN, a free-lance journalist, has conducted a special study of trade unionism in Africa. His articles appear in the *Christian Science Monitor*, the *New York Herald Tribune*, and other leading American and British publications.

ANGIE BROOKS, Assistant Secretary of State of Liberia, has served as Assistant Attorney General of Liberia and was Professor of Law at the University of Liberia. She was with the Liberian mission to the U.N. General Assembly from 1954 to 1963.

CARLOS GONÇALVES CAMBANDO, representative of the Angolan National Liberation Front (FNLA) in the United States, was previously FNLA representative in Great Britain.

GWENDOLEN M. CARTER is Melville J. Herskovits Professor of African Affairs and Director of the Program of African Studies at Northwestern University. Previously Sophia Smith Professor of Government at Smith College, she is the author of *The Politics of Inequality* and *Independence for Africa*, is co-author of *Government and Politics in the Twentieth Century*, and has edited a series of volumes on African governments.

JOSEPH CHICUARRA, a graduate student at Fordham University, is Mozambique National Liberation Front (FRELIMO) representative in New York.

M. W. KANYAMA CHIUME, formerly Minister of the Departments of Education and of Social Development and Information in Malawi, is now living in exile in Dar es Salaam. His publications include *Nyasaland Speaks* and *Nyasaland Demands Independence and Secession*.

D. V. COWEN, formerly Head of the Department of Comparative Law and Dean of the Faculty of Law at the University of Cape Town, represented the Basuto in negotiations with Great Britain for reforms—and, subsequently, for a new constitution—for Basutoland. His publications include *The Foundations of Freedom*.

VICTOR C. FERKISS is Associate Professor of Government at Georgetown University. His books include *Foreign Aid: Moral and Political Aspects* and *Africa's Search for Identity*.

THOMAS M. FRANCK is Director of the Center for International Studies and Professor of Law at New York University. Among the books he has written are *East African Unity Through Law* and *Legal Aspects of the United Nations Action in the Congo*.

JAMES T. HARRIS, JR., Director of Education and Training at Corning Glass International, was Program Associate in the Ford Foundation Overseas Development Program, Middle East and Africa, and served as Secretary-General of the National School of Law and Administration in Léopoldville.

GEORGE M. HOUSER, Executive Director of the American Committee on Africa, has traveled extensively in Angola, the Congo (Léopoldville), and other parts of Africa. His publications include *Erasing the Color Line*.

THOMAS KARIS is Associate Professor of Political Science at the Baruch School of Business and Public Administration, City College of the City University of New York. He is co-editor (with Gwendolen M. Carter) of a two-volume *Documentary Survey of Non-White Political Movements in South Africa*.

THE REVEREND MARKUS KOOPER is a petitioner at the United Nations for the South West Africa National Union (SWANU). Previously, he fought attempts by the government to relocate the Namas and was a petitioner for his tribe at the United Nations.

F. JARIRETUNDU KOZONGUIZI, presently studying law in London, is President of the South West Africa National Union. He helped form the United Front—a coalition of the African National, South African Indian, and Pan-Africanist congresses.

JACOB KUHANGUA, a student at the time of the conference, is now Secretary General of the South West Africa Peoples Organization (SWAPO), party-in-exile with headquarters in Dar es Salaam.

COLIN LEGUM, Commonwealth Correspondent for *The Observer* (London), is the author of *Pan-Africanism: A Short Political Guide*, co-author of *South Africa: Crisis for the West*, and editor of *Africa: A Handbook to the Continent*.

ALLARD K. LOWENSTEIN, an attorney practicing in New York, represented South West African tribes at the United Nations in 1959–60. He has taught political science at North Carolina State College and Stanford University, and is the author of *Brutal Mandate*.

JOHN A. MARCUM, Director of the African Language and Area Center and Professor of Political Science at Lincoln University, has traveled extensively and conducted research in Africa. His articles have appeared in *Pan-Africanism Reconsidered, New Forces in Africa, The New Leader, Africa Report*, and *Africa Today*.

ACHKAR MAROF, Ambassador of Guinea to the United Nations, was a member of the Delegation of Guinea to the U.N. General Assembly from 1959 to 1964.

BLOKE MODISANE, a South African free-lance writer, is the author of *Blame Me on History*, as well as numerous articles and short stories.

EDUARDO C. MONDLANE, President of the Mozambique Liberation Front (MLF), is Assistant Professor of Anthropology on leave from the Maxwell Graduate School of Citizenship and Public Affairs at Syracuse University. Previously, he served with the U.N. African Trusteeship Department.

PAUL KHOTSO MOONYANE is a student at Lincoln University. He has been a participant in Basuto Congress Party conferences.

WILLIAM E. MORAN, JR., is Dean of the School of Foreign Service at Georgetown University, Consultant to the National Planning Association on African and Latin American Studies, and a member of the Advisory Committee of the Bureau of African Affairs, U.S. Department of State. He is the co-author of *Handbook of African Economic Development*.

JOAO NHAMBIU, a graduate student in political science at the Wharton School of Finance and Commerce, University of Pennsylvania, is President of the National Union of Mozambique Students (UNEMO).

LEWIS NKOSI, a writer and former radio producer for the Transcription Centre in London, was on the editorial staff of *Drum*. He is the author of *Home and Exile*, as well as articles in the *Spectator, The Observer* (London), and *The Guardian* (London).

MORLEY NKOSI is a student at New York University. He has served as Vice Chairman of the Witwatersrand Region of the Pan-African Congress (PAC) and assistant to the PAC representative in London.

F. TAYLOR OSTRANDER, Assistant to the Chairman at American Metal Climax, is Vice President of the African-American Chamber of Commerce.

ALEX QUAISON-SACKEY, formerly Ghana's Minister of Foreign Affairs, was President of the Nineteenth Session of the U.N. General Assembly and served for a number of years as Ambassador and Permanent Representative of Ghana to the United Nations. He is the author of *Africa Unbound*.

SAUNDERS REDDING, Johnson Professor of Literature at Hampton Institute, is a member of the Executive Council of AMSAC. He is the author of *On Being Negro in America* and *An American in India*, and is a frequent contributor to American periodicals.

ROBERT I. ROTBERG is Assistant Professor of History and Research Associate at the Center for International Affairs, Harvard University. He is the author of *The Rise of Nationalism in Central Africa: The Making of Malawi and Zambia, 1873–1964* and *A Political History of Tropical Africa*.

LESLIE I. RUBIN, Professor of Comparative Government at Howard University, was National Vice President of the South African Liberal Party and served as a Senator representing the Africans in the South African Parliament. His published works include *The Constitution and Government of Ghana* and *This Is Apartheid*.

ZARICA JOHN SAKUPWANYA was a student at Lincoln University and the University of Rochester, and chief representative of the Mozambique National Democratic Union (UDENAMO) in the United States.

NDABANINGI SITHOLE, President of the Zimbabwe African National Union (ZANU), was previously National Chairman of the Zimbabwe African Peoples Union (ZAPU). He is the author of *African Nationalism*.

OLIVER TAMBO, Deputy President General of the African National Congress (ANC), since 1958, has appeared before the United Nations on behalf of the United Front and the South West Africa National Union. He established, with Nelson Mandela, the first African legal partnership in South Africa.

SAMUEL Z. WESTERFIELD, JR., is Deputy Assistant Secretary for Economics and Planning at the Bureau of African Affairs, U.S. Department of State. He previously served as Senior Adviser at the Office of International Affairs, U.S. Treasury Department and was Professor of Economics and Dean of the School of Business Administration at Atlanta University.

DOUGLAS L. WHEELER, Assistant Professor of History at the University of New Hampshire, has published articles in the *Rhodes Livingstone Journal*, *Missouri Historical Society Bulletin*, and *Studia* (Lisbon).

ARTHUR N. L. WINA, Minister of Finance of Zambia, was previously the United National Independence Party (UNIP) representative to the United States and the United Nations.

ALVIN W. WOLFE, Associate Professor of Anthropology and Sociology at Washington University, is the author of two monographs, *In the Ngombe Tradition* and *Field Guide to West and Central Africa,* as well as articles in *American Anthropologist, Toward Freedom,* and *Social Problems.*

EDDISON ZVOBGO, Executive Secretary of the Zimbabwe African National Union, was the official Zimbabwe African Peoples Union representative to the United States.

THE EDITORS

JOHN A. DAVIS, Chairman of the Department of Political Science, City College of the University of the City of New York, is President of the American Society of African Culture. He is the editor of *Africa Seen by American Negroes.*

JAMES K. BAKER is Executive Director of the American Society of African Culture. As a practicing attorney, he served as counsel for the National Association of Colored People in a number of civil-rights cases.